PROTECTING CANADIAN DEMOCRACY

Protecting Canadian Democracy:

The Senate You Never Knew

Edited by Serge Joyal

Canadian Centre for Management Development
Centre canadien de gestion

McGill-Queen's University Press
Montreal & Kingston • London • Ithaca

© Serge Joyal and Canadian Centre for Management
Development/Centre Canadien de gestion 2003
ISBN 0-7735-2593-9 (cloth)
ISBN 0-7735-2619-6 (paper)

Legal deposit second quarter 2003
Bibliothèque nationale du Québec

Printed in Canada on acid-free paper.

This book has been published with the assistance of the
Canadian Centre for Management Development.

McGill-Queen's University Press acknowledges the support of
the Canada Council for the Arts for our publishing program.
We also acknowledge the financial support of the Government of Canada through the Book Publishing Industry Development Program (BPIDP) for our publishing activities.

National Library of Canada Cataloguing in Publication

Protecting Canadian democracy: The Senate you never knew /
edited by Serge Joyal.

Includes bibliographical references and index.
ISBN 0-7735-2593-9 (bnd)
ISBN 0-7735-2619-6 (pbk)

1. Canada. Parliament. Senate.   2. Canada. Parliament.
Senate. – Reform.   I. Joyal, Serge, 1945–.

JL155.S46 2003   328.71′071   c2003-900578-x

This book was typeset by True to Type in 10/12 Baskerville

This book is dedicated to

Speaker of the Senate (1994–2001), senator (1970–2001), for his unfailing integrity and steadfast loyalty to the Senate.

Contents

Acknowledgments

This book would not have been possible without the intensive work and dedication of a large group of people. Our gratitude is first offered to the contributors, and I am deeply honored to have had the opportunity of working with each of them: Professor Janet Ajzenstat, Professor C.E.S. Franks, Senator Lowell Murray, PC, Professor Gil Rémillard, Dr Jack Stilborn, Professor David Smith, Professor Paul Thomas, and Professor Ronald L. Watts. Without their willingness to share their scholarship and expertise, there would not have been any book at all.

I wish to express my enduring gratitude to the president of the Canadian Centre for Management Development, Jocelyne Bourgon, PC, for her unfailing support. I must also convey my deep appreciation to the staff of the CCMD for their inestimable aid throughout the process of publishing this book. Gratitude is also extended to my current and former Senate colleagues who have contributed their time and resources to this project. Senator Michael Pitfield, PC, and Senator John B. Stewart took the time to review and comment on several drafts of this manuscript, allowing it to benefit from their knowledge of parliamentary institutions and history, as well as their extensive experience. Senator Jerry Grafstein also gave the book the benefit of his considerable knowledge of the history of federal political institutions.

I would also like to offer special thanks to those individuals who have facilitated the development of the book from the very beginning. Charles Robert, the Principal Clerk of Procedure of the Senate, has spent countless hours responding to inquiries about all aspects of the institution. He has worked tirelessly, providing advice and sound counsel drawn from his extensive knowledge of Parliament. Mark Audcent, the Senate Law Clerk and Parliamentary Counsel, has provided invaluable commentaries, suggestions, and research that have improved the quality and substance of the book. Mr Richard Paré, Director of the Library of Parliament, made himself available for repeated consultations and responded rapidly to all of our queries and requests for information. Andrew Turner, from my office, handled the complex challenge of coordinating the research and serving as liaison with the authors. Finally, also from my office, John Nagle supervised the collection of the statistical data, the creation of the supporting database, and the interpretation of the numerous tables and charts.

The Table Officers in the Senate also provided expert assistance and advice. Paul Bélisle, Clerk of the Senate, Gary O'Brien, Deputy-Clerk of the Senate and Principal Clerk of Legislative Services, Heather Lank, Principal Clerk of Committees and Private Legislation, Blair Armitage, Deputy Principal Clerk of Committees and Private Legislation, the committee clerks, the legislative clerks, and the indexers of the Senate Journals were exceedingly helpful in providing both information and comments.

Proper mention must also be made of several other individuals who took the time to review drafts of this book and offer suggestions for improving it, most notably James R. Hurley, former Constitutional Advisor in the Privy Council Office, and Professor Robert Howse, who is presently teaching at the University of Michigan. Jason Evans, a lawyer from my office, provided sound advice and meticulous revision in respect of my chapters. I must also thank several individuals from the Library of Parliament for their accurate and useful research: Mollie Dunsmuir, Peter Niemczak, Bryan O'Neal, and Claude Brind'Amour. The staff of the translation services of the Government of Canada and of Tessier Translation also provided a great deal of assistance. In addition, I express my thanks to Alain Landry and Marnie Kramarich for their editing and stylistic suggestions and to Daniel Poliquin, with his extensive professional experience as a translator, for refining the French version of the book.

The construction of the database on the composition of the Senate and the House of Commons was a challenging and demanding undertaking. I am very grateful to the people who helped with its construction and with the evaluation of the data: Harold Price, Lavagnon Ika, Shravan Chopra, Shamir Doshi, Robert Ferraco, Christian Legault, Adrian Martins, Alan Middleboro, Lorne Rogers, and Pierre Sauvé.

Finally, present and former staff members of my office who contributed to this project deserve special thanks: Pierre-Henri Aho, Philippe-Antoine Morin, Yannick Landry, Vincent Mac Neil, Chad Edmonds, Bernard Doucet, Brett Carr, Carl Bolduc, Alain-Robert Nadeau, Amanda Riddell, and Alain Bouchard.

This project has been a voluntary endeavour, and all of the professors contributed generously of their time and research. The Canadian Centre for Management Development financed the translation and publication of the book. McGill-Queen's University Press, and in particular Aurèle Parisien, Joan McGilvray and Claude Lalumière, reviewed with care the English and French manuscripts for publication.

Many of my Senate colleagues used a part of their research budget to help finance the development of the database. I am personally grateful for the support of Senator Eymard Corbin, Senator Wilfrid Moore, Senator

Nicholas Talyor, Senator Eugene Whelan, Senator Joan Cook, Senator Leo Kolber, Senator Richard Kroft, Senator Lise Bacon, Senator Shirley Maheu, Senator Marisa Ferretti-Barth, Senator Sharon Carstairs, Senator Rose-Marie Losier-Cool, Senator Aurélien Gill, Senator Tommy Banks, Senator Catherine Callbeck, Senator Daniel Hays, Senator Lucie Pépin, and Senator Philip Derek Lewis. In their capacities as Chairs of the Senate Liberal Caucus, Senator Ione Christensen and Senator Joan Fraser were also both supportive.

Serge Joyal, PC

Preface

The Canadian Centre for Management Development (CCMD) is pleased to be associated with the publication of *Protecting Canadian Democracy: The Senate You Never Knew*. This volume presents a thoughtful, well-researched, and well-crafted set of reflections on the future of the Senate of Canada. The Senate is a central feature of Canada's parliamentary democracy. Its responsibilities and activities are relevant to all Canadians and to how federal public servants interact with parliamentarians.

Reflections on and reforms to Canada's political and representative institutions are best articulated through collaboration between parliamentarians and experts. Through this dialogue, experience and practicality are blended with analysis and research in order to create rigorous, focused, and insightful reform. This volume is especially noteworthy for the non-partisan spirit that underscores each contribution and for the writing and research collaboration between parliamentarians and Canadian academic experts.

This book is to a large extent due to the dedication, the commitment, and the leadership provided by Senator Serge Joyal. His experience in the House of Commons and in the Senate, combined with his academic expertise of institutional matters, have contributed to the success of this undertaking.

Senator Serge Joyal and Senator Lowell Murray, by rising above partisan politics, have shown how those who serve in a national political institution can take the initiative to explore how to improve democratic government within Canada's constitutional framework.

CCMD is pleased to be a partner in the publication of this volume. By co-publishing this book with McGill-Queen's University Press, CCMD wants to promote a learning partnership among parliamentarians, the Public Service of Canada and the Canadian academic community.

Senator Joyal and his co-authors are to be commended for placing the Senate under critical scrutiny and for putting forward a set of reform

proposals for review and discussion. Their work represents a model of
how Canada's system of parliamentary government can be studied and
debated.

Jocelyne Bourgon
President
Canadian Centre for Management Development

Foreword

The proper study of Senate reform inevitably gives rise to important issues that touch many of the core principles and values that inspire the whole Canadian constitutional framework. It involves an elaborate set of topics and interests that are not always immediately apparent or obvious.

Despite all the discussions about Senate reform, few proposals seem to have thoroughly assessed the role and function of the Upper Chamber in our modern federal system of government, which is so ingeniously complex, centered as it is now on the constitutional guarantee of personal rights and freedoms, dual linguistic equality, the recognition of aboriginal status, entrenched regional identities, and strong provincial governments. It must also cope with the reality of our immediate proximity to the world's superpower.

Longstanding experience in public administration has taught me to approach anything as challenging as Senate reform with prudence and a reserve of humility. Nonetheless, I remain convinced that such reform is both desirable and feasible as long as certain precautions are not ignored.

In constitution-making it is important to bear in mind that the first step in reform is almost never the final step. To the contrary, the first step sets off a process of evolution usually quite rapid at first and gradually petering out. Focusing merely on the change and not on its consequences as far as the eye can see is to invite mistakes and chaos.

Equally, it is important to build on the genius of the system itself, to avoid trying to achieve some sudden change of direction by simply declaring it to happen. Development should always take account of the natural trend and momentum. These can be shaped and bent, but trying to break or stop them invariably leads to serious trouble. It is important, therefore, to build on what exists, not on what is envisioned as ideal. At the same time, it is essential to recognize what is uniquely Canadian, to avoid seduction by what can be taken discretely from other systems because it simply happens to look good in another context. Chances are that transplants would cause, in practice, grave distortions to our own system of government.

The Senate should not be a duplicate of the House of Commons, but a complement: a somewhat less partisan, more technical forum with a longer-term perspective. Appropriately designed Senate reform could provide greater counter-valence against the executive, more useful national debate and sharper administrative supervision – not only within the Senate itself, but in Parliament as a whole.

Constitutional institutions must be kept simple both so that they can be understood by the people and so that they can function efficiently and effectively with one another. Because a government is a large system with an overall equilibrium of its own, any change in one place is bound to have repercussions elsewhere – sometimes in surprising and far-off places, sometimes with far-reaching and even contradictory effects. Thus, in the final analysis, the most important rule of constitution-making is to keep changes as few as possible and to allow for the natural operation of politics to create conventions over time that can gently update and modify governmental arrangements as circumstances change.

The great British constitutional scholar Sir Ivor Jennings once said that, treated this way, a constitution that has lasted a hundred years should last forever and the well-being secured by such constitutional stability is one of the greatest gifts that governors can confer on both the individual citizen and on a society as a whole.

What is at the heart of the Canadian dilemma? It is how to mature as a country and develop a greater sense of unity and purpose not by passing through the crucible of national trauma – civil war, depression, or cataclysmic revolution – as other countries have done but through peaceful and rational evolution, through the operation of the law.

With the goal of advancing thoughtful proposals for Senate reform, several scholars have willingly applied their knowledge and learning to this subject. Their contributions can provide the foundation of understanding that is essential to the proper consideration of Senate reform. Taken together, their approach expresses a confidence in our reliance on open debate and free discussion, which, whatever the outcome, remains the best guarantee that we will continue to enjoy the benefits of peace, order, and good government.

Senator Michael Pitfield

NOTE

This foreword is in large part composed of excerpts adapted from a speech to the Empire Club, Toronto, 20 October 1983, and from testimony before the Special Joint Committee of the Senate and of the House of Commons on Senate Reform, 18 October 1983. See both of these for further discussion on this topic.

Introduction

The Senate is likely the least admired and least well known of our national political institutions. Its work attracts neither the interest of the media, the respect of elected politicians, the sympathy of the public, nor even the curiosity of academia. How paradoxical that very few Canadians have an understanding of the history, role, and operations of the Senate, and yet everyone seems to have an opinion on the institution. The conventional wisdom in our modern political culture is that the Senate is an outdated relic that has outlived its usefulness. Why is the Senate viewed with such contempt? Some argue that this legislative body designed by the Fathers of Confederation has become "an affront to federalism and democracy."[1] Such was the level of public discourse on the Senate when I was appointed to the Upper Chamber in November 1997.

The Senate of Canada is a house not so much divided as besieged, by politicians and commentators at either end of the political spectrum. On the left, the New Democratic Party has unreservedly championed the abolition of the Senate, condemning the Upper Chamber as a private club that exists to advance the interests of a well-heeled elite. On the right, one finds the Canadian Alliance advocating an American-style Senate with equal representation from every province. At times, prime ministers have diminished the Senate, either by abusing their power of appointment or by attempting to strip the institution of its legislative powers. In this context, it is not surprising that some federal cabinet ministers have publicly questioned the need for an upper chamber.[2]

This hostility for the institution was jarring given the exemplary qualifications and devotion to public life demonstrated by senators on both sides of the chamber. The more I became acquainted with my new colleagues, the more I came to appreciate their contributions to public life. Among many others, I think of Lise Bacon, who represented the interests of Quebec within Canada as the province's Deputy Premier (1985–94); Michael Pitfield, who served as Clerk of the Privy Council in the government of Pierre Trudeau; Dr Wilbert Keon, surgeon and founder of the

Ottawa Heart Institute; and Charlie Watt, an Innu leader who was instrumental in constitutional negotiations leading to the recognition of aboriginal rights in the *Constitution Act, 1982*.

Unfortunately, the accomplishments of the entire institution can be instantly discredited by the ill-advised actions of a single member. The attendance record of former Senator Andrew Thompson virtually monopolized national media coverage of the Upper Chamber, from December 1997 until he resigned after senators passed a motion finding him in contempt of the Senate.[3]

Even distinguished former senators have called the role of the Senate into question. In the summer of 1998, two former colleagues used the occasion of their retirement as an opportunity to propose reforms that would have substantially weakened the autonomy of the Upper Chamber and the effectiveness of Parliament itself. Former Senator Philippe Gigantès published a booklet[4] in which he gave credence to the idea of the Premiers making half of all Senate appointments, while Jacques Hébert, the former Government Whip in the Senate, announced his support for replacing the legislative veto of the Upper Chamber with a so-called "suspensive veto" – an initiative that would essentially reduce its powers to those of a government focus group.[5]

These events happened to coincide with the negative comments of a federal minister regarding the Senate.[6] These comments called for a response. On 13 August 1998, I wrote to the minister, stating that:

What our country dramatically needs is not an Upper Chamber that duplicates the attacks and maintains the tensions and prejudices conveyed in the House of Commons, but rather a forum in which the regional and linguistic differences that characterize us are reconciled, which speaks for this country as a whole and expresses its common values.

I then responded to Senator Hébert in a lengthy letter on 27 August 1998:

To remove the veto would be to remove the legislative function of the Upper Chamber. If we remove the Senate's absolute veto, we would, in fact, be undermining its role together with its utility.

This theme of preserving the fundamental character of Parliament and the values entrenched in its institutions was further expounded in an article published in the February 1999 edition of *Cité Libre*.[7]

A review of the existing academic literature on the Canadian Senate revealed a pronounced lack of interest among the nation's political scientists on the origins, purpose, and operating principles of this institution. Many of the current reference texts on the topic are more polemic than academic in nature, containing sweeping and dismissive statements that fail to seriously address or even consider the need for equilibrium in the constitutional

architecture of our parliamentary institutions.[8] As Lysiane Gagnon has written, "in the field of ideas, the avoidance of written and verbal confrontation
only leads to intellectual frailty and sterile conformism of the lowest order."[9]

The situation was aggravated by the fact that the last major academic
text on the Senate was published forty years ago.[10] This shortage of scholarship is astonishing when one considers that, in the past thirty years
alone, no less than twenty-eight government and political party proposals
on Senate reform have failed. There was an obvious need for current academic research on the constitutional principles underlying our parliamentary institutions in general and the Senate in particular. In spring
1999, I invited a group of respected scholars from the fields of history,
political science and constitutional law to contribute to an in-depth review
of the origin, role, and evolution of the Senate of Canada. Our goals were
to challenge the existing dogma surrounding this institution and to
expand the discourse beyond prefabricated models for Senate reform that
are often contemplated in isolation from the political, historical, and
sociodemographic realities of our country.

At the same time, we knew that any major new study on the Senate
would have to be accessible not only to academia but also to those in public life and other interested Canadians. The Senate is a national political
institution. Discussion over its role and purpose should not be confined to
the lecture halls of our universities; it should also take place in other
forums across the country. For this reason, our book draws not only from
the academic expertise of a number of distinguished scholars but also
from the practical experience of seasoned political professionals. In other
words, this volume serves two complementary functions: to inform and to
stimulate discussion.

Since this project began, a number of events have reinforced the necessity of our endeavours to produce this volume. For one, anti-Senate
rhetoric shows no signs of abating and remains void of any constructive
ideas or historical context.[11] Perhaps out of frustration at their inability to
achieve their political goals, some abolitionists have descended to slurring
the individuals who serve in the Senate.[12]

It also became clear from certain studies on the operation of the
House of Commons that the deficiencies observed there with regard to
its composition, the electoral system, the nature of parliamentary
debates, the operation of its committees, and the influence of the Executive on its members required an equal if not larger number of fundamental reforms. In fact, to be effective, the reform of one cannot occur
without a substantial review of the other. Those who merely propose simplistic solutions for Senate reform rarely mention this complementary
aspect of the two houses of Parliament. A poorly reformed Senate may
turn out to be incompatible with the kind of House of Commons we really want. In a speech to the Canadian Political Science Association, I
asserted that:

Before wanting to make the Senate another House of Commons, we should first solve the basic problems that undermine the democratic operation of that chamber and then act on the criticisms that have put a finger on the most obvious weaknesses in the operation of our system of responsible government.[13]

The June 2000 passage of Bill C–20 (the *Clarity Act*)[14] has further altered the fundamental role of the Senate by excluding any requirement of its consent to the wording of the question and the majority required in respect of any future referendum on the secession of Quebec.[15] On this subject, a letter (which I co-signed) dated 31 January 2000 to the Leader of the Government in the Senate stated:

Bill C–20 minimizes the role of the Senate in such a process to a mere consultative role. Such a role fails to recognize and respect the equal status of the Senate as one of the three components of the Parliament of Canada. Furthermore, the Senate, as the embodiment of the federal principle, has a duty to protect its equality so as to guarantee its unfettered ability to fulfil its constitutional function at all times in the future.

This legislation was an obvious example of a persistent trend. In one session[16] alone five bills were passed and one Government White Paper was introduced in the House of Commons excluding the Upper Chamber from a role in the review process[17] or reporting mechanism[18] of proposed legislation. The consequence of this diminished monitoring role for the Senate is a corresponding concentration of power in the hands of the executive branch. In my opinion, and in that of other Senate colleagues, this situation had to be addressed.[19]

In this context, an in-depth reflection on how to adapt the institution to contemporary needs was all the more urgent. Yet, as the late eminent scholar and former Senator Eugene Forsey observed, major constitutional changes are "not in the cards."[20] Given this situation, are there any improvements that could be implemented? The legal, constitutional, and political obstacles to Senate reform seem insurmountable.[21] Were we condemned to inaction? Fortunately, one hallmark of the parliamentary system in the British tradition is its capacity to evolve through conventional practices rather than through formal constitutional settlements. According to the unanimous decision of the Supreme Court in *Reference re Secession of Quebec*,

The global system of rules and principles which govern the exercise of constitutional authority in the whole and in every part of the Canadian state ... include constitutional conventions and the workings of Parliament. Such principles and rules emerge from an understanding of the constitutional text itself, the historical context, and previous judicial interpretations of constitutional meaning.[22]

The second avenue to institutional reform is through legislative initiatives within the competence of Parliament. Section 44 of the *Constitution Act, 1982* states the parameters in the following terms: "Parliament may exclusively make laws amending the Constitution of Canada in relation to the executive government of Canada or the Senate and House of Commons." In other words, a simple majority in both the Senate and the House of Commons can pass important institutional reforms of Parliament, without resorting to a constitutional amendment involving the provinces.

Notwithstanding the failure[23] of three major constitutional reform initiatives, our country has continued to evolve and adapt in the twenty years since 1982. Canada has undergone some fundamental economic, social, and political changes during this period. The last few years have seen a number of successful bilateral constitutional amendments, among them: educational reform in Quebec and in Newfoundland and Labrador, recognition of the equality of status for the linguistic communities of New Brunswick, implementation of the Nisga'a treaty creating a level of aboriginal self-government, and the creation of a fixed link from New Brunswick to Prince Edward Island. All of these changes were brought about by a constitutional amendment requiring the approval of the Parliament and the legislature of the concerned province.[24]

Equally important, in 1996, Parliament approved Bill C–110,[25] a bill that is "constitutional in nature" and that obliges the federal government to obtain the approval of five regions before introducing any formal resolution to amend the Constitution based on the seven-fifty formula. More significant, however, is the variety and number of reform initiatives through intergovernmental agreements, such as the Social Union, the Internal Trade Agreement, and the agreement on the transfer of the exercise of jurisdiction over manpower training. These broad-based transformations have been implemented by legislative or executive initiatives of the federal government, without recourse to complex amending formulae.

This book contends that the same dynamic – that of constitutional evolution without formal amendments to the Constitution – can be applied to the improvement of the functioning of the Canadian Senate. To be successful, however, it is necessary for the study to reflect on the origin, record and current function of the Senate within Parliament, as well as on the institutional principles and the political context in which it operates.

CHAPTER 1
BICAMERALISM AND CANADA'S FOUNDERS: THE ORIGINS OF THE CANADIAN SENATE

It seemed logical that a volume on the history, role and evolution of the Canadian Senate should begin with an analysis of the context in which the Upper Chamber was established in 1867. Having co-published *Canada's Founding Debates* in 1999, Janet Ajzenstat, Professor Emeritus of the

Department of Political Science at McMaster University, is eminently qualified to provide insight into the political and constitutional considerations
that led to the creation of the Canadian Senate.

Professor Ajzenstat's chapter assesses the influence of the colonial Legislative Councils as antecedents of the Senate. She also addresses whether or not
the House of Lords served a model for our Upper Chamber and discusses the
influence of the American Civil War on the architects of Canadian federalism. Her chapter does not stop at 1867, but continues with an account of the
Canadian Senate over the first fifty years of Confederation, examining the
adaptation to its legislative role in the life of the new Dominion. At the same
time, she provides a review of the corresponding evolution of the House of
Commons, assessing the degree to which the two chambers complement
each other. Finally, Professor Ajzenstat considers the valuable lessons that the
Confederation debates teach Canadians about our parliamentary institutions; namely, that these institutions were carefully designed to serve the vital
role of circumscribing the power of the executive branch of government.

CHAPTER 2
FORTY YEARS OF NOT REFORMING THE SENATE — TAKING STOCK

Over the past thirty years, the Canadian political landscape has sprouted
twenty-eight major proposals on Senate reform; proposals championed by
federal or provincial governments, commissions and political parties. All
of them failed. In fact, since 1867, there have only been two constitutional amendments regarding the Senate.[26] It seemed altogether appropriate
that this volume on the Senate should include a chapter that would evaluate these proposals and offer an explanation for their failure.

Dr Jack Stilborn directed research for the Special Joint Committee on
the Future of Canada in 1991 and is currently a senior research officer at
the Library of Parliament. At my request, he conducted a comparative
analysis of these twenty-eight proposals on Senate reform. His review identifies ways of improving the Senate within the current constitutional framework. Dr Stilborn's analysis highlights the conceptual weaknesses of these
constitutional proposals, offering a set of criteria for evaluating the feasibility of future Senate reform initiatives.

CHAPTER 3
BICAMERALISM IN FEDERAL PARLIAMENTARY SYSTEMS

Many mature democracies, including members of the G8, operate under
the regime of bicameralism; a system in which the legislative branch of government is divided into two autonomous chambers. Bicameralism is a common characteristic of large federal states (i.e., the United States, Germany,
Canada, Australia, and India) for obvious reasons: the Upper Chamber

can serve to balance national and sectional interests and, in some cases, provide a forum for the representation of minority groups. Short of creative and complex gerrymandering, unicameralism has difficulty achieving these objectives.

Canada was the first democracy to apply the Westminster parliamentary model to a federal state. This long tradition of institutional innovation is perhaps part of the reason why our country has produced such highly esteemed experts in the study of federalism and bicameralism as Ronald Watts, Principal Emeritus and Professor Emeritus of Political Studies and Fellow of the Institute of Intergovernmental Relations at Queen's University. Professor Watts immediately came to mind as someone whose knowledge and understanding would enrich the calibre of this volume. His chapter examines the particular features of upper chambers in federal systems of government. Professor Watts also contrasts the high degree of legislative autonomy enjoyed by subnational governments in Canada (i.e., the provinces) with the significantly more centralized political apparatus of most federations.

CHAPTER 4:
SENATE REFORM: BACK TO BASICS

The Senate was a key element of the compromise that made Confederation possible. Its constitutional architects designed an Upper Chamber that would reflect the federal status of the new Dominion while also serving as a mechanism for reinforcing government accountability. One of the reasons for the failure of so many proposals aimed at structural reform of the Senate was that they neglected to take these institutional characteristics into account.

Gil Rémillard, Professor at Montreal's École nationale d'administration publique, former Quebec Minister of Justice (1988–93) and author of *Le fédéralisme canadien*, draws from his substantial political and academic experience to provide the reader with an in-depth understanding of the Senate as a complementary chamber to the House of Commons. His chapter contrasts the role of the Upper Chamber, as the federal legislative body created to support regional and minority interests, with the mandate of provincial governments to advance the concerns of their particular province. Professor Rémillard addresses the question of whether the Senate should be an instrument for provincial power in Ottawa or a forum within Parliament for the representation of Canada's diverse regional, linguistic, cultural, and socioeconomic interests.

CHAPTER 5:
WHICH CRITICISMS ARE FOUNDED?

As I have mentioned, there is no shortage of criticism levelled at the Senate. Almost invariably, however, this criticism comes from those who are

least familiar with the Upper Chamber. One must distinguish the valid criticisms of the institution from the folklore surrounding the Senate and its
members. When evaluating such grievances, it is also important to consider the impact that any institutional reform of the Upper Chamber might
have on the constitutional equilibrium of the country.

Clearly, there is a need for an honest assessment of the institutional flaws
of the Senate, along with an examination of the prospects for constructive
change. Having served as a senator since 1979, Minister of State for Federal-Provincial Relations (1986–91), and Leader of the Government in the
Senate (1986–93), Lowell Murray is one of the most qualified authorities
in Canada to offer this assessment. His chapter contrasts the overall academic approach of this book by offering an insider's perspective on the
institution. Senator Murray identifies the valid criticisms of the Senate and
explores nonconstitutional avenues for parliamentary reform, while also
engaging the reader in a frank discussion on whether or not the Senate is
the best mechanism for the representation of sectional and regional interests at the federal level.

CHAPTER 6
THE CANADIAN SENATE IN MODERN TIMES

Although both are autonomous legislative chambers of the national Parliament, the Senate and the House of Commons serve different functions. The
Senate is designed to review government legislation and scrutinize the activities of the Executive, with an emphasis on the interests of underrepresented groups and regions. As Canada has evolved, so too has its political institutions. An appreciation of the changing role of the Canadian Senate is an
essential component of any informed discourse on parliamentary reform.

C.E.S. Franks, Professor Emeritus of Political Studies at Queen's University and author of *The Parliament of Canada*, is an internationally respected observer and analyst on government accountability and intergovernmental relations. His chapter traces the evolving role of the Senate from
1957, examining the patterns and the appropriateness of how the Senate
has used the legislative powers at its disposal. In the process, he addresses
two conflicting criticisms of the Upper Chamber; that it is either too active
in national affairs or, conversely, not active enough. Professor Franks also
evaluates the extent to which the legislative and investigative roles of the
Senate are complementary to those of the House of Commons.

CHAPTER 7
COMPARING THE LAWMAKING ROLES OF THE SENATE
AND THE HOUSE OF COMMONS

A comparative analysis of the legislative and committee activity of both the
Senate and the House of Commons is required in order to determine the

optimal contribution that the Senate can offer to Parliament. In his analysis of how the Senate studies and debates proposed legislation, Paul Thomas, Duff Roblin Professor of Government at the University of Manitoba, provides insight into the different yet complementary roles played by both houses of Parliament.

Professor Thomas notes that the real legislative influence of the Senate is largely overlooked. His chapter underscores the role of the Senate in scrutinizing the activity of both the public service and the executive branch of the federal government. Professor Thomas also assesses the substantial contribution of the Canadian Senate to public policy development and review through its special studies on such diverse issues as poverty, telecommunications, land use, and scientific research; observing that few of these studies were undertaken in the context of a legislative initiative already introduced by the government.

CHAPTER 8

THE IMPROVEMENT OF THE SENATE
BY NONCONSTITUTIONAL MEANS

Any changes to the Senate ought to be designed so as to improve the efficiency of the Upper Chamber and enhance its working relationship with the House of Commons and the federal Cabinet. Clearly, this would improve the efficiency of Parliament and government as a whole. Given the current political and social context, it is equally obvious that any sweeping constitutional amendment on the subject of Senate reform is neither feasible, nor really desirable, at this time.

In his chapter, David E. Smith, Professor of Political Studies at the University of Saskatchewan, provides a set of proposals for reform of the institution that are consistent with the founding principles of Senate and do not require amendments to the Canadian Constitution. His innovative text includes a "Declaration of Principles" that are intended to serve as a practical guideline for any future proposals to reform the Upper Chamber.

CONCLUSION
AND APPENDIX

The closing chapter is intended to stimulate debate on the constitutional role of the Senate. Initiatives are discussed that would improve the Upper Chamber, while respecting the principles on which the Senate was founded and ensuring the equilibrium of the constitutional architecture of Parliament. Specifically, the final chapter assesses the significance of the Senate's veto power, suggests changes to its appointment process, and examines the legislative independence of the Upper Chamber in the context of conflicting institutional and party loyalties. Any comprehensive

attempt at improving the Senate must address these three issues. Sectional interests, the rights of linguistic minorities, the status of Aboriginal peoples, and the role of Parliament in relation to the rights and freedoms
entrenched in the Charter are presented as the inescapable references by
which one must evaluate the merits of the Senate and any proposal for its
effective reform.

Finally, there is an appendix, which includes several charts and many statistics on the composition and operation of the Senate. The database from
which this important information was generated is now available to all
researchers and interested persons in an easily accessible format.

The academic research and critical reflection contained in this book will
hopefully serve as the basis for a debate that goes beyond the empty
rhetoric and prefabricated conclusions that have heretofore characterized
public discourse on the Canadian Senate. In fostering a better understanding of the nature of our parliamentary institutions and the values
they embody, we seek to stimulate a discussion of how our system of government should function. It is our hope that this open exchange of ideas
will result in successful proposals for the practical, real, and immediate
improvement of the Senate of Canada.

Serge Joyal, PC

NOTES

1 Simpson, *The Friendly Dictatorship*, 18.
2 Aubry, "Trio in Cabinet Quietly Hope to Scrap Senate," A9: "The House of
   Commons' anti-Senate coalition has the support of several prominent parliamentarians, including at least three closet abolitionists in [the federal] cabinet."
3 Senator Thompson attended only twelve sittings of the Senate from 1990 to
   1997, citing poor health (supported by medical certificates) as the reason for
   his chronic absence from the Chamber. When it was discovered that Senator
   Thompson was actually residing in Mexico, the Senate ordered him to appear
   in the Chamber. He failed to comply with this order and was found in contempt of the Senate. As a result, Senator Thompson was suspended without
   pay, prompting his resignation.
4 Gigantès and Erlington, *The Thin Book: Reforming the Senate.*
5 Marissal, "'Le Sénat a trop de pouvoirs', soutient l'ex-sénateur Hébert," B1.
6 On 5 June 1998, Intergovernmental Affairs Minister Stéphane Dion stated to
   the Canadian Press in Calgary that he was "not in love with the Senate we
   have." ("Dion dit non au Sénat élu," *Le Droit*, Monday, 6 July 1998, 17.)
7 Joyal, "The Senate: The Earth Is Not Flat."
8 For example, Peter Hogg, an otherwise rigorous scholar of constitutional law,
   tersely summarizes the agreement reached by the Fathers of Confederation

on the creation of an Upper Chamber, opining: "It is obvious that this plan was fatally flawed." (*Constitutional Law of Canada, 3rd ed.*, 241.)

9 Lysiane Gagnon, "Le Syndrome Dutoit-Boilard,"A13: "Dans celui (le domaine) des idées, le refus de la confrontation écrite et verbale ne mène qu'à la mollesse intellectuelle et au conformisme le plus sterile."

10 Kunz, *The Modern Senate of Canada, 1925–1963: A Reappraisal.*

11 Brown, "MPs Plan Demonstration against the Senate on June 8," A10: "Helping to organize the demonstration are three abolitionists from the Bloc Québécois, Jean-Paul Marchand, René Canuel and Gérard Asselin, and Reformer Rob Anders who wants an elected Senate... 'We all agree that we've got an out-of-touch, arrogant, tax-and-spend institution,' said Anders."

12 Bellavance, "Senator Files Defamation Suit against Bloc MP," A8. In April 1998, then Bloc Québécois MP Jean-Paul Marchand sent his constituents, at taxpayers' expense, an anti-Senate leaflet in which certain senators, myself included, were named as collecting a House of Commons pension along with their Senate salaries. In response, I launched a defamation suit in Québec Superior Court. Senator Céline Hervieux-Payette, who was also smeared by the leaflet, filed a similar action. Mr Marchand later apologized, calling his own actions "a deplorable mistake." Eventually, he agreed to pay an out-of-court settlement. On the other side of the chamber, former Senator Ron Ghitter (PC – Alberta) successfully filed suit against Rob Anders for remarks made by the Calgary MP in a Reform Party fundraising letter.

13 Joyal, "The Senate You Thought You Knew."

14 *An Act to give effect to the requirement for clarity as set out in the opinion of the Supreme Court of Canada in the Quebec Secession Reference* (S.C. 2000, c. 26).

15 Four Senate vacancies were filled by the Prime Minister just in time to defeat an amendment from the government side of the Senate. The amendment to Bill C–20 would have restored the constitutional role of the Upper Chamber regarding secession. The four senators appointed were Betty Kennedy (Ontario), Raymond Setlakwe (Québec), Raymond Squires (Newfoundland and Labrador), and Jane-Marie Cordy (Nova Scotia). The amendment was defeated on 29 June 2000 by a vote of forty-six yeas to fifty nays, with three abstentions.

16 36th Parliament, 1st Session (22 September 1997 – 18 September 1999).

17 Bill C–25: *An Act to amend the National Defence Act and to make consequential amendments to other Acts*; Bill C-32: *An Act respecting pollution prevention and the protection of the environment and human health in order to contribute to sustainable development*; Bill C–43: *An Act to establish the Canada Customs and Revenue Agency and to amend and repeal other Acts as a consequence*; Canada, Department of Finance, *Reforming Canada's Financial Services Sector: A Framework for the Future*, 80 (Proposed Measure 11).

18 Bill C–3: *An Act respecting DNA identification and to make consequential amendments to the Criminal Code and other Acts*; Bill C–52: *An Act to implement the Comprehensive Nuclear Test-Ban Treaty.*

19 In the previous two sessions of Parliament, the following legislation was

introduced to restore the Senate's status in the twenty-seven statutes from which it had been excluded since 1920: *An Act to better assist the Senate to serve Canadians by restoring its rights, opportunities and functions* (Bill S–31, 36th Parliament, 2nd Session), *An Act to maintain the principles relating to the role of the Senate as established by the Constitution of Canada* (Bill S–8, 37th Parliament, 1st Session).

20 From an unpublished speech by Eugene Forsey to a meeting of the Canadian Bar Association at Halifax, Nova Scotia, on 19 August 1985.

21 Joyal, *Legal, Constitutional and Political Imperatives to Senate Reform.*

22 [1998] 2 S.C.R. 217, para. 32.

23 The initiatives in question were: 1) *Constitution Amendment (Powers of the Senate)*, proposed by then Minister of Justice John Crosbie in House of Commons on 9 May 1985; 2) the Meech Lake Constitutional Accord (1987); 3) the Charlottetown Accord (1992).

24 In addition, one multilateral amendment relating to Aboriginal rights has been adopted.

25 *An Act respecting constitutional amendments*, S.C. 1996, c. 1.

26 In 1965, a mandatory retirement age for senators was set at seventy-five years. In 1982, the Senate was given a qualified veto over certain constitutional amendments.

PROTECTING CANADIAN DEMOCRACY

CHAPTER ONE

Bicameralism and Canada's Founders: The Origins of the Canadian Senate

Janet Ajzenstat

Scholars often suggest the modern world is moving toward unicameralism. Indeed, some think it is not moving quickly enough.[1] The argument is a familiar one: a senate (an upper house, a second legislative chamber) may be useful in a federal system as a forum for representation of the constituent states or provinces, but in the absence of federalism is probably unnecessary. At best the upper house duplicates the work of the lower; at worst it delays and obstructs. A single-chamber system is more efficient, more accountable, and more democratic.[2]

The strongest version of this argument maintains that the second chamber is especially inappropriate in parliamentary regimes as to require a majority vote in two legislative houses detracts from responsible government. It muddles the accountability of government to the peoples' representatives in the elective branch. Reason enough to prefer unicameralism? Some believe the fact that responsible government encourages accountability to the majority in the lower house and thus to the electorate is what makes the parliamentary system superior to the presidential one.

Canada's founders thought otherwise. They valued accountability but did not see it as the ne plus ultra of parliamentary politics. Just as important, or more important, was security for political dissent and respect for minority political rights. They were intimately familiar with the principle of responsible government and understood that concentrating power in an executive answerable to the majority promotes accountability, but they also believed such concentration of power poses dangers. A high-handed Cabinet can silence opposition using accountability as its excuse. They called crude majority rule of this kind "democracy" or "unbridled democracy" and believed it one of the classic forms of autocracy.

Throughout the nineteenth century and still at Confederation, political thinkers and parliamentarians regarded parliament as a system of checks and balances, not unlike the presidential form of government in this one respect at least. The Cabinet, the Commons, and the Senate (the three "branches" of the system) were believed equally prone to dreams of aggrandizement and power. Fortunately, or so the theory went, each branch jealously watched the others, checking imprudence and haste and reigning in the ambitions of elites. In this system, it fell to the Senate to exercise "the power of the check" on Cabinet and Commons. The Senate had the task of delaying or obstructing legislation when it appeared that a cabinet was attempting to use its majority in the Commons to silence dissent and suppress minorities.

Though the founders did not use the term "democracy" to describe this system (they spoke of mixed or balanced government, or the British constitution, or parliamentary responsible government) we today call this approach democracy. Liberal democracy traditionally values security for political minorities; it argues that only such respect is compatible with egalitarianism and that it is the condition of fruitful political deliberation for the public good. It is not wrong – indeed it is very right – to call the Fathers of Confederation and Canada's founding legislators liberal democrats. The founders' argument, we may say, is that bicameralism protects liberal democracy and that bicameralism is therefore more democratic than unicameralism.

A SYSTEM OF CHECKS AND BALANCES

The Fathers of Confederation and Canada's founding legislators exhibited an impressive knowledge of constitutional history and theoretical texts.[3] They cited British, American, and French authorities, studied European constitutions, and compared federal systems.[4] Though more likely to rely on Edmund Burke and John Stuart Mill than on the great philosophers of the seventeenth and eighteenth centuries, some at least knew Thomas Hobbes, John Locke, Montesquieu, and Rousseau. Mill's *Representative Government*, published in 1861, is the most often-cited book. Many had read the famous documents of US constitutional history, especially the *Federalist Papers*. They referred to sections of the American Constitution and to constitutions of the individual states.

They were familiar with the experiments in unicameralism that characterized the French Revolution and the period of the English Civil War. They remembered, some of them from first-hand experience, the proposals for abolition of the colonial legislative councils (the second chambers) that circulated at the time of the 1837–38 Rebellions.[5] They were, above all, the French-speakers as well as the English-speakers, knowledgeable about the British parliamentary tradition.[6] They read British newspapers and the accounts of debates in the British Parliament. Almost all of them were experienced parliamentarians and many had been involved in the struggle to establish responsible government in the individual colonies.

Recall the argument: the second chamber promotes democracy and protects minority rights by curbing high-handedness and arrogance in Cabinet and Commons. Underpinning this contention is the description of parliament as an institution with three independent and competing "authorities," or "branches": the Ministry and the two legislative houses. In the debates on colonial union in the Red River colony, James Ross noted approvingly: "The principle on which the British law is based is that there should be three branches of the legislature."7 In the Legislative Assembly of the united Canadas John A. Macdonald assured listeners that the general government of the new federation would replicate the British system of "King, Lords, and Commons."8 In 1869, Newfoundland's F.B.T. Carter, still attempting to appease the anti-confederates, observed that "The constitution [of the Dominion government] was composed of those three estates to which they were already so well accustomed – the monarch, the Senate, and the House of Commons, elected by the people; with that principle there was no disposition to interfere."9 The Cabinet was sometimes referred to as the "monarchic branch" since it consisted of ministers of the Crown; the Senate was the "aristocratic" house; and the Commons, the "democratic" house.

It was an important part of the argument that each branch had a degree of constitutional independence. Remember that the branches are to act as "checks and balances."10 Scholars have sometimes argued that the introduction of responsible government in British North America in the late 1840s "fused" the executive and legislative powers; Cabinet and Commons were no longer independent in the old sense. Textbooks contrasting the Canadian and American forms of government commonly argue that the former exhibits "fusion of powers" and the latter "separation of powers."11 It is easy to see how this usage came about. In parliamentary systems, ministers must have seats in the legislature, while in presidential systems they must not. But to suppose that Cabinet and Commons are "fused" takes us far from the founders' vision. They insist that Cabinet, Commons, and Senate are and should be constitutionally independent.

Consider James Gray Steven's argument for the independence of the second chamber. He is speaking in New Brunswick's lower house, the House of Assembly:

The Constitution of Great Britain had received the plaudits of all writers of history. The reason of this is because of the admirable checks which one branch has on another. We should, therefore, endeavour to prevent the usefulness of the upper branch being done away with by any remarks calculated to bring them, as an independent branch, into contempt.12

In the Legislative Assembly of the united Canadas, George Brown makes a similar contention:

The desire was to render the upper house a thoroughly independent body – one that would be in the best position to canvass dispassionately the measures of this house [the legislative assembly] and stand up for the public interests in opposition to hasty or partisan legislation.13

In the Canadian Legislative Council, Thomas Ryan asserts: "If the constituents of both houses are merely the same, you lose the power of the check, or at least you will not have it effectual, because you will have the same sentiments and feelings represented in this house [the Legislative Council] as in the other."[14]

And consider Peter Mitchell in New Brunswick's upper house:

We are told we must be swept away; that the majority are "effete, antiquated politicians," representing no one but ourselves and having no regard for the people's interests, desirous only to gratify our ambition, our selfishness, and our interests ... Does Mr. [Albert] Smith not know, and has he not often repeated the fact, that without the check, which the upper branch has been to hasty and reckless legislation in the lower house, our statute book would have been filled with injudicious and unwise statutes?[15]

The theory regards Cabinet ministers as potential tyrants, the ambitious leaders in the lower house as potential demagogues, and senators as potential oligarchs.[16] When all is working as it should, when the branches are free to check each other, the system forestalls the three classic forms of despotism: the despotism of the single tyrant (the "one"); the despotism of the "few"; and the despotism sometimes referred to as "unbridled democracy," the rule of popular leaders in the lower house who claim absolute and uncontested authority to speak for the "many."

Though almost all regarded parliamentary government as the remedy, partisan differences are evident. The Conservatives, or some of them, believe "democracy" the greatest threat. Their political memories reach back to Cromwell, Robespierre, and, in the colonies, Louis-Joseph Papineau at the time of the Rebellions – democratic despots all. The Liberals fear oligarchy and monarchic tyranny. In the Liberal imagination, a resurgence of Papineau's philosophy is unlikely, but a return to the bad old days of the colonial oligarchies – the Family Compact and Chateau Clique – is entirely possible. The Stuart monarchs of English history and the absolute rulers of continental Europe in the eighteenth century are the Liberal bogeymen.

John A. Macdonald encapsulates the theory in the following passage from his speech on "King, Lords, and Commons." Notice how quickly he runs it past his colleagues. There was no need to explain. All were perfectly familiar with the ideas.

We will enjoy here that which is the great test of constitutional freedom – we will have the rights of the minority respected. In all countries the rights of the majority take care of themselves, but it is only in countries like England, enjoying constitutional liberty, and safe from the tyranny of a single despot or of an unbridled democracy, that the rights of minorities are regarded.[17]

By the "minority," Macdonald does not mean ethnic or religious minorities, as commentators have sometimes supposed. (He discusses the issue of ethnic minorities elsewhere in the Confederation debates.) "Minority" here refers to the political minority, that is, the political opposition, in the Senate and Commons and in the populace at large. Macdonald is saying that the supreme benefit of parliamentary government is that it protects political opposition, the right to dissent. In most political systems the rights of the majority take care of themselves; despots of all sorts, even monarchic despots, seek to appease the majority in one way or another. The singular advantage of parliamentary democracies is that they protect the minority. Only in a parliamentary system must the majority refrain from ignoring or suppressing the complaints and interests of the political opposition.

Richard Cartwright makes the same point, drawing on the same theory:

No fear here [in the province of Canada], Mr. Speaker, for many a day to come at least, of perils which await us from the tyranny of hereditary rulers, or the ambition of aristocratic oligarchs. No, sir, no; and while it is true that here, as elsewhere, there are always dangers enough to retard our progress, I think that every true reformer, every real friend of liberty will agree with me in saying that ... our chiefest care must be to train the majority to respect the rights of the minority, to prevent the claims of the few from being trampled under foot by the caprice or passion of the many.[18]

Participants in the Confederation debates found a classic defence of the second chamber as guarantee against despotism in Mill's *Representative Government*:

A majority in a single assembly, when it has assumed a permanent character – when composed of the same persons habitually acting together, and always assured of victory in their own House – easily becomes despotic and overweening, if released from the necessity of considering whether its acts will be concurred in by another constituted authority. The same reason which induced the Romans to have two consuls, makes it desirable there should be two chambers: that neither of them may be exposed to the corrupting influence of undivided power, even for the space of a single year.[19]

Mill is inveighing against democratic despotism – Macdonald's "unbridled democracy." The single-chamber system can easily develop into a ruthless drive for party dominance. Bolstered by electoral victory, leaders in the majority party ignore the political opposition and deride minority views. Under the "corrupting influence of undivided power," the majority party strives to pass itself off as the only possible representative of "the people." Autocracy blooms in the guise of "democracy."

What is wanted is a system of "divided power." Cabinet decisions should run the gauntlet of debate in two "constituted authorities," two independent arenas of deliberation, the two legislative houses. It was certainly an important part of Mill's argument that representatives in the second chamber should be "independent," that is, should not have to rely on the elites in power for re-election, status, and income. Thus, arguments that appeared weak in the one house might be raised again in the other, perhaps with more success. The very idea that the debate must be rehearsed again in another chamber might well influence deliberations in the original house. The hope is that the Senate will force "second thoughts" on the Prime Minister and party elites in Cabinet, preventing them from using their influence in the Commons to silence opposition.

Thomas Ryan cites Mill with approval:

In [his] chapter on the second chamber ... [Mill] says: "That there should be in every polity a centre of resistance to the predominant power in the constitution – and in a democratic constitution, therefore, a nucleus of resistance to the democracy – I have already maintained and I regard it as a fundamental maxim of government." Now honourable gentlemen, I think a second chamber, constituted nearly the same way as the lower chamber, would be wholly ineffectual to stop the current of legislation coming from that chamber; the point, indeed, admits of very little question.[20]

How often today it is argued that, as a consequence of the principle we call responsible government, the party in office rules almost unopposed during its term. How often it is said that between elections we have a form of government resembling despotism. The founders, in contrast, believed that parliamentary responsible government supremely ensured that no party, clique, faction, or would-be single despot or demagogue could govern unchallenged. The Westminster system would protect the political dissent and opposition that guarantee freedom and deliberation.

Have we seen enough of the argument to believe bicameralism protects democracy? Over the years Canadians have convinced themselves that getting rid of the "aristocratic" body is the necessary step toward a more democratic politics and there is a certain superficial plausibility to the notion. It sounds as if it ought to be right. It certainly convinced the Canadian radicals of the 1830s. Out with the oligarchs, in with the democrats: that was their war cry. But if we listen to the parliamentarians of the next generation, the Fathers of Confederation and the founding legislators we will conclude that abolition of the Senate serves to concentrate power in the hands of the Prime Minister and his key consultants in Commons and in government. Without the Upper House, the centres of opposition in the Commons (the minority parties, and independent thinkers in the government caucus) lack essential reinforcement, making it that much less likely they will be able to reign in the undue ambitions of the "single despots."

INDEPENDENT SENATORS:
QUALIFICATIONS AND SELECTION

To explore the idea that the Senate protects minorities and promotes deliberation, we must look more closely at two issues: qualifications for appointment and the mode of selection. Can the Senate be independent if the individual senators are obliged to elites of the day for re-election, status, and salary?

A person eligible for appointment to the Senate must own property in the amount of four thousand dollars.[21] It is clear that the founders wished to see senators chosen from the wealthier class. The crucial question is whether they expected senators to *represent* that wealthy class? In a parliamentary system, does the upper house speak for the class or estate of the wealthy few? One reason for supposing that the founders did not think the Senate should speak only for property and money is that in the Canadian Constitution the Senate represents the regions of the federation. Surely, the Fathers did not suppose that senators would sit only for the rich in their locales. Nevertheless the question of Senate representation requires exposition.

In the eighteenth century and until some time in the nineteenth, the argument for the "three branches" was sometimes confused with the idea that English society was composed of three "estates" or classes, the monarchic (the class of "the one"), the aristocratic ("the few"), and the democratic ("the many"). I do not propose to tell the story of this confusion in full, or to explore developments in parliamentary practice.[22] It is enough to say that whatever the English Parliament may have been in its origins, even before the Glorious Revolution of 1688, the connection between social estates and representation in the branches of parliament was wearing away. It is true that only titled aristocrats sat in the House of Lords, but increasingly it was argued that they did not sit solely to represent and to benefit aristocrats. In theory, the connection between estates and branches was on the wane. In the popular mind, and no doubt in daily life, it lingered.

For the British North Americans, the crucial debate occurred in the British House of Commons in 1791. The bill before the House repealed the Quebec Act of 1774; the old province was divided into two jurisdictions, Upper Canada and Lower Canada, and each was given representative institutions, that is, a legislative assembly and legislative council.[23] Much of the 1791 debate was taken up with the question of qualifications for the legislative council. Everyone agreed there should be a second chamber. The colonists were to have the British Constitution in full: "King, Lords, and Commons." There remained the awkward fact that the colonies did not have a hereditary aristocracy; there was no lordly "estate."[24]

Convinced of the importance of ensuring the independence of the Upper House as a check on "democracy," Edmund Burke argued for the creation of a landed and titled class in the colonies. He appears to have been thinking in the old terms; the branches of parliament represent social estates or classes. Charles James Fox opposed him; hereditary titles would be an absurdity in the equalitarian conditions of North America.[25] Fox believed that whatever respect accrued to the members of the Upper House under the new regime should result not from titles or inherited position but from the members' greater wealth. "The extension of commerce and wealth in the province, which there was every reason to imagine would follow the introduction of the new constitution, would make them hold a fair weight in that constitution, and imperceptibly clothe them with that respect and influence that ought to belong to the aristocratical branch of a free government."[26] The idea that the Upper House should represent a permanent, aristocratic social stratum was utterly rejected.

Fox's argument prevails. In the Confederation debates sixty-five years later, we find Macdonald arguing: "The members of our upper house will be like those of the lower, men of the people, and from the people." Macdonald makes a special point of noting that when Parliament rises members of the Upper House "return to the people."

Springing from the people, and one of them, [the senator] takes his seat in the council with all the sympathies and feelings of a man of the people, and when he returns home at the end of the session, he mingles with them on equal terms and is influenced by the same feelings and associations, and events, as those which affect the mass around him.[27]

Macdonald and others in the Confederation debates still sometimes speak of "estates." But the idea that the branches of parliament speak exclusively for hereditary classes has dropped away. Between Burke's defence of a landed aristocracy and Macdonald's confident assertion that senators would be "of the people," affected by the feelings and associations of the "mass," there has been a major development in the philosophy of political representation.[28] Sir George Ross offers data to support Macdonald's contention. He notes that of the first 304 senators appointed after Confederation,

Not one can be said, either by heredity or factitious pre-eminence, to be less democratic than the chosen representatives of the people in the House of Commons. Very few, if any, represented either large estates or accumulated capital which would separate them in business or interest from their fellow citizens ... [In] no respect, either by education, environment or personal interests or pretentions are they different from their fellow legislators in the Lower Chamber ... So when we invest the Senate with a certain power, we are merely investing the democracy with a second voice in the councils of the nation.[29]

There remains the question of the property qualification. Senators are not to represent the propertied as a class, but we might ask whether they are expected to have a certain sympathy for the rich. Perhaps they are expected to represent business? But as Edmund S. Morgan argues, there is no precedent for the notion of corporate representation in British constitutional history. Parliamentarians of both legislative houses sit for territorially defined ridings (and for the country as a whole):

In England and America ... the community [and thus the electoral riding; the constituency] was geographically defined. It was the Isle of Kent or the borough of St. Mary's; it was Shropshire or Staffordshire, Norwich or Bristol; it was never the worshipful company of grocers or cordwainers, never the tobacco farmers' union or the association of ship owners. In the eighteenth and nineteenth centuries the fiction of representation was sometimes explained and defended as means by which all the different economic or social "interests" in a country had a voice in its government, but representation in England and America has never in fact been based on anything but geographically defined communities.[30]

It is the fact that senators do not sit for class, estate, or corporate interests that leaves them free to speak on all the issues that come before Parliament, and enables them collectively to support or check Cabinet and Commons. As Burke himself argued so persuasively in his address to the electors of Bristol, direct representation of corporate interests in Parliament constrains deliberation intolerably. In an effective Parliament, senators, like members of the Commons, must be able to speak freely. In John A. Macdonald's words, they must "sit down together and compare notes and discuss the questions that may come before [them], and ... be convinced according to the force of the reasons that may be advanced for or against."[31]

The property qualification and the fact that senators have a nonrenewable appointment (originally appointment for life) were meant to render the Upper House independent of the Crown and served as well to place the Upper House on a different footing from the Lower. Independence of the branches! If the Senate is to fulfil its function of checking the Cabinet it must have resources to enable it to resist the blandishments of the political executive. If it is to check the Commons it cannot be a mere duplicate of that house. Remember George Brown's contention: "The desire was to render the upper house a thoroughly independent body."[32] John A. Macdonald echoes him:

There would be no use of an upper house if it did not exercise, when it thought proper, the right of opposing or amending or postponing the legislation of the lower house. It would be of no value whatever were it a mere chamber for registering the decrees of the lower house."[33]

We come to the issue of selection. Should senators be appointed or elected? It was a major topic of debate at Confederation, more important, indeed, than the matter of qualifications. Agitation in favour of the elective upper house dated from the 1830s. When they were not arguing for abolition of the legislative council, the radicals of those years plumped for election, and the elective upper house proved in the end the one plank in their platform to interest later decades. The united province of Canada introduced elections for the legislative council in 1856.[34] Prince Edward Island adopted an elective upper house in 1862. In the Confederation debates some participants still see the elective second chamber as the necessary and progressive step, but they are in the minority.

One perhaps surprising feature of the debates is that we sometimes find Liberals arguing for an appointive Senate and Conservatives supporting an elective one. Brown's argument for the appointive upper house begins: "I have always been opposed to a second elective chamber ... I voted, almost alone, against the change when the council [in the Province of Canada] was made elective, but I have lived to see a vast majority of those who did the deed wish it had not been done."[35] Macdonald's begins: "The arguments for an elective council are numerous and strong; and I ought to say so, as one of the administration responsible for introducing the elective principle into [the Province of] Canada." He continues: "I hold this principle has not been a failure in Canada but there were causes – which we did not take into consideration at the time – why it did not so fully succeed ... as we had expected."[36]

Why did Liberals like Brown, traditionally more inclined to identify with the popular element, support appointment? Christopher Moore suggests that Brown for one favoured an appointive upper chamber because he believed it would have less legitimacy and would therefore be less forward politically and less inclined to interfere with responsible government, the principle for which Liberals had successfully campaigned for so many years.[37] Brown argues: "[What] was most feared was that the legislative councillors would be elected under party responsibilities; that a partisan spirit would show itself in the chamber; and that the right would soon be asserted to an equal control with this house over money bills."[38] Moore concludes that the Conservatives, or at least some of them, were willing to tolerate an elective house because they were less staunch in their support for responsible government.

It will not do to exaggerate the differences between the Liberals and the Conservatives on this issue. Macdonald comes down squarely for the appointive principle. The elected House had proved disappointing for several reasons. There was first the "enormous extent of the constituencies and the immense labour which consequently devolved on those who sought the suffrages of the people for election to the council." He also finds evidence of an "increasing disinclination on the part of men of standing, and political experience and weight in the country" to put themselves forward for election to the Upper Chamber. Young men of ambition, "those who have resolved to embrace the life of a statesman," were more likely to want seats in the Assembly.[39] It is perhaps a little surprising to find

Macdonald suggesting that province's legislative councillors were not men of the first rank, given that he required their approval to pass the Confederation resolutions. Brown is more politic: "I readily admit that if ever there was a body to whom we could safely entrust the power which by this measure we propose to confer on the members of the upper chamber, it is the body of gentlemen who at this moment compose the Legislative Council of Canada."[40]

Macdonald expresses admiration for the men who sat in the colonial legislative councils before the introduction of responsible government. The old colonial legislative councils, he says, commanded "great respect from the character, standing and weight of the individuals composing them." In other words, the councils appointed before responsible government were composed of exactly the kind of men Macdonald would like to see in an upper house. Unfortunately before responsible government, the councils "had little sympathy with the people or their representatives, and collisions with the lower house frequently occurred, especially in Lower Canada." The problem, it appears, is to ensure that the Upper House will be composed of persons of "standing," persons who have the weight and experience to oppose the people's representatives in the Commons, but who also have the prudence to defer to the Commons when deference is appropriate.

The dilemma as Macdonald describes it raises the issue of "deadlock." Would there come a time when the Upper House was too effective a curb, when the men of experience and standing that Macdonald so admires would bring Parliament to a halt? Curiously, neither Macdonald nor Brown thought there was much likelihood of deadlock. We have already seen that Brown believed an appointive upper house would see the wisdom of moderating its opposition to the elective body. Macdonald is of the same opinion: senators would not "set themselves deliberately at work to oppose what they know to be the settled opinions and wishes of the people of the country."[41]

It must be an independent house having a free action of its own, for it is only valuable as being a regulating body, calmly considering the legislation initiated by the popular branch and preventing any hasty or ill-considered legislation which may come from that body, but it will never set itself in opposition against the deliberate and understood wishes of the people.[42]

An obvious precaution against deadlock was to insert a clause in the new constitution to allow appointment of additional members to the Upper Chamber. Both Brown and Macdonald spoke against this idea, because they did not want to license "swamping," that is, appointment of legislative councillors by the ministry of the day "for the purpose of carrying out partisan schemes," and because they feared upsetting the Senate's distribution of seats by region.[43] Brown argues,

It was perfectly clear as argued by those who represented Lower Canada in the [Quebec] conference, that if the number of legislative councillors was made capable of increase, you would thereby sweep the whole protection they had from the upper chamber.[44]

Making the case against "swamping," Macdonald argues:

No ministry in Canada in future can do what they have done in Canada before – they cannot, with the view of carrying any measure or of strengthening the party, attempt to overrule the independent opinion of the upper house by filling it with a number of its partisans and political supporters. The provision in the constitution, that the Legislative Council shall consist of a limited number of members – that each of the great sections shall appoint twenty-four members and no more – will prevent the upper house from being swamped from time to time by the ministry of the day, for the purpose of carrying out their own schemes or pleasing their partisans. The fact of the government being prevented from exceeding a limited number will preserve the independence of the upper house and make it, in reality, a separate and distinct chamber, having a legitimate and controlling influence in the legislation of the country.[45]

Preserving the separateness and independence of the Upper Chamber from the machinations of the "monarchic" branch is an overriding concern for Brown and Macdonald. They know that without appropriate checks and balances, without an alert Senate, the elites that boast the support of a majority in the Commons are all too prone to ignore political dissent.

Nevertheless, at the London Conference of 1866–67, just before the Canada Bill was presented to the Westminster Parliament, the British Government insisted that the possibility of a deadlock between the houses required a provision allowing appointment of additional senators and Macdonald devised a formula to ensure that the additional appointments would not disrupt the regional representation in the Upper House. The result was section 26 of the *British North America Act, 1867*, which today allows the appointment of four or eight additional senators.

REPRESENTATION OF REGION

Consider again Brown's statement that Lower Canadians opposed the idea of appointing additional senators: If "the number of the legislative councillors was made capable of increase you would thereby sweep away the whole protection they had from the upper chamber."[46] We are reminded that the Canadian constitution gives the Senate two quite distinct tasks. The first is to "check" Cabinet and Commons. The second is to represent the regions of the Canadian federation, thereby "protecting" vulnerable constituencies. The first function is a feature of parliamentary regimes whether federal or unitary. The second is peculiar to federal systems. In the Confederation debates, representation of the constituent elements of the federation in the Upper House is one of the most hotly contested topics. The arguments have a familiar ring still today.

The formula devised by the Fathers owes much to the example of the American Senate though it does not adhere to it in all respects. The US system allows each state of the union two senators regardless of population, giving less populous states a great advantage. The *British North America Act, 1867*, in contrast, allocates seats in the Upper House on the basis of region. It overrepresents the smaller provinces, but not in the dramatic fashion of the United States. The Quebec Resolutions defined three "divisions," or regions of the new union, assigning to each twenty-four senators. Canada West and Canada East (still at this time referred to as Upper and Lower Canada, and soon to become Ontario and Quebec) each had twenty-four; the Maritimes as the third region had twenty-four, ten each for Nova Scotia and New Brunswick and four for Prince Edward Island, and then – a departure from the formula – Newfoundland was allotted an additional four.[47] It was a scheme open to challenge!

Legislators from Lower Canada feared, just as Brown suggests, that, without the security of a fixed number of seats in the Upper Chamber, the united English-speakers in Parliament might overwhelm the French. Hence their opposition to the idea of additional appointments at the behest of the Crown. The provinces on the periphery had a different gripe. The Quebec Resolutions of 1864, the first draft of the *British North America Act, 1867*, called for representation by population (rep by pop) in the Lower Chamber, a formula that would give Upper and Lower Canada, the giants of British North America, considerable political clout. Legislators from the Atlantic region and, later, from British Columbia complained that their provinces would be reduced to quasi-colonial status by this arrangement; they would be mere appendages of the central provinces. Some legislators argued for a scheme of representation in the Upper House that more closely approximated to the American system.[48] Some went so far as to demand enhanced representation for the small provinces in the Lower House in violation of rep by pop.[49]

In the end however, it was decided to the satisfaction of almost everyone that in a modern system of government the people's House, the Lower Chamber, must conform to the principle of representation by population. The hope was that the formula for regional representation in the Upper Chamber would be enough to offset the dominance rep by pop gave Ontario and Quebec, thus reassuring the periphery. Quebec in turn was to have a secure twenty-four seats and the guarantee that even if additional senators were appointed to break a deadlock the proportions of the regional distribution in the Upper House would be respected.

It is not too much to say that the fate of Confederation turned on the issue of regional representation in the Upper Chamber. As Brown argued:

The very essence of our compact is that the union shall be federal and not legislative. Our Lower Canada friends have agreed to ... representation by population in the lower house, on the express condition that they shall have equality in the upper house. On no other condition could we have advanced a step; and for my part I am quite willing that they should have it.[50]

WHAT HAPPENED AFTER 1867

Did the Senate fulfil the founders' expectations? Differences of opinion about the Senate's performance surface as soon as the ink dries on Confederation. This section reviews the arguments of the first fifty years. Recall the Senate's two tasks: to represent the regions and to exercise the "power of the check." How well did the Senate do as champion of the regions? In 1908 Senator Frederic Beique described the Fathers on regional representation in this fashion:

What led to adopting the constitution of the Senate at the time of confederation was that a part of the provinces were against the system of representation by population. As that system was forced by the larger provinces, it was thought proper that there should be compensation for the other provinces by having a Senate in which the members would be appointed otherwise than according to population.[51]

He captures the Fathers' argument exactly. From the beginning critics argued that the Senate would be better equipped to represent the regions if the provincial governments exercised the power of appointment or shared it with the federal level. In 1874, Ontario's David Mills demanded that the provinces be allowed to select Senators and to determine the means of doing so. He repeated his arguments in the House of Commons in 1886.[52] At the Interprovincial Conference of 1887, Quebec's Premier Honoré Mercier argued that it was generally admitted that the constitution of the Senate presented serious objections and that the power granted to the federal authorities to appoint to the Senate politicians belonging all to one party was a permanent source of danger of conflict between the two houses of the federal parliament and the executive.[53] He called for an elective upper house.

In a Commons debate of 1906 on reform of the Senate, G.H. McIntyre opted for a scheme of shared authority to appoint: "We find the anomaly that while the federal system is adopted and representation given in that way, the different parts of the Dominion coming into confederation have no power in the appointment of these senators." He continued: "I believe that a strong feeling exists among the Canadian people that the Canadian Senate has failed entirely to reach that standard which is desired and that it should be changed."[54]

Scholars sometimes cite as indication of the Senate's apparent failure to represent the regions the fact that other institutions soon took on the role. They note, for example, the aggressive defence of provincial rights by Mercier and by Ontario's premier Oliver Mowat at the 1887 Interprovincial Conference.[55] Another institution commonly believed to have trumped the Senate as champion of the provinces is Britain's Judicial Committee of the Privy Council, which prior to 1949 was Canada's final authority on the interpretation of the constitutional division of legislative powers. Eugene Forsey argued that the Senate had not had to protect the regions and provinces because the Judicial Committee of the Privy Council had so interpreted the British North America Act that the power of the national Parliament was steadily narrowed.

Canada is now the most decentralized federation in the world. So the national Parliament's power to work injury to regional interests has turned out to be much smaller than the Fathers had expected; and big, powerful, pushing provinces, working through the frequent federal-provincial conferences, have largely taken over the task of protecting the regions and provinces, even in matters under Dominion jurisdiction.[56]

Scholars are not all of one mind about the merits of the Judicial Committee of the Privy Council decisions. Those like Forsey who think the Fathers intended a strongly centralized union argue that the Law Lords' generous awards to the provinces subverted the founder's vision. But others argue that the Fathers intended a sturdy balance of federal and provincial powers and suggest that the Judicial Committee of the Privy Council's decisions conformed to the founders' design.[57] Nevertheless all agree the British judicial body was highly effective, perhaps more effective than the Senate, in upholding provincial powers.

But should we take the effectiveness of the Judicial Committee of the Privy Council as evidence that the Senate failed? Consider again the founders' scheme. They called for representation of the regions in a legislative and deliberative institution where the members would bring their knowledge of the regions into debates on national issues. None of the so-called usurping institutions (the provincial premiers, the interprovincial conferences, the Judicial Committee of the Privy Council, and – today – the machinery of executive federalism, the Supreme Court) fits this description. These other institutions may be effective in articulating and asserting provincial interests, but they do not articulate those interests in the formal, deliberative, and lawmaking process of the nation.

It is a peculiar feature of legislatures that the members represent both a particular constituency and the nation as a whole. Both members of the Commons and the Senate sit for their riding or region, and also for Canada.[58] Joseph Cauchon put the idea succinctly in the Confederation debates: "Our constitution is constructed upon the model of the British Constitution ... Each representative, although elected by one particular county, represents the whole country, and his legislative responsibility extends to the whole of it."[59] If members did not sit for the country as a whole they could not effectively debate measures in the national interest. There would indeed be no true national deliberation, and the Senate would have no "power of check." Consider the argument of Senator Ambrose Comeau, speaking in the 1908 debate on the Senate:

The supreme usefulness of this chamber [the Senate] depends ... upon ... its "national character," upon "the broad outlook" of its members; upon the maintenance of a just and equitable consideration, not only of the rights of every class of men and industry, but of each and every portion of the Dominion as well.[60]

It cannot be denied that this double obligation of parliamentary representatives, to speak for both locality and for the nation, poses a dilemma. Members are called on to reconcile the sometimes irreconcilable. Should we regard this feature of representative institutions as a deficiency? Perhaps it is a strength. The dilemma is ever present; the local interest cannot be neglected, but neither can the responsibility to consider local interests in the context of the national good. Note that there is no similar dilemma for the premiers in their role as provincial champions. They are free to defend their region single-mindedly. The role of integrating particular demands into the laws of the nation is a task for the national legislature.

This is not the place to compare at length courts and legislatures or federal-provincial decision-making committees and legislatures. I merely want to say that these bodies cannot do the job of upholding regional rights in just the way the Senate is called to do, and the fact that regional interests are articulated by other institutions does not mean that those interests should not be represented in Parliament as well. If the Senate is not, and by its very nature cannot be, the single-minded defender of provincial perspectives, it is in a better position than other institutions to represent them in the broadest deliberations and to remind those with a vision of the national good not to silence regional demands.

R. MacGregor Dawson argues: "It would be idle to deny that the Senate has not fulfilled the hopes of its founders; and it is well also to remember that the hopes of its founders were not excessively high."[61] Of course the Fathers knew contestation with the premiers and the partisans of locality would continue after Confederation. It is well known that Macdonald would have preferred a strong central government, but he was always surrounded by provincial champions: George-Etienne Cartier, George Brown, Oliver Mowat. The strength of local feeling in the Maritimes is well attested. The founders could not have believed representation of regions in the Upper Chamber would be enough to satisfy local feeling. I do think they regarded that representation as necessary. Would they be disappointed if they returned today? Surely not. Canadians, immersed in the daily headlines, see a history of crisis and turmoil. But in the world's eyes, this country ranks as a supremely successful federation: peaceful, wealthy, civil, and enduring.

There remains the second function of the Senate, its role as one of the three branches of Parliament. Though they clearly expected the Senate to refrain from obstructing the will of the elective house unduly, the founders just as obviously wanted a chamber that would query hasty or ill-considered legislation and would remain on the watch for attempts by the political executive to silence opposition.

Did the Senate live up to expectations in this second area? Some early critics thought the Senate was not aggressive enough. In 1886, Senator Lawrence Geoffrey Power argued "the truth is that this chamber as presently constituted, does not fulfil satisfactorily any of the objects for which the Senate is intended." Echoing the legislators of the 1860s he continues: "A second Chamber which is a mere echo of the Lower House is of no value in the constitution. If the second Chamber has no independence – if it never rejects a measure which is adopted by the ruling party in the Lower House or if it never largely amends such a measure, of what value is it?"[62] In the same debate Senator George Alexander argued that the framers designed the Senate of the Dominion to be a "safe-guard to prevent all maladministration from either the one or the other of the two great political parties of the country."[63] He too contends that it had not lived up to the task.

G.H. McIntyre is another convinced the Upper House had been ineffective as check on Cabinet and Commons. In the 1906 debates on Senate reform, he complains:

Would I be wrong in saying that it would seem as if it were necessary to inoculate the sleeping senators with some germ that would stimulate them to activity and a sense of duty? Something should be done, I think, to make those gentlemen feel that they are put upon their honour – something that would create a proper *esprit de corps* among them in regard to other matters than a mere attention to dignity.[64]

But McIntyre is no abolitionist. He asks:

What would abolition mean in Canada? ... It would put the business of Canada in the absolute control of the House of Commons, and not only that, but in the absolute control of the majority of that House, or a caucus of that majority. Would that be wise? ... The abolition of the Senate would mean leaving the destinies of this country under the control of an absolute democracy rather than a limited one.[65]

He continues: "In every polity, there should be some centre of resistance against predominant power, or that power will become absolute." Shades of J.S. Mill! McIntyre's mind buzzes with ideas to make the Upper House more effective. He wants to limit senatorial tenure to one term, "not to exceed the legal term of three parliaments."[66] In any case senators should retire before the age of eighty. As I noted above, McIntyre proposed that the provinces and federal authorities share the power to appoint. Giving power of appointment to the provinces would strengthen the Senate as regional champion. Taking some power from the federal government would enhance the Senate's independence, making it more effective as check on the Cabinet.

Robert MacKay, writing in 1926, shares McIntyre's opinion that the Senate must be a "centre of resistance." But unlike McIntyre he believes the Senate has fulfilled this role admirably. Noting that, "The Senate has never defeated the real will of the people or obstructed it when that will was clearly expressed," he continues:

A government which comes into power through the mechanics of election cannot be said to represent the opinions of the people on all public questions, though it may on the specific issue or issues upon which the election turned. The autocracy and arrogance of a political party which has conquered at the polls, and which through questionable means can maintain itself in office, is an ever-present danger in Canadian politics. No Government, however large its majority, however overwhelming may have been the defeat of its opponents, has an unlimited mandate ... A check upon the majority of the House of Commons is a sound requirement in Canada. This the Senate has been when its majority has been politically opposed to the majority in the Commons. On such occasions the Senate has not abused its power. On the contrary, it has been the guardian of the rights and interests of the people against the Government and temporary party majorities.[67]

High marks for the Senate from MacKay! Note the reference to "the autocracy and arrogance" of governing parties fresh from electoral victories. Such governments are an "ever present danger." Note the description of the Senate as "guardian of the rights and interests of the people"! If Sir John A. Macdonald had been alive in 1926, if John Stuart Mill had been writing, they would have seconded Robert MacKay!

And note MacKay's helpful reminder that "A government which comes into power through the mechanics of election cannot be said to represent the opinions of the people on all public questions." Parliament is more representative, more inclusive when the Senate insists on respect for dissenting voices.[68] MacKay cites Sir Clifford Sifton, writing in 1917:

According to my experience, the will of the people is very often better expressed after a check, and after a period of searching and critical discussion which generally arises from such a check, than it is in the first instance. It must also be remembered that under our system, the power of the Cabinet

tends to grow at the expense of the House of Commons ...The Senate is not
so much a check on the House of Commons as it is upon the Cabinet, and
there is no doubt that its influence in this respect is salutary.[69]

Both MacKay and Sifton believe the Senate is a more effective check
when its majority is politically opposed to the majority in the Commons.
To reinforce the point MacKay cites MP Frank Oliver:

I have been in Parliament since 1896 ... I have seen the Senate go counter to
a Liberal Government, and I have seen it go counter to a Conservative Government. I am bound to say that, in my humble judgement, the Senate is of
most use when, by reason of its majority not being in accord with the majority of the Commons, political alliances do not govern the judgement of Senators as thoroughly as they do when the majority is the same in both Houses.
It is when the Senate is liable to bring upon itself the objuration of the Government and its supporters that it justifies its existence and protects the
interests of the people.[70]

We must ask whether the Senate is in fact more likely to oppose when its
majority is not in accord with the majority in the Commons. As Jeffrey Simpson notes, early in the century it was evident that Canadian politics had
evolved into extended periods of one-party rule. "Once partisanship
became the overriding criterion for Senate appointments, one-party dominance produced a long series of senators from the governing party. This
development in turn frequently gave the Senate lop-sided majorities that
persisted regardless of any changes in the Commons." Through "no fault of
its own, the Senate sometimes found itself completely out of step with the
prevailing mood of the country."[71] When Laurier came to power in 1896
his Liberal majority in the Commons faced a Conservative majority in the
Senate. When Conservative Robert Borden took over in 1911 he faced a
Liberal majority in the Senate. The question is whether the out-of-step Senate is more likely to amend legislation coming up from the lower house.

Sir George Ross thinks not. He notes that from 1867 to 1903 the Conservative party was paramount politically in the Senate. For twenty-four
years of that period the same party was in control of the House of Commons. He finds "but very little difference in the number of Bills amended
or rejected by the Senate during those two different periods."[72] Whether
the houses are in step or out of step, whether the Conservatives or the Liberals dominate both, whether it's a Conservative Senate and Liberal Commons or Liberal Senate and Conservative Commons, the figures are in the
same ball park. The Senate amended perhaps one quarter of the Bills and
rejected outright no more than three percent. Ross concludes that party
influence counts for little.

Interesting findings! Ross's assertion points to the idea that under the
constitution members of the Senate have the independence hoped for by

the founders. An independent Senate can perhaps act as effective check on Cabinet and Commons even when the same party holds the majority in both houses.

John G. Bourinot notes that in the session of 1888 "twenty-six Commons bills were amended out of the one hundred and three sent to the upper house." The majority of these amendments were "verbal and unimportant." However he also contends that:

From time to time the senate makes amendments that show how thoroughly its members understand and are competent to consider certain subjects; and the sometimes hasty legislation of the commons – hasty because that body is often overweighted with business – is corrected greatly to the advantage of the country.[73]

He makes this observation to support his argument that more legislation should be introduced in the Upper Chamber.

Note that McIntyre, Bourinot, MacKay, Sifton, and Oliver are all wedded to the idea that the Upper Chamber should exercise "the power of the check." McIntyre and Bourinot think the Senate's performance could be improved; they have ideas for reform. But just as much as MacKay, Sifton, and Oliver, they believe the Senate must act as counterweight to Cabinet and Commons.

It is time to turn to the parliamentarians and scholars who criticize the Senate because they find something objectionable in the very idea of the "power of the check." These are the critics who think it undemocratic for an out-of-power party ensconced in the Upper Chamber to thwart the will of the elected majority in the Lower House. We have already had a hint of this view in Mercier's suggestion at the 1887 Interprovincial Conference that the power granted to the federal authorities to appoint to the Senate politicians belonging all to one party is a permanent source of danger of conflict between the two houses of Parliament and the Executive. Most of the observers we have seen so far think that at least a degree of conflict between the houses is salutary. Mercier, in contrast, suggests conflict should be avoided.

In the 1886 Commons debates on the appointment process, David Mills argued that the Senate "as at present constituted" is objectionable because "it is in no way amenable to public opinion; it is not controlled by the intelligent public opinion of the country."[74] How often above did we find parliamentarians and authors arguing that the Senate would be useless if it merely replicated the opinions and arguments of the public as represented in the Commons. But Mills, like Mercier, wants a Senate that answers to the prevailing majority in the manner of the Commons. The out-of-step Senate is inherently objectionable:

If there were a change of Government, and the administration of public affairs should pass into the hands of those not in political accord with the

Senate, it is plain, I think, that we should have a deadlock in our legislation and our administration.

Mills has other criticisms. He argues that the Senate is too lazy to conduct effective research. (He compares the Canadian Senate and the British House of Lords, to the Senate's disadvantage.) He never loses sight of his provincial rights agenda. But our concern here is with his belief that the Senate should be in step with current opinion, amenable to the "intelligent public opinion" of the country. His original 1874 motion on Senate selection is worth quoting in full:

The present method of constituting the Senate is inconsistent with the Federal principle in our system of Government, it makes that body independent of the people and the Crown, and is in other material respects defective, and ... the appropriate steps should taken to secure such amendments of the British North America Act as to make the Senate directly responsible to the people in the several provinces of the Dominion.[75]

In the 1886 debate in the Upper House, Senator Richard Scott argued: "We live in a democratic age, when a chamber constituted as the Senate is, differs entirely from any other legislative body on the face of the globe." A nominated chamber, he concludes, "is entirely repugnant to the first principles" on which Canada is governed.[76] The principle of selection, he said, should be brought into harmony with public opinion.

Randall White suggests that by the time Laurier came to power the Senate's "most immediately controversial feature had become its tendency to artificially extend the influence of the former federal governing party, most recently defeated by the voters at the polls." Recurrent "bouts of righteous indignation at the essentially undemocratic interventions of an appointed Senate, in an increasingly democratic national political system, drew attention away from any positive role the Senate might have played as defender of regional interests."[77] For those seized with such "righteous indignation," I suggest, it is the very idea of opposition to the majority that incenses.

We are now a long way from the founders' vision. The Fathers wanted a Constitution that would temper majority rule. They wanted assurance that the Upper Chamber could challenge the vaulting ambition of a political Executive supported by electoral majority. In the unchecked Executive they saw a threat to political freedom. In the regime they prescribed they saw security for freedom and dissent, including the dissent of regions.

McIntyre called the Fathers' form of government "limited democracy." We call it liberal democracy. It is democratic because the representation of political interests and argument is broad, acknowledging contributions from the political minority as well as the majority that supports the party in office. It is democratic because, as Clifton suggests, the "will of the people is very often better expressed after a check, and after a period of searching and critical discussion which generally arises from such a check."[78]

THE SENATE IN A DEMOCRATIC AGE

"We live in a democratic age."[79] At the time Senator Scott was speaking the term "democracy" was undergoing a change of meaning. In the Confederation debates, it usually referred to a form of rule in which leaders claimed absolute and uncontested authority to speak for the *demos*. The Fathers of Confederation did not call themselves democrats because they did not believe any one party should have uncontested authority. By the 1880s, "democracy" could be used to describe any form of government in which participation by the people is encouraged. It was becoming a term of approbation.

G.H. McIntyre's insight remains helpful.[80] "Democracy" as we now use it includes two sharply opposed notions: it sometimes refers to "limited democracy," or liberal democracy, which believes tolerance of political opposition is crucial, but it may also refer to "absolute democracy," crude majoritarianism, which is suspicious of opposition, "checks," delays, and obstruction. What is clear is that insofar as our understanding of "democracy" moves toward the "absolute" end of the scale, respect for the second chamber is in danger.[81]

Is the party of absolute democracy now in the ascendancy in this country? Surely not. And yet in the quest for accountability to the majority Canadians have now gone very far in stripping away parliamentary features that the founders regarded as essential. The provincial second chambers went years ago. The federal Senate has proved more resistant, grounded as it is in the British North America Act. But Canadians have found ways to demean the Senate using the media and the classroom. We have forgotten its role as check on Cabinet and Commons, a fact that has surely contributed to the concentration of power in the Cabinet and especially in the hands of the Prime Minister. (Remember Sifton's observation that, in parliamentary regimes now, the Senate is not so much a check on the House of Commons as it is upon the Cabinet).

And how Canadians complain about the concentration of power in Cabinet! We describe Executive dominance as a form of autocracy. We argue that Parliament does not pay attention to political minorities and does not allow effective political participation and deliberation. Yet we apparently believe that further streamlining is necessary, that further trimming the institutional "checks" will curb Executive dominance, thus increasing democracy. Confusion reigns in our thinking about Parliament!

It might be suggested that any regime with a free electorate and competing political parties will protect political dissent and encourage political deliberation in the legislature. In the unicameral systems of the provinces we rely on the media, a network of political interest groups, competition among the parties, and habits of mind formed by living in a parliamentary democracy. Do these safeguards suffice? Individual premiers can be very powerful, surely more powerful than the founders' formula would tolerate. In the larger provinces especially, with their substantial immigrant populations, dissatisfied "identities," and marked urban-rural cleavages we might do well to resurrect provincial bicameralism. It has been suggested that Quebec re-establish its Upper Chamber.[82] A highly interesting proposal! What better way to assert Quebec's constitutional independence and distinctiveness, while affirming an essential element of Canadian parliamentary tradition and history?

The Second Chamber as the Canadian founders intended it had the vital function of checking the potential for highhandedness in Cabinet and Commons. It was given the task of securing the respect for political dissent that promotes deliberation about the common good. It was to ensure that no clique, no faction, not even the party commanding the majority in the Commons – especially not the party commanding the majority in the Commons – could rule unchallenged. When bicameralism was working well, when the dash of moderation prescribed by Macdonald and Brown was evident, it would take some of the sting out of the winner-take-all electoral system. Parties and interests losing a general election would sometimes, perhaps often, retain a voice in Parliament. Confidence in the efficacy of the vote would be reinforced, and parliamentary representation and the idea of deliberation strengthened. (Why should the passions of the present and dreams of the future be the sole and overriding influence in our political debates?)

Liberal philosophers like to believe that good government results from good institutions rather than good hearts. Given a well-designed system like parliamentary liberal democracy, it should not be necessary to rely on political virtue in our leaders or in the general populace. As Immanuel Kant famously argues, the good regime can be operated by a race of intelligent devils with results of benefit to all. But I do not think that good institutions will always stand against the assault of ignorance, hostile intention, or – perhaps the greatest danger – political utopianism. And these are exceptional times in Canada. During the debates on the Meech Lake and Charlottetown Accords Canadians indulged in an orgy of constitutional utopianism. We allowed ourselves to dream of a radically New Constitution, a New Canada. We were ready to jettison the proven institutions of liberal democracy for a future whose outlines we could barely discern.

It is time to make our liberal democracy work. It is time to revisit the founders' bicameralism. We must summon to our aid whatever forbearance, moderation, prudence, street-smarts, and statesmanship we have left. For the fact is that humans have not discovered a better system of government for the modern world than parliamentary liberal democracy.

NOTES

1 Arend Lijphart suggests that more nations would adopt unicameralism if it were not for the sheer difficulty of amending constitutions; Lijphart, "Foreword: 'Cameral Change' and Institutional Conservatism," xi.

2 Longley and Olsen, *Two Into One*, Chapter 1.

3 For the arguments of the legislators, see the debates on Confederation from 1865 to 1873 in British Columbia, the Red River colony, the Maritimes, the Province of Canada, and Newfoundland. A selection of these debates is found in Ajzenstat et al., *Canada's Founding Debates*. For the arguments of the elites who drafted the British North America Act at the 1864 Quebec Conference (the Fathers of Confederation), see Browne, *Documents on the Confederation of British North America*.

4 A number of legislators consulted Thomas D'Arcy McGee's *Notes sur les gouvernements fédéraux passés et présents*. McGee describes federal systems and confederacies ancient and modern, including the (then) federal constitution of New Zealand.

5 Abolishing the upper house or humbling it in some other fashion was a major objective of the Canadian rebels. See the report by Louis-Joseph Papineau's agent, John Arthur Roebuck, *Colonies of England, A Plan for the Government of Some Portion of Our Colonial Possessions*. A good recent account of debates on the role of the second chamber in Upper Canada can be found in McNairn, *The Capacity to Judge, Public Opinion and Deliberative Democracy in Upper Canada, 1791–1854*, 288–95.

6 For a defence of the upper house as a vital part of the parliamentary constitution, see Pierre Bédard's "Prospectus" for the journal *Le Canadien*, November 1806. Bédard was perhaps the most eminent Canadian constitutional scholar of our early history. He was also the first leader of the French Canadian party in the Legislative Assembly of Lower Canada. His leadership in the popular house and his sterling defence of the principle of parliamentary responsible government make his support for the second chamber the more impressive. Another constitutional teacher of importance was Étienne Parent; see especially *Le Canadien*, 18 February 1824, and 8 September 1842. Still another constitutional authority was Lord Durham. He was regularly cited in the Confederation debates. At the time of the Confederation debates Durham is still routinely cited as a constitutional authority. In *Report on the Affairs of British North America*, he argued that the colonial legislative councils had been "little calculated to answer the purpose of placing the effective check which I consider necessary on the popular branch of the legislature," but elsewhere he praises the Legislative Council of Lower Canada: "The Colony has reason to congratulate itself on the existence of an institution which possessed and used the power of stopping a course of legislation that, if successful, would have ... overthrown every guarantee of order and national liberty" (Craig, *Lord Durham's Report*, 59; see also 80–1, 168–9).

7 Ross, Red River, Fort Garry Convention, 31 January 1870, in Ajzenstat et al., *Canada's Founding Debates*, 68.

8 Macdonald, Canadian Legislative Assembly, 6 February 1865, in Ajzenstat et al., *Canada's Founding Debates*, 70.

9 F.B.T. Carter, Newfoundland House of Assembly, 23 February 1869, in Ajzenstat et al., *Canada's Founding Debates*, 59.

10 See, for example, Lord Gosford's Report of 1837 on British North America, 6: "the system of checks and balances is often considered the peculiar feature of the British Constitution."

11 Keith Archer et al., *Parameters of Power, Canada's Political Institutions*. For a better view of the Westminster constitution, one consonant with the argument of this chapter, see Aucoin, "Accountability: The Key to Restoring Public Confidence in Government."

12 Stevens, New Brunswick House of Assembly, 23 June 1866, in Ajzenstat et al., *Canada's Founding Debates*, 96.

13 Brown, Canadian Legislative Assembly, 8 February 1865, in Ajzenstat et al., *Canada's Founding Debates*, 88.

14 Ryan, Canadian Legislative Council, 20 February 1865, in Ajzenstat et al., *Canada's Founding Debates*, 93.

15 Mitchell, Legislative Council of New Brunswick, 16 April 1866, in Ajzenstat et al., *Canada's Founding Debates*, 96.

16 For the history of this idea see Fink, *The Classical Republicans: An Essay in the Recovery of a Pattern of Thought in Seventeenth Century England*; see also the review of Fink in Leo Strauss, *What is Political Philosophy? and Other Studies*, 290–2. Strauss illuminates the difference between modern and ancient theories of mixed government, implicit in Fink's account. The modern theory, following the seventeenth-century philosophers Hobbes and Locke, insists that governments adhere to the principle of human equality. The ancient argues that good government must take account of men's natural inequalities.

17 Macdonald, Canadian Legislative Assembly, 6 February 1865, in Ajzenstat et al., *Canada's Founding Debates*, 206.

18 Cartwright, Canadian Legislative Assembly, 9 March 1865, in Ajzenstat et al., *Canada's Founding Debates*, 18–9.

19 Mill, "Considerations on Representative Government (1861)," 513–9. The introduction to the World's Classics edition of Mill's *Representative Government* notes that Mill crucially influenced British debates on the reform of the franchise in 1867, but it fails to point out that he was at least as influential in the design of the new nation just then coming into being in British North America. What attracted the British North Americans was Mill's support for the principle of responsible government and his defence of the second chamber. His position on reform of the electoral system received less attention.

20 Ryan, Canadian Legislative Council, 20 February 1865, in Ajzenstat et al., *Canada's Founding Debates*, 93.

21 *British North America Act, 1867* (now called the *Constitution Act, 1867*), section 23 (3).

22 See Ajzenstat, *The Political Thought of Lord Durham*, chapter 6.

23 The merits of the 1791 Constitution were the subject of furious debate in

the colonies, and scholars even today are not of one mind. Did the framers mean to recreate the British Constitution and parliamentary system in full? Or did they think they were devising a truncated system appropriate for a dependency?

24 Few members of the British Parliament believed the seignieurial class in Lower Canada formed an effective aristocratic estate.

25 *The Parliamentary History of England,* vol. 29, especially the debates of 6 and 11 May 1791. Since Fox was commonly regarded as a spokesman for popular interests, his insistence on the equal importance of the Upper Chamber is noteworthy. The entire debate is fascinating. Here is the Mother of Parliaments sitting down in the great age of constitution-making to put on paper a version of the famous unwritten constitution! It is also the occasion of the quarrel between Burke and Fox on the French Revolution, a quarrel directly relevant to the issues before them in the Canada Bill.

26 *The Parliamentary History of England,* vol. 29, 11 May 1791.

27 Macdonald, Canadian Legislative Assembly, 6 February 1865, in Ajzenstat et al., *Canada's Founding Debates,* 82. He is describing an appointive legislative council.

28 It was a development to which indeed Burke made a signal contribution. His "Speech to the Electors of Bristol," influential in its day, is still instructive.

29 Ross, *The Senate of Canada, Its Constitution, Powers and Duties Historically Considered,* 69–70.

30 Morgan, *Inventing the People, The Rise of Popular Sovereignty in England and America,* 41.

31 Macdonald, Canadian Legislative Assembly, 13 March 1865, in Ajzenstat et al., *Canada's Founding Debates,* 461.

32 Brown, Canadian Legislative Assembly, 8 February 1865, in Ajzenstat et al., *Canada's Founding Debates,* 88.

33 Macdonald, Canadian Legislative Assembly, 6 February 1865, in Ajzenstat et al., *Canada's Founding Debates,* 80.

34 Existing life members retained their seats. Some of the most thoughtful arguments on all issues of Confederation emerge from exchanges among appointive and elective members in the Canadian Legislative Council. For the debate on the subject of the elective upper house in the new constitution, see Ajzenstat et al., *Canada's Founding Debates,* 88–95.

35 Brown, Canadian Legislative Assembly, 8 February 1865, in Ajzenstat et al., *Canada's Founding Debates,* 83.

36 Macdonald, Canadian Legislative Assembly, 6 February 1865, in Ajzenstat et al., *Canada's Founding Debates,* 78–9.

37 Moore, *1867: How the Fathers Made a Deal,* 108ff.

38 Brown, Canadian Legislative Assembly, 8 February 1865, in Ajzenstat et al., *Canada's Founding Debate,* 84.

39 Macdonald, Canadian Legislative Assembly, 6 February 1865 , in Ajzenstat et al., *Canada's Founding Debates,* 79.

40 Brown, Canadian Legislative Assembly, 8 February 1865, in Ajzenstat et al., *Canada's Founding Debates*, 88. Brown later felt he had earned a Senate appointment by his efforts on behalf of Confederation. Cartoons of the period cruelly depict him in doggy form, begging for a senate "bone." But when Old Mother Macdonald went to the cupboard, it was bare.

41 Canadian Legislative Assembly, 6 February 1865, in Ajzenstat et al., *Canada's Founding Debates*, 82.

42 Canadian Legislative Assembly, 6 February 1865, in Ajzenstat et al., *Canada's Founding Debates*, 80.

43 Macdonald, Canadian Legislative Assembly, 6 February 1865, in Ajzenstat et al., *Canada's Founding Debates*, 79–80.

44 Brown, Canadian Legislative Assembly, 8 February 1865, in Ajzenstat et al., *Canada's Founding Debates*, 88.

45 Macdonald, Canadian Legislative Assembly, 6 February 1865, in Ajzenstat et al., *Canada's Founding Debates*, 79–80.

46 Brown, Canadian Legislative Assembly, 8 February 1865, in Ajzenstat et al., *Canada's Founding Debates*, 88.

47 The Quebec Resolutions, 8 and 9; see in Ajzenstat et al., *Canada's Founding Debates,* 465–6.

48 See Albert J. Smith in the New Brunswick House of Assembly, 27 June 1866 and the debate that followed the next day, in Ajzenstat et al., *Canada's Founding Debates*, 271–5. Smith finds it offensive that Canada (Canada East and West) will be represented by forty-eight senators, while the three Maritime provinces together will have only twenty-four. In Newfoundland, George Hogsett argues that the province's paltry four members would be "out-voted on every question affecting the policy of Newfoundland" (House of Assembly, 23 February 1869, in Ajzenstat et al., *Canada's Founding Debates*, 98–9). Both men prefer the American scheme.

49 See the debate in the New Brunswick House of Assembly, 31 May 1865, in Ajzenstat et al., *Canada's Founding Debates*, 111–12.

50 Brown, Canadian Legislative Assembly, 8 February 1865, in Ajzenstat et al., *Canada's Founding Debates*, 286.

51 Beique, in Canada, Senate, *Debates*, 24 March 1908, 641.

52 Mills, in Canada, House of Commons, *Debates*, 14 May 1886, 1272–3. The idea had already surfaced in the Confederation debates.

53 "Minutes of the Interprovincial Conference held at the City of Quebec from the 20th to the 28th October, 1887, inclusively," in Cloutier, *Dominion Provincial and Interprovincial Conferences from 1887 to 1926*, 7–27.

54 McIntyre, in Canada, House of Commons, *Debates*, 30 April 1906, 2285.

55 Simpson, *Spoils of Power: The Politics of Patronage*, 312.

56 Forsey, "The Canadian Senate," 276. Forsey also argues that regional representation in Cabinet has demoted the Senate's role. It is a factor mentioned frequently by other scholars.

57 See Sabetti and Waller, "Introduction: Crisis and Continuity in Canadian

Federalism," 2: "The Canadian constitutional system gave the national government such formidable power and influence over provincial governments as to place the latter in a position of nearly colonial subordination to the national government." Contrast the argument in Romney, *Getting It Wrong: How Canadians Forgot Their Past and Imperilled Confederation*, and Vipond, *Liberty and Community, Canadian Federalism and the Failure of the Constitution*.

58 Edmund Burke is the great authority here. And see Morgan, *Inventing the People*, especially chapter 2, "The Enigma of Representation."

59 Cauchon, Canadian Legislative Assembly, 6 March 1865, in Ajzenstat et al., *Canada's Founding Debates*, 448.

60 Comeau, in Canada, Senate, *Debates*, 24 March 1908, 647.

61 Dawson, *The Government of Canada*, 307.

62 Power, in Canada, Senate, *Debates*, 3 May 1886, 331.

63 Alexander, in Canada, Senate, *Debates*, 3 May 1886, 328.

64 McIntyre, in Canada, House of Commons, *Debates*, 30 April 1906, 2286.

65 McIntyre, in Canada, House of Commons, *Debates*, 20 January 1908, 1518.

66 McIntyre, in Canada, House of Commons, *Debates*, 20 January 1908, 1513; and see Canada, House of Commons, *Debates*, 30 April 1906, 2276.

67 MacKay, *The Unreformed Senate of Canada*, 136–7.

68 On dissent and political deliberation in the years before Confederation, and the decline of confidence in deliberation in our own day, see especially the introductory and concluding chapters in McNairn, *The Capacity to Judge, Public Opinion and Deliberative Democracy in Upper Canada*.

69 MacKay, *The Unreformed Senate of Canada*, 136; Sifton, "The Foundation of the New Era," 50.

70 Oliver, in Canada, House of Commons, *Debates*, 11 June 1914, 5294–5, cited in MacKay, *The Unreformed Senate of Canada*, 236n1.

71 Simpson, *Spoils of Power*, 313.

72 Ross, *The Senate of Canada, Its Constitution, Powers and Duties Considered*, 74ff.

73 Bourinot, *Federal Government in Canada*, 99–100.

74 Mills, in Canada, House of Commons, *Debates*, 14 May 1886, 1272–3.

75 Mills, in Canada, House of Commons, *Debates*, 14 May 1886, 1275.

76 Scott, in Canada, Senate, *Debates*, 3 May 1886, 334.

77 White, *Voice of Region: The Long Journey to Senate Reform in Canada*, 106–8.

78 Sir Clifford Sifton, cited in MacKay, *The Unreformed Senate of Canada*, 136.

79 Senator Richard Scott, in Canada, Senate, *Debates*, 3 May 1886, 334.

80 Compare Macpherson, *The Real World of Democracy*, on liberal and non-liberal democracy.

81 Examining the impetus behind efforts to abolish or reform the Senate, Ian MacGregor concludes that dissatisfaction with the upper house stems from partisan considerations rather than any clear sense that the Senate was failing to meet expectations; MacGregor, "A History of Senate Reform in Canada, 1867–1957."

82 Descoteaux, "Un Nécessaire contrepoids," A8.

CHAPTER TWO

Forty Years of Not Reforming the Senate

Jack Stilborn

INTRODUCTION

Discussion of Senate reform has been a near-constant feature of the Canadian political landscape over the past forty years. This chapter examines the major government and parliamentary proposals for reform developed during this period.

All of the proposals ended in failure, but this does not mean that they are no longer useful. The proposals identify the major reform options and provide insightful explorations of their relative merits and weaknesses and, thus, a kind of cognitive resource base for any future consideration of Senate reform. Their history offers instruction about the obstacles that must be surmounted if future reform proposals are ever to be adopted and implemented. The reports are especially noteworthy for the light they shed on evolving public expectations. They are all the products of consultative processes and, in the case of the parliamentary reports, reflect the work of committee members with wide political experience. The reports are thus particularly helpful in identifying assumptions, some of them questionable, that have crept into the Senate reform debate. Many of the issues raised in these proposals remain important, and any future attempt to improve the Senate needs to build upon what we can learn from the reports, rather than merely repeating their errors.

The chapter is structured in two parts, reflecting its two central purposes. In part 1, which reviews the proposals, an attempt is made to relate key elements of the proposals to the major arguments relied upon to justify them and to any arguments developed to critically respond to other proposals and to public expectations. This approach is intended to counterbalance the tendency, especially evident in the pressure-cooker atmosphere of task forces and parliamentary committees, to reduce past proposals to short summaries of their key recommendations and lose sight of their supporting arguments, which are arguably at least as important.

A fundamental theme of part 2 is that discussions of Senate reform in Canada have suffered from a chronic lack of adequately specific attention to the problems that reform is intended to remedy. This has fostered recurring vagueness about how, precisely, a reformed Senate would make things better. These problems may explain the long-standing tendency for debate about reform to be dominated by relatively transitory assumptions about what is needed and how it should be achieved. Perhaps as a result of this, public support for Senate reform has never attained the degree of intensity or duration required to propel significant change.

PART 1:

MAJOR PROPOSALS AND THEIR KEY ARGUMENTS

The Proposals: An Overview

Beginning in the 1960s, the issue of Senate reform began to be pursued with new urgency. Heightened public and governmental attention reflected developments both in Quebec, where the Quiet Revolution was fostering new autonomist pressures, and in Western Canada, where perceptions of the unresponsiveness of central institutions were exacerbating long-standing resentments.

More broadly, the new prominence attached to Senate reform in the 1960s reflected the innovative style – and focus on institutions and processes – characteristic of the federal government of that era. The emergence of the provinces as independent policy-making entities also required a broad adjustment of federal-provincial relationships.

Four decades of sporadic discussion have produced some important shifts in the content of Senate reform proposals. During the 1960s and 1970s, the emphasis was on the rehabilitation of the appointed Senate, by means of some degree of provincial involvement in the appointment of senators.

One group of proposals would have involved the provinces in one half of Senate appointments, while leaving the other half exclusively in the hands of the federal government.[2] A second group of proposals for an appointed Senate relied heavily on the West German "Bundesrat model," and would have given exclusive provincial control over appointments.[3] The Senate thus would have become a kind of proxy for the provincial governments, and it was anticipated that the process of accommodating provincial concerns might shift from the domain of intergovernmental relations and First Ministers' Conferences to the federal legislative process itself. Controversy over the desirability of this development became, indeed, a central element in debate over the proposals, with some proponents of decentralization opposing a Bundesrat Senate on the grounds that it would shift powers to the federal government and reduce the scope of provincial influence.

Beginning in the early 1980s, the prevailing fashion in Senate reform proposals underwent a substantial shift. The assumption underlying successive proposals came to be the equation of elected status with legitimacy, from which it seemed to follow that the Senate could not have a major and durable impact on the legislative process unless it, like the House of Commons, was a product of democratic electoral choice-making.

The major proposals calling for an elected Senate are the 1984 report of a special joint committee of the Senate and House of Commons (Molgat-Cosgrove), the 1985 report of the Royal Commission on the Economic Union and Development Prospects for Canada, the 1985 report of the Alberta Select Special Committee on Upper House Reform, and the 1992 proposal of the Special Joint Committee on a Renewed Canada.4 It should be noted that the first of these proposals responded to a 1983 discussion paper that provides the first favourable treatment by the federal government of the option of direct election, while the most recent proposal is reflective of the criteria and guidelines set out in a general framework proposal released by the federal government in September 1991, which the Committee had been created to study.5

The Charlottetown proposal of 28 August 1992, the last proposal in the recent cycle, is very much in the tradition of the proposals for an elected Senate dating back to the early 1980s.6 Indeed, its central novelty is that it combines within one proposal many of the procedural and structural options that had previously been seen as competing alternatives.

In the remainder of part 1, these proposals are compared with respect to the three major architectural components involved in major reforms to the Senate: methods of selecting senators (including electing them); the regional distribution of Senate seats; and the powers to be exercised. Drawing partly on these comparisons, part 1 then concludes with a discussion of the purposes underlying the proposals, and the expectations these imply.

Methods of Selecting Senators

APPOINTED SENATE PROPOSALS

Proposals of the 1960s and 1970s for a reformed appointed Senate do not oppose elected upper houses universally. They argue, instead, that the election of the second chamber is incompatible with the parliamentary system, or would require sacrifices outweighing the advantages gained.

Thus, for example, a 1978 Government of Canada paper setting out the rationale underlying Bill C–60 argues that an elected Upper House is a viable option in a congressional system founded on the separation of powers, such as that in the United States.7 It is claimed, however, that the dependence of the Executive on the confidence of the elected Lower House in a parliamentary system makes the election of the Upper House inappropriate. An elected Senate, simply by virtue of being elected, would undermine the supremacy of the House of Commons and foster confusion. Two elected Houses would complicate the question of ultimate responsibility and thus undermine parliamentary government.

This basis for rejecting an elected Senate was repeated in the 1979 report of the Pepin-Robarts task force.[8] It argues that the Australian experience (which involved serious deadlock between the Upper and Lower Houses during the mid 1970s) illustrates the problems that can arise in a parliamentary system when there is a conflict between two popularly elected Houses. It also argues that an electoral process would tend to enhance the role of political parties, so that party concerns, rather than regional concerns, would tend to dominate the activity of an elected Upper House.

These arguments were also made in 1978 by the Government of British Columbia.[9] This proposal argues that giving an elected Senate modest powers (perhaps in the form of a suspensive veto) would not necessarily be a permanent solution to the problem of conflict between the Houses. The point is made that elected senators might justifiably feel entitled to unrestricted powers and would exert continuing pressure in this direction. A supplementary approach is taken in the 1972 Molgat-McGuigan report, which argues that an elected Senate would be less able to represent minorities and Canadian diversity than an appointed Senate[10]; representatives of even the least numerous ethnic and other minorities can be systematically appointed to the Senate, while an electoral process is less likely to achieve their representation.

ELECTED SENATE PROPOSALS

Early proposals for an elected Senate share the view that elected status is a prerequisite for the legitimate exercise of influence, and several make this claim explicitly. The 1985 Alberta Select Committee, for example, argues that only a directly elected Senate "would enjoy legitimacy and would be able to exercise fully the significant political and legislative powers necessary to make a valuable contribution to the Canadian Parliament."[11] A similar view is apparent in the 1984 Molgat-Cosgrove report, which argues that the central objective of enhanced regional representation can only be achieved by reforms that "ensure that senators have more political authority."[12]

The assumption that representative legitimacy and elected status are closely connected also underlies the 1985 Macdonald Commission proposal. It argues that "The Senate is part of Parliament, and Parliament is pre-eminently a representative body. For that reason ... we join those who have argued that the Senate should be an elected body."[13] Similarly, the Beaudoin-Dobbie proposal of 1992 concludes:

If we wish to establish a strong and effective institution to ensure the responsiveness of the central government to regional needs, that institution needs to have the legitimacy which comes from having been chosen directly by the people.[14]

The Charlottetown proposal would have enabled provincial govern-ments to choose between two methods for the selection of senators: direct election by the people of the province or election by the provincial legis-lature.[15] Although neither option (nor the need for more than one) is justified explicitly, the first at least conforms with major Senate reform pro-posals since the early 1980s in its apparent assumption about the relation between election, legitimacy, and the potential effectiveness of the Senate. The second option – election by the provincial legislature – was included during the final stages of negotiations, in order to obtain agreement by Quebec. The resulting Senate would, therefore, likely have consisted of two cohorts of senators: indirectly elected senators from (at least) Quebec and senators directly elected by the people in other parts of Canada.

The existence of two representation options places the Charlottetown model in tension with the argument, made in the other proposals, that there is an important distinction between representing provincial legisla-tures or governments (mandated to deal with issues in the provincial juris-diction) and representing the people of the provinces in national decision-making. It also raises issues of internal consistency, since questions about the legitimacy of indirectly elected senators appear unavoidably to be implied by the rationale for directly electing other senators. The status of the representation provided by indirectly elected senators would, in prac-tice, depend partly on the procedures used to elect them. They could, for example, be selected according to procedures that would ensure that a province's cohort of senators would mirror its political diversity. Alterna-tively, procedures placing the power to select entirely in the hands of a government majority could result in senators more closely akin to proxies of the provincial government. The Charlottetown agreement does not preclude either of these possibilities. It therefore opened the door to a considerable variation, at least initially, in the kind of representation provincial populations would have in the Senate.

CONCLUDING OBSERVATIONS

The main development among proposals for selecting senators is a deci-sive shift in fashion from appointive systems to elective systems, which appears to have taken place in a very short time during the early 1980s. This was not the result of a sudden revelation concerning the relation between elected status and legitimacy. The authors of earlier appointive proposals had routinely acknowledged this relation, before going on to advocate appointive systems on the grounds that they would achieve desir-able results, without posing the danger to responsible government associ-ated with elected upper houses.

Any attempt to explain the perception shift that occurred in the early 1980s is necessarily speculative, since the more recent proposals do not extensively address the concerns about election raised in earlier proposals. They simply assert, as a self-evident truth, that only elected status can provide the Senate with the needed legitimacy. They assume that the influence available to a reformed appointed Senate would not be enough to do the job that a second chamber charged with representing the underpopulated regions needs to do.

The unstated assumption that may explain the perception shift concerns the extensiveness of the intervention that would be needed from a reformed Senate and, perhaps, the degree of resistance towards adequate regional representation present in Canada's existing political process. Earlier proposals included regional representation among a range of useful tasks that the Senate could perform and assumed that provincial appointment processes could confer the needed degree of legitimacy. Later proposals appear to be more pessimistic. The watershed development underlying this shift was almost certainly the National Energy Plan, which provoked furious resentment in Alberta following its announcement by the federal government in October 1980.[16] It would appear that the depth of this resentment crystallized long-standing pressures for greater responsiveness from central institutions into a desire for something more tangible: a Senate that would provide the West with enough "clout" to ensure the protection of its interests, and specifically the preclusion of future National Energy Plans.[17]

Electoral Systems

A number of possible electoral systems have been proposed. The rationales for these systems focus, in general, on their effectiveness in reflecting the complexion of political opinion within the electorate as well as on issues of comprehensibility to the electorate and administrative complexity.

THE MOLGAT-COSGROVE REPORT (1984)[18]

The Vote. The Molgat-Cosgrove report argues for single-member Senate constituencies and plurality voting on the grounds that proportional representation involving the selection of candidates from lists drawn up by their political party would foster greater dependence of candidates on their party. This, in turn, would reduce the likelihood of nonpartisan conduct in the Senate and increase the probability that partisan considerations would prevail over regional considerations in the voting of senators. The report also argues that because most Canadians have no experience with such a proportional system, and its operation would not be transparent to voters, this could undermine the legitimacy of a reformed Senate.

Constituencies. The Molgat-Cosgrove report proposes that single-member constituencies should be drawn with special attention to geographic, community, linguistic, and cultural factors in order to embody natural communities. This is presented as self-evidently desirable.

Timing and Terms. The Molgat-Cosgrove report recommends triennial elections, each of which would renew one-third of the Senate's membership. The elections would be held on fixed dates. Separate elections are supported on the grounds that Senate elections coinciding with national House of Commons elections would be overshadowed by campaigns focused on electing a government. Senators elected separately would have more authority as regional representatives. Separate elections would also, it is claimed, increase the likelihood of successful campaigns by independents.

ALBERTA SELECT COMMITTEE (1985)[19]

The Vote. The Alberta Select Committee proposal recommends plurality voting in multiple-member province-wide constituencies. This is defended, first, on the grounds that plurality voting is already a part of the Canadian electoral tradition. It is claimed that an elected Senate would involve changes that are radical enough without being accompanied with experimental electoral systems. It is also argued that proportional representation systems have been tried in various Canadian jurisdictions and subsequently abolished.

Constituencies. Province-wide constituencies are defended on the grounds that smaller constituencies would render senators less distinguishable from members of the House of Commons and that provinces would be best represented as wholes by representatives not tied to localities or distracted by purely local concerns.

Timing and Terms. The Alberta Select Committee argues that Senate elections should be held simultaneously with those for provincial legislatures. A central basis for this is the view that provincial perspectives would be at the forefront of public attention during provincial elections and would thus be highlighted in Senate elections. It is also argued that, if Senate elections were to coincide with provincial elections, the ties binding senators to national political parties would be reduced, making senators likely to represent regional interests rather than national party positions.

THE MACDONALD COMMISSION (1985)[20]

The Vote. This report advocates proportional representation to correct the tendency of plurality voting, or "first-past-the-post" systems, to underrepresent minority parties. Canada, the report argues, has shown a persistent tendency for political parties in the House of Commons to have very few members from some regions, even though their popular vote in these regions is not vastly less than that of the successful political parties. This situation can lead, in turn, to cabinets in which some regions are not adequately represented. The relatively large constituencies involved in Senate proposals would, it is further argued, exaggerate these distortions. If a plurality voting system were employed, Senate reform could turn out to be a step backwards in representation. It is recognized that a proportionally elected Senate would frequently not give a majority of seats to political parties governing with a majority in the House of Commons. The report's central response to this is to curtail the powers of the Senate, so that the House could ultimately prevail. It is also argued that a distinctive electoral process could enable the Senate to compete with the House of Commons for legitimacy in the eyes of the Canadian public and that this might have interesting long-term consequences.

Constituencies. The Macdonald Commission report recommends six-member constituencies on the grounds that this number is large enough to allow a system of proportional representation to operate.

Timing and Terms. The Macdonald Commission report proposes that Senate elections should be simultaneous with those for the House of Commons. Simultaneous elections, it is claimed, would reduce the danger of major contrasts between the party composition of the House of Commons and that of the Senate and thus of possible "paralysis" if a House dominated by elected members of one party were to confront a Senate dominated by elected members of another.

THE BEAUDOIN-DOBBIE REPORT (1992)[21]
The Vote. The Beaudoin-Dobbie proposal recommends a proportional representation system involving: (a) the nomination of slates of candidates by parties; (b) the ability of independent candidates to run; (c) the promotion, by parties, of gender equality and of the representation of Canada's diversity; and (d) the option, for voters, of selecting candidates from several party slates. Rationales for this proposal are: that it would make it unlikely for the party composition of the Senate merely to duplicate that of the House of Commons; that it would reflect accurately the party preferences of voters in the various regions and avoid translating regional votes into monolithic single-party blocks of senators; and that it would better represent minorities.

Constituencies. The Beaudoin-Dobbie committee argued that excessively large constituencies distance candidates from voters and heighten the reliance of voters on party affiliations. At the same time, candidates are forced to become more dependent on party assistance, giving an advantage to widely known party notables and creating barriers for independent candidates. The committee thus recommended that constituencies be no larger than required by an electoral system achieving proportional representation based on multi-member constituencies electing at least four senators.

Timing and Terms. The Beaudoin-Dobbie Committee called for fixed electoral terms and elections separate from those of either the House of Commons or provincial legislatures. It argued that maximizing the effectiveness of regional representation should be the central criterion in decisions about matters such as timing and length of terms and that separate elections would distance Senate elections from those for the House of Commons and enable them to be less partisan, thus reducing the likelihood that party affiliation would dominate the legislative behaviour of senators.

Staggered terms are opposed on the grounds that they would reduce the size of the pool of senators to be elected at each election and thus impede the capacity of the electoral system to deliver proportional representation. The length of the non-staggered terms recommended is six years, which is claimed to avoid the risk of isolating senators from electors implicit in systems employing longer terms.

THE CHARLOTTETOWN PROPOSAL (1992)

The Charlottetown agreement did not specify an electoral system for the proposed Senate. It merely prescribed that elections to the Senate should be simultaneous with those for the House of Commons and indicated that federal electoral legislation would be "sufficiently flexible" to allow provinces and territories to provide for gender balance in their cohorts of senators.[22] The absence of an electoral system proposal makes it impossible to determine which of the lines of argument in preceding proposals may be most applicable.

The Charlottetown agreement did not exempt provinces in which senators are elected by provincial legislatures from the simultaneity requirement. It may be that a simultaneity requirement would have special importance in these cases. Senatorial selection by provincial legislators in the context of a national election campaign might help to "federalize" the focus of the selection and mitigate possible concerns (raised in the preceding section) relating to the representational status of senators selected by provincial legislatures.

CONCLUDING OBSERVATIONS

The proposals reviewed in this paper, in general, devote considerable attention to the detail of recommended electoral systems. Considered in retrospect, they provide a useful overview of the advantages and disadvantages of the major alternative electoral systems for a reformed Senate. The discussion provided in these reports is also insightful in identifying the place of political parties and partisanship and how it is to be handled in a body intended to represent regional interests as central issues influencing the choice of an electoral system Interestingly, consensus about the importance of this question was not accompanied by agreement on the answer.

The Molgat-Cosgrove proposal reflects the view that voting along lines of party affiliation by senators would tend to undermine the representation of regional interests and concerns and that ways must therefore be found to reduce the prominence of political parties in Senate politics.

The Alberta Select Committee proposal takes a somewhat different tack. It focuses on discouraging the influence of the national political parties while assuming, apparently, that the affiliation of senators with provincial political parties would foster the representation of provincial interests and concerns.

The Macdonald Commission takes a contrasting approach, arguing that political parties are important, and deeply entrenched, representational vehicles in Canada and that a reformed Senate should use them to enhance regional representation rather than attempting to minimize their influence. This approach is reflected in the endorsement of an electoral system embodying proportional representation, which is seen (along the lines earlier developed in the federal government's 1983 Discussion Paper) as a means of bolstering legitimacy by ensuring that regions will be better represented in party caucuses and cabinets.

The Beaudoin-Dobbie report does not address this issue explicitly. It does, however, emphasize the value of proportional representation in distinguishing the composition of the Senate from that of the Commons. The capacity of the Senate electoral system to do this by reflecting party preferences accurately is, indeed, the decisive consideration in the Committee's choice of an electoral system. This would not have made sense if it had been assumed that party affiliations would become unimportant in a reformed Senate.

The absence of an electoral system recommendation in the Charlottetown agreement prevents this proposal from confirming an otherwise modest trend towards recognizing political parties as potential vehicles for regional representation and away from seeking to develop arrangements intended to encourage the displacement of party affiliation by regional affiliation. It is far from clear that this approach would support the underlying objective of elected Senate proposals: enhancing the legitimacy of the Senate. In order for it do so, the substantial numbers of Canadians who view party discipline and partisan voting in the House of Commons as a barrier to the representation of the interests of citizens would have to see it, simultaneously, as a means to the effective representation of regions in the Senate.

The Redistribution of Seats

APPOINTED SENATE PROPOSALS

Many of the proposals for a reformed appointed Senate developed during the 1960s and 1970s called for a redistribution of Senate seats. Typically, there was minimal explanation of this. It appears to have been regarded as

Table 1   Redistribution of Seats under Appointed Senate Proposals

	Molgat-McGuigan	Bill C–60	Ontario (1980)	Beige Paper	Lamontagne	Pepin-Roberts
Ontario	24	24	26	20	24	12
Québec	24	24	30	20	24	12
BC	12	10	12	9	12	8
Alberta	12	10	10	8	12	6
SK	12	8	8	5	10	4
MA	12	8	8	5	10	4
NS	10	10	10	4	10	4
NB	10	10	10	4	10	4
NL	6	8	6	3	8	4
PEI	4	4	4	2	8	2
NWT	2	1	1	*	1	0
Yukon	2	1	1	*	1	0
Nunavut	N/A	N/A	N/A	N/A	N/A	N/A
TOTAL	130	118	126	80	126	60

* The Beige Paper indicates that this distribution is only illustrative, for the purpose of establishing proportions. It is stated that the territories should have full voting rights, although a seat distribution is not specified.

NB: The 1978 proposal of the government of British Columbia asserted that equal regional representation was still the best basis for distributing Senate seats, but that British Columbia's emergence as a region needed to be recognized and reflected. However, a numerical distribution was not included in the proposal. Consequently, this proposal is not included in this table.

self-evident that the existing distribution of seats needed to be adjusted to reflect population growth in the Western provinces, while remaining politically acceptable elsewhere. This assumption is reflected in the proposed distributions shown in table 1.

ELECTED SENATE PROPOSALS

Proposals for an elected Senate reflect the existence of two competing approaches to distribution focusing, respectively, on adjustments to the current distribution so that it will better reflect demographic realities that have emerged since 1867 or on the allocation of an equal (or near equal) number of Senate seats to each province. The relative importance of these two considerations in the various proposals is apparent in table 2.

Alberta Select Committee (1985). The Alberta report contains both negative and positive arguments in favour of an equal distribution of seats among the provinces. On the negative side, it argues that representation by population would cause the Senate to duplicate the House of Commons and would not provide a balance of provincial viewpoints. It is also argued that equal regional representation is based on the assumption that regions are the authentic subnational units of Canada. This assumption

Table 2   Redistribution of Seats under Elected Senate Proposals

	Molgat-Cosgrove	Macdonald	Alberta	Beaudoin-Dobbie*	Current**
Ontario	24	24	6	30 / 20	24
Québec	24	24	6	30 / 20	24
BC	12	12	6	18 / 12	6
Alberta	12	12	6	18 / 12	6
SK	12	12	6	12 / 8	6
MA	12	12	6	12 / 8	6
NS	12	12	6	10 / 8	10
NB	12	12	6	10 / 8	10
NL	12	12	6	7 / 6	6
PEI	6	6	6	4 / 4	4
NWT	4	4	2	2 / 2	1
Yukon	2	2	2	1 / 1	1
Nunavut	N/A	N/A	N/A	N/A	1
TOTAL	144	144	64	154 / 109	105

* Proposal sets out two possible distributions (with a third being recommended in a Liberal Party dissent).
** Permanent seats only.

is rejected, and regions are portrayed as being merely "artificial" group-ings of provinces.

The alternative to these approaches – the representation of provinces – is supported on the grounds closely akin to those set out in a proposal developed by the Canada West Institute four years earlier.[23] It is argued that Canadians identify with their provinces rather than their regions. Equal representation of provinces is called for on the grounds that it is the only distribution that would give Canadians a balanced process of federal government.

Molgat-Cosgrove (1984), Macdonald Commission (1985), and Beaudoin-Dobbie (1992).[24] These proposals oppose provincial equality in the Senate. The Molgat-Cosgrove proposal argues that disparities in size between Cana-da's largest and smallest subnational units are much greater than in the United States, for example, where the largest state contains only about 10 percent of the population. Equal numbers of seats, it is claimed, would grossly overrepresent the smaller provinces. The Committee con-cludes that substantial overrepresentation is desirable, but that this must be balanced against demographic realities and that the appropriate dis-tribution should be based on a principle of equality weighted according to population.

The Macdonald Commission proposal incorporates the Molgat-Cosgrove distribution of seats, although it does not provide a specific rationale for this.

The Beaudoin-Dobbie proposal accepts the position of the Alberta proposal that the central basis upon which Senate seats should be distributed is provincial (or territorial) rather than regional. It goes on to argue that, since the purpose of a directly elected Senate is to represent the people of the various provinces, the distribution of seats cannot entirely ignore the principle of representation by population. Instead, the distribution should seek to balance requirements of this principle against the need for enhanced representation for people living in the smaller provinces. It is argued, as well, that there is no general principle of federalism that requires provincial equality in upper houses and that, if such a principle were to be applied consistently in a directly elected Senate, it would require equal numbers of seats for the territories as well as the provinces. Two possible distributions are then recommended for consideration, on the grounds that they each respond to the various considerations that must be reflected in a distribution of seats that is fair to everybody.

The Charlottetown Agreement (1992). The Charlottetown agreement proposed a Senate in which seats are distributed on the basis of provincial equality, with each province receiving six Senate seats and the Northwest Territories and the Yukon each receiving one. While the agreement does not present a rationale for the equality of seats, background notes subsequently released by the federal government claim that:

This agreement responds to and reconciles three visions of Canada – equality of provinces, equality of citizens, and equality of English and French linguistic and cultural communities.[25]

This comment may suggest that the Charlottetown agreement reflects an endorsement of the arguments made in previous proposals that favour provincial equality, rather than simply an accommodative gesture, by the larger provinces. This possibility is strengthened by the explicit commitment to "the principle of equality of the provinces" contained in the Canada clause proposed in the Charlottetown agreement.

CONCLUDING OBSERVATIONS

The evolution of attitudes to the distribution of seats in a reformed Senate may be seen by comparing the average regional distributions of the earlier appointive proposals with those of the more recent elective proposals. The appointed Senate proposals of the 1960s and 1970s recommended only a modest shift of seats from Central Canada to Outer Canada. They would have increased the proportion of seats assigned to the West by transferring seats from Atlantic Canada in greater proportions than from Central Canada. In contrast, the elected Senate proposals of the 1980s have recommended a more pronounced shift of seats from Central Canada to

Table 3   Regional Percentages of Senate Seats in Two Groups of Proposals

	Central Canada (%)	Atlantic Canada (%)	Western Canada (%)
Existing Senate	46	29	23
Appointive Proposals	42	24	34
Elective Proposals	27	32	37

Outer Canada and have involved increases in the proportion of seats allocated to both Atlantic Canada and Western Canada.

It is noteworthy that equality of seats is assumed to be needed for adequate representation, in those proposals that recommend it, rather than being concretely demonstrated to be necessary. The only report that tackles the issue in a substantive way – the Beaudoin-Dobbie proposal – departs from the provincial equality model by allocating 40 percent or 37 percent of the Senate's seats to Central Canada, 20 percent or 24 percent to Atlantic Canada, and 39 percent or 37 percent to the West, for a breakdown very similar to those of earlier appointive proposals.

The Beaudoin-Dobbie report criticizes the assumption that there would be a significant difference, in practice, between a provincially equal Senate and one embodying a less extreme degree of overrepresentation of the smaller provinces. The report argues that, in either case, the senators of an individual province will usually not be able to determine legislative outcomes. Their success as regional representatives (and thus the effectiveness of a reformed Senate in performing this role) will therefore depend more on their ability to enlist support from senators representing other provinces and to create cross-provincial voting coalitions than on their number.

The central reality illustrated by these proposals, however, may be that the distribution of seats remains, as it was in 1867, so heavily freighted with symbolic considerations and intergovernmental posturing that arguments ultimately play a role of minimal importance in outcomes. Thus, in the Charlottetown agreement, the equality of provinces in the Senate was affirmed, but only after protracted bargaining that resulted in compensatory measures elsewhere.[26] The cycle of Senate reform proposals ending with this agreement suggests that provincial equality of seats, or something closely approaching it, has likely emerged as the benchmark against which future proposals will be assessed, but that it is far less clearly a feature that is genuinely needed.

Powers

Both the proposals for a reformed appointed Senate and the more recent proposals for an elected Senate undertake to replace the extensive (but normally unused) powers of the existing Senate with more limited powers whose full use is anticipated and would be generally accepted. Most of these proposals argue that these powers would enable the Senate to be more effective, while at the same time preventing it from being so powerful that it could deadlock the legislative process or complicate the practice of responsible government.

APPOINTED SENATE PROPOSALS

Broadly similar powers are recommended in the various proposals for a reformed and appointed Senate that emerged during the 1960s and 1970s. The proposals involving appointments by both federal and provincial governments favoured suspensive vetoes, ranging from sixty days in the case of Bill C–60 to six months in the case of the Molgat-Cosgrove report.[27] Bill C–60 also originated the idea of a double-majority voting procedure for measures of linguistic significance. It was proposed that these measures require majorities of both French-speaking and English-speaking senators and that the rejection of such a measure by the Senate require its subsequent passage by a special majority in the Commons in order to become law.

The general direction of the Bundesrat (provincial appointment) proposals is similar to that of earlier proposals. They would replace the inclusive power to veto legislation with suspensive vetoes, in some cases accompanied by a power of absolute veto over a limited class of legislation. Thus, for example, the Pepin-Robarts report recommends that approval of the Upper House not be required for legislation within exclusive federal jurisdiction, that suspensive vetoes be available with respect to matters of concurrent federal and provincial jurisdiction, and that Upper House approval be required for treaties dealing with matters in the provincial jurisdiction or (with a two-thirds majority) for the exercise of the federal spending power within the federal jurisdiction.[28] The establishment of a role for the Second Chamber in the review of federal appointments was also popular.

ELECTED SENATE PROPOSALS

Molgat-Cosgrove Committee (1984).[29] This Committee recommended that a reformed Senate have the following powers:

- a suspensive veto of up to 120 sitting days, which applies to all legislation except supply bills, which would not be subject to any delay;
- the power to amend any bill except a supply bill (with the House of Commons having the power reject an amendment, which would ensure passage of the original bill, after a delay of at least sixty sitting days);
- the power to initiate bills relating to internal matters (including the Senate's budget), with other supply bills being initiated only in the House of Commons;

- an absolute veto over legislation or other initiatives relating to official languages (with voting by a double-majority procedure, requiring majorities of the whole Senate and of French-speaking senators) and, subject to a thirty-day time limit, the power to ratify order in council appointments to federal agencies whose decisions have important regional implications.

After affirming the principle that the Senate should not be a "confidence chamber," the Molgat-Cosgrove report argues that an absolute veto over ordinary legislation would make the government, in effect, responsible to both Houses. This would substantially complicate the parliamentary process, by requiring the government to serve two (potentially opposed) masters. The example of Australia is used in support of the claim that deadlock between the Houses is the central danger created by an absolute veto. A suspensive veto avoids this danger and the need for double-dissolution procedures (with the probability of proliferating elections) to which the possibility of deadlock gives rise.

The Committee's concern about the potential threat to responsible government posed by an assertive Senate also led it to propose limits to suspensive veto powers. The Committee argued that powers of delay over supply bills could paralyse public administration and that the denial of power to overturn the government requires denial even of a suspensive veto over appropriations bills.

An absolute veto over legislation of linguistic significance in conjunction with a double-majority voting procedure is also proposed. This is justified on the grounds that it is necessary for an effective procedure to provide "additional protection for the French language and culture" – claimed to be one of the original purposes of the Senate.

Alberta Select Committee (1985).[30] The Alberta Committee recommended that the proposed Senate have:

- the power to initiate any legislation (except a money or taxation bill, with the exception of bills concerning its own operational budget);
- a 180-day suspensive veto over constitutional amendments;
  a ninety-day suspensive veto over money or taxation bills;
- the power to amend any bill (the Commons could override this by re-passing the bill with a larger majority in percentage terms than passed the amendment in the Senate);
- the power to veto any bill except a supply bill (Commons can override a veto on money or taxation bills by a simple majority);
- the power to ratify non-military treaties.

According to the Alberta Select Committee, a suspensive veto is insufficient to ensure effective influence on the legislative process. If the Senate were an elected body, the central basis for limiting its powers to a suspensive veto would disappear and the fate of legislation would be determined by whichever House could summon the largest majority. Constitutional change is excepted from this argument, however. The Committee argues that the amending formula ensures that provincial interests will be protected and that additional protection is unnecessary. Money bills are likewise excepted, reflecting the traditional role of the House of Commons with respect to money bills.

The power to ratify non-military treaties is proposed on the grounds that social and economic impacts within particular provinces may be involved. Military treaties are excepted, however, because delays in this area may threaten national security. This report states that possible powers such as the ratification of public service and judicial appointments properly belong to "other federal bodies." Finally, the Alberta Committee argues that the Senate has a role in protecting language and cultural rights and that a majority of its witnesses supported a double-majority voting procedure as a means of accomplishing this.

Macdonald Commission (1985).[31] Under this proposal, a reformed Senate would have:

- a suspensive veto of six months on all ordinary legislation;
- an absolute veto over measures having special linguistic significance (to be voted following a double-majority voting procedure a majority of all senators in addition to all French-speaking senators).

Declaring that Senate reform should aim to ensure regional sensitivity and temper majority rule and not override the principle of responsible government, the Macdonald Commission report argues that the present powers of the Senate, if actually used, could seriously complicate the practice of responsible government. The potential contribution of the Senate to regional responsiveness can be achieved with a suspensive veto, and a veto of six months would ensure that regional viewpoints were fully considered. This would be a sufficiently long period to "give pause" to unrestrained majorities in the House of Commons.

The Macdonald Commission report claims that the Senate can function as both a regionalist and a dualist chamber and that in this latter mode it can contribute to representing and reconciling the interests of French- and English-speaking Canadians. An absolute veto over legislation of special linguistic significance is proposed (in conjunction with double-majority voting) as a means of enabling the Senate to perform this second role.

The Beaudoin-Dobbie Proposal (1992).[32] Under this proposal, a reformed Senate would exercise:

- powers to amend or defeat ordinary legislation, provided that (a) the House of Commons could override Senate votes in the case of deadlock and (b) a double-majority procedure would apply to measures affecting French language or culture;
- the power to delay ordinary legislation by up to 180 days, with such legislation deemed to have passed if not voted within that period;
- powers to amend or defeat supply bills (with the Commons being able to override Senate votes by simple majority) and/or to delay such bills for up to thirty days;
- the power of ratification of appointments of the governor of the Bank of Canada, heads of national cultural institutions, and heads of regulatory boards and agencies.

The central rationale for these powers is that they would work in concert with other features of the proposed Senate to enable effective representation of regional interests, while avoiding the dangers of deadlock and the paralysis of Parliament. In order to achieve this balance, the Senate is given relatively unrestricted powers to amend or defeat legislation, and deadlock is avoided by legislative overrides and limitations on the power to delay. Throughout its arguments, the Committee stressed the continuity of this proposal with elected Senate proposals of the mid–1980s.

The proposal to make legislation relating to the French language and culture subject to a double-majority voting procedure is defended on the grounds of widespread consensus, both among previous reports and among Canadians. The proposal to endow the Senate with a power to ratify appointments is supported on the grounds that such agencies can have significant impacts on all regions of Canada.

The Charlottetown Proposal (1992).[33] The Charlottetown agreement recommended that a reformed Senate have:

- the power to delay ordinary legislation for up to thirty sitting days, or to defeat or amend it; this would, with certain exceptions (see below), trigger a joint sitting with the House of Commons (outcome determined by simple majority);
- the power to delay revenue and expenditure bills for up to thirty calendar days, or to defeat or amend (the Commons could then re-pass with a simple majority);
- the power to amend or defeat, by means of a double-majority procedure (majorities of both all senators and Francophone senators voting), bills materially affecting French language or culture (no House of Commons override);
- the power to amend or defeat, by simple majority, bills involving "fundamental tax policy changes directly related to natural resources" (no House of Commons override);

- the power to initiate bills, except money bills;
- the power to ratify federal appointments to be set out in legislation, after a delay of not more than thirty sitting days of the House.

The structure of the powers proposed for the Charlottetown Senate establishes a number of distinctions between classes of legislation, accompanied by attempts to tailor powers to the various classes. Such an approach holds the promise of enabling the Senate to be relatively influential over the fate of some types of federal legislation, while ensuring that the House of Commons will prevail elsewhere. While it can thus be defended, generally, on the grounds that it preserves the supremacy of the Lower House, it also requires specific defences of the powers established for each special category of legislation.

A second noteworthy feature of the powers proposed in the Charlottetown agreement arises from the reliance on joint sittings of the House of Commons and Senate as the ultimate means for determining the fate of most bills. The joint sitting procedure would have placed substantial power in the hands of senators under conditions of minority government, or small government majorities, while tending to minimize their impact where large government majorities exist in the Commons. Varying the Senate's legislative "clout" according to the size of Commons majorities could be supported by the argument that there should be particularly stringent limits on the capacity of a government with weak national support, and possibly minimal support in some minority regions, to pass legislation impacting on these regions. However, minority/small majority government situations do this anyway, and the "Charlottetown Senate" would have been least effective when other checks on the capacity of governments to act were also least substantial.

CONCLUDING OBSERVATIONS

The various proposals reviewed above share a common understanding of the central challenge posed by the task of defining the powers of a reformed Senate. The powers need to be great enough to enable the Senate to meet expectations, but not so great as to enable the Senate to warp roles appropriate to the House of Commons and to bring the processes of government to a halt through legislative deadlock.

The persisting consensus has been that the first step in meeting this challenge should be a substantial decrease in the formal legislative powers of the Senate, combined with an attempt to ensure that the full use of the remaining powers will be seen as legitimate. The practical powers of the Senate to influence legislation could thus increase, while the formal powers and danger of legislative deadlock would be reduced.

The trend over the last forty years, from this starting point, has been to increase the Senate's formal powers (although not enough to equal those presently in existence) and seek ways to increase its legitimacy sufficiently to enable its powers to be used. Thus, the earlier appointive proposals generally reflect the view that the federal legislative process can be made to respond to regional interests through the Senate's use by of suspensive vetoes. In the case of the Bundesrat proposals, suspensive vetoes are supplemented, or in some cases replaced, with absolute vetoes over narrowly defined classes of legislation that affect provincial jurisdictions. The elected Senate proposals, with certain exceptions, broaden the absolute veto powers of the Senate, while relying on Commons overrides to maintain the supremacy of the Lower House and responsible government.

The other noteworthy trend involves the drawing of distinctions among policy fields, enabling the enhanced practical powers of a reformed Senate to be restricted to defined classes of legislation. Initially, for example, the establishment of a class of legislation relating to Canada's official languages (first proposed in Bill–60 of 1978) envisioned an absolute Senate veto that could be overridden by a special majority in the House of Commons. The elected Senate proposals of the 1980s supported absolute Senate vetoes over legislation relating to official languages (or the French language and culture), subject to a double-majority voting procedure within the Senate and not reversible by the House of Commons.

The Charlottetown proposal attempts to give Alberta the vital core of what has been advocated in the movement for a "Triple-e" (equal, elected, effective) Senate by making the Senate more powerful than the House of Commons on matters of tax policy relating to natural resources. This represents a significant step in the gradual evolution of reform proposals towards increased Senate powers. It also inevitably raises the possibility of analogous provisions relating to sectors determined to be of central importance in other regions.

Considered collectively, recent proposals do not provide a fully convincing demonstration that Senate reformers can "have their cake and eat it too," i.e., make the Senate powerful enough to protect regional interests while, at the same time, avoiding a threat to the supremacy of the House of Commons. The arguments for this approach focus on demonstrating the need for heightened powers over classes of legislation seen to be distinctively related to central roles of the Senate, given that the regular powers being proposed would not permit the Senate to prevail over the Commons in these areas. But these arguments are not related back to the consideration that has led proponents of reform to share the belief that routine powers need to be reduced in the first place, namely the need to enable governments to govern. In particular, they do not explain how matters such as official languages can be simultaneously of such vital importance that special legislative powers for the Senate are justified and of sufficiently limited importance that the defeat of Government bills concerning them would not imply a question of confidence, or raise doubts about the capacity of a government to govern. While this concern is arguably of limited importance where there is only one class of legislation subject to special Senate powers, it becomes potentially more significant as natural resources and (potentially) other such matters are added to the list.

Purposes And Expectations

Canadian Senate reform proposals have typically given rather cursory attention to the purpose of the Senate before turning to the details of reform. This has left relatively unexplored a crucially important group of questions relating to the problems that Senate reform is intended to address and to the expectations of reformers about what Senate reform can achieve. This section relies on implications of the details of reform proposals, as discussed above, along with claims and arguments where they have been provided, to identify the purposes apparently envisioned for the Senate in the various reform proposals. On the basis of this examination, it suggests that assumptions about what Senate reform needs to achieve, and expectations about what it can achieve, have risen markedly over the course of forty years of discussion.

APPOINTED SENATE PROPOSALS
Mixed Appointment Models. According to the Molgat-McGuigan report, released in 1972, regional alienation and the emergence of separatist movements, combined with new concerns about domination by the central provinces, reinforce traditional views of the need for a regionally representative Upper House.[34] Bill C–60 (1978) took a similar approach. The purpose of the Upper Chamber was to protect the interests and represent the concerns of provinces and regions.[35]

Evidently, these proposals assumed that appointed senators could exercise enough influence upon the legislative process to be effective representatives of the regions and could achieve this through powers limited to a suspensive veto. This suggests that this Committee believed that effective regional representation required only a relatively modest alteration of the status quo. Modest intentions and expectations are further suggested by the minimal degree to which seats are redistributed (implying, perhaps, that outlying regions need only a moderate increase in "clout") and by the fact that the federal government would continue to appoint one half of the Senate.

The mixed appointment feature may suggest, indeed, that regional representation is not the dominant purpose of the Senate in these models. These models would likely have achieved only a slightly different balancing of federal and provincial perspectives within the Senate (and within the legislative process as a consequence). They would not have resulted in the emergence of the Senate as a single-purpose advocate, in

Ottawa, of regional interests. Nor was this likely thought, at the time, to be needed.

Provincial Appointment Proposals. Regional representation as a distinctively important purpose of the Senate achieves clearer prominence in proposals for a Senate wholly appointed by the provinces. In 1979, the Pepin-Roberts Commission, for example, argued that a council appointed by provincial governments could combine the representation of regional interests with the institutionalization of the processes of executive federalism, in which members of the council would act as proxies for their provincial governments on matters affecting provincial jurisdictions.[36] The 1980 Quebec Liberal Beige Paper adopted a similar approach, arguing that increased functional interdependence between the levels of government creates a need for an institution that enables the provinces to influence federal initiatives that impact on provincial jurisdictions.[37]

Some provincial appointment proposals explicitly equate regional representation with provincial representation. In its 1978 proposals, for example, the British Columbia Government argued that the purpose most clearly articulated by the Fathers of Confederation was "the representation of provincial interests in the making of national laws."[38] It is claimed that the Senate has failed to do this effectively.

The shift away from the mixed appointment model to provincial appointments, combined with the role (in several of these proposals) of provincial governments in selecting senators, suggests an important shift in underlying purpose. The "Bundesrat Senate" does not attempt to balance regional representation with other purposes. It first serves the purpose of regional representation, with other purposes playing a highly subsidiary role. Secondly, regional representation is clearly equated with provincial representation in these models, and provincial representation is equated with the representation of provincial governments rather than the direct representation of the people in each province.

The potential impact of a provincially appointed Senate is moderated by two features: it is an appointed body exercising only (for the most part) suspensive vetoes, and its most significant (i.e., longest suspension or, in some cases, absolute) veto powers are restricted to classes of federal legislation affecting provincial jurisdictions. These features, together with the fact that the major redistributions of seats proposed are from the Atlantic provinces to the West, rather than from the large provinces to the small provinces, have implications for the practical meaning of the regional representation that "Bundesrat Senate" models would have achieved. In practice, this "regional representation" would have amounted to a modest increase in the influence of provincial governments, collectively, within the federal legislative process. Provincial influence relating to federal legislation affecting provincial jurisdictions would have increased more significantly. The relative numbers of senators from

Outer Canada and Central Canada would not, however, have been greatly altered (although representative weight would have migrated from the
East to the West).

As with the mixed appointment models, one may infer that the practical
meaning of "regional representation" emerging from Bundesrat models
tells us what their creators thought was needed. The central problem was
seen as a problem of insufficient influence in Ottawa by the governments
of the provinces, both large and small. More fundamentally, it was assumed
that any feelings of alienation or exclusion then being experienced by people in Canada's regions could be addressed by increased provincial influence over, primarily, federal impacts within provincial jurisdictions.

ELECTED SENATE PROPOSALS

Proposals for an elected Senate continue to assert that the need to
enhance regional representation is the fundamental reason for Senate
reform. Interestingly, some have undertaken explicitly to state and justify views about what regional representation is and why it is needed. This
may suggest an awareness, on the part of authors, that they were express-
ing a new and possibly controversial conception of the Senate's traditional purpose.

The 1984 Molgat-Cosgrove Committee report, the 1985 Alberta Select
Committee report, and the 1985 Macdonald Commission report, adopt
substantially the same argument. They portray the central purpose of the
Senate as regional representation and equate this with representation on
a provincial basis, rather than the representation of Canada's traditional
regions. All three reports argue that representation on a provincial basis
does not mean the representation of provincial governments; representation within the federal legislative process is portrayed as having the potential to undermine the intergovernmental process (Molgat-Cosgrove, Alberta) and as incorrectly employing provincial governments, rather than
federal members of the House of Commons and senators, to represent
regional interests relating to national issues (Macdonald Commission).
The reports differ, however, on whether representation on a provincial
basis requires equal representation; the Molgat-Cosgrove and Macdonald
Commission reports take the position that it does not.[39]

The discussion of the purpose of the Senate in the 1992 proposal of the
Beaudoin-Dobbie Committee reflects both the insights reached in previous studies and the assumptions underlying the federal government's
1991 framework proposal, which the Committee was created to study. It is
argued, fundamentally, that regional representation should be the primary purpose of the Senate because enhanced representation, particularly of
the outlying regions within the central government, remains a major need
within the country. Furthermore, differences among the provinces make it
difficult to adequately represent their populations on the basis of the traditional regions and require regional representation to be understood as

provincial representation. Finally, it is argued that provincial governments have no mandate to represent their populations on national issues and that the form of representation sought from a reformed Senate, therefore, requires senators to represent the people of the provinces, rather than provincial governments.[40]

Architectural features of the proposals just reviewed confirm what is actually said about the purpose of the Senate. In recommending an elected Senate, for example, these proposals reflect a redefinition of the representational problem to be addressed by Senate reform. The focus shifts from provincial governments to the people of the provinces, and the Senate comes to be seen as a central institutional mechanism for remedying popular feelings of alienation and exclusion.

With respect to the distribution of Senate seats, these proposals defend their recommendations on the basis of arguments about the fair treatment of the populations of the various provinces and abandon appeals based on the treatment of Canada's traditional regions. They also, perhaps reflecting this, involve more radical redistributions away from Central Canada. Furthermore, the heightened representational status that would be possessed by elected senators is reflected in the recommendations concerning Senate powers contained in these proposals, which prescribe generally greater powers than were envisioned in earlier proposals.

OBSERVATIONS

While elected Senate proposals retain the language of "regional representation" traditionally used to define a purpose of the Senate, they appear to reflect a substantial shift in thinking about what the Senate should actually accomplish within our legislative system. This shift in thinking was fully reflected in the culminating proposal of this group: the Charlottetown agreement.

The Charlottetown proposal for Senate reform does not spell out the purpose that it is supposed to serve. A fact sheet distributed by the federal government in September 1992 declares that the Upper House is "designed to give the less populous regions a greater say in the policy-making process of Parliament" and that the proposed Senate would give "the less populous provinces more clout in the legislative process."[41] The architecture proposed for a reformed Senate, involving the redistribution of seats on a provincial basis and special powers relating to regionally sensitive matters, reflects the stated intentions of its proponents in much the same way as earlier elected Senate proposals.

The fact that the Charlottetown proposal leaves the door open for elections by provincial legislatures as an alternative to direct election has implications for its implicit purpose just as it has been seen to have potential implications concerning the legitimacy of senators. It creates the possibility that a Senate modelled on the Charlottetown proposal would have provided several kinds of representation, endowing its general purpose of regional representation with a plurality of specific meanings in practice.

If the Charlottetown model is taken as an expression of what is needed in order to fulfil the purpose of regional representation, it thus may add something to preceding proposals. More clearly than its antecedents, it may suggest that "regional representation" had come after forty years of discussion to express expectations so divergent, from region to region across Canada, that they could no longer be met by an institution that handles all issues, relating to all regions, in the same way.

PART 2:

TAKING STOCK

The various commission, task force, and parliamentary reports reviewed in this paper provide an impressive set of ideas, options, and arguments for consideration in the development of future Senate reform proposals. At this level, the value of these proposals, as a "resource base" that can, and should, be given close attention by future proponents of reform speaks for itself.

The potential usefulness of the proposals extends beyond their provision of a *tour d'horizon* of options and technical issues, however. Future reformers may benefit even more substantially from thinking about why these proposals did not get implemented. While the full story of the demise of each of these proposals is vastly complex, and would have to include a range of political and intergovernmental dynamics entirely unrelated to the substance of the proposals, this should not preclude attention to a simple possibility. The proposals may have failed, in part, because they simply were not persuasive enough. It is not impossible that Canadians considered them, approximately on their merits, and remained unconvinced that they were urgently needed and unprepared to provide the sustained support that is required in order to bring about Senate reform in Canada.

To the extent that the proposals failed "on their merits," Senate reform is unlikely to come about until more convincing, and more convincingly argued, proposals are developed. In particular, attention needs to be directed towards four central challenges that remain in the wake of our most recent cycle of attention to Senate reform.

The Conceptual Challenge

It is self-evident that any attempt to reform the Senate must be guided by a clear conception of what the Senate is supposed to contribute to our political process and why this contribution should be sought from an upper legislative chamber instead of some other institution or process. This challenge has several aspects that warrant separate discussion.

One aspect is the need to clearly define the problem, or unmet need, in the Canadian political system that warrants a reform of the Senate. Many Senate reform proposals have been extremely limited in their discussion of this aspect, if not entirely silent.

For example, most recent Senate reform proposals assume that regional representation, in order to enhance governmental responsiveness, is a fundamental purpose of the Senate and needs to be strengthened. This is sometimes portrayed as an intention of the Fathers of Confederation, although it is not explained why Canadians today are obliged to accept this intention while, at the same time, ignoring the other purpose envisioned in 1867: special representation for the interests of the propertied class.

Proposals that attempt to relate the need for increased regional representation to present needs rather than traditional assumptions have, since the early 1980s, frequently focused on the existence of regional resentment and alienation, particularly in Western Canada. While this represents a useful beginning to the formulation of a problem, it is far from being precise enough to sustain a proposal for specific reforms.

First of all, the notion of regional "alienation" introduces a highly abstract and even metaphysical concept into our definition of the problem that Senate reform is expected to address. It fosters discussion at a level of abstraction that makes it virtually impossible to know what, specifically, is needed to resolve the problem, or what outcomes would demonstrate its successful resolution. The challenge, here, is primarily to shift attention back to a more pedestrian, but practically useful, level of discussion and focus on the concrete political problems that have given rise to dissatisfaction among Canadians. If, as has been suggested elsewhere in this chapter, Western resentment over the National Energy Plan of the early 1980s is the central source of the most recent wave of sentiment concerning the Senate, then this event needs to be reflected, explicitly, in the practical tests applied to proposals for reform. Had it been in effect during the early 1980s, would the proposal have resulted in the Senate stopping or substantially changing the National Energy Plan?

Similar attention is needed to the notion of "regional representation" in order to maximize its usefulness as a source of practical guidance about how unmet needs can be addressed. Like the concept of "alienation," it introduces a level of considerable abstraction into a discussion that may really be about relatively concrete sources of dissatisfaction. Furthermore, it encourages us to make a very problematical assumption: that changes to our representative institutions are what is needed in order to address dissatisfaction in the West and elsewhere. As it has been used by proponents of the reforms examined in this chapter, however, the concept is open to a number of significantly different interpretations, including some that have more to do with power than representation in any literal sense and to which purely representative processes may not be directly relevant. The language of "regional representation" obscures the possibility that dissatisfaction may need to be addressed by greater legislative power on the part of some regions, or by enhanced communication from the centre to the regions, explaining and justifying decisions rather than merely by more visible (or audible) representation of regional perspectives within the parliamentary process. It also deflects attention from the question of how much power is needed – a question of fundamental importance if greater legislative power on the part of some regions is the key to resolving issues of regional discontent.

Questions about the practical meaning of alienation and representation, and how much power is needed by regions, are of central relevance to a second dimension of the conceptual challenge: establishing that the upper legislative chamber is the appropriate mechanism to address the needs that are currently unmet. If the need is for a means to prevent the passage of legislation that is deeply offensive to a single region or province (as the "National Energy Plan test" described above may suggest), then a legislative chamber is inherently unsuitable, however constructed or empowered. As the Beaudoin-Dobbie proposal pointed out in 1992, even the equal representation of all provinces still leaves each province as a minority, and therefore able to ensure a legislative outcome compatible with provincial interests only where coalitions with other provinces can be created. Procedural arrangements, such as double-majority voting procedures for proposals in specified policy areas, can deal with exceptional cases but are unsuitable for dealing with substantial numbers of such cases. Thus, it may well be that policy fields of central interest to individual provinces need some other form of protection, such as legislative or administrative devolution, and that the attempt to address concerns about federal action within them through Senate reform is fundamentally misguided.[42]

A further dimension of the conceptual challenge is to translate a vision of the needs that require Senate reform into a more specific set of roles that can provide a basis for the design of the institution. Many proposals have included roles (e.g., the protection of human rights and sober second thought roles such as in-depth committee studies or detailed review of legislation) that are essentially extraneous to what is claimed to be the central role of the Senate. In so doing, they have ignored the practical reality that each additional role is likely to dilute the effectiveness of the Senate in performing central roles. This concern would seem to be raised by proposals for an elected Senate that, for example, take for granted its retention of traditional roles as a chamber of sober second thought but do not address the fact that the basis for the suitability of the Senate as a place of second thought is that, since they are free from the pressures of constituency and electoral duties, senators have the time to consider issues in a manner different from that of the House of Commons. It is doubtful that elected senators could continue to do this.

More generally, this aspect of the conceptual challenge requires that the various major and minor roles envisioned for the institution be coherent in serving (or at least not impeding) its fulfilment of fundamental purposes.

Forty years of debate about Senate reform has not provided a fully convincing response to the conceptual challenge of Senate reform. Indeed, it remains far from clear that an Upper Chamber is the appropriate mechanism to meet the expectations that have taken shape in the course of this debate.

The Challenge of Institutional Design

A second challenge that will continue to face proponents of Senate reform is the development of a set of institutional arrangements (selection process, distribution of seats, powers) that would enable a reformed Senate to fulfil its purpose. This process requires a series of trade-offs, and forty years of discussion suggest that several of these are far from easy to make. Indeed, it is possible that they should be seen as dilemmas, reflecting permanently unresolvable contradictions, rather than challenges that can in principle be addressed by a sufficiently well-calculated balancing of institutional attributes.

SELECTION: PURSUING LEGITIMACY IN A SCEPTICAL WORLD

A Senate that meets expectations must possess the legitimacy needed for substantial influence, but the direct elections that have come to be seen as necessary to achieve this would appear to be in unavoidable tension with the task of regional representation. The legitimacy challenge needs to be seen as a dilemma because attempts to combine the reliable representation of regional interests and the credibility associated with elected status would almost certainly lose one or the other. For example, the nine-year nonrenewable terms proposed by the Molgat-Cosgrove committee as a way of making elected senators sufficiently independent from parties to permit them to faithfully represent regional views would have had the practical effect of reducing their elected status to a virtual formality, exerting no influence on their behaviour and (for senators well into their terms) long-forgotten by voters. It is hard to see how it would have conferred significant legitimacy.

On the other hand, attempts to make political parties the vehicles of regional representation by transforming the Senate, in effect, into an opposition House collide with the reality that, unless political parties are content to remain purely regional protest parties, they are under ceaseless pressure to develop policies that can result in their election in Ontario and Quebec. While such an arrangement might protect the interests of minority regions on occasion, there is room for considerable doubt about whether it could do so as general rule, especially on "zero-sum" issues where the advantage of one region may be expected to provoke the wrath of others (and most especially where these others include the populous provinces). Nor, in a democratic age, does a reformed appointment process promise the degree of legitimacy that is needed, if regional representation requires the capacity to block, change or substantially delay measures passed by the elected House of Commons.

REGIONAL REPRESENTATION – TOO MUCH IS NOT ENOUGH

An effective Senate must distribute a sufficient number of seats to the underpopulated regions to inspire confidence that their representatives could ensure the protection of their interests, while at the same time providing the populous regions with a plausible share (sufficient, at least, to be accepted at the intergovernmental bargaining table). Here, again, a direct statement of the challenge suggests that it poses a dilemma, rather than pointing to a possible trade-off. As has been argued above, even an equal distribution of seats among the provinces does not place the representatives of any province in a position to protect its residents from federal legislation to which they object, no matter how passionately their views and votes might be applied in a reformed Upper Chamber. If more modest forms of protection would meet expectations, then this dilemma grows less troubling. But, even here, elected Senate proposals have not provided any basis for a belief that the interests of the smaller provinces might furnish a basis for their representatives to form and maintain the voting coalitions that would be required if the protection of minority regions were to be achieved, even minimally.

POWERS: BLOCKING WITHOUT USURPING

An effective Senate must possess sufficient power to be able to stop (or inspire the amendment of) legislation unacceptable to minority regions while, at the same time, it must not have the power to bring about permanent deadlock between the Houses, which would impede the capacity of governments to govern and undermine the role of the House of Commons. Forty years of discussion leave considerable room for doubt that there is a trade-off that can simultaneously serve the expectations that have come to be expressed in the demand for regional representation and also be compatible with requirements of the Westminster model of responsible government.

While reform proposals have been careful to stipulate that the Commons retain its status as the exclusive "confidence chamber," the possibility that measures duly passed by the Commons could be blocked by an elected Senate opens the door to a seeming anomaly: a government having the confidence of Parliament but not the capacity to obtain support for its legislative program.[43] The practical outcome in such a case would almost certainly be the same as that of a loss of confidence under present arrangements: the resignation of the government and an election.[44] Thus,

while a powerful Senate might well increase efforts to accommodate the
interests of minority regions, it would not do this without risks. Senators
acting on the basis of a specific mission to protect regional interests, and
subject to no institutional imperatives favouring compromise, might be
expected to be extremely difficult to accommodate. And failures to accommodate them could result in parliamentary stalemates followed by plebisc-
itary elections focused on regional controversies – clearly something that
Canada does not need.

Powers clearly inferior to those of the House of Commons remove the
possibility of deadlock and the dangers that accompany it, but they may as
a result be insufficient to ensure that the Senate can live up to expectations
that it will achieve effective regional representation in Ottawa. There are
also practical difficulties. Inferior powers may not be sufficient to persuade
potential senators to endure the rigours and uncertainties of elected
office, resulting in problems of recruitment. Furthermore, an elected
Senate with insufficient powers could easily become an institutionalized
source of regional complaint within the legislative process; the actions of
such a Senate would not be restrained by the accountability for outcomes
and incentives to compromise that accompany significant legislative
power.

DILEMMAS, OR MERELY PROBLEMS NOT YET RESOLVED?
All institutions embody balances among competing, and sometimes logi-
cally opposed, requirements. The fact that the proposals reviewed in this
chapter attempt to develop such balances is not therefore objectionable in
principle. On the contrary, the proposals are useful because they explicitly recognize these challenges and display considerable ingenuity in their
responses.

It remains true, however, that ingenuity is not the only factor that determines whether satisfactory balances can be found. The factor that ultimately determines whether a balance will be satisfactory is its relation to
the purpose that it is intended to serve. That is why it is so critically important to address, as precisely as possible, the purposes and expectations that
underlie proposals for Senate reform. Viewed in relation to the expectations that appear to have propelled the shift to elected Senate proposals in
the early 1980s, what might once have been viewed as challenges of design
have come to look more and more like dilemmas. As such, they suggest
that what is needed now is critical reflection about expectations, rather
than greater ingenuity in trying to meet them.

The Intergovernmental Challenge

If a Senate reform proposal meets the foregoing technical challenges, and
requires constitutional change or the active cooperation of provincial governments, it must then survive the process of intergovernmental negotia-

tions and agreement. At this level, a proposal becomes subject to an open-ended and highly unpredictable group of influences. These may include symbolic issues, interpersonal relations between First Ministers, substantive political issues across the full range of government activity (including tensions that have no relation to the Senate), and genuine concerns about the substance of the proposal.

The effect of the process of intergovernmental negotiation and agreement on recent proposals has impeded progress in addressing the two challenges discussed above: clarity about purpose and coherence of institutional design. The Charlottetown process illustrates this impact vividly. It was launched with a federal discussion paper that provided useful explorations of a number of issues and options and involved a Joint Committee report proposing various arrangements on the basis of a relatively detailed rationale. The result of the final round of intergovernmental discussion, however, was a proposal that combined various elements previously viewed as competing alternatives. It was also studiously silent about the underlying purpose that the proposed institution was intended to serve. If this pattern is of general applicability, it suggests that success in meeting the challenge of intergovernmental agreement may have to be purchased by compromising the substantive merit of proposals, at the cost of undermining their attractiveness to citizens. The intergovernmental challenge may therefore pose a more serious obstacle to successful Senate reform than the mere need to obtain intergovernmental agreement about change.

The unique circumstances that have applied to individual proposals in the past make it difficult to arrive at specific lessons concerning features of proposals that favour intergovernmental agreement, or discourage it. The history of attempts at Senate reform in Canada does, however, clearly demonstrate the importance of sensitivity to the need for intergovernmental support, in proposals that require constitutional change or provincial cooperation. In so doing, it demonstrates that reforms falling exclusively within the federal jurisdiction, or within the jurisdiction of the Senate itself, possess an enormous practical advantage. They can be put into effect far more easily than reforms requiring intergovernmental agreement and are more likely to reach the implementation stage without having lost internal coherence and thus potential effectiveness.

The Effectiveness Challenge

The challenges discussed above each, in their separate ways, relate to the potential effectiveness of a reformed Senate. Reforms that do not reflect a clear purpose, achieve internal consistency, or meet the test of intergovernmental acceptability are unlikely to be effective, assuming they can be implemented at all. There is an additional effectiveness challenge: the one posed – by the expectations that have come to be attached to Senate reform – to the capacity of an institution that, no matter how extensively reformed, will remain an institution of Parliament.

During the forty-year period when the reform proposals discussed above appeared, in their several waves, the role of elected parliamentarians and lower houses within systems of government based on the Westminster model was undergoing substantial attention, both from scholars and participants. The verdict that had emerged in Canada by the late 1970s contained significant notes of pessimism. It reflected general agreement that the role of the backbench member of the House of Commons had undergone a serious long-term erosion, brought about by a wide range of factors including the impact of the broadened franchise and the progress of social pluralism on the nature of electoral constituencies (and the credibility of any individual claiming to represent them); the rise of organized interest groups and corporate lobbying involving the direct representation of particular interests to government, along with the new capacity of governments to "go around" members of the House of Commons and access public opinion directly through polling and related consultative initiatives; the vast increase in the volume and complexity of legislation generated by the modern state, which imposed unprecedented pressures on the time and policy capacity of Parliament and its individual members; and the emergence of modern disciplined political parties, upon which individual members had become increasingly dependent for policy and organizational support at election time and for perks and career advantages afterwards.

Perceptions of the erosion resulting from these various factors had resulted, by the early 1980s, in widespread concern that Parliament was in danger of being reduced to a virtual rubber stamp within the policy process. There were even perceptions that, in the blunt words of a widely used political science text of that era, members of Parliament remained policy generalists who were "functionally disqualified from having a substantive impact on government policy decisions."[45]

It is, to say the least, ironic that during the period covered by this paper, expectations about what the Senate could do if it were made more like the House of Commons grew steadily, seemingly in virtual tandem with the rise of pessimism about what the House of Commons could do if it were not significantly changed. While some of the early appointed Senate proposals allude to a possible role of the Upper Chamber in counterbalancing the power of the Executive (and thus imply that Senate reform could contribute to the broader reform of parliamentary institutions) later proposals are virtually devoid of these references. They seem entirely oblivious to the possibility that elected senators might be subject to some or all of the representational and functional challenges then being widely ascribed to elected members of the House of Commons. Yet to the extent that elected senators were to incur comparable limitations, their capacity to remedy problems as deep-seated as regional alienation was thought to be, during this period at least, is surely open to question.

Several of the Senate reform proposals considered in this paper address Senate reform as an issue of parliamentary reform and explore how changes to both the Senate and the House of Commons might contribute to the efficacy of Parliament. Their recommendations concerning the House of Commons remain relatively modest, however, and their focal interest in the Senate as a mechanism of regional representation precludes direct discussion of the broader challenges facing parliamentary institutions.[46] It is impossible to determine whether this shortcoming had a material impact on the fate of the proposals. One wonders, however, whether a public increasingly cynical about the elected politicians already in existence may have experienced mixed emotions when it contemplated proposals that may have seemed to promise only the creation of more politicians without substantively addressing the roots of public cynicism.

CONCLUDING REMARKS

In the years since the demise of the Charlottetown proposal, Senate reform has ceased to be a matter of urgent public or political interest. As a result, the proposals explored above now stand relegated to that special public sector limbo known as "the shelf." The fundamental claim of this chapter is that it would be a serious waste if they merely remain there and are not actively examined and used as a basis for progress when Senate reform makes its inevitable reappearance among the front-burner issues of governance. The proposals provide an extremely useful "resource base" for future thinkers about Senate reform, both because of what they contain and because of the questions they leave unanswered.

NOTES

1 This chapter draws on factual and comparative information provided in Stilborn, *Senate Reform Proposals in Comparative Perspective.* The opinions and conclusions developed below are those of the author alone and are not to be attributed to the Parliamentary Research Branch or Library of Parliament.

2 This group of proposals includes a White Paper (Canada, *The Constitution and the People of Canada*); Bill C-60 of 1978 (the somewhat belated translation of the Paper into legislative language); Canada, Special Joint Committee of the Senate and the House of Commons on the Constitution of Canada, *Report* (referred to below as Molgat-MacGuigan); and Canada, *Report on Certain Aspects of the Canadian Constitution* (referred to below as Lamontagne).

3 Variations on the Bundesrat model were proposed in: British Columbia,

Reform of the Canadian Senate, (referred to below as BC); Canada, Task Force
on Canadian Unity, *A Future Together — Observations and Recommendations*
(referred to below as Pepin-Robarts); Ontario, Advisory Committee on Confederation, *Reports (First and Second),* 1978 (referred to below as Ontario);
and Constitutional Committee of the Quebec Liberal Party, *A New Canadian
Federation,* 1980 (referred to below as Beige Paper). This latter proposed an
intergovernmental rather than a parliamentary body, but it has been included
in this chapter because it was a major focus of ensuing governmental discussion. All these proposals envisioned a Senate appointed and recalled by
provincial governments, and acting on their instructions.

 4 See, respectively, Canada, Parliament, House of Commons, *Report of the Special
Joint Committee of the Senate and of the House of Commons on Senate Reform*
(referred to below as Molgat-Cosgrove); Canada, *Royal Commission on the Economic Union and Development Prospects for Canada, Report,* vol. 3, (referred to
below as Macdonald Commission); Alberta, Legislative Assembly, *Report of the
Alberta Select Special Committee on Senate Reform;* and Canada, Parliament, *Report
of the Special Joint Committee of the Senate and of the House of Commons on a
Renewed Canada.*

 5 See Canada, Department of Justice. *Reform of the Senate: A Discussion Paper,* and
Canada. *Shaping Canada's Future Together: Proposals,* 16f.

 6 See Canada, *Consensus Report on the Constitution: Charlottetown,* and Canada,
Draft Legal Text [of the Consensus Report on the Constitution].

 7 Canada, *Constitutional Reform: House of the Federation,* 13–14.

 8 Pepin-Robarts, 97.

 9 BC, 20ff.

10 Molgat-McGuigan, 35.

11 Alberta Select Committee, 24.

12 Molgat-Cosgrove, 13.

13 Macdonald Commission, 88.

14 Beaudoin-Dobbie, 44–5.

15 Charlottetown Agreement, 4.

16 The long shadow cast by this program and its central role in the rise of Western discontent during this period are respectively illustrated and documented
by Roger Gibbins, *Conflict & Unity – An Introduction to Canadian Political Life,*
especially 28ff and 178ff.

17 The new set of assumptions and the explicit conviction that meaningful
regional representation requires power rather than merely "input" are
apparent in the seminal 1981 study that marks the origin of the modern cycle
of electoral Senate reform proposals and the "Triple-E" reform movement.
See McCormick, Manning, and Gibson, *Regional Representation: The Canadian
Partnership.*

18 See Molgat-Cosgrove, 24ff.

19 See Alberta Select Committee, 27ff.

20 See Macdonald Commission, 88ff.

21 See Beaudoin-Dobbie, 45ff.

22 See Charlottetown Agreement, 4ff.

23 See McCormick, Manning, and Gibson, whose discussion of what should be the appropriate geopolitical unit of representation had a strong impact on the work of the Alberta committee. It argues that provinces have become the authentic regions of which Canada is composed and that any representation scheme denying this "political reality" would be met with justifiable skepticism by many Canadians (110–11).

24 See Molgat-Cosgrove, 28ff, Macdonald Commission, 89, and Beaudoin-Dobbie, 51.

25 Canada,"Responsive Institutions – Fact Sheet," 2.

26 In the proposal, which proved highly controversial in British Columbia and Alberta (especially), to establish a floor for the proportion of Québec seats in the House of Commons, at 25 percent.

27 See Bill C–60, 1978, S. 67, and Molgat-Cosgrove, 34.

28 See Pepin-Robarts, 98.

29 See Molgat-Cosgrove, 29ff.

30 See Alberta Select Committee, 31ff.

31 See Macdonald Commission, 91.

32 See Beaudoin-Dobbie, 52ff.

33 See Charlottetown Agreement, 5, and Canada, *Draft Legal Text*, 5f.

34 Molgat-McGuigan, 34.

35 See Canada, Constitutional Conference (1968), *The Constitution and the People of Canada*, 30ff.

36 Pepin-Robarts, 97.

37 Beige Paper, 52.

38 BC, 9.

39 See, respectively, Molgat-Cosgrove, 19; Alberta Select Committee, 14ff; and Macdonald Commission, 87ff.

40 Beaudoin-Dobbie, 41–2.

41 Canada, "Responsive Institutions – Fact Sheet," 1–2.

42 If regional representation, in the narrow sense described above, were recognized as primarily the task of other institutions than the Senate, this would repeat a shift in the focus of debate that occurred at an earlier point. Especially since the early 1980s, the courts and human rights commissions have emerged as the specialized institutions to which Canadians look for the primary protection of human rights, although some earlier Senate reform proposals envisioned the protection of human rights as a central role for the Senate.

43 The Australian example, where the Senate provoked a constitutional crisis by refusing to pass the budgets of the Labour Government in 1974 and 1975, is often cited as an example of the potential danger posed by a Senate powerful enough to block measures passed by a majority of the lower house within a system of government based on the Westminster model. See, for example, Archer and Maddox, "The 1975 Constitutional Crisis in Australia," 50ff.

44 As in the Australian constitutional crisis of the 1970s, which is often cited as

an illustration of the inherent tensions between an elected and partisan
upper house, and in the Westminster model of responsible government.

45 Van Loon and Whittington, *The Canadian Political System: Environment, Structure and Process*, 635–7.

46 For example, the Government of Canada's 1991 proposals and the Beaudoin-Dobbie Committee report in which they were studied both directed attention
to the need for reforms of the House of Commons in conjunction with Senate reform, but offered relatively limited proposals and did not relate them to
the general concerns described above.

CHAPTER THREE

Bicameralism in Federal Parliamentary Systems

Ronald L. Watts

INTRODUCTION

A bicameral parliament or legislature is not only a feature of Canada but also of most mature democracies and particularly of nearly all federal political systems. In considering the role of the Canadian Senate, a general comparative analysis of second chambers in federal parliamentary systems may provide a context within which to consider the particular nature of our own Senate and its prospective adaptation and evolution.

THE INTERNATIONAL AND THEORETICAL CONTEXT

The Widespread Use of Bicameral Legislatures

The roots of modern bicameralism can be traced to ancient Greece and Rome,[1] but the more immediate predecessors of modern second chambers were those established in Britain and Europe from the fourteenth century onward.[2] The combination of bicameralism and federalism dates from the Philadelphia Convention of 1787, establishing the first modern federation, the United States of America. Subsequent major federations created in the nineteenth and twentieth centuries, Switzerland (1848), Canada (1867), the German Confederation (1871), Australia (1901), Germany (1949) and India (1950), all established bicameral federal legislatures.

Indeed, bicameralism is a ubiquitous contemporary feature of both unitary and federal democratic political systems. In May 1999, the Inter-Parliamentary Union database included details of 178 parliamentary democracies of which sixty-six were bicameral,[3] and a meeting of the Forum des Sénats du Monde in Paris in February 2000 noted that between the early 1970s and 2000 the number of countries with bicameral legislatures had increased from forty-five to sixty-seven.[4] More significant is that of twenty-four contemporary federations all but two have bicameral legislatures at the federal level. These two exceptions – Micronesia and the United Arab Emirates – are relatively small, having populations of 135,869 and 2,445,989, respectively.[5] Furthermore, it is worth noting that two other federations – Pakistan and Nigeria – that experimented earlier with unicameral federal legislatures eventually replaced them with bicameral ones.[6] It is also noteworthy that in some federations, such as the United States and Australia, nearly all the state legislatures (with one exception in each) are also bicameral.

The Rationale for Bicameral Legislatures

Underlying this widespread establishment of bicameral legislatures are two main rationales. These relate to the roles of second chambers in legislative review and representation of regional interests.

A primary function of most second chambers is *legislative review*. Bicameral systems add an element of deliberate "redundancy" into the legislative processes, which can form an important part of the checks and balances within a democratic government.[7] Just as a second opinion is sought and valued in every walk of life, whether medicine, science, or day-to-day family problems, so a second chamber may look afresh at legislative proposals and uncover difficulties not noticed in the first chamber.[8] Furthermore, the delay required by review of legislation may provide more opportunity for media attention and public debate on issues so that there is time for political pressure to be brought to bear on the first chamber to reconsider its legislation. This is particularly important where legislative proposals may have been prepared in haste and passed in the first house under strict party discipline. Thus, the "sober second thought" of a second chamber, as Canada's first Prime Minister, Sir John A. Macdonald, put it, may provide protection against the danger of rash judgements by an unchecked lower house. At the 1787 Philadelphia Convention drafting the United States Constitution, James Madison argued that the two purposes of a second chamber are "first, to protect the people against their rulers, secondly to protect the people against transient impressions to which they themselves might be led."[9]

The value of legislative review applies in both unitary and federal political systems. If democracy is defined simply in terms of majority rule with each citizen counting as equal, then it might be argued that a second legislative chamber imposing constraints upon a majority of the directly elected representatives in a popularly elected first chamber represents a limit upon full democracy. The extent to which this is the case, however, would clearly vary according to the way members are selected and the composition of the second chamber, i.e., the degree to which it is itself democratic in character. Furthermore, if democracy is defined in broader and more sophisticated terms, not simply as rule by majority vote but rather as requiring political decision-making after extensive public debate involving input from a wide range of bodies and individuals within society assisted by extensive media coverage, then the elements of delay and second thought may themselves be democratically valuable. In addition, depending upon the membership of the second chamber, such a body may also provide an opportunity to bring particular forms of expertise to bear on the debate of an issue before parliament finally confirms its decisions. One study of unicameral and bicameral legislatures has pointed out that "the presence or absence of a second chamber cannot determine whether a parliament will be an effective democratic institution,"[10] since the method of selection, composition, powers, and processes of the second chamber are all critical factors. Nevertheless, it is significant that, as noted in the preceding subsection, a substantial number of the national legislatures of contemporary political regimes that style themselves as democratic have found bicameral legislatures, with the second chamber performing the function of legislative review, desirable, and the number has been increasing not decreasing.[11]

Representing regional interests at the federal or national level is a second major role that second chambers have played in the vast majority of federations and, indeed, even in many unitary states.[12] Representation in the lower houses of most federations has been based on population. But this means that the more populous states or provinces will have a preponderant influence in the lower house through their greater proportion of representatives. As a counterbalance to this, the creators of federations have generally chosen to provide the less populous states and provinces an improved voice in deliberations at the federal level by giving them weighted or even equal representation in a federal second legislative chamber. This has been intended to ensure that different state or provincial viewpoints would not be simply overridden by a majority of the population concentrated in the larger states or provinces. In addition, in most federations their designers have chosen a different method for selecting members in the second chamber in order to facilitate the expression of regional interests. For instance, members in one house may be elected to represent single-member constituencies, while those in the second chamber may be elected by proportional representation.

The essence of federal systems as political systems is that they are intended to be based not solely on majoritarian principles but upon the recognition and accommodation of diversity. This has almost invariably been translated in the institutions of the federal legislature into a majoritarian first chamber and a non-majoritarian representation of regional interests in the second chamber. In this respect, federal second chambers have filled two roles: first, as a device to check the power of majoritarian elements that might otherwise dominate the governmental process and, second, to ensure adequate representation of regional and minority interests and viewpoints. In terms of democratic principles, this represents a more refined view of democratic government as involving not simply majority rule but also the accommodation and protection of distinct regional groups and minorities within a constitutional framework. Thus, as Kenneth Wheare has noted, while there is no logical requirement for the federal government of a federation to contain a second chamber based on regional representation, "it is often essential if federal government is to work well."[13] In the words of Campbell Sharman writing about the Australian Senate, "Bicameralism is the natural ally of federalism: both imply a preference for incremental rather than radical change, for negotiated rather than coerced solutions, and for responsiveness to a range of political preferences rather than the artificial simplicity of dichotomous choice."[14]

It is important to be clear here about what is meant by the concept of "representation of regional interests." Four points need to be made. First, what are the regions whose interests are to be represented? In most contemporary federations the regions represented in the federal second chamber are the constituent units of the federation identified in the constitution: the states, provinces, cantons, länder, etc. In this respect, Canada has been unique among federations in distinguishing constitutionally, for purposes of representation in the Senate, between regions (groups of provinces, originally three and now four groups, each of which is represented by twenty-four senators) and individual provinces (the units of regional government).

Second, provincial or state representation in federal second chambers provides representation of minority interests, but primarily for federal minorities which themselves constitute a majority in each of one or more states or provinces (as typically is the case in multilingual or multinational federations). It does not necessarily enhance the representation of those federal minorities which do not constitute a majority in any province or which instead of being concentrated within particular states or provinces are diffused throughout the federation. An example of this latter type of minority is the Black minority in the United States, which, while a significant minority, is not a majority in any one state. Ultimately, a federal system represents a form of territorial distribution of power within the polity and, therefore, is more suited to situations where the internal diversity is geographically based rather than those where the internal differences are unrelated to geography. When it is argued that the role of the second chamber is that of enhancing minority representation, it is important, therefore, to distinguish whether the reference is to regionally concentrated minorities served through a state or provincial basis of representation in the federal second chamber, which is the typical pattern in federations, or to minorities which are not territorially concentrated and which therefore may be better served and protected by schemes of proportional representation, reserved seats filled either by election or appointment, or constitutionally stipulated minority rights enforced by the courts.

Third, the representation of regional interests in a federal parliament through its second chamber has two aspects. One is that of providing a forum for the direct expression of regional viewpoints on issues of federal policy. Effectiveness in this regard will depend on the degree to which the representatives are seen to express the views of the regional electorates, legislatures, and governments. Consequently, in different federations representation within the federal second chamber has usually taken one of three forms or a combination of them: direct election by the state or provincial electorate, indirect election by the state or provincial legislature, or members delegated by state or provincial governments. Rarer is a rather more indirect form of regional representation, i.e., appointment of regional representatives by the central government. The second aspect is that of ensuring, by weighted or equal representation of the constituent units in the federal second chamber, that the voices of the smaller provinces or states are not submerged by a majority dominated by the more populous provinces or states. In the case of the origin of the Canadian Senate, clearly the first of these dimensions was not given substantial weight since provincial electorates, legislatures, and governments were given no voice in the appointment of senators. There was, however, some effort to deal with the second aspect, although this was moderated by applying the notion of regional equality to groups of provinces rather than directly to individual provinces as in most other federations.

Fourth, it could be argued that, since the creation of the Canadian federation in 1867, the provinces have grown substantially in importance and that the supposed failure of the Senate to perform the function of provincial representation at the federal level now arises because the Senate was not originally designed to fulfill that function. Certainly that has been the case and senators cannot be blamed for not performing a function that was not envisaged in the original formulation. Nevertheless, any current review of the role of the Senate will have to take account of those changed circumstances and of the lessons other federations provide. These point to the importance, for the survival and effective development of a federation, of having a federal second chamber that provides an adequate channel for the representation of provincial interests in federal policy-making and which thus serves as a vital process for the reconciliation of these interests.

In addition to the two primary functions of legislative review and representation of regional interests that federal legislative second chambers have performed, note must also be taken of *other useful functions* that second chambers have often performed. Reference has already been made above to the representation of non-regional minority interests, although in most federations this has been considered secondary to the representation of the views of the fundamental regional building blocks of the federation, i.e., the constituent provinces or states. Another is that of conducting investigative studies of particular events or areas of policy, particularly those with long-term implications.[15] Others have included the approval of senior federal bureaucratic and judicial appointments, approval of treaties, and the scrutiny of executive action.

While second chambers in democratic regimes have generally performed a variety of useful functions, all of which must be taken into account in assessing their full role and in considering appropriate reforms to the Canadian Senate, this chapter places a deliberate emphasis upon the important role that second chambers within the federal legislature have played in providing a channel for the representation of regional and provincial interests in federal policy-making. The reason for this emphasis is that a crucial factor in the relative stability and effectiveness of federations generally has been the extent to which their federal institutions have enabled the differing and distinct viewpoints of their provinces and states, the basic constituent units, to be taken into account and reconciled within the processes of federal policy-making. Some federal second chambers, despite their designers' intentions, notably the United States Senate, have come to function more as a national decision-making body or, as in Australia, primarily as an opposition party house. But, comparative studies of federal second chambers have indicated that in almost all federations, including even these cases, the ostensible representation of regional interests in the federal second legislative chamber has been a vital requirement.[16] Thus, in considering Senate reform in Canada, its wider significance for the future stability and development of the federation as a whole is of particular importance.

Nonparliamentary and Parliamentary Legislatures

An important factor affecting the role of federal second chambers is whether the form of the federal government is based upon the separation of powers between the executive and legislature or upon the relative fusion of the executive and the lower legislative house through a parliamentary executive responsible to the popularly elected house of the legislature.[17] The two modern federations that preceded Canada, the United States with its presidential-congressional organization and Switzerland with its collegial fixed-term executive, emphasized the separation of the executive and legislature. The Latin American federations have generally followed the US model.

Canada, on the other hand, was the pioneer in combining federal and parliamentary institutions, but many others have since followed that pattern. Two types of parliamentary executives are found in federations. There are those based on the originally majoritarian British institutions

at Westminster as found, for example, in Canada, Australia, India, and
Malaysia. Then there are those following European traditions of responsible cabinet government, often based on coalitions, as found in Austria,
Germany, Spain, and Belgium. Some of these parliamentary federations
are constitutional monarchies (e.g., Canada, Australia, Malaysia, Spain,
and Belgium), while some are republics with heads of state elected
either directly or by an electoral college (e.g., Austria, Germany, and
India).

There is a third category, which might be called the hybrid presidential-
parliamentary form of executive. France is a non-federal example, but Russia is a federal example incorporating a directly elected federal president
having significant executive powers combined with a parliamentary cabinet responsible to the federal legislature.

Because Canada is a parliamentary federation and unlikely to abandon
its parliamentary character, this chapter will concentrate upon reviewing
parliamentary federations, although for comparative purposes reference
will be made from time to time to federal second chambers in nonparliamentary federations. The combination of parliamentary with federal institutions places some limits on the role that second chambers may play.[18]
Where there is a separation of powers between the executive and legislature as in the United States, the Latin American federations, and Switzerland, normally the two federal legislative houses have had co-equal powers (although in the United States the Senate does in fact have some
additional powers relating to ratification of appointments and treaties).
Where there are parliamentary executives, the difficulties that would be
involved in having two "confidence" chambers mean that the house that
controls the executive (invariably the popularly elected first chamber) is
the more influential, and the powers of the second chamber, either
through constitutional stipulation or political convention, are more limited. Often in parliamentary systems the usefulness of the second chamber has been seen more as that of being complementary to the confidence chamber.[19]

The more limited role of second chambers in parliamentary legislatures has sometimes raised questions about whether in these instances
their second chambers provide sufficient capacity for legislative revision
and regional influence in federal decision-making. This concern is further reinforced by the usual strength of party discipline within parliamentary federations. Nevertheless, some of the federal second chambers, such as the Australian Senate and the German Bundesrat, have
been able to exercise considerable influence by virtue of their composition and ability in practice to provide significant checks on the legislative
process. Indeed, Lijphart, in his threefold classification of second chambers based on their formal powers and on their democratic legitimacy,
judged not only the nonparliamentary federations of the United States
and Switzerland but also the parliamentary federations of Australia and

Germany to be strongly bicameral while classifying Canada as weakly bicameral.[20] Notwithstanding Canadian experience, the continued operation and influence of federal second chambers in most other federations indicates that, while parliamentary institutions may place some limits on the role of federal second chambers, they have nevertheless frequently played an important role in contributing to their effectiveness as federations.

Processes of Change and Adaptation

Federations are never static. All federations have had to adapt to changing conditions and circumstances. This applies as well to the operation of their federal second chambers. Adaptation may take one of two general forms. The first is that of constitutional amendment. In most federations the basic features of the federal second chamber are set down in the constitution since the federal second chamber represents a basic element in the constitutional framework, and therefore fundamental changes require amendments to the constitution. In the case of Canada, the relevant procedures for constitutional amendments relating to the Senate are set out in the *Constitution Act, 1982*, sections 38–39 and 42(b and c), requiring assent by a majority in both Houses of Parliament and by the legislative assemblies of at least seven provinces representing 50 percent of the total population. Furthermore, section 41(b) requires unanimous consent of the provinces for any change in the number of senators to which a province is entitled. A provision (s. 47) stipulates that, if the Senate has not adopted a resolution to amend the *Constitution* within 180 days and the House of Commons again adopts the resolution, an amendment may be proclaimed without Senate approval. This was intended to prevent the Senate from blocking its own reform and was apparently justified on the ground that, in any case, assent by the required majority of provincial legislatures would ensure that the House of Commons alone would not be able to impose the amendments. The essential point is that, as in most federations, constitutional amendment relating to the federal second chamber is intended to require a wide measure of formal consensus and, therefore, is difficult to achieve.

The second form of adaptation is that of evolutionary changes through the development of practices and conventions not requiring constitutional amendment.[21] Such evolutionary changes without formal constitutional amendment have occurred frequently in the federal second chambers of other federations, although such changes have had to fit within the basic constitutional framework. A classic and oft-cited example relates to the introduction of direct elections for senators in the United States. Originally, the Constitution of 1789 (art. I, s. 3) specified that senators would be selected by the state legislatures. However, by 1912 the practice had developed in more than half the state legislatures of choosing senators from candidates named by the parties in the primary elections, thus in practice making a significant change in the process of selecting senators. Eventually, the passage of the Seventeenth Amendment in 1913 formally amended the Constitution to bring it more into line with practice by requiring direct election of senators.

Experience elsewhere suggests then that, while changes to certain fundamental features of the federal second chamber may ultimately require constitutional amendment, in a situation where formal constitutional amendments are difficult to achieve, there remains considerable scope for change and even transformation through incremental pragmatic adjustment.[22] In considering such evolutionary adjustments to the role of the Canadian Senate, it will be important to ensure that pragmatic political compromises work towards a coherent evolution and that they are not undertaken in isolation from a more general parliamentary reform or the overall operation of the federal system.

A REVIEW OF SECOND CHAMBERS
IN FEDERAL SYSTEMS

Bicameralism within Federations

We have already noted that all the major contemporary federations have bicameral federal legislatures as an essential feature of their federal character. But while most federations have found it necessary to establish bicameral legislatures, there is enormous variation among them in their role, method for selecting members, composition, and powers. In this section we shall review the bicameral legislatures of a range of major parliamentary federations: Canada, Australia, Austria, Germany, India, Malaysia, Spain, and Belgium. While the focus is on parliamentary federations, references will also be made to the nonparliamentary federations, particularly the United States and Switzerland, to draw attention to contrasts between parliamentary and nonparliamentary federations. Table 1 sets out variations in the role, selection, composition, and powers of these second chambers in federations, and table 2 summarizes the particular combination of elements incorporated in the federal second chamber of each of these federations. In considering these various examples, it will be important to note not simply the formal constitutional structures but also the operating dynamics of the way in which they actually function.

In the contemporary world, twenty-four federations and quasi-federations can be identified,[23] but in selecting the parliamentary and nonparliamentary examples referred to above for review, the focus is on examples particularly relevant to Canadian issues. The remaining contemporary federations are generally less relevant to the Canadian context. The four Latin American federations, Argentina, Brazil, Mexico, and Venezuela, are

Table 1   Variation in Role, Selection Composition, and Powers of Second Chambers in Major Federations

Role	Selection	Composition	Powers
1 Legislative chamber only (e.g., Canada, USA, Switzerland, Australia, Austria, India, Malaysia, Spain, Belgium) 2 Combined legislative and intergovernmental role (e.g., Germany, South Africa)	1 Appointment by federal government (no formal consultation) (e.g., Canada 1867, Malaysia 58% of seats) 2 Appointment by federal government based on nominations by provincial governments (e.g., Canada: Meech Lake Accord proposal) 3 Appointment ex officio by state governments (e.g., Germany) 4 Indirect Election by state legislatures (e.g., USA 1789–1913, India, Malaysia 42% of seats, Austria) 5 Direct election by simple plurality or majority (e.g., USA since 1913, Switzerland) 6 Direct election by proportional representation (e.g., Australia) 7 Choice of method left to cantons (e.g., Switzerland until 1999) 8 Mixed (e.g., Malaysia, Belgium, Spain)	1 Equal "regional" representation (e.g., Canada for groups of provinces) 2 Equal state representation (e.g., USA, Australia, and 42% of Malaysian senate) 3 Two categories of cantonal representation (e.g., Switzerland) 4 Weighted state representation: 4 categories (e.g., Germany) 5 Weighted state representation: multiple categories (e.g., Austria, India) 6 Additional or special representation for others including aboriginals (e.g., Malaysia, India) 7 A minority of regional legislature representatives plus direct election (e.g., Belgium, Spain)	1 Absolute veto with mediation committees (e.g., USA, Switzerland) 2 Absolute veto on federal legislation affecting any state administrative functions (e.g., Germany for about 60% of federal legislation) 3 Suspensive veto: time limit (e.g., Malaysia, Spain) 4 Suspensive veto: matching lower house vote to override (e.g., Germany for some) 5 Deadlock resolved by joint sitting (e.g., India) 6 Deadlock resolved by double dissolution then joint sitting (e.g., Australia) 7 Money bills: brief suspensive veto (e.g., India, Malaysia)

all bicameral, but follow the United States example of presidential-congressional institutions and lack the long, stable history of the United States. Nigeria, Pakistan, Ethiopia, Comoros, and Yugoslavia have all been wracked by political instability and turmoil. Micronesia and United Arab Emirates do provide examples of unicameral federal legislatures, but as noted earlier both are relatively small with populations of less than three million. South Africa, while predominantly federal in form, is highly

Table 2   Selection, Composition, and Powers of Federal Second Chambers

USA: (1789)	Senate: direct election since 1913 (by simple plurality); equal state representation; absolute veto (mediation committees).
Switzerland: (1848)	Council of States: direct election with majority requirement determined by each canton; cantons with either 1 or 2 representatives; absolute veto (mediation committees).
Canada: (1867)	Senate: appointed by federal government; equal regional representation for groups of provinces (some exceptions); absolute veto (legally).
Australia: (1901)	Senate: direct election (by proportional representation); equal state representation; absolute veto (but followed by double dissolution and joint sitting)
Austria: (1920)	Bundesrat: elected by state legislatures; weighted representation (range 12–3); suspensive veto (may be overridden by simple majority in lower house, the Nationalrat).
Germany: (1949)	Bundesrat: state government ex officio delegations + weighted voting (3, 4, 5, or 6 block votes per state); suspensive veto on federal legislation overridden by corresponding lower-house majority, but absolute veto on any federal legislation affecting state administrative functions (60% of federal legislation); mediation committees.
India: (1950)	Rajya Sabha (Council of States): elected by state legislatures (plus small number (5%) of additional representatives for special representation); weighted representation (range 86–12); veto resolved by joint sitting.
Malaysia: (1963)	Dewan Negara (Senate): 42% elected by state legislatures (plus 58% additional centrally appointed representatives for minorities); equal state representation (for 42% of total seats) offset by inequality for appointed senators; suspensive veto (6 months).
Spain: (1978)	Senate: 208 directly elected members and 51 appointed by parliaments of 17 Autonomous Communities; categories of 4, 3, or 1 directly elected senator(s) per province (sub-units of Autonomous Communities) supplemented by representation of 1 or more (related to population) appointed by each autonomous parliament; suspensive veto (2 months).
Belgium: (1993)	Senate: combination of directly elected (40), indirectly elected by linguistic Community councils (21), and co-opted senators (10); variable representation specified for each unit; equal competence with House of Representatives on some matters but on others House of Representatives has overriding power.

centralized and indeed quasi-federal in character by comparison with Canada, although its federal second chamber, the National Council of Provinces, as an adaptation of the German Bundesrat, does have some interesting features. The Russian federation has a second chamber, the

Council of the Federation composed of 178 members, where each of the eighty-nine territories is represented by two members (the head of state administration and the chair of the state legislature), but its mixed presidential-parliamentary institutions make it less relevant to the Canadian context.

The Role of Federal Second Chambers

The role envisaged for a federal second chamber is clearly a major determinant of its design, including the method of selecting members, its composition, and its powers. The primary role of most of the federal second chambers in parliamentary and nonparliamentary federations surveyed here has been legislative, both to review legislation for possible improvements and to bring regional and minority interests and concerns to bear on federal legislation. The German Bundesrat stands out by contrast with the others in performing an additional and equally important role as an institution facilitating intergovernmental co-operation and collaboration. It is able to do this because, unlike other federal second chambers, it is composed of instructed delegates of the länd governments and, in addition to its suspensive veto over all federal legislation, it possesses an absolute veto over federal legislation affecting state legislative and administrative responsibilities. Under the German pattern for the constitutional distribution of legislative and administrative responsibilities, large areas of federal legislation are administered by the länder (in Canada the jurisdiction over criminal law follows this pattern) with the result that in practice the Bundesrat has had an absolute veto over 60 percent of all federal legislation. This gives the Bundesrat strong leverage and makes it the central focus for intergovernmental negotiations.[24] This model heavily influenced the South Africans in the design of their national second chamber, the National Council of the Provinces, in their new 1996 Constitution, although some significant modifications to the German model were made.

Federal second chambers have also performed a number of other valuable secondary roles.[25] These have included in various instances conducting investigative studies through special committees, the approval of senior federal bureaucratic and judicial appointments, the approval of treaties, and the scrutiny of executive policies and action (although in parliamentary systems this last function is usually left primarily to the lower house, to which the cabinet is responsible).

Selection of Members

There is considerable variety in the ways in which members of federal second chambers are selected and these have an impact upon the role that the second chambers may perform within the federal institutions. In three federations, Australia since its inception in 1901, the United States since 1913, and Switzerland (by individual cantonal choice but eventually in all cantons), members of the federal second chamber are directly elected by the citizens of the constituent units. In the United States from 1789 to 1912, members of the federal Senate were indirectly elected (i.e., selected by the state legislatures), but the Seventeenth Amendment in 1913 changed that to direct election. Indirect election by state legislatures is currently the case for all members in the Austrian Bundesrat and the vast majority of members in the Indian Council of States. In the case of India a small number of seats (initially twelve out of 216) were reserved for centrally appointed members to represent literature, art, science, and special minorities. A third pattern occurs in Germany, where the members of the Bundesrat are delegates of their länd governments, holding office ex officio as members of their länd cabinets and voting in the Bundesrat as a block on the instructions of their länd governments. A fourth pattern, found among federations only in Canada, is the appointment of all senators by the Governor General (in effect by the Prime Minister), these appointees holding office until retirement at seventy-five. The federal second chambers of Malaysia, Belgium, and Spain have a mixed membership. In Malaysia, twenty-six of the sixty-eight Senate seats (42 percent) are filled by indirect election by the state legislatures. The remaining forty-two seats (58 percent) are appointed by the head of state acting on the advice of the federal government, nominally to represent special interests and racial minorities. The Spanish Senate has 208 directly elected members and fifty-one representatives appointed by the seventeen Autonomous Community legislatures. In Belgium, forty of the seventy-one senators are directly elected, twenty-one are indirectly elected by the Flemish, French, and German Community Councils, and ten (six Flemish and four French) are appointed by the directly elected senators.

In those federations where the members of the federal second chamber are directly elected, they are generally representative of the interests of the regional electorates rather than of the regional governments. While directly elected representatives are usually more responsive to the wishes of their electorates, in parliamentary systems where party discipline tends to be stronger this may be a moderating factor. Nevertheless, where the second chamber is not a "confidence" house, party discipline has usually not been as strong as in the lower house. Where members are indirectly elected (i.e., appointed by the state legislatures), they are also generally representative of regional interests, but regional political party alignments within the state legislatures have a particularly significant influence upon selection. Where, as in Germany, members of the second chamber are ex officio instructed members of the constituent governments, it is primarily the views of those governments (often coalition governments) that they represent, and therefore only indirectly those of the länd electorates. Where all senators are appointed by the federal government and for lengthy terms, as in Canada, senators have had in comparative terms the least credibility as spokespersons for regional interests, even when they are residents of the regions they represent.[26] This has reinforced the perception of provincial premiers as the more legitimate and, therefore, major spokespersons for provincial interests on the federal scene. Nor has the public legitimacy of the Senate been helped by recent examples of appointment of elderly persons just short of retirement in order to ensure passage of a particular bill. Federal appointment of members of a federal second chamber can, however, provide a means for ensuring representation for some particular minorities and interests (either intraprovincial minorities or non-territorially based minorities). It was to ensure representation of particular minorities and interests that the Indian Constitution of 1950 provided for twelve centrally appointed members out of a total not to exceed 250 members in the Council of States and that the Malaysian Constitution currently provides for a substantial portion (forty-two out of sixty-eight senators) to be appointed by the federal government. In this respect, it is noteworthy that the Canadian Senate is substantially more representative of women, aboriginal people, and visible minorities than the elected Canadian House of Commons, thus more accurately reflecting the Canadian population in these respects.[27] The mixed basis of selection of senators in Spain and in Belgium is the result of compromises intended to obtain the benefits of different forms of selection for members of the federal second chamber. These latter examples suggest that selection of members in a federal second chamber need not be confined to only one form and that a mixed basis of selection may serve to meet a variety of needs.

It is common for members of the federal second chambers in federations to have longer terms than those in the first chambers, often double the length, with a rolling membership that is renewed in parts.[28] Australia is an example where half of the Senate is elected every three years. This means that the second chamber cannot be dissolved by the government (except in the special circumstances leading to a double dissolution to break deadlocks between the chambers). In those cases where members of the second chamber are indirectly elected (i.e., appointed by state legislatures or governments), terms for these members are often tied to the regional elections (e.g., Spain and Germany).

How do the different methods of selection affect the other functions of the second chamber besides that of representing regional interests? In relation to legislative review, the evidence seems to suggest that this function is performed equally well by elected or appointed members in a second chamber. Where there are appointed members with relevant expertise, members may use their expertise in the delivery of policy to draw attention to technical and administrative problems with bills. On the other hand, in terms of political impact, the greater political legitimacy of directly elected or provincial government delegates may enhance their ability to act as a check on the lower house, as Australian and German experience illustrates. This is particularly the case in situations where the balance of power in the second chamber is held by parties other than the majority in the lower house.[29] With regard to the representation of non-regional minorities, either the use of proportional representation for second chamber elections or the appointment of some members (but a minority of the total membership) seems to have been the preferred arrangement in practice.

Composition of Second Chambers

The nature of the regional distribution of seats in a federal second chamber has an important impact on the role it plays. In all federal bicameral legislatures, the membership of the second chamber has been based on representation of the constituent states or regions. Indeed, this is also true of about a quarter of unitary states.[30]

It is often declared that equality of state representation in federal second chambers is the norm in federations. This assumption is derived from the American precedent where the debate over whether representation in the federal legislature should be in terms of population or in terms of states was particularly intense at the Philadelphia Convention in 1787. The struggle between the large and small states for influence was resolved by the "Connecticut Compromise" whereby a bicameral solution was adopted. This based one house, the House of Representatives, on population and the other house, the Senate, on equal representation of the states. The compromise ensured that differing state viewpoints would not be simply overridden in the Congress by a majority of the population concentrated in a few large states.

In fact, however, in only two of the ten federal second chambers listed in tables 1 and 2 are the states equally represented. These are the United States and Australian senates. Recognizing that equal state representation may have significant unequal consequences[31] most other federations have not incorporated equal state or provincial representation in their federal second chambers. In recognition, however, of the need to counterbalance the possible dominance of the larger states or provinces in federal deliberations, most federations have made some effort to weight representation in the federal second chamber in favour of the smaller regional units and minorities. In the case of the Malaysian Senate, the seats filled by indirectly elected senators are in fact equally distributed among the states (two per state), but the remaining 58 percent of seats which are filled by centrally appointed senators have not followed a consistent pattern of balanced state representation, and the influence of party considerations in these appointments has meant in practice a considerable variation in the net representation of each state.

In most other federations, the relative population of the constituent units has been a factor in their representation in the federal second chamber, although generally there has been weighting to favour the smaller units. The degrees of weighting have varied. In Switzerland, there are two categories of representation in the Council of States: twenty cantons have two representatives each and the six "half cantons" have only one each. The German Constitution (art. 51) establishes four population categories for länd representation in the Bundesrat: länder have three, four, five, or six block votes in the Bundesrat. Each länd is guaranteed three votes, but länder with over two million inhabitants have four; those with more than six million, five; and those with over seven million, six. In India, Austria, and Spain, the range of state representation in their second chambers is wider, being, from largest to smallest, 86–12 in India and 12–3 in Austria. In Spain, for the directly elected senators there have been four, three, or one representative(s) per province (the provinces are subunits within the seventeen Autonomous Communities). In addition, legislators from each of the seventeen Autonomous Community may select at least one senator plus one more for each million inhabitants. Thus the number of indirectly elected senators per Autonomous Community varies between one and seven.[32] In Belgium, the differential representation of each Community and region in the Senate is specified in the Constitution. The twenty-one Community seats elected by and from within the Community Councils are allocated ten to the French-speaking Community, ten to the Dutch-speaking Community, and one to the German-speaking Community. Of the forty directly elected senators, fifteen are French-speaking and twenty-five are Dutch-speaking, recognizing a population difference. For some especially significant issues, however, article 43 of the Constitution requires majorities within both the French-speaking and Dutch-speaking members of the Senate.

Canada, as is the case with so much about its Senate, is unique among federations in basing Senate representation not on individual provinces but on regional groupings of provinces with the four basic regions having twenty-four seats each, plus an additional six for Newfoundland and one each for the three territories. The effect of this arrangement and the pattern of historical evolution has been that some relatively populous provinces like British Columbia and Alberta have only six senators each, while the much smaller provinces of Nova Scotia and New Brunswick have substantially more with 10 senators each, a factor further eroding the legitimacy of the Senate in the eyes of the residents of the western provinces. A particular factor complicating the design of the Canadian Senate is the fact that Canada's most significant linguistic minority, the French-speaking majority within Quebec, is concentrated in the second most populous province. In many other federations where the major linguistic minorities are often concentrated in smaller provinces, the weighting of senate representation in favour of the smaller constituent units also favours these minorities. But in Canada, equality or weighting in favour of the smaller provinces would lead to underrepresentation of Canada's major linguistic minority concentrated in Quebec. That is one of the factors that has made a resolution to contentions over equality or weighted provincial representation in the Senate particularly difficult.

It is worth noting in passing that in some federations, notably Switzerland, Spain, and Belgium, there are provisions permitting or, in some instances in Spain and Belgium, requiring senators to hold dual membership (i.e., membership at the same time in the legislatures of the constituent units). In Germany, of course, this is true of all Bundesrat members who are there ex officio as members of their länd governments. These arrangements increase sensitivity in the federal second chamber to the interests and concerns of the constituent units and in some cases, most notably Germany, have facilitated intergovernmental consultation and collaboration. It is sometimes argued that in the Canadian context such an arrangement would result in a provincial stranglehold over all federal legislation, creating serious confrontations within Parliament. German experience, where the Bundesrat has had in practice an absolute veto over 60 percent of federal legislation, suggests otherwise. There, the Bundesrat has, over time, served instead to co-opt the provincial governments into supporting federal objectives and policies. Indeed, those Canadian provincial premiers, such as Premier Lougheed, who in the 1970s resisted such a "House of the Provinces" reform, recognized the potential threat to their autonomy. The problem in Germany has been not that of heightened contention within Parliament, but rather the tendency to inertia arising from "the joint decision trap" produced by the requirement of joint intergovernmental agreement on all major policies by both levels of government.[33] Other federations, however, have prohibited simultaneous dual membership in federal and provincial legislatures to avoid conflicting demands upon the time of their parliamentarians, a path that Canada followed after an initial period in which such dual membership was permitted.

Powers of Second Chambers Relative to First Chambers

Where there is a separation of powers between the executive and legislature, as in the United States of America and Switzerland, normally the two federal legislative chambers have had equal powers (although in the United States the Senate has some additional powers relating to ratification of appointments and treaties). In federations with parliamentary institutions, the house that controls the executive (invariably the first chamber) normally has more power, even where the constitution has formally allocated nearly equal legal powers. Furthermore, as a consequence, in these federations, the powers of the second chamber in relation to finance bills are usually limited. Generally in parliamentary federations, in cases of conflict between the two houses, provisions for a suspensive veto, for the lower house to override the second chamber by a two-thirds vote, for joint sittings where members of the second chamber are substantially outnumbered by members of the lower house, or for double dissolution have usually rendered the second chamber weaker, although the degree varies (see table 1, column 4, and table 3 for examples). This has sometimes raised concerns within these federations about whether their second chambers provide sufficient capacity for legislative revision and regional influence in federal decision-making. This concern has been further reinforced by the usual strength of party discipline characteristic of parliamentary institutions. Nonetheless, some of the federal second chambers in parliamentary federations, such as the Australian Senate and the German Bundesrat, have been able in practice to exert considerable influence. In the Australian case, this has been due to the Senate electoral system, which, differing from that of the House of Representatives, has produced a different party composition, and to the ability of the Senate to stand up to the House of Representatives through the mechanism of double dissolution.[34] The particular membership of the German Bundesrat and its absolute veto over all federal legislation involving administration by the länder (in practice about 60 percent of all federal legislation) have been major factors in its influence.

Table 3 outlines the relation with the lower house of selected federal second chambers setting out their powers in terms of ordinary legislation, financial legislation, dispute resolution and constitutional amendments. The information in table 3 and the processes for resolving disputes between the two houses in each federal legislature set out earlier in table 1, column 4, and table 2 give some indication of the general balance between houses within each federation. In such an assessment, the extent to which the perceived political legitimacy of the federal second chamber has strengthened or weakened its relative power and influence in relationship to the lower house is also to be factored in. In this respect, the most powerful and influential federal second chambers have been those in the United States, Switzerland, Germany, and Australia. By contrast, the federal second chambers in Malaysia, India, and Spain have been considerably weaker, clearly occupying more of a complementary role. The Belgian Senate is closer to the latter group, although it is somewhat stronger. The Canadian Senate is something of an anomaly. In purely legal constitutional terms it is more similar to the first group of examples, but because the manner of appointment of its members has undermined the public perception of its legitimacy (it is the only federal second chamber composed wholly of centrally appointed members), its relative influence, while significant, has been substantially less than a literal reading of the Constitution would suggest. Thus, its role is basically complementary to that of the House of Commons. Any consideration of Senate reform will need, therefore, to be placed within the broader context of parliamentary reform as a whole.

Assessment of Effectiveness

Literature assessing second chambers comparatively is relatively limited, the most notable recent examples being Lijphart (1984), Tsebelis and Money (1997), Patterson and Mughan (1999) and Russell (2000). Additionally, in literature comparing federal systems, Sharman (1987) and Watts (1999) include attention to second chambers in federal systems.

Lijphart assessed second chambers in twenty-one democracies (including unitary systems) in terms of a threefold classification based on their *formal powers* relative to the first chamber and on their *democratic legitimacy*. His criteria were symmetry and congruence: a symmetrical legislature being one in which both houses have similar powers and a congruent legislature being one in which both houses have similar composition. A bicameral system was judged strong if it was symmetrical and incongruent, weak if it was either symmetric and congruent or asymmetric and incongruent, and insignificant if it was asymmetric and congruent. Among the federations included in his analysis four (Australia, Germany, Switzerland, and the United States) were assessed as symmetrical (or only moderately asymmetrical) and incongruent, and thus judged to be strongly bicameral. The Canadian federal Parliament was considered extremely asymmetrical and incongruent, and hence weakly bicameral.

Tsebelis and Money analysed the interactions between chambers in the legislative processes in some fifty bicameral countries using the game theory models of co-operative and nonco-operative behaviours. They analysed two methods of achieving compromises between chambers: the shuttling of proposed legislation between houses, as in Canada, and the joint conference committee method in which selected members of each house meet to negotiate compromises as in the United States, Switzerland, Germany, Russia, and South Africa. They show that the details of the rules governing each method have predictable consequences for legislative outcomes and that the details of this interaction are critical to understanding both behaviour within each house and the legislative outcomes that are generated.

Patterson and Mughan, from their analysis of second chambers in nine countries including the federations of Australia, Canada, Germany, and Spain, reach a number of conclusions. One is that by comparison with the United States, second chambers in parliamentary systems generally draw less power and prestige than first chambers.[35] They also conclude that second chambers in parliamentary systems, whether federal or not, are contested institutions whose existence is commonly a matter of dispute. They attribute this to the majoritarian emphasis inherent in parliamentary systems and the emphasis in such systems upon the concentration rather than dispersal of power.[36] Their third conclusion is that nevertheless second chambers are important and influential parliamentary institutions. Their fourth conclusion is that in parliamentary systems the behaviour of second chambers is structured more by their legislative review function than by their representative function.[37] Finally, they conclude that second chambers generally are becoming more assertive in relation to first chambers in part due to partisan competition, in part due to lack of respect for the second chambers typically shown by members of the first chamber, and in part due to divergent views in the two chambers about the nature of democracy itself as majoritarian or non-majoritarian.[38] The net effect, they argue, is that second chambers are becoming more important as shapers of policy than in the recent past.

Russell studied a range of second chambers in both unitary and federal parliamentary systems in order to bring a comparative perspective to the process of reforming the House of Lords in the United Kingdom. Federal examples included for in-depth analysis in her study were Australia, Canada, Germany, and Spain. She noted the high degree of heterogeneity in these examples arising from their differing histories, traditions, and political institutions.[39] She suggested that Lijphart's analysis puts insufficient emphasis upon legitimacy as a factor determining the strength of bicameralism.[40] She advocates three interlinked elements that are required for a second chamber to be effective.[41] First, the second chamber must have a composition distinct from the first chamber. For this, method of appointment, composition, and party balance are important. Second, the second chamber must have moderate to strong powers if its impact is to be adequate. Third, the perceived legitimacy of a second chamber is critical to its success. A second chamber even with a distinct composition and nominally adequate powers will, she argues, remain ineffective without a public perception of legitimacy. Because of this, she believes that territorial representation of constituent units in the second chamber is best expressed through direct election.

Sharman explores the relationship between federalism and bicameralism. He concludes that there is no necessary logical connection,[42] but notes that both are based on the concepts of constitutionalism and dispersal of power. Both imply preferences for incremental change, negotiated solutions, and responsiveness to a wide range of political preferences. Thus, second chambers make an important contribution to the values implicit within federal political systems.

Watts suggests that to obtain the confidence of the citizens in the different units, the shared institutions of the federal government and legislature must meet two criteria: genuine representativeness of the internal diversity within the federation and effectiveness in federal government decision-making.[43]

CANADIAN SENATE REFORM PROPOSALS
IN COMPARATIVE TERMS

The Pressures for Abolition or Reform

The Canadian Senate has in fact done more useful work than it is usually credited with in the legislative review process and in conducting investigative reviews.[44] On the other hand, in comparative terms it is clear from the foregoing that of all the federal second chambers the Canadian Senate has the least perceived public legitimacy in the representation of regional interests within the federal legislature.[45] Lack of satisfaction with the role and functioning of the Senate has over the years led to many calls for reform or even abolition.[46] As long ago as 1926, R.A. Mackay wrote a book entitled *The Unreformed Senate of Canada.* Most Canadians agree that the Senate should be reformed, but disagreement about what reforms would be appropriate has to the present day left it substantially unreformed. This led C.E.S. Franks to declare that the Senate in its present form "remains as it has for 131 years an anomaly, a peripheral institution of government, sometimes a nuisance, occasionally of value."[47]

A substantial number of Canadians, in the face of continued frustration with the failure to reform the Senate have come to argue for abolition. But the experience of other federations suggests that this would be a serious mistake. As noted earlier, virtually all other major federations of any significant size have found it necessary to establish and maintain bicameral federal legislatures. The exceptions represent a few relatively tiny or unstable federations. An examination of the pathology of federations would include the splitting of Pakistan in 1971, which followed the failure of its unicameral legislature to reconcile the deep fissures between East and West Pakistan.[48] Not surprisingly, the federation of Pakistan (formerly West Pakistan), which was subsequently established after the departure of what became Bangladesh, adopted a bicameral federal legislature. While there are a few unicameral federal legislatures, in these instances the resulting predominance of simple majoritarianism has usually increased minority insecurity and had a corrosive impact upon any ability to generate a consensus among the diverse groups that usually constitute a federation. Most federations have found an effective federal second chamber essential for the operation of the federation as a federation, and Canadian proposals for abolition oversimplify the issue by failing to recognize this essential requirement for an effective federation. In any case, abolition of the Canadian Senate would require a constitutional amendment under article 41 of the *Constitution Act, 1982* and hence the unanimous assent of all ten provinces, a difficult process at best. Abolition of the Senate, therefore, far from solving the problems of Canadian federation, is likely to exacerbate them. The real issue is not abolition of the Senate, but what kind of reform is desirable and achievable.

Table 3   Powers of Selected Federal and Quasi-federal Second Chambers

	Ordinary legislation	Financial legislation	Dispute resolution	Constitutional Amendments
AUSTRALIA Senate	Bills are introduced in either house. Upper house may amend or reject any legislation.	Must be introduced in lower house. Upper house may not amend but may "request" amendments, or reject.	Dissolve both houses of parliament, followed after elections by joint sitting if necessary.	Must pass at least one house with absolute majority and then pass referendum by majority and with majorities in more than half the states.
AUSTRIA Bundesrat	Bills are introduced in lower house. Upper house can object within 8 weeks, but cannot amend.	Upper house cannot object to federal budget.	Lower house can override upper house veto by simple majority.	Passed by lower house only, but if one-third of upper house members demand it, there must be a referendum.
BELGIUM Sénat	Two kinds of legislation: "ordinary" bills start in lower house and pass automatically unless 15 Senators demand a review within 15 days (Sénat then can consider for 60 days); "bicameral" bills, covering, e.g., foreign affairs, need support of both chambers.	Treated as ordinary legislation.	Lower house can override upper house veto on "ordinary" legislation, but not on specified matters.	Require both houses to be dissolved, and two-thirds majority in both new houses.
CANADA Senate	Bills are introduced in either house. Upper house may amend or reject any legislation.	Must be introduced in lower house. Upper house may amend but not increase costs.	No means of resolving disputes – bills may shuttle indefinitely.	Senate can only block for 180 days, but must also be assented by legislative assemblies in two-thirds of provinces, comprising 50% of population.*

Table 3   continued

	Ordinary legislation	Financial legislation	Dispute resolution	Constitutional Amendments
GERMANY Bundesrat	Upper house sees and comments on all legislation before introduction in lower house. After lower house reading, bills return to upper house for approval.	Treated as ordinary legislation, except budget which is introduced in both houses simultaneously.	Joint committee recommends a compromise which usually cannot be amended. Then upper house has veto on bills affecting the states (around 60% of bills), lower house has last word otherwise.	Must be passed by two-thirds majority in both houses
INDIA Rajya Sabha	Bills are introduced in either house. Reviewing house has 6 months.	Most such bills must be introduced in the lower house, but budget is introduced in both houses simultaneously and upper house has 14 days to review (lower house is decisive).	If upper house passes unwelcome amendments, rejects the bill, or fails to consider it within 6 months, joint session decides.	Must be passed by two-thirds majority in both houses and majority of total membership of both houses.
MEXICO Cámara de Senadores	Bills are introduced in either house. Both houses may amend or reject legislation.	Must be introduced in lower house. Upper house has 30 days to review. Lower house has last word.	Two-thirds majority in lower house over rules upper house veto. Lower house may call a joint mediation committee, but has the last word.	Must be passed by two-thirds majority in each house, and by half of all states.
RUSSIA Council of the Federation	Bills are introduced in lower house. Upper house cannot amend bills but may reject within 14 days.	Treated as ordinary legislation.	Joint committee recommends a compromise which may be overridden by two-thirds majority in lower house.	Some must be passed by three-fifths majority in both houses, others treated as ordinary legislation.
SOUTH AFRICA National Council of Provinces	Bills are introduced in either house. For ordinary legislation upper house members have 1 vote each. For bills affecting provinces each province casts 1 block vote.	Must be introduced in lower house, but otherwise treated as ordinary legislation.	Joint committee recommends a compromise which may be overridden by two-thirds majority in lower house.	Must be passed by two-thirds majority in lower and 6 out of 9 provinces in upper house, voting as blocks.

Table 3   continued

	Ordinary legislation	Financial legislation	Dispute resolution	Constitutional Amendments
SPAIN Senado	Bills are introduced in lower house. Upper house has 2 months to review, or 20 days in case of urgency, and may introduce amendments with an absolute majority.	Treated as ordinary legislation.	Lower house can override upper house amendments. Upper house veto may be overridden by an absolute lower house majority or a simple majority after 2 months delay.	Most changes must pass by three-fifths majority in both houses. Joint committee can propose compromise, which requires two-thirds majority in lower house and absolute majority in upper house. Also subject to referendum if requested by one-tenth of members of either house.**
SWITZERLAND Ständerat	Bills are introduced in either house. Both houses have veto power over legislation.	Treated as ordinary legislation.	Joint committee recommends a compromise. If this is rejected the bill fails.	Passed by both houses, and requires a referendum with majorities in a majority of cantons.
UK House of Lords	Bills are introduced in either house. Upper house may amend or reject legislation. However, by convention upper house does not reject legislation implementing government's manifesto commitments.	Bills classified as "money bills" must be introduced in lower house. Upper house may only delay for 1 month.	Lower house can override upper house veto approximately 1 year after bill's introduction if reintroduced in new parliamentary session.	Treated as ordinary legislation except bill to extend life of a parliament, which Lords can veto.
USA Senate	Bills are introduced in either house. Senate can amend or reject any legislation.	Must be introduced in lower house, but otherwise treated as ordinary legislation.	Shuttles indefinitely, but joint committee, with non-binding outcome, may be called at any time.	Must be passed by two-thirds majority in both houses, and ratified by three-quarters of states within 7 years.

Source: Russell, M. Reforming the House of Lords. London: Oxford University Press, 2000, 34–8, with some modifications.

* Some amendments require assent of all provincial legislatures. There is provision also for bilateral federal-provincial amendments.

** Major changes are subject to a more rigorous procedure.

In this section we turn to a review of proposals for Canadian Senate reform, assessing them in relation to the actual experience of comparable examples in other federations.[49] In reviewing various proposals for Senate reform in Canada, two major considerations will need to be borne in mind. One relates to the objectives of reform. In spite of other positive achievements, the Canadian Senate in comparative terms suffers from a perceived lack of public legitimacy as a body representing regional and provincial interests within the federal Parliament; that constitutes one major weakness of the current Senate that requires correction. Proposals for reform, therefore, need to be assessed in terms of how this fundamental weakness might be remedied. It is sometimes argued that it is equally important that forms of social diversity other than regions or provinces should be represented in the second chamber, such as linguistic, cultural, ethnic, religious, professional, vocational, and gender differences, as for instance argued in the Wakeham Report.[50] While sometimes special provision has been included for such representation in the second chamber, one characteristic that stands out among other *federal* second chambers is the primary emphasis placed upon representation of the constituent units of the federation, whether of their electorates, legislators, or governments. The adequacy of regional voices in the federal legislature through the federal second chamber seems to have been found in most cases to be essential to the effective operation of the federation, a requirement consistently underestimated in many discussions of Senate reform within Canada. An important objective for a more effective federation in Canada, therefore, must be the reconciliation of federal and regional interests within Parliament, and the Senate can make a major contribution to that end.[51]

The second consideration relates to the degree of practicability. Senator Eugene Forsey once noted in 1985, "there are two types of Senate reform proposals: the practicable and the impractable" and added that Canadians spend most of their time pursuing the impracticable – those that would require formal constitutional amendments to bring them into effect – rather than seeking more modest changes that could be done without getting into the hopeless morass of comprehensive constitutional change.[52] Not only the Supreme Court judgment on Bill C–60 regarding Senate reform[53] but the subsequent procedures for constitutional amendment enacted in the *Constitution Act, 1982* make it clear that major constitutional amendments relating to the Senate require the assent of the provinces. Changing the method of appointment, composition or powers set out in the *Constitution* would require assent by seven provinces representing 50 percent of the federal population,[54] and in certain circumstances changing provincial representation may require unanimous assent of the provinces.[55] After three decades of failures in efforts at comprehensive constitutional reform culminating in the rejection of the Charlottetown

Consensus Agreement in 1992 and the further complicated requirement for the consent of the five regions created by the federal Parliament with Bill C–110 (*Constitutional Amendments Act, 1996*), these rigid processes for constitutional amendment appear to evoke little enthusiasm among Canadians today. The issue then is what Senate reforms might be practicable either through unilateral amendments within the limited scope of section 44 of the *Constitution Act, 1982* or through incremental nonconstitutional reforms developed by convention or practice, and whether such reforms would be sufficient to restore the perceived public legitimacy of the Canadian Senate.

There have been many proposals for the reform of the Canadian Senate. For example, a draft document prepared for the Senate identifies twenty-six distinct Senate reform proposals in the period 1969–92 alone.[56] For the purposes of this chapter, rather than attempting to assess each of these twenty-six proposals, broad groups of proposals will be assessed in comparative terms. This will be undertaken primarily in relation to how they might remedy the perceived lack of public legitimacy of the Senate as a federal institution, and in terms of their practicability for implementation in a context where there is broad public reluctance to undertake formal constitutional amendment. Among the types of reform proposals that will be reviewed are those for mixed appointments, for a "House of the Provinces," for an elected Senate and for a reformed appointment process.

During the 1970s and 1980s, there were a large number of proposals for replacing the existing Senate with a body composed of delegates of provincial governments who would act on the instructions of those governments. These proposals were inspired by the apparently extremely successful example of the German federal second chamber, the Bundesrat, although often modifications to fit particular Canadian circumstances were added. Among these proposals were those advanced by Peyton Lyon (1962), Donald Briggs (1970), Ronald Watts (1970), Ronald Burns (1973), the Government of British Columbia (1978), the Committee on the Constitution of the Canadian Bar Association (1978), the Ontario Advisory Committee on Confederation (1978), the Task Force on Canadian Unity (Pepin-Robarts; 1979), the Constitutional Committee of the Quebec Liberal Party (Beige Paper; 1980), and the Government of Alberta (1982).[57] Indeed, until proposals for a popularly elected senate emerged in the 1980s, the advocacy of a Bundesrat-type federal second chamber was almost unchallenged as a model for replacing the existing Senate.

Typically, these proposals envisaged a council composed of provincial delegates voting under instruction from provincial governments, with each province having a number of votes that varied with, but was not proportionate to its population. The council would exercise an absolute veto over the use of federal "overriding" powers such as the spending power and dis-allowance, the emergency power, federal legislation administered by the provinces (such as criminal law), Supreme Court appointments, appoint-ments to specified agencies, and most constitutional amendments, but would have only a suspensive veto on other federal legislation. Underlying these proposals was the belief that such a second chamber would achieve two primary objectives: a clear provincial voice in federal deliberations and the facilitation of intergovernmental collaboration by processes that are more explicit and open to public scrutiny. The clear success of the German Bundesrat in both these respects provided the inspiration for these pro-posals in Canada.

Nevertheless, these proposals met with determined opposition from Mr Trudeau's federal government, which feared that it would give provincial governments too large a voice and introduce a divisive element in federal deliberations. Such fears were clearly based on a failure to understand the actual operation of the German Bundesrat, which, apart from sensitizing federal governments to regional concerns, has in practice equally sensi-tized and integrated the länd governments into national deliberations and has drawn them into an interlocking collaborative federalism.[58] Indeed, it was because they leaned towards a centralized form of federalism that the South Africans chose to follow (with modifications) the German model in establishing the National Council of Provinces as a second chamber in their new Constitution. In this respect, those Canadian provincial premiers who opposed a Bundesrat type of second chamber, because in such an arrangement they would find themselves co-opted by the federal govern-ment, understood much better the realities of the operation of the Ger-man Bundesrat than did the federal government opponents of such an arrangement for Canada.

But while some of the Canadian criticism of these proposals may have been misguided and based on an inadequate understanding of how the Bundesrat has operated in practice in Germany, there are some valid reasons for caution about applying the German model to Canada.[59] Fundamental is the significance of the very different form of the Cana-dian distribution of powers between federal and provincial govern-ments, which places much more emphasis upon the exclusive jurisdic-tion and autonomy of each order of government, whereas in Germany the emphasis is upon the interdependence of the federal-state-local governments.[60]

Indeed, the logic of the distribution of powers within these two federa-tions is quite different.[61] In Canada the constitutional emphasis has been upon the relative autonomy of each order of government. Most responsi-bilities are assigned exclusively to one level of government or the other and each order of government has generally been assigned executive responsibilities in the same fields for which it has legislative authorities.

This reinforces the autonomy of each government and its accountability to the electorate not only for the adoption of policies but also for implementing them. It is true that this is moderated by the constitutional specification of a few areas of concurrent jurisdiction; examples include the constitutionally defined federal legislative, but provincial administrative, responsibilities relating to criminal law and the practical necessity, because of overlaps in jurisdiction, for considerable intergovernmental co-operation and for federal funding in some major areas of provincial jurisdiction. Nevertheless, by contrast with the general Canadian pattern, in Germany a major feature of the distribution of powers has been the assignment of legislative and administrative responsibilities in most areas to different levels of government. The Constitution assigns most of the major areas of legislative authority to the federal Parliament, but it assigns the administrative responsibility for a large portion of federal legislation to the states. It is this which provides the context and rationale for the Bundesrat's unique role as an intergovernmental federal second chamber. Since such a large portion of German federal laws are administered by the states, the Bundesrat was designed to be a forum where the representatives of the state governments that have to administer these federal laws may participate in designing and approving the laws that they will have to administer. Indeed, the German Constitution grants to the Bundesrat an absolute veto on all federal laws involving administration by the states, and this has in practice applied to more than 60 percent of all federal legislation.[62] This is what has made the Bundesrat such an influential institution in the federal legislative processes.

It is interesting to note that, in the past decade, the Germans themselves, under the strains of reunification and European integration, have become more critical of the role that the Bundesrat has come to play in the highly integrated and interlocked German federalism, which has displayed increasing inertia.[63] This has led to proposals for reforms that would increase the possibility for more autonomous action by each level of government and that would also affect the role of the Bundesrat.[64]

In terms of practicability, the replacement of the current Senate in Canada by a House of the Provinces along lines similar to the German Bundesrat would require a major constitutional amendment, a process which as we have already noted is likely to find nothing like the support that would be necessary to carry it through. While it is undoubtedly true that the current processes of intergovernmental collaboration typified by "executive federalism" have serious deficiencies, the effort to couple the more effective institutionalization of those processes as occurs in some other federations with a complete replacement of the current Senate by a new House of the Provinces is unlikely to be a practical prospect in the current conditions in Canada.

Proposals for Indirect Election

A number of federations have second chambers composed wholly or in part of members indirectly elected by state legislatures. Such a scheme would make these members more clearly regional spokespersons than centrally appointed senators. This idea was proposed by the federal government in 1978 through Bill C–60. The proposal was that for each province half the senators would be elected by the provincial legislators representing parties in proportion to the party vote in the most recent provincial election, and half would be elected by the members of the House of Commons from each federal party, electing a number of senators in proportion to the popular vote received by the party in the most recent federal election. The result would be that both federal and provincial parties would be represented in the federal second chamber, and in all likelihood no single party would have a majority. The second chamber proposed by Bill C–60 also would have had only a suspensive veto. These proposals were intended to achieve more effective representation of the people of the provinces without threatening the primacy of the House of Commons in the way that direct election might.

Three points are worth noting about this proposal. First, indirect election of all or part of a federal second chamber by state or provincial legislatures has occurred in a considerable number of federations, such as Austria, India, Malaysia, Spain, Belgium, and, prior to 1913, the United States. Such members have in practice provided a strong regional voice (certainly stronger than centrally appointed senators) in deliberations within the federal second chamber. Nevertheless, their perceived political legitimacy is generally somewhat less than that of directly elected senators, and it is significant that in both the United States (since 1913) and in Switzerland (by individual cantonal choice at different times) indirect election by state or cantonal legislatures has been replaced totally by direct election. In the Canadian context, it is significant that the Bill C–60 proposals for indirect election received little public support at that time.[65]

Second, the Bill C–60 proposal that half the senators be elected by federal members of the House of Commons is a rarely found feature in federal second chambers elsewhere. The closest example, although not strictly comparable, is the arrangement in Belgium where in a senate of seventy-one members, ten are chosen (co-opted) by the directly elected members in the Senate itself, but the Lower House has no role in the appointment of those senators. As the examples of India, Malaysia, Spain, Belgium, South Africa, and Russia illustrate, it is not unusual to have a mixed membership in the federal second chamber with different forms of election or appointment, but in none of them has it been thought appropriate for members of the federal lower house to elect or appoint members of the second chamber.

Third, as the Supreme Court[66] made amply clear at the time, the reforms proposed in Bill C–60 in 1978 would have required a constitutional amendment involving assent of the provinces. The subsequent *Constitution Act, 1982* has clearly reinforced this requirement. Thus, such changes also raise questions about their practicability at the present time.

Proposals for Direct Election

In the 1980s considerable support arose for establishing a Senate whose members would be directly elected by the people of Canada. Among significant proposals were those advanced by the Canada West Foundation,[67] the Special Joint Committee of the Senate and the House of Commons on Senate Reform , the Royal Commission on the Economic Union and Development Prospects for Canada, the host of proposals during the later 1980s and early 1990s for a "Triple-E" (elected, equal, effective) Senate advanced by groups in western and Atlantic Canada,[68] the proposals of the Government of Canada (1991), and the Charlottetown Consensus Agreement (1992).

These proposals tackled head-on the issue of giving the federal second chamber full public legitimacy by advocating direct election of senators and reallocation of the geographical distribution of seats in the Senate. It was clear from a wide number of public opinion surveys at that time that direct election of senators was the most publicly supported method of selection and that appointment of senators by the federal Executive was considered inappropriate in a democracy. Most of these proposals for a directly elected Senate, following the precedents of elected federal second chambers in some other parliamentary federations, advocated some form of proportional representation to differentiate the method of election to the Senate from that to the House of Commons.[69]

In arguing for an elected Senate, some advocates, notably those supporting the "Triple-E" proposals, cited the United States and Switzerland as examples while failing to recognize that the different nonparliamentary form of executive-legislature relationship in both makes them inappropriate models for Canada with its parliamentary institutions. But Canadian critics of the proposals for an elected senate who have argued that an elected federal second chamber is inappropriate in a parliamentary system have failed to acknowledge that some parliamentary federations elsewhere have wholly directly elected senates (e.g., Australia) or a majority of directly elected senators (e.g., Spain and Belgium). This indicates that directly elected second chambers are not necessarily incompatible with parliamentary institutions. Even the recent Wakeham Commission in Britain, as noted above, has recommended direct election for the regionally representative component of a reformed House of Lords.

In terms of the powers of an elected Senate, some Canadian proposals for an elected senate would have substantially reduced these to a suspensive veto. This would give pause to unrestrained majorities in the House of Commons by making them consider fully the varying regional viewpoints, but would ultimately allow the will of the majority in the House of Commons to prevail.[70] These proposals would have provided a substantially weaker Senate than that of Australia or Belgium, with their wholly or largely directly elected senates. Other Canadian proposals, believing that there is little point in establishing an elected Senate in order to introduce a significant element of intrastate federalism and then make that almost meaningless by giving it a weak suspensive veto in order to reconcile it with responsible government, have advocated somewhat stronger powers.[71] A number of "Triple-e" Senate proposals have emphasized the importance of an "effective" Senate if it was to be meaningful. Another alternative Canadian example was that of the Charlottetown Consensus Agreement,[72] which proposed that the ultimate resolution of differences between the two federal Houses should be a simple majority in a joint sitting where, because of the difference in the sizes of the Chambers, the House of Commons would have a substantially larger number of votes. This would follow the precedents for the ultimate resolution of differences between the two federal legislative chambers in the parliamentary federations of Australia and India, where, to ensure such a balance, the lower houses have at least double or more than the membership of the upper houses, thus ensuring that the lower house predominates on issues of confidence in the executive.[73] Another alternative would be the requirement of a two-thirds majority in the lower house to override a second chamber veto, as is required in Russia and South Africa.

An issue which is sometimes raised in relation to an elected Senate is the role of political parties in such a body.[74] Both the McCormick-Manning-Gibson and the Special Joint Committee proposals for elected senates would have deliberately minimized the influence of political parties to ensure that regional interests would not be overridden by voting predominantly along party lines. No doubt such views were influenced by the experience of directly elected federal chambers elsewhere, especially Australia, where voting in the second chamber has regularly followed party lines. Efforts to avoid party voting in an elected federal second chamber are, however, misguided. They neglect the fundamental importance of parties in policy formation within parliamentary systems and the fact that an important contribution an elected Senate could bring to policy-making at the federal level is in providing stronger regional viewpoints within party deliberations and caucuses within the federal institutions. To press for a Senate isolated from political parties is to confine it to virtual irrelevance in a parliamentary system where parties are a fundamental part in the policy process. Nevertheless, since the Senate is not a "confidence house," strict party discipline would be less essential than in the House of Commons, so the loosening of party discipline in the Senate and some degree of independence would be desirable.

Canadian proposals for an elected Senate have usually taken one of two approaches in relation to the regional allocation of seats. One is to advocate equal representation for provinces. The United States and Switzerland are often cited as precedents, but inappropriately: both are nonparliamentary in their institutions, and in any case in Switzerland there is a different representation for cantons and half cantons. In fact, among parliamentary federations Australia is the only precedent for equal state representation. Most other parliamentary federations have instead used some form of weighted representation related to population, but favouring smaller states in their federal second chambers. Not surprisingly, therefore, a number of Canadian proposals for elected second chambers have advocated some form of weighted representation for provinces.[75] The Charlottetown Consensus Agreement[76] recommended equal provincial representation, but attempted to deal with the problem of substantially reducing Quebec's representation in such a senate by guaranteeing to Quebec 25 percent of the seats in a House of Commons that would predominate in a joint setting because under these proposals the House of Commons would have been six times the size of the proposed Senate.

In terms of practicability, the various proposals for an elected senate (including altered composition and powers) would clearly require a formal constitutional amendment. Although such proposals might have a greater prospect of considerable popular support than others, the process of constitutional amendment with the degree of provincial legislative consensus required would, nevertheless, make it a difficult process. An alternative would be to simply replace appointment by direct election, leaving the composition and powers unchanged. Doing this while leaving the powers unchanged and without introducing a deadlock resolution process such as exists in Australia, might open the way to serious problems in the operation of responsible government. Furthermore, leaving the composition unaltered would leave unresolved the serious underrepresentation of the western provinces in the Senate.

A Reformed Appointment Process

One approach to Senate reform that raises fewer issues of practicability is that of changing the method and term of appointment. This would not necessarily require a formal constitutional amendment, but merely the development of new conventions and practices on the basis of which the Prime Minister would recommend appointments to the Governor General.

Here there are three general possibilities. One is to follow the model of the Wakeham proposals in the United Kingdom and create an independent Appointments Commission to nominate individuals to the Prime Minister. The desirability of this option is open to question.

A second is for the Prime Minister in making recommendations to the Governor General to submit names recommended by the provincial premiers. This would certainly improve the legitimacy of the Senate as a body representing provincial interests within federal deliberations and was the interim reform to the method of appointing senators included in the Meech Lake proposals. However, subsequent public discussion seemed to indicate no great enthusiasm for replacing appointment of senators by the federal government with appointment by the premiers. Consequently, the tentative June 1990 First Ministers' Agreement (never implemented) would have established a commission to prepare specific proposals for an elected Senate. These were to include more equitable representation of the less populous provinces and territories and effective powers to ensure that the interests of the residents of the less populous provinces and territories would figure more prominently in national decision-making, reflect Canadian duality, and strengthen the Government of Canada's capacity to govern on behalf of all citizens, while preserving the principle of responsibility of the government to the House of Commons.[77]

A third option is for the Prime Minister, in making nominations to the Governor General, to accept as a convention the practice of naming those who have emerged as winners in an electoral process within the relevant province. This process has been advocated within Alberta and on one occasion was followed, although somewhat reluctantly, by Prime Minister Mulroney. His successor Prime Minister Chrétien has, however, steadfastly refused to follow that precedent and give up the political leverage of prime-ministerial appointments.

Although this option has sometimes been advocated as a first step towards a fully elected senate, it does have some weaknesses. One criticism that is sometimes offered is the difficulty of getting all provinces to agree to such a convention. But it would not need to be applied uniformly from the outset. As noted below, experience elsewhere provides precedents for regional variations in the introduction of elections to federal second chambers. More serious is that such a convention would not resolve the major problem of seat distribution and would thus continue to leave the western provinces significantly underrepresented. Since the allocation of Senate seats is set out in the Constitution, this particular problem can be corrected only by a formal constitutional amendment. Nor would a convention solely regarding appointments deal adequately with the question of the accountability of senators unless their terms of office were also modified so that senators, once appointed, would not continue to sit until the age of seventy-five.

If such a practice of election prior to appointment were to become a convention, it would be important also to develop conventions about how conflicts between the two elected Houses would be resolved so that the basic principles of responsible government are not undermined. In relation to the development of conventions limiting the exercise of the constitutional powers of the second chamber, both British and Canadian experience provides examples. There are precedents elsewhere for an evolutionary process leading to an elected federal chamber, although the two outstanding examples of such a development occurred in the United States and Switzerland, neither of which incorporates institutions of responsible government. In the United States, up until 1913 the state legislatures selected senators, but by that year over half the state legislatures relied on prior primary elections in choosing senators. Finally, in 1913 a constitutional amendment made direct election the requirement for all senators. In Switzerland, from 1848 to 1999, the choice of method of selection to the federal second chamber was left to each canton to decide. Eventually, however, one after the other, all the cantons opted for direct election. The new Swiss Constitution of 1999 has merely constitutionalized the status quo by requiring that all members of the federal second chamber be elected, although the cantons retained the power to regulate the elections to the federal second chamber (art. 150). It is of interest to note that the Charlottetown Consensus Agreement, 1992, section 7, would, as a compromise proposal, have allowed provinces and territories to choose either indirect or direct election to the Senate, with the expectation that, as in Switzerland, popular pressure upon provincial legislatures would over time lead to the eventual adoption of direct election in all the provinces and territories.

There are, of course, a number of other areas where the effectiveness of the Senate could be improved by developing practices and conventions in relation to the legislative review process in general, to committee work, to review of subordinate legislation, to conduct investigative studies and so on.[78] These are vitally important. Ultimately, however, the area that most needs attention is in strengthening the role of the Senate to represent the regional dimension of Canadian life in the deliberations of Parliament, because it is in that respect that our federal institutions have in recent experience exhibited an especially serious weakness.[79]

CONCLUSIONS

Bicameralism, far from being regarded as undemocratic, has been widely regarded as enhancing democracy, and in most federations federal second chambers, as an arena both for legislative review and for representing regional interests in the decision-making at the federal level, have been considered essential to the effective operation of the federation. Abolition of the Canadian Senate would, therefore, almost certainly be counterproductive and would make Canada unique among major contemporary federations.

The review of the roles, appointments, composition, and powers of *federal* second chambers indicates considerable variety, but two lessons emerge. One is that in federations, almost invariably, one of the primary roles of federal second chambers has been to provide a forum where regional viewpoints may be brought to bear and reconciled in the deliberative processes within the federal institutions. Second, in this respect, the Canadian Senate, despite its formally strong constitutional powers and relative effectiveness in legislative review and the performance of other functions, is in comparative terms among federal second chambers the weakest in representing regional interests. This is because of its perceived lack of legitimacy as a regionally representative body due to its method of appointment and composition.

This comparative review, therefore, points to the need for reforms to the Canadian Senate to remedy this particular deficiency. Any reforms directed at this objective should, of course, ensure that the roles performed by the current Senate in the revision and scrutiny of government policy, as well as various secondary tasks, are at the same time preserved and strengthened. Many proposals for reform that have been advanced can be related to experience elsewhere. But most of these proposals would require formal constitutional amendment, a process for which the Canadian public, after three decades of failure or incomplete efforts to achieve full comprehensive constitutional change, has little enthusiasm. There is a need, therefore, to focus instead on the development of conventions and practices to remedy the deficiencies of the current Senate. Nevertheless, there are some reforms that can be achieved only by formal constitutional amendment. What is required is a process of pragmatic evolutionary adaptation. But mere tinkering will be insufficient. The more effective operation of Canada as a federation requires sufficient significant changes to ensure that the Senate can be publicly perceived as a genuine forum for regional interests within deliberations at the federal level. To meet this objective, it will be useful to bear in mind the major lessons from experience in other parliamentary federations, while also keeping in mind the particular conditions required for a Canadian solution.

NOTES

1 Tsebelis and Money, *Bicameralism*, 17–19.
2 Tsebelis and Money, *Bicameralism*, 21; Russell, *Reforming the House of Lords: Lessons from Overseas*, 20.
3 Russell, *Reforming the House of Lords: Lessons from Overseas*, 22.
4 Forum des Sénats du Monde, *Bicameralism in the World*, 1.
5 As of July 2002, source: Central Intelligence Agency, *The World Factbook 2002*.
6 Watts, "The Organization of Legislative and Executive Institutions: The Comparative Relevance for Europe of Canadian Experience," 151–5.

7 Russell, *Reforming the House of Lords: Lessons from Overseas*, 21; Patterson and Mughan, *Senates: Bicameralism in the Contemporary World*.

8 Russell, *Reforming the House of Lords: Lessons from Overseas*, 21.

9 Patterson and Mughan, *Senates: Bicameralism in the Contemporary World*, 14.

10 Constitution Unit, *Checks and Balances in Single Chamber Parliaments: A Comparative Study*, 3.

11 Russell, *Reforming the House of Lords: Lessons from Overseas*, 22–4.

12 Watts, *Comparing Federal Systems*, 83–4, 92; Russell, *Reforming the House of Lords: Lessons from Overseas*, 22.

13 Wheare, *Federal Government*, 87–90.

14 Sharman, "Second Chambers," 96.

15 Russell, *Reforming the House of Lords: Lessons from Overseas*, 173–6.

16 Watts, *Comparing Federal Systems*, 83–97.

17 Watts, *Comparing Federal Systems*, 84–90.

18 Watts, *Comparing Federal Systems*, 96.

19 An examination of this role of the Canadian Senate is undertaken in the chapter by Gil Rémillard in this volume.

20 Lijphart, *Democracies: Patterns of Majoritarian and Consensus Government in Twenty-One Countries*, 97–101.

21 The Canadian context for such changes is considered more fully in the chapter by David Smith in this volume.

22 Watts, *Comparing Federal Systems*, 121–3.

23 Watts, *Comparing Federal Systems*, 10.

24 Watts, *Comparing Federal Systems*, 26, 38, 78, 97.

25 Russell, *Reforming the House of Lords: Lessons from Overseas*, 165–222.

26 Russell, *Reforming the House of Lords: Lessons from Overseas*, 52–5, 252.

27 See appendix.

28 Russell, *Reforming the House of Lords: Lessons from Overseas*, 257, 297.

29 Russell, *Reforming the House of Lords: Lessons from Overseas*, 64.

30 Russell, *Reforming the House of Lords: Lessons from Overseas*, 31.

31 See, for instance, Lee and Oppenheimer, *Sizing Up the Senate: The Unequal Consequences of Equal Representation*.

32 Russell, *Reforming the House of Lords: Lessons from Overseas*, 67.

33 Scharpf, "The Joint Decision Trap: Lessons from German Federalism and European Integration."

34 Sharman, "Second Chambers," 94–5.

35 Patterson and Mughan, *Senates: Bicameralism in the Contemporary World*, 338.

36 Patterson and Mughan, *Senates: Bicameralism in the Contemporary World*, 338–40.

37 Patterson and Mughan, *Senates: Bicameralism in the Contemporary World*, 240–2.

38 Patterson and Mughan, *Senates: Bicameralism in the Contemporary World*, 342–6.

39 Russell, *Reforming the House of Lords: Lessons from Overseas*, 76–7.

40 Russell, *Reforming the House of Lords: Lessons from Overseas*, 253–4.

41 Russell, *Reforming the House of Lords: Lessons from Overseas*, 254–7.

42 Sharman, "Second Chambers," 96.

43 Watts, *Comparing Federal Systems*, 83.

44 As Paul Thomas indicates in his chapter in this volume.

45 Watts, *Comparing Federal Systems*, 97; Russell, *Reforming the House of Lords: Lessons from Overseas*, 252.

46 See, for instance, Hoy, *Nice Work: The Continuing Scandal of Canada's Senate*, 296–304.

47 In an article entitled "Not Dead Yet, But Should It Be Resurrected? The Canadian Senate," quoted in Patterson and Mughan, *Senates: Bicameralism in the Contemporary World*, 155.

48 Watts, *Comparing Federal Systems*, 113–14.

49 See Stilborn, in this volume.

50 Royal Commission on the Reform of the House of Lords, *A House for the Future*, 3.

51 See, for instance, Royal Commission on the Economic Union, Report, 87.

52 Cited by Hoy, *Nice Work: The Continuing Scandal of Canada's Senate*, 296.

53 *Reference re Legislative Authority of Parliament of Canada in Relation to the Upper House*, [1980] 1 S.C.R. 54.

54 *Constitution Act, 1982*, ss. 38(1) and 42(1)(b) and (c)

55 *The Constitution Act, 1982*, s. 41(b)

56 The specific details of individual senate reform proposals are examined more thoroughly in Stilborn, in this volume.

57 See Smiley and Watts, *Intrastate Federalism in Canada*, 121.

58 See, for instance, Watts, *Comparing Federal Systems*, 26, 78.

59 Smiley and Watts, *Intrastate Federalism in Canada*, 123–5.

60 Watts, *Comparing Federal Systems*, 27–8.

61 Watts, *Comparing Federal Systems*, 36–7, 78.

62 Watts, *Comparing Federal Systems*, 96–7.

63 Jeffery, *Recasting German Federalism*; Scharpf, "The Joint Decision Trap: Lessons from German Federalism and European Integration."

64 See, for instance, Bertelsmann Foundation, *Disentanglement 2005. Ten Reform Proposals for Better Governance in the German Federal System*.

65 Special Joint Committee, Report, 19.

66 *Reference re Legislative Authority of Parliament of Canada in Relation to the Upper House*, [1980] 1 S.C.R. 54.

67 McCormick, Manning, and Gibson, *Regional Representation: The Canadian Partnership*.

68 For a review of these, see Watts, "The Federative Superstructure," 325–9.

69 For example, Royal Commission on the Economic Union, Report, 87–92.

70 For example, Special Joint Committee on Senate Reform, Report, 29–31; Royal Commission on the Economic Union, Report, 91.

71 Smiley and Watts, *Intrastate Federalism in Canada*, 130–3, 156.

72 Charlottetown Consensus Report on the Constitution, Final Text, s. 12.

73 In Australia the joint sitting occurs only if the Senate again rejects a bill following a double dissolution and elections for both houses.

74 Smiley and Watts, *Intrastate Federalism in Canada*, 133–5.

75 An example being the Special Joint Committee on Senate Reform, Report, 28–9; for a survey of various such proposals, see Watts, "The Federative Superstructure," 328.

76 Charlottetown Consensus Report on the Constitution, Final Text, ss. 8, 12, 21.

77 Watts, The Federative Superstructure," 326.

78 For example, Special Joint Committee on Senate Reform, Report, 35–7; Smiley and Watts, *Intrastate Federalism in Canada*, 135–9.

79 Royal Commission on the Economic Union, Report, 91–2.

CHAPTER FOUR

Senate Reform: Back to Basics

Gil Rémillard,
with the collaboration of Andrew Turner

INTRODUCTION

The last century was characterized by a decentralization of the powers exercised by democratic states. Governments viewed decentralization as an effective way to enhance both the quality of and control over the exercise of their powers. In fact, regardless of the type of political system, democratic states now increasingly tend to divide the exercise of their power as a more effective way to put in place the rules of effectiveness, transparency, and accountability that have become the pillars of the new public governance.

This tendency is particularly apparent in the legislative branch. As a result, bicameralism has now become the rule in the vast majority of democratic countries, particularly among federations.[1]

Canada experienced this development in a particular context, since, in 1867, it was the first country to attempt to reconcile the rules of federalism with those of Westminster-style responsible government. The challenge was not an easy one. A number of Canadian delegates to the London Conference of 1866 were well versed in the conventions of responsible government, which they had managed to obtain from Britain for its North American colonies fifteen years earlier. However, their knowledge of federalism was much more limited, even though relations between London and its North American colonies, as well as those between Canada East (Quebec) and Canada West (Ontario), were based on certain rules of decentralization quite similar in certain respects to those of federalism.

It should also be said that the Fathers of Confederation were quite familiar with the American federal system, which had just gone through a traumatic civil war. History therefore shows us that the choices they made in drafting Canada's Constitution of 1867 were primarily informed by their intimate knowledge of the strengths and weaknesses of the American and British systems. Their work reflects an attempt to incorporate the best elements of each political system and to make them more functional in the interests of the new Dominion.

The Senate of Canada is the result of those efforts. The Fathers of Confederation were mindful that they were designing a system in which the various government institutions would have to interact, and they specifically designed a system in which the two houses of Parliament would have distinct and yet complementary characteristics. Thus, in their view, each house had to possess different attributes and strengths, allowing them to make a meaningful contribution to the legislative process. The two chambers would be complementary, with the work of the one improving that of the other, thereby bettering the quality of governance in the new country. The House of Commons, directly elected on the basis of representation by population, would hold the executive accountable as required by the responsible government model. The Senate, however, would play a different role.

In the minds of the Fathers of Confederation, the Upper House would serve primarily as a chamber of legislative review, applying sober second thought to the work of the Lower House in order to catch any errors or oversights. Moreover, it would properly reflect the principle of participation, which forms the basis of federalism, counterbalancing the dominance of the more populous regions in the House of Commons by giving the regions an equal voice in the Senate. The Upper House would also represent the national minorities in Parliament, that is the English-speaking population of Quebec and the Francophone populations of the other provinces.

For the Senate to play this important role, the Fathers of Confederation wished to confer five features on the Senate: *independence, long-term perspective, continuity, professional and life experience,* and *regional equality.*

The Fathers of Confederation thus determined that the Upper House would be an appointed body possessing legislative powers nearly equal to those of the Lower House. Even the most ardent reformers among the Fathers, such as George Brown and Jonathan McCully, believed that the second elected chamber would undermine responsible government by acting as a rival to the House of Commons. It was also feared that the government would suffer from legislative slowdowns caused by disputes between the two chambers if they both had mandates from the people.[2]

It was also thought that there was a danger the government might escape the actual control of Parliament because a vote of nonconfidence in one chamber could be nullified by a vote of confidence in the other. However, while recognizing that, in accordance with the principles of responsible government, a government enjoying the confidence of the House of Commons should usually be able to have its legislation passed by Parliament, the Fathers of Confederation believed that there was no point in having a Senate if it could be easily circumvented by the Lower House.

They therefore came to the conclusion that establishing the Westminster model in the federation entailed an appointed Senate with full legislative authority, except the power to augment or include monetary provisions in bills.

From the start of Confederation, the Senate has come under tough criticism. Numerous reform proposals designed to change its role or abolish the institution have been brought forward over the years. Among other things, the Senate has been criticized as being a house of retirees enjoying the favour of the powers that be and as essentially rubber-stamping government legislation.

While those criticisms appeared valid for a good part of the twentieth century, the situation is now much changed.[3] Due to a combination of changes within the Canadian system of government, media scrutiny, public interest, and increased activity among the senators themselves, the Senate, in the past twenty years, appears to be increasingly playing the role for which it was originally designed.

In addition, the globalization and regionalization of economies, together with the advent of the World Trade Organization (WTO) and the North American Free Trade Agreement (NAFTA), have consistently changed Canadian federalism over the past ten years, causing it to evolve in a context that much more effectively enables the Senate to play an important role in our parliamentary system.

Having regard to this new context, in this chapter, I will examine how the Senate functions as a complementary chamber to the House of Commons. It will begin by briefly examining the role of Parliament in general and then focus on the specific contributions of the Senate: legislative review and regional representation. Second, I will offer some thoughts on the essential characteristics that the Senate of Canada should have at the dawn of this new century. The chapter will conclude with an examination of some of the new responsibilities the Senate could take on in future in light of our evolving political context, both nationally and internationally.

PART 1:
THE SENATE AS A COMPLEMENTARY LEGISLATIVE CHAMBER

The Senate is the second house of Parliament, and, in order to understand how it must complement the House of Commons, it is necessary first to consider the role of Parliament as a whole.

Section 17 of the *Constitution Act, 1867* clearly states: "There shall be One Parliament for Canada, consisting of the Queen, an Upper House styled the Senate, and the House of Commons." Parliament comprises these three elements, which together perform a wide variety of functions. In our bicameral system, each of the two houses contributes in its own way to those functions. In some cases, one or the other house may take the initiative, but, for Parliament as a whole to perform its duties properly,

interaction between the two houses is essential and must occur on a complementary basis. For this to occur, certain conditions must be met.

The Senate Must Conduct Complementary Debate

Of all the core functions of Parliament, the most fundamental to the exercise of democracy is debate. It is through the process of debate that all
other functions are performed. Parliamentary debate serves to draw public attention to policy questions, provokes an exchange of ideas and the
reflection that is essential to the formulation and implementation of policy for the country. Open and full debate guarantees that the interests of
the various sections of society are taken into account before legislation is
enacted or a decision made. The process of debate itself is as important as
the decision taken. Debate fosters the development of policy options and
helps to legitimize the ultimate decision for those who may have advocated a different outcome.

In one of the most famous Canadian constitutional cases, former Chief
Justice Sir Lyman Duff described public debate as essential to the proper
functioning of Parliament. The institutionalization of open public debate,
he found, was a key constitutional principle evident not only in the provisions of the *Constitution Act, 1867*, which established Parliament, but in the
preamble as well:

Under the constitution established by [*The Constitution Act, 1867*],
legislative power for Canada is vested in one Parliament consisting of the
Sovereign, an upper house styled the Senate, and the House of Commons.
[...]
The preamble of the statute, moreover, shows plainly enough that the constitution of the Dominion is to be similar in principle to that of the United
Kingdom. The statute contemplates a parliament working under the influence of public opinion and public discussion. There can be no controversy
that such institutions derive their efficiency from the free public discussion
of affairs, from criticism and answer and counter-criticism, from attack upon
policy and administration and defence and counter-attack; from the freest
and fullest political proposals.[4]

While the House of Commons is responsible for debating all statutory
measures proposed by the government, the Senate considers those same
measures after the House of Commons has debated, amended, and passed
them. The Senate may thus first follow the debates in the House of Commons, gauge their perspective and impact and determine public opinion.
It is not necessary for the Senate to consider each bill in detail, but it
may, in certain cases, decide to examine them more carefully, considering
questions of drafting, institutional impact, public concern or policies and
principles related to the Canadian public interest.

In other words, each chamber makes an important contribution by guaranteeing public debate on legislation and on government policies and activities in general. Just as Parliament's function of promoting public discussion would be incomplete without the debates of the House of Commons, so too would the work of Parliament be incomplete without the "sober second thought" of the Senate, which can carefully scrutinize those policies that, as a result of their administrative complexity or significant impact on the public, require further reflection before enactment. It is in this respect that the role of the Senate, when properly played, truly complements that of the House of Commons.

It is the House of Commons that enables a majority party to form the government and affords the opposition the opportunity to criticize government policy. However, this fundamentally democratic model has evolved considerably since 1867, and, with the emergence of strict discipline within party caucuses and the evolution of parliamentary rules, the possibility of defeating a government whose party had a majority in the House of Commons has all but evaporated. Since the late 1960s, parliamentary convention has dictated that all confidence votes be announced in advance, eliminating the possibility of a surprise government defeat. While this evolution of the principle of parliamentary responsibility is a happy one, the government's control over its powers has nevertheless increased.[5]

However, as the constitutional convention of confidence does not apply to the Senate, debate there may be conducted with greater freedom from party discipline. However, senators who vote against a bill introduced by their party know they are not jeopardizing the life of the government. We will return to this question and show that senators of the governing party are increasingly voting against bills from the Commons. The Senate's contribution to the core functions of Parliament may therefore be substantially different from that of the House of Commons.

The Senate Must Be Representative of the Regions

The Upper House was assigned specific contributions by the Fathers of Confederation, and it is unlikely that the provinces would have agreed to unite themselves had this not been the case.[6] The continuing importance of this founding compromise was stressed by the Supreme Court in its 1980 *Reference re Legislative Authority of Parliament in Relation to the Upper House*. In that reference, a response to the Senate reform proposals contained in the Trudeau Government's 1978 Constitutional Amendment Bill, the Court quoted Lord Sankey, LC, in *Re: The Regulation and Control of Aeronautics in Canada*, stating that:

Inasmuch as the Act embodies a compromise under which the original Provinces agreed to federate, it is important to keep in mind that the preservation of the rights of minorities was a condition on which such minorities entered into the federation, and the foundation upon which the whole structure was subsequently erected. The process of interpretation as the years go on ought not to be allowed to dim or to whittle down the provisions of the original contract upon which the federation was founded ...[7]

The Court then went on to say that:

... it is not open to Parliament to make alterations which would affect the fundamental features, or essential characteristics, given to the Senate as a means of ensuring regional and provincial representation in the federal legislative process.[8]

The second role the Fathers of Confederation assigned to the Senate, which was to provide for the *equality of the regions and to represent the minorities*, emerged from the Canadian federative compromise. For the smaller provinces, which counted on their representation in the Senate to make up for their small numbers in the House of Commons, this was one of the most important elements of the federal system. Influenced by the model of the American Senate, the Fathers viewed the Senate as the best way to ensure that the concerns of the less populous regions could be presented and debated in Parliament, consistent with the principle of participation, which is the very basis of federalism. This is also the thrust of section 22 of the *Constitution Act, 1867*:

In relation to the Constitution of the Senate, Canada shall be deemed to consist of *Four* Divisions:
1   Ontario;
2   Quebec;
3   The Maritime Provinces – Nova Scotia and New Brunswick, and Prince Edward Island;
4   The Western Provinces of Manitoba, British Columbia, Saskatchewan and Alberta;
which Four divisions shall (subject to the Provisions of this Act) be equally represented in the Senate ...

The necessity of providing the regions with this protection was discussed extensively in 1867. In *Reference re Legislative Authority of Parliament in Relation to the Upper House*,[9] the Supreme Court stressed that:

the system of regional representation in the Senate was one of the essential features of that body when it was created. Without it, the fundamental character of the Senate as part of the Canadian federal scheme would be eliminated.

This function of the Senate, which was at the very heart of the federative compromise in 1867, is still there today. Unlike the American Senate, where each state is represented by two senators, who, at the time, were appointed by the states themselves, the Fathers of Confederation wanted Canada's senators to be truly from the regions they represented, but not to hold a mandate from the government of a province or directly from the people. Thus, in the minds of the Fathers of Confederation, senators were to be "representative" in the sense that the people of the region would have a common identity with their senators, but senators were not to be mandated by the people, like the members of the House of Commons.

The Fathers also wanted to assign the Senate the important function of ensuring that minorities, originally the Anglophone population of Quebec and Francophone minorities in other provinces, would be represented in the Senate. Subsection 23(6) of the *Constitution Act, 1867* states that "in the Case of Quebec, [a senator] shall have his Real Property Qualification in the Electoral District for which he is appointed." Certain electoral districts were chosen for the Anglophone minority that composed them. Results enabled senators to be representative of the minorities and to speak in that capacity in the debates and proceedings of the Senate.

The Characteristics the Fathers Invested in the Senate Are Still Present Today

Much of the role the Fathers of Confederation originally designed for the Senate is still functional today, even though certain aspects of Canadian politics have evolved beyond what might have been imagined in 1867. Consider, among other things, the importance of political parties, the establishment of the Charter of Rights and Freedoms in 1982, the growth of co-operative and executive federalism, and the economic phenomenon of globalization, all realities that completely have transformed the social, political, and economic context of Canadian federalism. But despite all that, the main functions and responsibilities of the Senate are still as valid today as they were in 1867.

The question that now arises is whether the Senate performs its various roles well. Since its creation, many commentators have called for a thorough reform or simply the abolition of the Senate. As noted above, while their criticisms might have been justified scarcely twenty years ago, the situation is different today.

Essential or Fundamental Characteristics of the Senate

In recent years, the Senate has become a legislative chamber that is more sensitive to the attributes the Fathers of Confederation wished to assign to it and thus entrenched in the Constitution:

a) independence;
b) long-term perspective;
c) continuity;
d) professional and life experience;
e) regional equality in accordance with the principles of federalism.

These five attributes were central to the analysis the Supreme Court conducted of the Senate in the 1980 reference,[10] and they still constitute the very basis of the Senate's existence.

INDEPENDENCE

Throughout almost the entire twentieth century, the Senate conducted itself as a legislative chamber in which the majority legislated in a manner strictly consistent with the wishes of the various Liberal governments that came to power during those years. However, matters have changed in the last decade and a half.

It is interesting to note that it was only once his majority was firmly in place that Brian Mulroney became the first Prime Minister since Diefenbaker to suffer defeat in the Senate. On that occasion, eight Conservative senators voted with the opposition against a proposal to merge the Canada Council with the Social Sciences and Humanities Research Council, resulting in the defeat of a bill arising from a mini-budget.[11] Likewise, since Prime Minister Chrétien established a majority for his party in the Senate in 1996, the Senate has frequently amended Government bills, often with senators of the governing party being the instigators of the amendments. In numerous other cases, senators from the same party as the Prime Minister have moved amendments to Government bills squarely against the government's wishes, voted against the government motion, or otherwise publicly expressed dissent. For example, the 1996 bill to cancel the Pearson Airport contract was defeated when one Liberal senator voted with the Conservative opposition. In another example, despite an imminent election call in October 2000, and the desire of the government to have the legislation passed quickly, Liberal senators took the time they needed to study the citizenship bill,[12] debated extensively and publicly expressed serious reservations during lengthy hearings held by the Senate Committee. The debate on third reading was interrupted by the election, and the bill died on the Order Paper.

In one particularly interesting display of nonpartisan behaviour, Liberal senator Michael Kirby criticized the Liberal Government's legislative initiative relating to split-run magazines, while Conservative senator Lowell Murray responded by congratulating the Liberal Government on its bill.[13] In 1999, the government's extradition bill received intense public scrutiny by Liberal senators who vigorously debated amendments that would have prohibited extradition unless assurances that the death penalty would not be imposed were made by the country requesting extradition. The following year, in a lengthy three-month debate, both in committee and on the floor of the Senate, many Liberal senators sharply criticized a bill that was of the utmost importance to the government, the Clarity Bill.[14] A number of Liberal senators moved significant amendments, including measures to include the Senate in the decision on the clarity of the referendum question and required majority, even after they had been publicly rejected by the government. Lastly, as it was a direct consequence of the Supreme Court opinion on the secession of Quebec,[15] the bill was passed by a slim majority.

Thus, over the past fifteen years, it would appear that senators have spoken out increasingly freely, less restricted by party discipline. However, it would be an exaggeration to suggest the party line no longer exists. In fact, there are still significant constraints on the independence of senators. The Speaker is appointed by the Governor General on the recommendation of the Prime Minister, in accordance with section 34 of the *Constitution Act, 1867*. As in the House of Commons, there is a Government Leader, Deputy Leader and Whip, appointed by the Prime Minister, while membership on Senate committees and the now-salaried committee chair positions are also subject to significant government influence.

These various aspects of political intervention compromise the Senate's independence to some degree, although it is still essential that an Upper Chamber be independent in order to perform these functions. This was recently acknowledged by the Wakeham Commission on the reform of Britain's House of Lords. While observing that it was impossible to exclude political parties altogether from a modern legislative body, the Commission recognized the value of protecting the independence of all members, regardless of party:

We share the view that even those members of the second chamber who are affiliated to a party should be prepared to deal with issues on their merits and should exercise a certain independence of judgment.[16]

This principle was adopted by the Appointments Commission recently established by the British government. This Commission is an independent body charged with appointing independent Life Peers to the House of Lords, and its published selection criteria attach paramount importance to independence.[17] Thus, as a result of these reports, the British government has undertaken to establish a statute-based Appointments Commission and to maintain an independent element in the House of Lords consisting of 20 percent of the total membership.[18]

The independence of senators must remain an important characteristic if they are to offset the essentially partisan nature of the House of Commons. If members are elected under their party's banner, which thus gives the Prime Minister virtually absolute control over his caucus, senators should be appointed on the basis of their personal merits so as to avoid excessive political control by the government.

Knowing that it is possible for governments to dominate the House of Commons, the framers of our Constitution wanted to include independent legislators in the federal Parliament. As Sir John A. Macdonald contended:

There would be no use of an Upper House if it did not exercise [...] the right of opposing or amending or postponing the legislation of the Lower House [...] it must be an *independent* House [...] for it is only valuable as being a regulating body, calmly considering the legislation initiated by the popular branch, and preventing any hasty or ill-considered legislation ...[19]

George Brown, another Father of Confederation and a Reformer, confirmed and elaborated this view:

The desire was to render the upper house *a thoroughly independent body* – one that would be in a position to canvass dispassionately the measures of this house [the legislative assembly] and stand up for the public interests in *opposition to hasty or partisan legislation.*[20]

The Supreme Court acknowledged this in its opinion on the *Legislative Authority of Parliament in Relation to the Upper House.*

In creating the Senate in the manner provided in the Act, it is clear that the intention was to make the Senate a thoroughly independent body which could canvass dispassionately the measures of the House of Commons.[21]

The Fathers of Confederation also wanted to guarantee this independence by setting what were at the time stiff conditions for prospective senators. In essence, the qualifications for Senate membership enumerated in the *Constitution Act, 1867* were designed to ensure that senators would have the necessary means to guarantee their independence: financial security, extensive prior professional and life experience and secure tenure. Section 23 requires that senators be at least thirty years old,[22] be Canadian citizens,[23] have at least $4,000, own more than $4,000 in property[24] and be residents of the province for which they are appointed (and, in the case of Quebec, own property in the specific electoral district).[25] Section 29 initially provided that senators would enjoy tenure for life and, after the *Constitution Act, 1965*, until the age of seventy-five.

Like judges, senators, as determined in 1867, had to be permanently appointed and it had to be virtually impossible to remove them. They can only be removed for the reasons enumerated in section 31, such as conviction for a serious crime. Even in such cases, the *Constitution Act, 1867* provides in section 33:

If any Question arises respecting the Qualification of a Senator or a Vacancy in the Senate the same shall be heard and determined by the Senate.

This seems to be an additional protection, ensuring that the removal of a senator cannot occur by arbitrary executive act, but only on the decision of the senator's peers. Such removal has occurred nine times since Confederation.

In theory, the Senate has all the basic elements to guarantee its independence. The fact remains, however, that, in the twentieth century, it did not always assert it in practice, and its reputation has suffered as a result. It is therefore impossible to consider reforming the Senate without establishing rules that, while remaining realistic, could ensure a certain degree of political independence in the Senate.

LONG-TERM PERSPECTIVE

The ability to view legislation and issues from a long-term perspective is another fundamental feature of the Senate, and, in order to ensure it, the Fathers enshrined life tenure for senators in section 29 of *the Constitution Act, 1867*. While it was later limited to membership until the age of seventy-five, the Supreme Court warned in the Senate Reference that:

At some point, a reduction of the term of office might impair the functioning of the Senate in providing what Sir John A. Macdonald described as "the sober second thought in legislation."[26]

The average term of a senator is now ten to twelve years, the equivalent of three or four parliaments or electoral cycles.[27]

The frequent renewal of the government's electoral mandate (every five years at most) is the essential cornerstone of democracy, and it ensures that the members of the House of Commons accurately reflect the views of their constituents. The Senate complements the House by providing Parliament with a more long-term view. As a result of their extended tenure, senators can devote themselves to extensive and time-consuming studies with greater ease than can members of the House of Commons, whose planning horizons are dominated by the need to face re-election every four to five years.

The Standing Senate Committee on Social Affairs, Science and Technology, for example, conducted a two-year, five-phase study of the state of the Canadian health-care system in 2000–02.[28] If such a study were undertaken by the House of Commons, it would take up nearly half of the members' entire term and, in this particular case, would have risked being disrupted by the fall 2000 election. Moreover, there would be considerable pressure to generate short-term results that would bolster the members' immediate electoral chances, rather than focusing on the underlying issues and developing solutions that are ultimately in the best long-term interests of the country.

Recent statistics show that terms in the House of Commons are increasingly short.[29] As the House of Commons evolves and member turnover becomes more rapid, preserving the long-term view of senators will become even more important in maintaining Parliament's balance in its role as legislator and in a perspective of continuity.

CONTINUITY

Continuity is a characteristic that flows from the same constitutional provisions designed to secure independence and long-term perspective. The result is a Parliament that incorporates a component of stability even when a general election generates a nearly complete turnover of the membership in the House of Commons, as occurred for instance in 1993.[30]

The consistency of experience in the Senate's membership is the result of the lengthy tenure that the Constitution assigns to senators. Although the Senate also renews itself, the renewal process is more gradual and regular. Thus, while new senators are appointed in almost every calendar year, at any point in time a majority of senators have been in the Senate for at least the equivalent of two parliaments. The continuity thus entrenched in the system serves as the means of preserving institutional memory in a system in which the electoral process can regularly create a substantial change in the makeup of the House of Commons. As trends indicate the average tenure of members of the House of Commons has declined steadily in the last fifty years, such institutional memory is all the more important, particularly since it is augmented by the senators' professional and life experience.

PROFESSIONAL AND LIFE EXPERIENCE

Because senators were to be appointed, the Fathers of Confederation defined eligibility criteria that would tend to bring legislators with experience into office. Sections 23(1) and 23(4) of the *Constitution Act, 1867* limited membership to persons over age thirty and required a senator to be successful enough to own land and to be financially secure. The importance that the Fathers attached to experience is further emphasized when one remembers that the average life expectancy in 1867 was less than sixty years.[31]

Having breadth and depth of experience in Parliament obviously lends itself to the formulation of better laws and policies. Legislators with experience in a particular field, be it agriculture, education, medicine, or any other, have specific and invaluable insights into government policies on these matters. While elections may return experienced people to the

House of Commons, there are no guarantees. Through its use of the power to appoint senators, the government can fill these potential "gaps" and correct any distortions that may result from the electoral process, allowing for the participation in Parliament of individuals who have knowledge or expertise that would not otherwise be brought to bear on the development of public policy.

REGIONAL EQUALITY IN ACCORDANCE WITH THE PRINCIPLES
OF FEDERALISM

The Senate is one of the compromises that made Confederation possible. The federal principle ensures that all regions would have an equal voice and opportunity to participate in Parliament. Without it, neither Quebec nor the Maritime provinces would have agreed to join because Ontario would have dominated both Parliament and the Executive Government. The Supreme Court also emphasized that the regional breakdown of the Upper House was an essential characteristic of the institution and a fundamental feature of the Canadian federal system.[32]

Section 22 of the *Constitution Act, 1867* provides for the representation of four regions: Ontario, Quebec, the Maritime Provinces (New Brunswick, Nova Scotia, and Prince Edward Island), and the Western Provinces (Alberta, British Columbia, Manitoba, and Saskatchewan).[33] In a federation as vast and sparsely populated as Canada, this notion of the equality of regions is the essential complement to the House of Commons, which is composed on the basis of proportionate equality of electors. The Fathers also took steps to ensure that senators were *representative* of the Canadian public. Accordingly, section 23(5) provides that a senator "shall be resident in the Province for which he is appointed." Section 31 provides that the seat of a senator who ceases to reside in the province for which he was appointed becomes vacant.

Is regional representation an essential characteristic of the Senate? While members of the House of Commons are mandated to represent a specific group of people in a clearly defined constituency, senators have a broader regional perspective. Even today, equality of regions continues to be the best basis for the distribution of seats. Thus, in accordance with the principles of federalism, while the House of Commons represents the people, the Senate is essentially constituted on a regional basis.[34]

Conclusion

In concluding this first part, we observe that the experience of the past fifteen years has proven that the Senate is now more effectively performing the functions originally assigned to it by the Fathers of Confederation. However, it is still far from being a truly effective Upper Chamber.

In the UK, the recent Royal Commission on the Reform of the House of

Lords (Wakeham Commission)[35] has determined the main roles of an Upper Chamber in the Westminster parliamentary model:

- it should bring *a range of different perspectives* to bear on the development of public policy;
- *it should be broadly representative* of British society; people should be able to feel that there is a voice in Parliament for the different aspects of their personalities, whether regional, vocational, ethnic, professional, cultural or religious, expressed by a person or persons with whom they can identify;
- it should play a vital role as one of the main "checks and balances" within the unwritten British constitution; *its role should be complementary to that of the House of Commons* in identifying points of concern and requiring the Government to reconsider or justify its policy intentions; if necessary, it should cause the House of Commons to think again; the second chamber should engender second thoughts;
- it should provide *a voice for the nations and regions* of the United Kingdom at the centre of public affairs.[36]

The British government accepted these principles as the basis for proceeding with Lords reform in their November 2001 White Paper, *The House of Lords: Completing the Reform.*[37]

Although Canada's political and social context is quite different from that of the UK, these fundamental functions and characteristics of an Upper Chamber described by the Wakeham Commission remain at the heart of the operation of a parliamentary system such as ours. If we add the regional representation principle, which is characteristic of federalism, we have before us the features that should guide us in reforming the Senate in order to meet the challenges of the new century.

PART 2:
REFORM PROPOSALS TO MAKE THE SENATE A MORE
COMPLEMENTARY AND EFFICIENT LEGISLATIVE CHAMBER

In this second part, we shall consider what nonconstitutional reforms could be made to the Senate. Such reforms must essentially enable the Senate to perform more effectively its functions as a complementary chamber to the House of Commons.

Increasing the Independence of Senators

The first such reform concerns the independence of the Senate. We have already observed the importance of ensuring the real independence of senators in the first part of this chapter. In fact, one must return to the original intent of the Fathers of Confederation, who made the independence of senators a key feature of the Upper House in 1867. This independence must be re-examined in the current political context with a view to freeing senators from the partisan constraints that prevail in the House of Commons.

In that context, the first obstacle to the political independence of senators is the appointment process. It is a good idea that senators be appointed. If they were elected, senators would lose their "representative" quality and become "representatives" with a direct mandate from the people of an electoral district, in the same way as members of the House of Commons. That would be a major change that would then lead us to completely rethink the Senate's role, something that would not be desirable. The principle of Senate appointments is still as valid today as it was in 1867. Section 24 of the *Constitution Act* provides as follows:

The Governor General shall from Time to Time, in the Queen's Name, by Instrument under the Great Seal of Canada, summon qualified Persons to the Senate; and, subject to the Provisions of this Act, every Person so summoned shall become and be a Member of the Senate and a Senator.

In practice, the power of appointment is exercised on advice of the Prime Minister, who is accountable to the House of Commons. The method of selection of senators was also assessed by the Supreme Court in the Senate Reference. In its opinion, the Court stated that "To make the Senate a wholly or partially elected body would affect a fundamental feature of that body."[38] It emphasized that an appointed Upper Chamber was part of the original design of the Canadian Parliament and that this could not be brushed aside lightly.

In 1867, electing senators was generally believed to be inconsistent with the principle of responsible government, which is the key to democracy in a Westminster system. Many of the Fathers of Confederation who opposed the election of senators were motivated to do so by their experience with the establishment of responsible government in the colonies. Fathers from Ontario and Quebec had also seen a partially elected Upper House in action in the United Province of Canada and were convinced that an elected Senate would contribute nothing useful to Parliament. A noted reformer of his day, George Brown declared:

I have always been opposed to a second elective chamber, and I am so still, from the conviction that two elective houses are inconsistent with the right working of the British Parliamentary system.[39]

So senators were not to "represent" the people; that is to say they were not to have a mandate from voters. Nonetheless, senators were expected to be fully "representative" of the people. In other words, senators were to be legislators whom the people of their province would recognize and identify with. Sir John A. Macdonald expressed this very clearly:

In this country we must remember that the gentlemen who will be selected for the [Senate] stand on a very different footing from the peers of England ... The members of our upper house will be like those of the lower, men of the people, and from the people. The man put into the upper house is as much a man of the people the day after as the day before ... Springing from the people, and one of them, he takes his seat in the council with all the sympathies and feelings of a man of the people, and when he returns home, at the end of the session, he mingles with them on equal terms and is influenced by the same feelings and associations, and events, as those which affect the mass around him.[40]

That is a key element in the proper functioning of Parliament as a whole. For senators to contribute to Parliament's work, they need not *represent* the people, but they must be *representative* of the people. This is what was to enable senators to play a key role with regard to minorities.

During the debates leading up to Confederation, the representatives of Lower Canada (Quebec) clearly expressed the important role that the Senate was to have with respect to linguistic minorities. Sir George-Etienne Cartier believed that one of the essential roles of the Senate would be the protection of the Francophone minority. In speaking of the Upper House in 1865, he declared that the institution "is our security."[41] Sir Hector-Louis Langevin shared these sentiments. In 1865, he affirmed that:

Under Confederation there will no longer be domination of one race over another, and if one section should be desirous of committing an act of injustice against another section, all the others would unite together to prevent it. But suppose that an unjust measure was passed in the House of Commons of the federal legislature, it would be stopped in the Legislative Council; for there we shall be represented equally with the other sections, and that is a guarantee that our interests will be amply protected.[42]

This theme is still as important today as it was in 1867. Canada's population today is one of the most diverse in the world. The House of Commons is composed of people who have a mandate to represent the electorate of their riding, but, by virtue of the electoral process, the result of almost every election is distorted and will not be fully representative of the population. Segments of the population, notably minority groups, may have special needs and concerns but may not be numerous or concentrated enough to elect a representative to the House of Commons. The appointment of senators complements our electoral system by securing parliamentary representation for these groups.

For example, the House of Commons has never been representative of the population on the basis of sex. In the latter half of the twentieth century, women generally made progress in gaining seats in the House of Commons, but their progress reached a plateau with the 1997 general election, and, by 2000, women had lost ground both in the number of candidates seeking election and in the number elected. Essentially, there appears to be a "glass ceiling" of just over 20 percent for women in the House of Commons, even though women constitute a majority of the population.[43] In the meantime, the exercise of the power of appointment has seen the number of women in the Senate rise to 34 percent in recent years.[44]

Similarly, Aboriginal communities in Canada are small and dispersed enough that the electoral process is unlikely ever to produce representatives in numbers comparable to their proportion of the general population. Even if no Aboriginal were returned in a general election, Aboriginal people would recognize and identify with at least some of their national legislators.[45]

The power to appoint senators also offers an opportunity to select individuals who will bring personal experience and expertise in a policy area that is needed in Parliament generally. As the complexity of policy and legislation increases, securing the participation of experienced and expert people becomes increasingly vital to the performance of Parliament's core functions.

In the United States, senators are elected. The American Senate is composed of two senators from each state. Senators have longer terms and responsibilities, which, in some respects, are different, as regards treaty ratification for example. However, the situation in the United States is quite different from our own: Americans have a presidential system, ours is a parliamentary regime. Ministerial responsibility thus does not apply to the US Congress. In the American system, the executive is not required to maintain the confidence of Congress in order to remain in government. Understanding these differences is fundamental.

In Canada, if senators were elected and derived their legitimacy directly from the people, the issues would be entirely different. Ministerial responsibility would have to be rethought and representation of minorities would have to be viewed differently. An elected Senate would thus constitute a major change that could only be done by means of a constitutional amendment and a full revision of the operation not only of the Senate, but of the government as a whole.

Western Canada has previously made this one of its main constitutional demands, and legitimately so. However, the increasing importance of executive federalism in recent years has made those demands less urgent. In fact, all the provinces openly claim that their governments are in the best position to defend their interests in Ottawa. An elected Senate might well considerably undermine the importance of the provincial governments in the development of national policy. Federal-provincial conferences might no longer have the same impact. Elected senators in one province could be from a political party different from the one forming the provincial government, with all the consequences that might have for building the consensuses so necessary to our type of federalism.

The same would be more or less true if the provinces appointed senators. This other way of constituting a second chamber works well in Germany. The members of the second house, the Bundesrat, are, to all intents and purposes, delegates from the Länder. For us, that would mean a considerable attenuation of our executive federalism. The provincial delegations led by their premiers or a provincial minister would no longer have the same role to play in federal-provincial conferences.

The 1987 Meech Lake Accord provided a middle ground to avoid this consequence. The Accord provided that senators would be appointed by the federal government from lists submitted by the provinces. Canada is an enormous, sparsely populated country composed of clearly defined regions. Federal-provincial conferences remain the most appropriate way to protect and promote regional interests, while at the same time developing national policies. The Meech Lake Accord recognized this by proposing to entrench annual federal-provincial economic conferences in the Constitution. In order to ensure the independence of the institution, the following changes must be made in the way senators are selected.

- The Prime Minister's power to appoint senators must be circumscribed by a clearly defined set of selection criteria brought to the public's attention by the government, which would table them in the Senate and in the House of Commons. Those criteria would be defined at the government's discretion but would have to be published prior to every appointment.
- The political independence of senators should also be reinforced by prohibiting senators from taking part in party caucuses alongside members of the House of Commons. The idea would not be to sever senators' political affiliations. That would be unrealistic. Since the Senate is a legislative chamber, it is all together reasonable, and even desirable, for the government to have the means to facilitate passage of its legislation. However, having senators and MPs attend the same caucus is unnecessary and would undermine senators' credibility.
- The Prime Minister must also avoid appointing senators to Cabinet, apart from the Leader of the Government in the Senate. By definition, a minister of the Crown ought not to sit in the Senate, given that the principle of ministerial responsibility does not apply in the Upper Chamber.

These three changes can all be achieved without amending the Constitution. They would bring greater independence and increased credibility to the Senate, which would in turn be better placed to take on new responsibilities.

New Responsibilities for the Senate

As a complement to the House of Commons, the Senate could take on new responsibilities consistent with the evolution of Canadian society.

CONDUCT SPECIAL STUDIES

Following the Second World War, democratic governments expanded their fields of activity. Parliament, which then sat only three or four months a year, was soon overwhelmed by increasingly complex bills. It was at that time that the Senate undertook to conduct special studies in certain important areas of activity. Many of those studies have had a considerable influence on the course of both government policy and public opinion. The *Report on Poverty in Canada* (1971), the five major reports on science policy (1970–77), and the series of reports on the mass media (1970) are still cited to explain certain aspects of the present context.

The special study should be one of the most important aspects of the Senate's work. Recent activity reports for the latest five-year period indicate that, in any given year, thirty-four special studies are undertaken by the Senate. That is in addition to the average of fifty Government bills usually studied in the calendar year. Senators will often tackle issues that are of no interest to elected parliamentarians, or even controversial ones that members of the House of Commons would prefer to avoid, such as special studies on euthanasia, palliative care, and marijuana, which were recently the subject of special studies.

ENSURE COMPLIANCE WITH THE CANADIAN CHARTER OF RIGHTS
AND FREEDOMS

Likewise, the advent of the *Canadian Charter of Rights and Freedoms* in 1982 also had an impact on the Senate's legislative work. When a bill becomes the subject of concern in Senate committees, it is very often because that bill involves the Charter. In a number of cases, the Senate has made amendments to remedy perceived Charter problems, and the House of Commons has passed them. Examples of these include the *Act to amend the Judges Act* (1999), the *Act to amend the Canada Evidence Act*, and the *Canadian Human Rights Act* (1998). In the fall of 2001, the Senate formed a special committee to study the new anti-terrorist measures contained in Bill C–36. Its concerns about the protection of individual rights induced the government to rethink certain measures.

In 2001, the Senate established a Standing Committee on Human Rights, confirming its new role as a Charter watchdog. This role is particularly well suited to the Senate and should occupy it increasingly, given the tendency of various governments to legislate on very delicate matters such as privacy. The bioethics sector is another field which should be the subject of special studies in the Senate since it will be the focal point of our societal debates in the coming years.

DELEGATED LEGISLATION

The Senate could also expand its role as auditor of federal government legislation. The regulatory power is playing an expanding role in the public administration. And yet, to a very large degree, it escapes the political control of the House of Commons. Delegated legislation also occurs at the federal-provincial level, where, under our Constitution, one order of government may delegate to another the administration of one of its exclusive fields of activity to the extent that it does not abandon it.

Compared to the Australian and British experience, the Canadian regime for parliamentary supervision of regulations is clearly less developed. As the British have demonstrated, the Upper House is well qualified and well disposed to perform this work, leaving members of the House of Commons free to pursue other roles and functions that contribute to Parliament's efficacy. The Senate should therefore devote more significant amounts of time and resources to monitoring regulations and delegated legislation in general in order to consider the effects on the public interest.

THE STUDY OF TREATIES AND OTHER INTERNATIONAL COVENANTS

The Senate could also play a more active role in scrutinizing Canada's treaties and international obligations in general. As a middle power, Canada has always pursued its international objectives primarily through multilateral organizations and is already party to some 4,000 international treaties, which unfortunately are not classified in any kind of systematic fashion. Multilateral trading arrangements, such as the WTO and NAFTA, are evidence of an international community that is becoming increasingly a system of laws based on agreements that include binding and enforceable mechanisms for dispute resolution. Part of Parliament's legislative authority is slowly migrating to the supranational level. This controversial development, which has both proponents and opponents, confronts Canada with the challenge of preserving sovereignty while simultaneously respecting and promoting the new international order. While this has happened largely with Parliament's consent, Parliament cannot function at its best in ignorance of developments in the realm of international agreements to which Canada is a party. These international agreements are often complex, and the Senate, as a result of its continuity, could develop special expertise in order to gain a better understanding of issues such as, for example, the globalization of the economy or of bilateral free trade agreements that Canada is signing with a growing number of countries.

The globalization and regionalization of the economy have had a major impact on the way we govern and administer. International trade has an increasing impact on policy, particularly in a country such as Canada, where exports account for 41 percent of GDP.

The Senate could thus have a major role to play in studying the effects of treaties and other international governance for Canada and the provinces. As we know, under Canada's Constitution, Ottawa has sole authority to sign treaties. However, those treaties must be integrated into domestic law through federal statutes, in areas of federal jurisdiction, and by provincial assemblies, in treaty matters under the jurisdiction of the provinces. The process is complex and involves the two orders of government in an often difficult process of negotiation before Ottawa can sign a treaty or agreement. Free trade agreements are a particularly important example of this. The Senate could play a highly useful role in facilitating a clear understanding of treaty issues and prepare the way for their implementation in Canadian law, both federal and provincial, without, of course, interfering in provincial jurisdictions.

It would be wise to institutionalize scrutiny of international agreements that affect Canada's legislative sovereignty, its role in the globalizing world economy, and its commitment to a rules-based international order. The Senate Foreign Affairs Committee, or a new committee formed specifically for the purpose, should systematically analyze the effects of all international treaties, and, in order to combine the expert and lengthy studies by the Upper House with the views of the elected representatives of the Lower House, its report should be considered by a joint committee of the House of Commons and the Senate. The population of Canada would stand to gain much from these kinds of studies, which could make the public aware of more complex and difficult aspects of international activity but which are so important for Canada.

Conclusion

By reason of its independence and continuity, along with its ability to represent and reflect the Canadian public, the Senate could play a more important political role than the one it currently performs. Through special studies and in other ways, the Senate should be involved to a greater degree in all matters concerning the Charter of Rights and Freedoms. It could also serve as a guardian of the public interest in the adoption of government regulations, an area beyond the oversight of the House of Commons. The Senate's study of international agreements to which Canada is a party would also be necessary if Canada wished to grasp all the implications of those commitments for the country's sovereignty. However, to better perform these new functions, the Senate must review some of its existing methods, notably those concerning its legislative and veto powers.

SHOULD THE SENATE INTRODUCE LEGISLATION?

The Senate's power to initiate legislation should also be reconsidered. No one would deny that the Constitution gives senators the power to introduce, approve, and send legislation to the House of Commons for study by that chamber. In fact, several governments have introduced a substantial number of their bills in the Senate in order to lighten the legislative agenda in the House of Commons. One wonders whether it is desirable for senators to be the first in line to study government legislation.

One of the main roles the Senate was originally intended to play is that of reviewing legislation. It would be logical to conclude, therefore, that the introduction of legislation in the Senate is inconsistent with this role. When the government introduces a bill in the Senate, it removes the function of review from the Upper Chamber, forcing the House of Commons to assume this role intended for the Senate. This example illustrates the wisdom of examining all reform proposals in the context of our parliamentary system. Reforms that appear attractive at first glance may actually conflict with the intended role of the Senate and undermine the complementarity of the two chambers and the efficient operation of Parliament as a whole.

HOW SHOULD THE SENATE USE ITS VETO?

According to the Constitution, the Senate may veto a bill referred by the House of Commons. The exercise of this power of veto is tantamount to killing a bill. The Fathers of Confederation gave that power to the Senate to make sure that MPs would understand the importance of its role. However, since that time, the situation has changed profoundly and democratic legitimacy has a different meaning today than in 1867.

In its 1981 opinion on patriation, the Supreme Court defined the notion of legitimacy for the first time.[46] In the Court's view, legitimacy is the exercise of power in accordance with the will of the people. Consequently, when a bill under study clearly derives from the electoral mandate of the government, the Senate must recognize the democratic will. Law professors Jacques-Yvan Morin and José Woerling argue that:

Surely the principle of democracy is reason enough to prevent the Senate from opposing the will of the elected representatives of the people, at least where the government has received a mandate for its proposed legislation from the public at the last general election.[47]

The Senate's refusal to pass legislation approved by the House of Commons, except under special circumstances, would raise the question of the legitimacy of its veto power in a democratic society such as ours. Indeed, the future of the Senate may well hinge on this question.

The Senate exercised its veto only forty-four times in the twentieth century.[48] In recent years, the Senate has shown an increased willingness to use its veto. Four of the five post-Second World War Senate vetoes have occurred in the past decade.

In the last twenty-five years, various specific reform proposals have raised the issue of its veto.[49] In 1978, Bill C–60 would have allowed the House of Commons to overturn the Senate's veto after sixty days but, due in part to the provisions affecting the veto, was declared unconstitutional by the Supreme Court in the 1980 Upper House Reference. Limits on the ability of the federal government to unilaterally modify the composition of the Senate and its veto have since been reinforced by the 1982 constitutional amending formula.

In 1985, the federal government put forward a constitutional resolution that would have enabled the House of Commons to overturn a Senate veto on money bills after thirty days and on non-money bills after forty-five days. Although eight provinces supported the resolution, the Quebec government chose not to be a party to the discussion because Quebec did not recognize the 1982 Constitution. Even though more than seven provinces representing over 50 percent of the population indicated their acceptance of the proposal, the government of Prime Minister Mulroney chose not to proceed with the amendment because it did not want to appear to be isolating Quebec. The 1992 Charlottetown Accord would have limited the Senate's ability to delay money bills to thirty calendar days.

Despite the failure of these and many other reform initiatives, it is nevertheless conceivable that the nature and scope of the Senate veto could be reviewed when the country is again in a position to discuss constitutional reform. At that time, a balance will have to be struck between the Senate's composition, the appointment process, and the powers of the institution, including its veto. Until then, however, the Senate will have to make prudent use of its legislative veto to kill a bill. Before opting to use its veto power, the Senate must conduct an extensive study of the issues raised by the bill. The public can only be pleased to see the Senate devote serious study and reflection to difficult issues. However, Canadians would be much less accepting of the Senate if it were to reject legislation passed by the democratically elected House of Commons without clear and compelling reasons.

The Senate should, on its own initiative, first conduct all the studies and debate necessary to a clear understanding of proposed legislation and ensure that the public grasps all its ramifications as well. Senators may then prepare amendments designed to improve a bill, rather than simply voting down legislation that has been passed by the House with a direct mandate from the Canadian people.

While many commentators would limit the powers of the Senate to a suspensive veto, this issue can only be settled through a reform of the Constitution. A discussion of possible reform proposals on this subject is beyond the scope of this chapter, which addresses the prospects of nonconstitutional proposals.

CONCLUSION

All the various attempts to reform the Senate have failed, mainly because their authors attempted too much. They called for extensive constitutional revisions requiring difficult consensuses between the provinces and within the same federal state. And yet new life needs to be breathed into the Senate as soon as possible.

It would appear to be possible to do this first of all without a constitutional review. Simple political and administrative changes could make the Senate a truly complementary legislative chamber to the House of Commons. Of course, not all can be done by purely administrative means. But that would be a first step, which would enable us to establish ways of proceeding and to create attitudes that, once checked to ensure they work, should be institutionalized.

We must reconsider the attributes with which the Fathers of Confederation endowed the Senate in 1867. They are still valid and must be developed. The future of the Senate depends on its independence and the quality of its members. The Canadian people will realize the Senate's true value once they understand that it enables them to better understand the major issues facing us as a society and as human beings.

Globalization of the economy, developments in communications, innovation and new technologies, deregulation, and demographic phenomena, all these things require our governments to rethink both their structure and the way they operate. The Senate could become a pillar in this new government edifice, tuned in to a public that is better informed and more sensitive to the stimulating but also, in many respects, disturbing international environment.

The Senate should have the necessary independence to examine the impact of government decisions on the fundamental rights and freedoms of Canadians. The government is increasingly developing its electronic communications with citizens. An online administration is necessary to ensure efficiency in government. However, it also entails many dangers, particularly with regard to privacy. While the Office of the Privacy Commissioner of Canada is the administrative monitoring and control agency in this area, the Senate could play the role of political overseer in the broader sense of that term. The Senate has already been heading in that direction since it created a standing committee to study specific questions relating to rights and freedoms.

Now more than ever the environment is a factor in the development and implementation of national policies. At the same time, the WTO, the International Monetary Fund, NAFTA, and bilateral trade agreements have a considerable impact on the way we govern. The Senate is an ideal forum for debating the ramifications of changes in the global economy and environment on government policies. By its very definition, the Senate ought to have the required experience and continuity to provide the long-term perspective that is missing from our political system.

In this context and with its independence, the Senate could develop important links with the public service. The Clerk of the Privy Council could be involved as an advisor, recommending research themes and questions that could be studied by the Senate. Senators and public servants could be encouraged to work more closely on a variety of important issues, such as those involving public health and confronting the government with a precautionary principle. This principle is now enshrined in our domestic law[50] and compels the government to conduct a careful risk assessment before making a decision. In case of doubt, the government must be cautious and never make any decision that could jeopardize the health of Canadians. We do not yet know the full impact of this new principle on the responsibility of politicians and public administrators. However, we know that it could considerably change our political and administrative decision-making mechanisms. In fact, the precautionary principle means that, before making a decision, our leaders must do everything in their power to obtain the necessary information on the consequences of their decision. Whether it be genetically modified organisms (GMOs), new drugs, materials, and so on, the government must now use every means at its disposal to be adequately informed. At the political level, the Senate could play an important role in this area, ensuring that the House of Commons and the government have the necessary information to make all their decisions in a manner consistent with this new precautionary principle.

According to the theory of federalism, the second chamber must represent the federated states, while the first chamber represents the people. In Canada, however, the application of this theory must be understood in the context of our political reality. If the theory were strictly applied, the result could be a greater centralization of power in Ottawa. Provincial interests might no longer be discussed at the federal-provincial conferences that can be held virtually anywhere across Canada but rather in the Senate in Ottawa. For this reason Senate renewal must not occur at the expense of executive federalism, which must be protected and developed. The best way to proceed for the moment is by means of administrative and political change. Let us take the time to assess the impact of these new functions and responsibilities that require no constitutional review, then see whether it would be a good idea to entrench them in the Constitution. The important thing for the time being is to sketch the backdrop that represents our aspirations. The framework for achieving them will follow at a later date. Let us not make the mistake of doing it the other way around.

NOTES

The author wishes to thank Andrew Turner, MA, International Relations, for his contributions to this article.

1 As Ronald Watts has pointed out in his chapter, only a handful of very small federations currently operate with a unicameral system.

2 The Fathers of Confederation from the United Province of Canada had first-hand experience with an elected upper chamber. From 1856 until Confederation, vacancies in the Legislative Council were filled by election. By 1867, all but seven members of the Legislative Council were elected, and the Fathers of Confederation concluded that an elected upper chamber was inconsistent with the Westminster model and responsible government.

3 See Bonenfant, *La Vocation manquée du Sénat canadien*, 51; also Pelletier, "La Réforme du Sénat canadien à la lumière d'expériences étrangères."

4 *Reference re Alberta Statutes*, [1938] S.C.R. 100, 132–3.

5 This trend has been charted by a number of observers and commentators. For example, see Savoie, *Governing from the Centre*, and Marshall, *Ministerial Responsibility*.

6 For a thorough discussion of the Senate and Confederation, see Ajzenstat, this volume.

7 *Re: The Regulation and Control of Aeronautics in Canada*, [1932] A.C. 54, 70.

8 *Reference re Legislative Authority of Parliament in Relation to the Upper House*, [1980] 1 S.C.R. 54, 78.

9 See also Janet Ajzenstat, this volume.

10 *Reference re Legislative Authority of Parliament in Relation to the Upper House*, [1980] 1 S.C.R. 54, 76.

11 The Fiscal and Economic Statement of the Minister of Finance, Hon. D. Mazankowski, PC, in the House of Commons on 2 December 1992.

12 Bill C–16: *An Act respecting Canadian citizenship*.

13 See *Debates of the Senate* of December 1995, starting at page 2446 for Senator Kirby and starting at page 2481 for Senator Murray.

14 Clarity Act (*An Act to give effect to the requirement for clarity as set out in the opinion of the Supreme Court of Canada in the Quebec secession reference*), 2000, c. 26.

15 *Reference re Secession of Quebec*, [1998] 2 S.C.R. 217.

16 United Kingdom, *Report of the Royal Commission on the Reform of the House of Lords*, 102.

17 House of Lords, House of Lords Appointment Commission, *Annex A: Criteria Guiding the Assessment of Nominations For Non-Party Political Members Of The House Of Lords*.

18 Great Britain, *The House of Lords: Completing the Reform*.

19 *Parliamentary Debates on Confederation of the British North American Provinces*, Québec, 1865; Ottawa, 1951, 571, cited in Kunz, *The Modern Senate of Canada*, 11. (Emphasis added.)

20 *Debates of the Canadian Legislative Assembly*, cited in Ajzenstat, ed., *Canada's Founding Debates*, 14. (Emphasis added.)

21 *Reference re Legislative Authority of Parliament in Relation to the Upper House*, [1980] 1 S.C.R. 54, 77.

22 Subsection 23(1).

23 Subsection 23(2).

24 Subsection 23(3).

25 Subsections 23(5) and (6).

26 *Reference re Legislative Authority of Parliament in Relation to the Upper House,* [1980] 1 S.C.R. 54, 76.

27 See appendix for statistics.

28 Canada, Parliament, Senate, The Standing Senate Committee on Social Affairs, Science and Technology, *Study on the State of the Health Care System in Canada. Work Plan. (August 2001).*

29 See appendix for statistics.

30 See appendix for statistics.

31 Statistics Canada, *Health Statistics at a Glance,* see table entitled "Life Expectancy at Birth."

32 *Reference re Legislative Authority of Parliament in Relation to the Upper House,* [1980] 1 S.C.R. 54, 76.

33 Many have argued that this division should be revisited. Although the Constitution does not specifically define what constitutes a senatorial region, but given the development of the country, it seems reasonable to conclude that a region entails a geographic entity with shared historic, economic, and political realities. On these grounds, a strong case can certainly be made that British Columbia has a claim to status as a senatorial region unto itself. Indeed, Bill C–110, enacted in 1996 following the 1995 referendum, was amended to recognize British Columbia as a distinct region. The regional division is, however, entrenched in the Constitution and cannot be altered without constitutional amendment.

34 Watts, this volume, offers a detailed examination of regional representation in second chambers.

35 Although not an exact parallel to the Senate, as it is not a federal chamber, the similar method of appointment and the complementary relationship between the Upper House and Lower House in both Parliaments allow for some comparisons to be made.

36 United Kingdom. *Report of the Royal Commission on the Reform of the House of Lords,* 3. (Emphasis added.)

37 Great Britain, *The House of Lords: Completing the Reform.*

38 *Reference re Legislative Authority of Parliament in Relation to the Upper House,* [1980] 1 S.C.R. 54, 77.

39 Quoted in Ajzenstat, ed., *Canada's Founding Debates,* 83.

40 Ajzenstat, ed., *Canada's Founding Debates,* 81–2.

41 Waite, *The Confederation Debates in the Province of Canada, 1865,* 115.

42 Legislative Assembly of Canada, cited in Ajzenstat, ed., *Canada's Founding Debates,* 298.

43 For a full discussion of the limitations on the participation of women in Canadian political institutions, see Tremblay and Andrew, *Femmes et représentation politique au Québec et au Canada.*

44 See appendix for statistics.

45 See appendix for statistics.

46 *Opinion on repatriation,* (1981) 1 S.C.R. 753.

47 Morin and Woerling, *Les Constitutions du Canada et du Québec, tome premier, 2e édition,* 205.

48 Audcent, *The Senate Veto: Opinion of the Law Clerk and Parliamentary Council,* appendix 1.

49 See Stilborn, this volume, for a more extensive discussion.

50 *114957 Canada Ltée (Spraytech, Société d'arrosage) v. Hudson (Town),* [2001] 2 S.C.R. 241.

CHAPTER FIVE

Which Criticisms Are Founded?

Lowell Murray

I have spent most of my adult life in and around politics and government, federal and provincial, and more than twenty-three of these years in the Senate. This background leaves me open to accusations of bias and self-interest. So be it. I believe I am as intimately familiar as anyone in the country with the role the Senate plays in our parliamentary democracy, and with the Upper House's shortcomings, real and imagined. More importantly, when it comes to shortcomings, I am well qualified to distinguish between real deficiencies and the lurid, uninformed caricatures of the Senate painted by some journalists and other commentators who never come near the place nor pay the slightest attention to what goes on here. (A Toronto journalist who wrote at length of the Senate's faults, was himself appointed to the chamber, where he made his colleagues wait thirteen years for his retirement speech in which he apologized for what he had written in ignorance.)

I respect the principled position of those who despise the idea of the Senate because it is a non-elected legislature. They are wrong, however, when they infer that this appointed body lacks legitimacy in our Canadian parliamentary democracy. Historical and constitutional legitimacy cannot be so lightly dismissed, and the Senate has plenty of both.[1]

The Senate was a "deal breaker" in the negotiations that led to Confederation in 1867. Quebec and the Maritime Provinces insisted on an Upper House with equal representation from three regions as a counterweight to Ontario's numerical advantage in the House of Commons. The Fathers of Confederation also wanted to create a further check on the executive government and its elected Commons majority. They decided this would be best accomplished by an appointed Senate whose members had life tenure.

These decisions were not taken casually. At the Quebec Conference, where Confederation's constitutional resolutions were drafted, design of the Upper House took up more time than any other single issue. Unlike most of today's comment on the Senate, it was a serious debate in which all the arguments and alternatives were canvassed. The Senate's historical and constitutional importance – and its positive contribution to our country's governance over the years – makes it worthy of far more serious attention and analysis than it has received in recent years.

The questions that ought to be considered are (1) whether Canada's parliamentary democracy would have been better – and would still be better – without the Senate created in 1867 and (2) whether any of the current proposals for a "new" second chamber would be an improvement. In my opinion the evidence answers a clear "No" to both questions. To answer these questions would require a thoughtful examination of the role the Senate plays. It would also need a more searching look at how our parliamentary and federal systems would be affected by creating one or another of the "new" senates dreamt of by their various advocates.

It is worth noting that the appointed Senate created in 1867 was in some important respects just a few generations ahead of its time. Today, non-elected judges legislate, and non-elected boards, commissions, agencies, and ombudsmen exercise great hybrids of quasi-judicial, quasi-legislative, quasi-regulatory, quasi-administrative, and delegated authority in every field from human rights to broadcasting to tax collection. These bodies have a large influence on many aspects of our national life. Their activities and decisions affect the lives of millions. Their accountability is, to egregiously understate the case, ill defined. The supervision of their activities by our elected representatives, to the extent that their arms-length status permits any such supervision, is casual and episodic at best. Their administrative and much of their deliberative process is hidden from public view. They are subject to almost no critical scrutiny by the nation's media. Compared to these elite, almost autonomous public bodies, the Senate is a paragon of transparency and accountability.

Any legislation originating in the Senate must be approved by the elected Commons. Our deliberations are open. The committee that runs our internal administration meets in public, unlike its Commons counterpart. Attendance in the Senate is recorded and is publicly available, unlike in the House of Commons and provincial legislatures. Senators suffer financial penalties if they do not comply with attendance regulations.

Canadians' knowledge of the Senate's role, particularly in the legislative process, is scanty at best. The only time they hear about it is when there is a real or potential confrontation with the Commons over the delay, amendment, or in very rare instances, defeat of a government Bill. In most cases, such confrontation occurs for one of three reasons. First, because there is a serious defect of constitutional principle in a proposed Bill. Witness the Chrétien Government's attempted denial of access to the courts for contractors claiming redress for cancellation of the Pearson Airport project, and the same government's attempt to put off to a more congenial political time the redrawing of electoral boundaries undertaken following the 1991 census. Second, because there is an identifiable group of Canadians adversely affected by the Bill and whose views have been inadequately championed in the Commons. The Conservative Government's refugee determination legislation (in 1988) and its Unemployment Insurance reforms (in 1989) or the Liberals' Unemployment Insurances changes (in 1996) and amendments to the Canada Pension Plan (in 1997) are examples. In most of these cases, the Senate succeeded in amending the Bills. And third, because there is a major partisan political issue, such as the Liberal delay of the Canada-United States Free Trade Agreement in 1988 and the Goods and Services Tax in 1990.

As Conservative Government leader in the Senate 1986–93, I argued against the decision by the opposition Liberal majority to block the 1988 Free Trade Agreement until the government had obtained a new mandate in a general election. Still, they had precedent on their side – the 1911 Naval Service Act, held up by Conservative senators for the same reason. When the Mulroney Government was returned to office, the Senate Liberals ceased their opposition. Some other actions by the opposition majority during the Mulroney years are less defensible. In particular their effort, over a three-month period, to obstruct the Goods and Services Tax Bill and to prevent it from being voted on, was an unprecedented abuse of Parliament. The thirteen-month delay in passing the Conservative Unemployment Insurance Bill also struck me as too much. That the motivation for these actions was primarily partisan was demonstrated by the sequels: the next Liberal Government reneged on its clear pledge to abolish the Goods and Services Tax, without drawing a word of criticism from any Liberal senator. Once on the government side, the same Liberal senators who had fought tooth and nail against the Conservative Unemployment Insurance changes, acquiesced without a word of dissent to far more punitive treatment of the unemployed in a bill brought in by their own government in 1996.

Such abuses are exceptional. Overall, the Senate has made a high quality contribution to the federal legislative and policy process and continues to do so today. Indeed, if the truth be known, of the three components of Parliament – Crown, Senate and Commons – only the Senate is performing as it should.

Consider the Crown. When, in the past thirty years, has a Prime Minister – or for that matter a Governor General – been heard speaking of the central place of the Crown in Canada's parliamentary democracy? When has the representative of the Crown been heard speaking of the office as the transcendent, continuing symbol of our existence as a nation, above the political fray, the ultimate safeguard of our constitutional liberties? Governors general speak eloquently of the values that unite Canadians, but never about the significance of their office as the embodiment and defender of those values. They are almost as embarrassed as senators to describe the role that history, tradition, and the Constitution have reserved for them. The office has been held by dedicated and highly respected Canadians. Yet its significance in our parliamentary democracy is unappreciated and misunderstood by the mass of Canadians. Most people wrongly believe it to be completely ceremonial and utterly powerless. That is the fault of successive generations of politicians, of an educational system that has never given the institution due study, and of past vice-regal incumbents themselves.

The Crown has become irrelevant to most Canadians' understanding of our system of government. However, its deterioration is not as serious as that of our other parliamentary component, the House of Commons. As individuals, members of the House of Commons are better paid, better staffed and equipped in both their constituencies and in Ottawa, have better access to research and travel than has ever been the case. Clearly they set great store by their role as champions of their constituents, helping them to navigate the federal bureaucratic maze in search of attention, assistance, redress, and sometimes simple justice. God bless them and their dedicated, overworked staffs for this. No one who knows the system doubts the need for this service.

However, the Commons as an institution has to a considerable extent forgotten its purpose. For the record, and in a single phrase, the role of the Commons, as Gladstone reminded his elected supporters, is "not to govern, but to hold to account those who do." In Canada, the Commons has been losing ground to the Cabinet steadily for more than thirty years. In terms of holding the government to account, it is today more form than substance.

How many Canadians know that the government's annual spending Estimates are "deemed" on a fixed date to have been approved by the various standing committees, whether or not they have ever been defended by a minister or examined by members of the House of Commons? Committees have three months to examine those Estimates and to criticize policy and administrative shortcomings, and during the rest of the year there are "Opposition Days" when members of the House of Commons can choose the subject and bring on a vote. This "supply" process is the foundation of the British and Canadian system of responsible government. Yet it is mostly lost in the shuffle of other committee and House business. Contrast this, incidentally, with the critical (but nonpartisan) work of the Senate in the annual Estimates and Supply process.

The Commons has become programmed to the needs of the Executive Government and to the convenience of members of the House of Commons and party caucuses. Legislation is routinely fast-tracked through the House by government use of time allocation and closure at every stage. Cabinet ministers are rarely required to guide their legislation through the Commons and its committees, or even to be in the Chamber. House duty is considered fit only for a quorum of backbenchers on both sides and parliamentary secretaries to ministers. Most important ministerial policy announcements are made to "client groups," friendly media or party gatherings, not to the House. Why do members of the House of Commons, whatever their party affiliation, put up with – indeed, why are they complicit in – this continuing erosion of their authority and responsibility? And have you seen what passes for debate, even among party leaders, (especially among party leaders) in the Commons? For the most part, it is the reading of scripted speeches, and no reference let alone reply to arguments raised by the previous speaker. Several generations of members of the House of Commons and parliamentary journalists have come and gone, believing that the forty-minute daily travesty known as the Question Period is the essence of responsible government.

There is a sense among members of the House of Commons, and among Canadians who give it a thought, that something is gravely wrong with the institution. In response to this, a cottage industry has grown up in Ottawa seeking to devise "make work" projects for members of the House of Commons and their committees. This consists of travel, policy studies that are better done by the Senate, and pseudo-ministerial activity to keep them occupied. Some proposals would let members of the House of Commons into the process of appointing judges and senior government officials. Others concentrate on fixing the relationship between members of the House of Commons and their constituents, which is really not broken. All this misses the point, which is that, over the past thirty years, government has gradually slipped away from Parliament.

The conventions by which members of the House of Commons used the power of the purse to hold ministers accountable are not really operative anymore. Whether it is cause or effect, the Cabinet system itself is today dislocated from its traditional parliamentary moorings. The authority, responsibility, and accountability of individual ministers are blurred by the proliferation and ascendancy of the Cabinet committee system and by the wide-ranging mandates of the central agencies. Political partisanship is an indispensable element in our democratic system and our parliamentary system, yet political parties have been reduced to near irrelevance. They are fund raising and Election Day machines with little serious, continuing role or influence in the policy process.

The dysfunction of important institutions such as Crown, government, Commons and political parties – and their relationship to one another – is a complex subject. It would be quite an exaggeration to suggest that the Senate compensates for all the inadequacies elsewhere and that it alone keeps our democracy on a relatively even keel. It is a fact, however, that the Senate – almost alone among our political institutions – has evolved to meet new needs and challenges. Most important, it provides some check on the power of the Cabinet and its Commons majority without challenging or offending today's democratic culture. We make corrections and improvements to government legislation without engaging in confrontation or creating stalemate with the Commons. We produce, in a largely bipartisan committee process, a substantial body of thoughtful policy advice, based on good quality research and exhaustive discussion with knowledgeable Canadians. And, contrary to the working assumption of many of our critics, journalistic and otherwise, repeated studies have shown that the Senate's work is cost effective.

Rather than the useless appendage decried by various and sundry critics, the Senate in fact proves its usefulness over and over again. Take, for instance, the Senate committee system. Upon my appointment to the Senate in 1979, I was fortunate to be named to two Standing Committees conducting in-depth studies of important policy questions. The Foreign Affairs Committee under the chairmanship of the late Senator George Van Roggen of British Columbia produced a comprehensive, three-volume report on Canada-United States trade, which during the 1980s was considered one of the most authoritative works in the field. The committee had no sooner exhausted this subject than Van Roggen persuaded us to turn to a study of Canada's relations with Middle Eastern countries. Then he turned the committee's attention to international financial institutions and the debt problem of developing countries, an inquiry that reported in 1987. More than fifteen years have gone by, and a lot of history, since the last of these three studies was completed, but they stand out as high quality contributions to policy debate and development in this country. The National Finance Committee, under the chairmanship of Senator Douglas Everett of Manitoba, concluded a study of regional development policy in 1982 that is still worth consulting by anyone interested in the hard economic and social policy choices in this field. There is a long list of other Senate committee studies that have contributed significantly to public debate and understanding and to government policy.

I have served on nearly every Senate committee, and at various times have been chairman of four of them – "Official Languages," "Banking, Trade and Commerce," "Social Affairs, Science and Technology," and "National Finance." Year after year, when legislation comes to the Senate or our committees conduct special policy studies, hundreds of Canadians beat a path to our door. Small business and big corporations, trade unions, environmental and social action groups, professional organizations, farmers, fishermen, the unemployed, students, educators, and sometimes even provincial governments and opposition parties line up. They all want to be heard, more of them than we can possibly accommodate to any reasonable timetable. Why is this? It is certainly not because the Senate provides a good public platform for airing their views. On the contrary, for all the media attention Senate committees get, we might as well meet behind closed doors. Nor is it because they have any realistic expectation that a grievance voiced to a committee will necessarily result in an immediate amendment (although sometimes it does), defeat of a government measure, or a quick change in public policy.

Quite simply, they keep coming back to us because they have found that the Senate, and senators, exercise influence, directly and indirectly, at many levels of the policy and legislative process in Ottawa and throughout the country. They believe that this influence is, or with their help can be, constructive. They have found that, usually, they get an informed hearing and a substantive discussion of their case. I cannot ever recall a witness walking away from a meeting with a Senate committee, proclaiming that the experience had been a waste of time, or professing dismay at the extent of partisan infighting and point scoring among committee members. I have often, however, heard such comments from witnesses who attended Commons committees.

Continuity of membership brings greater parliamentary experience and institutional memory to Senate debates and to committee deliberations than is present in the Commons. Some senators have over a period of years in office acquired expertise in certain fields. Generally, there is longer experience and a wider field of occupational and professional backgrounds in the Senate. This gives them a greater familiarity with the issues they confront. Free of the constant preoccupation with re-election, they can and do devote more time to this work. All these benefits derive from the appointment of senators, and most of them would be unlikely to survive the transition to an elected Senate.

During the year 2000, there were two parliamentary debates of historic constitutional importance in which, observers almost unanimously agree, the Senate's contribution far eclipsed that of the Commons in quality and usefulness. The land claims and self-government agreement reached by the federal and British Columbia governments with the Nisga'a people was given treaty status and entrenched in the Constitution when Bill C–9 was passed. Bill C–20 sought to define the circumstances under which the federal government would negotiate the secession of Quebec, or of any province, in the event of a provincial referendum on that subject.

The Senate divided, although not strictly along party lines, on both Bills, and debate was intense and prolonged, in both the Chamber and in committee. One of the factors that made the debates of high interest and importance was the participation of a large number of senators who were intimately familiar, from a perspective of more than twenty years' direct experience, with the issues involved. Several of our six aboriginal senators had been leaders, either outside or inside Parliament, in the successful campaign to entrench aboriginal rights, including treaty rights, in the *Constitution Act, 1982*. Other colleagues had been prominent in the "patriation" debates that culminated in the *Constitution Act, 1982*. Still others had participated as federal ministers, provincial premiers, members of Legislative Assemblies, or advisors to federal and provincial governments in constitutional discussions from John Robarts's Confederation of Tomorrow Conference of 1967, through the Victoria conference of 1971, the federal-provincial negotiations of the later 1970s and 80s and the Meech Lake and Charlottetown Accords of more recent times. The two most senior bureaucrats advising the Trudeau government at the time of the *Constitution Act, 1982* were by the time of the 2000 debates, members of the Senate. The debates, which were quite simply the best informed and most thorough that could possibly be imagined, could not have occurred anywhere but in the Senate.

Faced with the evidence, nay-sayers reply that, well, of course there are some good people in the Senate, doing some good work. However, they are exceptions to the generality, which is one of dozing time-servers. Absenteeism, indolence, conflict of interest, they say, are the norm in the Senate. And of course they always have an example or two ready to be produced to illustrate the charge. The fact is, the Senate is not a perfect institution, nor are senators infallible people. There are delinquencies: some of them inexcusable, but these are no more general in the Senate than they are in the Commons or in the parliamentary press gallery. The abolitionists who make their case on the basis of the Senate's performance rather than on principle have a very poor case.

Abolition of the Senate would increase the already excessive control of our governmental institutions by the Cabinet and bureaucracy. The dominance of central Canada would be even more pronounced in a unicameral Parliament. And the mostly positive contribution of the Senate to legislation and policy would be lost. Abolition, however, would do less damage to Canadian federalism, and to our parliamentary democracy, than some of the current proposals for a "reformed" Senate. The so-called "Triple-E" Senate (equal, elected, effective) is a prime example of what I mean. The "Triple-E" Senate is in every important respect the identical twin of the United States Senate. Its Canadian advocates ignore the fundamental differences between the Canadian and United States parliamentary systems and between our respective federal systems. The executive head of the United States Government, the President, is elected apart from members of the Congress. His Cabinet is chosen from the population at large, not from the elected representatives in the Senate and House of Representatives. He and his Cabinet do not need to have the confidence of the Congress in order to keep governing.

A Canadian "Triple-E" Senate operating on the United States federal principle and the United States Congressional principle would easily paralyze our system of parliamentary government, which may well be the intention of some of its advocates. In Canada, there can be only one "confidence" chamber, the House of Commons. How could this be maintained with a Second Chamber democratically elected and with powers equal to that of the Commons? It could not be. The "Triple-E" Senate would be a fundamental challenge to the basic principles of responsible government. The House of Commons would be permanently and significantly weakened.

Equal representation in the Senate from each state is said by some of its proponents to be inherent in the federal principle. It is, but of United States federalism. In that country, the state governments have far less constitutional power than Canadian provinces, and greater need to be represented qua states in the national legislature.

If the proponents of the "Triple-E" Senate want to make a coherent case, they should advocate that the entire United States Congressional system be transplanted here, not just one of its components. An argument might be made that a country with our regional and cultural diversity would be better served by the more flexible United States system than by our model where party solidarity and discipline are needed to maintain a viable government and a credible alternative government. So far, however, no one has made this principled case. Instead, people want to import the United States Senate without any of the checks and balances – fixed terms, the presidential veto, etc. – and insert it holus-bolus into the Westminster system of responsible government.

Some would have us stick with an appointive or, at most, indirectly elected chamber, the appointing or electing to be done by the provincial governments and/or legislatures. Senators would in effect be delegates of provincial governments at the centre of the national Parliament. The model most often referred to is the German *Bundesrat*, members of which are appointed by and responsible to the different *länd* governments.

This system makes sense in Germany. The constitutional role of the states, or *länder*, is not really comparable to that of a Canadian province. To submit all federal legislation to an effective provincial veto would transform our federal parliament into a permanent federal-provincial conference and undermine the foundations of responsible government.

The power that would be exercised by this "reformed" Senate, whether elected or appointed, would have to come from somewhere, and the immediate loser would perforce be the House of Commons. This seems not to have occurred to some members of the Commons who continue to advocate a second chamber that would soon overtake their own, already weakened House in terms of real power. Senators, elected at large in their respective provinces, would be quick to claim greater political authority and legitimacy than their Commons counterparts who had been elected from smaller constituencies. Elected models with the powers of the German or Australian upper houses would draw their influence at the expense of the provincial governments and legislatures. This point was readily apparent to Alberta Premier Peter Lougheed, who in 1978 dismissed a proposed "House of the Provinces" put forward by the federal Progressive Conservative caucus.

Underlying much of the agitation for a radically different Senate has been the perceived need for stronger regional representation at the centre. Support for this idea has been strongest in western Canada, which has a historic, and to a considerable extent justified, sense of grievance against the eastern-dominated federal government and Parliament and against eastern-dominated economic and financial institutions. The Liberal Government's National Energy Program in the early 1980s and the Conservative Government's decision in 1986 to award the CF-18 aircraft maintenance contract to a Montreal firm rather than to a Winnipeg contractor were among the flash points that ignited and reignited western alienation and propelled the drive for a new Senate. Compounding the sense of injustice was and is the fact that western Canadian provinces are grossly underrepresented in the present Senate.

When the parliamentary institutions of the new Confederation were being debated, much emphasis was placed on providing a forum where the smaller regions would be sure of a hearing on an equal basis. This was one of the important roles the proposed Senate would play. Equal regional representation would balance the representation-by-population principle in the elected House of Commons. It has not really worked out that way for several reasons.

First, regional power in Ottawa was assumed and exercised, almost from the beginning, by so-called regional "barons," elected to the House of Commons, appointed to the Cabinet, or occupying prominent posts in opposition parties. The names of Cartier, Lapointe, and Marchand from Quebec; Gardiner, Hamilton, Mazankowski, and Axworthy from the prairies; Sinclair, Laing, Fulton, and Green from British Columbia; Pickersgill, Jamieson, Nowlan, Crosbie, Leblanc, and MacEachen from Atlantic Canada come to mind. These members of the House of Commons were prominent political figures in their regions. In the Commons, they were leading spokesmen when in opposition and senior ministers holding important portfolios when in government. Compared to these big hitters, senators from those regions have been relatively insignificant in terms of real power and influence at the centre.

Second, the legislative powers assigned to the provinces, which may have seemed in 1867 to be of local rather than national significance, took on critical importance as society evolved and with it the role of the state. Their responsibility for education and health, for economic infrastructure such as roads and electrical power, and for industrial development gave provincial governments great importance in the lives of citizens. Over the years their taxing and spending, cumulatively, and in the case of the bigger provinces, singly, gave them fiscal and economic clout rivalling that of Ottawa. The notion of watertight, exclusive jurisdictions was overtaken by the complexities of modern life, and in many fields of activity both orders of government became players. This interdependence created "executive federalism," the quiet, continuing process of negotiation and accommodation by which federal and provincial ministers and officials have ordered our affairs for most of the past forty years. Provincial governments, often headed by strong personalities who contended with federal prime ministers on major issues, hardly felt the need for senators to speak for their provinces in Ottawa.

Senators are members of caucus and in a few cases of Cabinet. Once the policy is settled in those bodies, the tradition of party solidarity and the need for it in order to ensure stable government in the Westminster system usually take precedence over other considerations. During my time in the Senate, there have been two crucial and conspicuous occasions when regional concerns might have moved senators to bolt the party line. One was the 1981 resolution to patriate the Constitution with an amending formula and a charter of rights. Both government and opposition in the Quebec legislature opposed this. Of fifteen Liberal senators from Quebec, only two voted against the resolution, notwithstanding serious misgivings that I know were held by some others. The same was true of the contentious National Energy Program, which went through the Senate with little or no protest, and certainly no dissenting votes, from Alberta or Saskatchewan Liberal senators.

It needs to be said that "Triple-E" advocates, who believe that elected senators from their regions would be impervious to the call of party loyalty and could be counted on to support the perceived regional perspective instead, are not thinking realistically. "Triple-E" senators, like most parliamentarians, would have party affiliations. It also needs to be pointed out that in the examples cited above, a straight regional vote in the Senate would have had almost no chance of defeating the National Energy Program. Politicians and most of the people in the energy-consuming provinces supported it. As for the patriation resolution, I believe it would have sailed through on a vote by regions. After all, the governments of nine provinces had signed on. Decisions such as the CF-18 maintenance contract are made by executive fiat, and there is no opportunity for any parliamentary body to overturn them. No institutional reform can prevent governments from sometimes making decisions that are inimical to the interests of one or other of our regions. The people of those regions almost always punish the government severely at the first opportunity; nor do they forgive and forget quickly. Federal elections of the past twenty years provide dramatic evidence of this.

None of this is to say that the Senate has become irrelevant to the defence of regional interests at the centre. General elections produce some unbalanced and unfortunate results. The continuity and, in recent years, better balance of party and regional representation in the Senate makes it possible to compensate for these unpredictable outcomes.

The most obvious, and lately most usual, use of the Senate is as a source of Cabinet ministers from provinces or regions where a government's Commons representation has been eliminated or drastically reduced at an election. Thus, three of the four elections won by Mr Trudeau brought almost no Liberal members of the House of Commons from the west to

Ottawa and the Prime Minister brought senators from that region – at one point, four of them – into his Cabinet. Likewise, Mr Clark in 1979 appointed three cabinet ministers from the Senate in order to make up for the lack of francophones in his Commons caucus. After the 1997 election Mr Chrétien went to the Senate for Cabinet representation from Nova Scotia, where no Liberal members of the House of Commons had been elected. Waiting for, and trying to hasten, the restoration of the party's political fortunes in regions where it has been shut out electorally, senators provide representation and a continuing regional political connection with the national parliamentary caucus.

The Senate's ability to act as a check on the government has on occasion taken on a significant regional dimension. Following the 1993 election, Liberal members of the House of Commons supporting the Chrétien Government occupied all but one of the thirty-two seats in the Atlantic region. For the next four years, Conservative senators from that region provided almost the only parliamentary debate and serious questioning of government policies affecting Atlantic Canadians. Tory senators from Quebec and Liberal senators from the west often played the same role when their parties were in opposition.

It goes without saying that the Constitution presents an important barrier to significant reform of the Senate. Some would-be reformers have therefore hatched ingenious proposals to make radical changes without the bother of going through the constitutional amending process and obtaining the consent of Parliament and at least seven provinces representing 50 percent of the population. Most such proposals involve the creative use, or misuse, of the Prime minister's prerogative to nominate senators.

It is suggested, for example, that the Prime Minister could decide to appoint only candidates who had been elected in Senate "elections" in the province. Proponents of this formula justify it by pointing out that the United States Senate began as a body of individuals appointed by the states. It wasn't until the early 1900s, led by Oregon, that states began electing their senators. Soon all of the others followed suit. If the Prime Minister started filling Senate vacancies from Alberta with candidates who had won an election in that province, other provinces might imitate them and in due course we could have an entirely elected senate. So the reasoning goes.

There are obvious and valid objections to this scheme. There is no provision for successful candidates to present themselves for re-election, ever, and no way to guarantee that any informal provision, for example a letter of resignation, signed by the successful candidate and dated four or six years ahead, could be legally binding. Until the constitution is changed, the elected senators would have the constitutional right to stay until the age of seventy-five. Let us assume, however, that all the senators, once elected, respected a fixed term and were re-elected or replaced every four or six years. This elected senate would have all the nineteenth-century powers of the present Senate, and would, being elected, exercise those powers. The status of the Commons, the "confidence" chamber elected on the more democratic basis of representation-by-population, albeit a representation-by-population somewhat modified as Canadians are wont to do, would soon be eclipsed. We would then have an extremely powerful elected second chamber, but with the same underrepresentation of western Canada that exists today. You need a constitutional amendment to right that imbalance.

The elected senators would have no reason to exercise the restraint that has guided the present Senate in the exercise of our legislative veto and other powers. The point here is that it would be quite risky to proceed to an elected senate without at the same time negotiating at least its powers in relation to those of the Commons, and its regional distribution of seats. To the extent that Senate elections conducted under provincial aegis produce a Senate that is more "provincial" in the source of its power, the reform should also not be consummated without some consideration of the balance of power in the federal-provincial relationship. All these are issues for constitutional negotiations.

This same consideration leads me to reject another proposed "wrinkle" in the exercise of the prime-ministerial prerogative. It is suggested that Senate appointments be made only from lists submitted by provincial governments, or produced by indirect election in their legislatures. The Meech Lake appointments process, in which Prime Minister Mulroney nominated senators from lists submitted by provinces, was a transitional stage intended to expedite a comprehensive reform of the Senate. Provincially chosen senators should not become a permanent part of the federal parliament so long as the Senate has the power of life and death over government legislation.

Other, more fanciful, proposals would have the Prime Minister agree to appoint only from lists submitted by some neutral, non-political nominations body. This would produce a "non-political" senate. Such an idea would be unworkable in the extreme. We would have a Senate composed of 105 legislative Lone Rangers, "loose fish" as Sir John A. Macdonald called them, with everybody voting as an independent on every issue. They would have no loyalty to any political party, no commitment to any political program. Yet they would have tenure to the age of seventy-five, and collectively they would have veto power over all government legislation. A Prime Minister who lent himself to such a process, and a Commons that put up with it, would be out of their minds.

The formation of parliamentary parties as an organizing principle provides the country and Parliament with a government and one or more alternative governments. It enables the work of Parliament to get done. In the case of the Canadian Senate, whose legislative veto power has been unchanged since the nineteenth century, our political loyalties and commitments exercise a moderating influence on any temptation to throw our undoubted constitutional weight around in the parliamentary system. In the ideal world envisioned by advocates of a non-partisan Senate, neither the nominating committee nor the appointees would be accountable to anybody. The Prime Minister of Canada is responsible to the House of Commons, accountable, as its leader, to a national party, and every four or five years must submit to the judgment of the voters.

I appreciate, and do not contest, the principled objections to the traditional appointments system, based as it is on prime-ministerial patronage. However, none of the alternatives I have mentioned would be an improvement, and some of them would be destabilizing to our parliamentary system, if tried under the present constitutional provisions governing the Senate. Anyway, has the system of prime-ministerial appointments produced such awful results for Parliament and the country?

The frequently heard complaint that the Senate is full of political bagmen and organizers is an exaggeration. No more than a handful of senators have ever been party fundraisers and this is a relatively small part of their public activity. They are recruited as fundraisers because they are successful in business and the professions and are known to have the respect of their peers. For that reason they are always in demand as fundraisers for hospitals, universities, and all the charitable causes. This background makes them obvious candidates for the present Senate. Most of them have done valuable work in the Senate's legislative and policy process. Many of the critics, however, never look behind the unfair and inaccurate clichés they are so fond of repeating.

Is it an abuse of the appointments prerogative when a Prime Minister names a retired Commons colleague to the Senate? Or is it an opportunity for the former members of the House of Commons to continue to be useful in public affairs and for the country to have the advantage of that experience? The charge that these people go to sleep or treat the office as a sinecure is also untrue. Former Liberal ministers such as George McIlraith, Maurice Lamontagne, Romeo Leblanc, and Allan MacEachen and former Tory members of the House of Commons such as Jacques Flynn, Orville Phillips, Jack Marshall, James Balfour, and Heath Macquarrie distinguished themselves in the Senate, as any fair reading of the record would demonstrate. The same is true in most cases of the former provincial premiers who have served in the Senate (four from Nova Scotia in my time, two from New Brunswick, one from Prince Edward Island, one from Manitoba, and one from Alberta) and a host of former provincial Cabinet ministers and opposition leaders from every province.

In addition to those who had made their names in federal or provincial politics before becoming senators, prime ministers have also appointed former senior bureaucrats in federal and provincial governments (the names of six former deputy ministers now serving actively in the Senate come quickly to mind) and successful people from business, the professions, universities and the voluntary sector.

The patronage prerogative lets the Prime Minister compensate somewhat for imbalances of gender and race in the elected House. Recent prime ministers have seized the opportunity. In nine years, Mr Mulroney appointed more women than all his predecessors combined. Mr Chrétien topped that record in less than six years. Prime Minister Diefenbaker appointed the first aboriginal person to the Senate. There are now six aboriginals vigorously participating in the work of the Senate and its committees.

Since the introduction of the retirement age at seventy-five, a few notorious absentees have given the Senate an extremely bad press. I doubt that the problem is more prevalent in our Chamber than in other legislatures. That being said, I believe there is a higher obligation on us. None of us is in the Senate by right, nor have we been chosen by the electors. It is an extraordinary privilege that is granted to us, to be full participants in the national legislative process and to have tenure. Therefore, we owe a greater duty to be conscientious in the performance of our duty.

The attendance rules have been tightened up lately, and the financial penalties for non-attendance have been increased. However, we owe it to Parliament and the country to close off the avenues of potential abuse that still exist. The right to invoke "public business" as an excuse for absence needs to be limited and better defined than it is. When prolonged illness keeps a senator from attending, an insurance plan should be in place to protect them, similar to those available in the private sector. And there is a constitutional provision regarding Senate attendance that can be changed by the two Houses of Parliament, without involving provincial consent. Section 31 (1) of the *Constitution Act, 1867* stipulates that the place of a senator shall become vacant if for two consecutive sessions of Parliament he fails to attend. This provision was enacted at a time when a parliamentary session could not be expected to last more than a few months. In recent times, sessions often go on for two years or more. We could easily amend this section by imposing a lower maximum number of absences, perhaps more than one-third of sittings in two consecutive calendar years, that would result in the forced retirement of a senator.

Critics are prone, far too easily so, to making public accusations of malfeasance and corruption regarding the Senate. When applied to the institution as a whole these are grossly unjust. The incidence of such scandal is no greater than in any other political body. In two decades in the Senate, I am aware of charges being laid against five senators. Two were acquitted, one died before the trial could proceed, and two were convicted.

Canada's criminal law is clear enough about the more serious offences that can be attributed to a public official, whether elected or appointed. I refer here to things such as bribery, fraud, influence peddling, and breach of trust. The Rules of the Senate state clearly that a senator may not vote on any question in which he or she may have a pecuniary interest not available to the general public. Criticism, usually undocumented, is sometimes heard to the effect that senators quietly abuse their positions by mixing private interest with their public responsibilities. It is suggested that such abuse, while it may not directly break the criminal law or the Senate rules, is at least unethical.

As it is impossible to draft rules that could contemplate every conceivable situation, it seems to me that the best way to deal with these matters is for the Senate to establish an ethics committee. The operating principle behind the creation of such a committee should be that it is far from sufficient for senators to stay within the four corners of the criminal law and the Senate Rules. A higher standard of conduct is required, which it is not necessary to codify since it should be apparent to the informed conscience of a reasonable person. The ethics committee would be authorized, on its own initiative or on receipt of a complaint, to investigate and call a colleague to account. The committee could expose and censure the conduct of a colleague, or submit a resolution of censure to the Senate. It might even have authority to advise a colleague formally on whether a particular affiliation or activity outside the Senate would place the senator in a potentially compromising position or bring Parliament into disrepute.

Tightening our attendance rules, creating an ethics committee and other such improvements will not assuage those who hold a principled objection to the Senate as presently constituted. Nor will the useful contribution of the Senate to so many aspects of Canada's governance. For the principled objector, the Senate's definitive, existential flaw, that it is a non-elected legislative chamber, nullifies its virtues – as a check on Cabinet and its Commons majority, a solid contributor to the legislative process, a place of policy study and ideas, a unique source of continuity, institutional memory, stability, regional perspectives, and gender and racial balance.

The constitutional hurdles to abolition or major change are real, and they are significant. Since the expiry of the Meech Lake Accord and with it the agreement – in 1990 – to conduct a new round of negotiations aimed exclusively at Senate reform, the issue is one of a multitude of bargaining chips in any constitutional discussion. The idea of a single-item agenda was swept away with the Meech Lake Accord, various interests insisting that the issue of Quebec's political adherence to the 1982 Constitution could not be resolved unless and until other matters – aboriginal rights, Senate reform, improvements to the Charter – had also been settled. This is the phenomenon that Brian Mulroney described in terms of "paralyzing linkages" and warned the provincial premiers about in 1986 *before* he agreed to embark on the Meech Lake, or Quebec, round.

So, the questions a provincial advocate of Senate reform must answer
are: "How badly do you want it?" and "What constitutional concessions are
you willing to make, in order to pay for it?" Just such questions confronted Premiers in the 1992 process that led to the Charlottetown Accord.
Something approaching the "Triple-E" Senate was agreed upon but as part
of a comprehensive agreement. In the event, the tradeoffs, including a
guarantee to Quebec of 25 percent of Commons seats in perpetuity and
recognition of an "inherent" aboriginal right to self-government proved to
be more than the political traffic could bear, and the Accord was rejected
in a referendum by voters in eight of the ten provinces and by the northern territories.

In a word, it looks as if the principled objectors will have to live with the
present, unelected Senate for a while yet. The only constitutional amendment that might conceivably stand a ghost of a chance is one that would
redress the underrepresentation of the western provinces in the Chamber. The injustice is so flagrant that perhaps it is not too much to hope
that other regions and the federal government would co-operate to correct it, to the point of not exacting a constitutional price of their own in
return.

Meanwhile, it is unfortunate for Canada's parliamentary democracy that
one of the two Houses of Parliament is almost unknown in any substantive
way by the Canadian people. And that the Canadian people, who are entitled to more informed and thorough reporting on their parliamentary
institutions, are so badly served by media comment that serves mainly to
misinform and to perpetuate hackneyed myths about the place.

The Senate is an integral part of our national political system. It is not
going to disappear or radically change any time soon. There is no shortage
of useful work to be undertaken. For example, I believe the Senate should
consider "specializing" in a number of areas of national importance that
need more serious and continued attention than they are now getting.
Such national institutions as the federal public service, the armed forces
and Royal Canadian Mounted Police, the legal and judicial system, public
broadcasting, and the National Capital Region need far more fundamental examination and debate than Parliament gives them now. The Senate
should "adopt" these institutions as its areas of continuing study. The focus
should not be on day-to-day operations and policy but on mandate, recruitment, contribution to national life, morale, ethical standards, and forward
planning. The Senate would provide information and assessments for the
House of Commons and for public debate. Members of the House of
Commons would decide whether and how to act on our findings. The institutional memory and continuity of the Senate would be used to good
advantage in this way.

Television coverage of our committees is now permitted, indeed
encouraged. We should open the Senate chamber itself to the television
cameras and do more of our work in Committee of the Whole. I know that

television coverage has not enhanced the reputation of the Commons, in fact the contrary is true. The inevitable comparisons could only be to the Senate's advantage.

NOTE

1 As other chapters in this book show.

CHAPTER SIX

The Canadian Senate in Modern Times

C.E.S. Franks

THE CANADIAN SENATE IN MODERN TIMES: INTRODUCTION

More has been written about the Canadian Senate than about any other major institution of Canadian parliamentary government. At the same time the Senate is the least studied institution, because most academics and journalists have been satisfied with the accepted image of the Senate as a dusty, obscure Arcadia filled with aged and retired political warhorses – once characterized by former Prime Minister Mulroney as "has-beens and never-weres" – whose main concern, apart from enjoying a good, comfortable life, is to preserve private wealth and the interests of big business, the "lobby from within."[1] Most of what is written about the Senate does not look at what it does but at how it might be reformed, and in particular reformed to give it a more powerful role in federal-provincial relations.[2]

Notions about the Senate embody a confusion of many contradictions; though widely criticized for being ineffective and lackadaisical, its committees and committee investigations are often better than those of the Commons; though senators are often attacked as being political hacks who owe their appointments and allegiance to party and Prime Minister, on average its members are more experienced and by and large have higher qualifications than those of the Commons; though senators are appointed on the basis of province and region, regional and provincial representation are among the least well-performed of its functions; though the public thinks Senate appointments are rich sinecures, its members (like those of the Commons) are actually paid less than, for example, judges, senior civil servants, and many school principals; though accused of being unrepresentative, it has a higher proportion of women in it than does the Commons, and the first Aboriginal Canadian in Parliament was an appointed senator. Regardless of the useful work it does, and its sometimes crucial role in politics, the Senate's public image and approval rating remain, to say the least, low.

As a result of these contradictions and problems, Canada has in effect wound up with three quite different Senates. The first is the actual Senate as it exists as a living institution, composed of real people doing real things. The second is the imaginary Senate as it is portrayed in the press and perceived by the public – a comfortable rest home filled with aging political warhorses put out to pasture and bloated plutocrats defending the interests of money and business. The third Senate is found in the many hypothetical senates conceived by would-be reformers, the most well-known of which at present is the "Triple-ᴇ Senate" – elected, equal, and effective. The real Senate, which is the least well-known of all, will be the focus of this paper.

This paper examines the activities of the Senate in recent years, with a close look at the 1984–2001 period, during which the majority in the Senate oscillated between the government and the opposition. In this period, the Senate was politically more active, and in certain instances more partisan, than earlier studies suggest would have been likely. Having looked at this recent history, the paper then examines two aspects of the Senate: first, its role in the legislative process, especially in relation to that of the House of Commons and, second, the investigative role of its committees. This section explores the too-often ignored real Senate and its work. Finally, the Senate's role in modern parliamentary government in Canada is assessed.

This examination concludes that the Senate performs very well and makes an important contribution to the Canadian parliamentary system. Unfortunately, the good work of the Senate is largely ignored as both the media and critics focus on accusations of partisanship and scandal. This weakness limits the ability of the Senate to perform its functions more effectively, as its work can too easily be dismissed by opponents as illegitimate partisan activity.

THE EARLY MODERN SENATE, 1957 TO 1984

The modern Senate emerged by gradual degrees, and the selection of a specific date of origin is thus an unavoidably arbitrary judgment. It is clear, however, that many of its characteristic patterns of activity date from the end of the lengthy period of Liberal government that continued from the McKenzie King era through the Second World War and beyond. When Progressive Conservative Prime Minister John Diefenbaker took office in 1957 after defeating the Liberals, who had held power without interruption since 1935, seventy-five of the incumbent senators supported the Liberal Party and only seven the Progressive Conservatives.

In the public proceedings of the Senate, this Liberal majority did not consider itself to be or act as an opposition to the new Conservative Government. After four years of peaceful coexistence, however, the Liberal dominated Senate did oppose the Diefenbaker Government on two important issues. In May 1961, after months of private and public wrangling, the governor of the Bank of Canada, James E. Coyne, was asked to resign by the Prime Minister. Coyne favoured tight money and disagreed with the government's fiscal policy, a key part of its economic strategy. When Coyne refused this request to resign, the government introduced a bill into the Commons declaring the Office of governor of the Bank of Canada vacant.[3] This bill was pushed through the Commons by Diefenbaker's huge Conservative majority, with the government refusing to allow Coyne to testify before a parliamentary committee.

When the bill reached the Senate, the Liberal majority claimed the issue was a matter of rights and of the integrity and reputation of one individual. reading, the Senate, on a strictly partisan vote, passed the bill on to its Banking and Commerce Committee, where Coyne appeared as the sole witness through seven sittings lasting a total of thirteen and a half hours. The Committee rejected the bill, whereupon Coyne, in accord with a promise he had made in his testimony, promptly resigned. The bill at this point had lost its purpose and was dropped. In the Coyne affair, the Senate gave a distinguished public servant his day in court, something the government had not allowed the Commons to do.

In terms of broad questions of governance rather than individual rights, it was not tenable to have the governor of the Bank of Canada publicly disagreeing with the government and thwarting its economic policies. Even many Liberal senators would have agreed on this. However, the press accepted the line taken by the Liberal senators – that the Coyne Affair was a matter of individual rights and due process, not of who was ultimately responsible for economic policies and governing the country. The Senate succeeded in portraying this Coyne affair as a nonpartisan issue of rights and the Diefenbaker Government was roundly criticized for this "bill of attainder" directed at one official. Soon after the Liberals had been returned to power in the 1963 election, Parliament passed a Government bill that required the governor of the Bank of Canada to obey formal instructions from the government of the day. The Liberal Government made certain that the Coyne affair could not be repeated.

The other, and less noteworthy, instance of the Diefenbaker Government's legislation being rejected by the Senate also occurred in 1961, when Liberal senators insisted on amendments to Commons legislation amending the Customs Act to give the government more discretionary powers over levying tariffs. The government refused to accept the amendments, and the bill was allowed to die.

From 1963 to 1984 the actual day-to-day operations of the Senate did not impinge much on public awareness. However, discussions of Senate reform formed a large part of ongoing constitutional discussions, and, in

1965, legislation was passed which established a mandatory retirement age of seventy-five for senators. Most importantly, however, the basis for the Senate's reputation for committee investigations began to emerge during this period. Several Senate committees conducted useful investigations, including ones into concentration in the media (Davey) and aging in Canada (MacLean). Senator Davey commented about his work on the Senate committee on the media, saying that:

I would never work longer or harder in my life than I did for the next two years. Fifteen hours a day was the norm. Incidentally, special Senate studies like this are a great bargain for Canadians. In far less time and for far less money, our study did a better job than could possibly be done by any royal Commission.[4]

These investigations typically focused on subjects not being addressed by the House of Commons, enabling senators to raise issues that would not otherwise be considered by Parliament. This activity has greatly expanded and is now one of the major components of the Senate's work. In addition to this, to avoid its chronic problem of being deluged with bills passed by the House of Commons towards the end of a session, the Senate began the practice of pre-studying bills by referring their subject matter to Senate committees while the actual bills were still under consideration in the Lower Chamber. This evened out some of the workload of the Senate and allowed its committees to examine bills without undue time pressures. This practice of pre-study was especially helpful in handling the extremely complex tax legislation of 1971. Previously, senators "had almost always dutifully swallowed their pride and passed legislation no matter how late it was received, while complaining of the indignity of being taken for granted."[5]

The work of the Upper House went largely unnoticed throughout this period as there were no high-profile conflicts with the government. This was the beginning of a recurring pattern in which the useful work of the Senate has been ignored by the media.

Up until 1984, the Senate continued in its traditional role as the secondary chamber in a parliamentary democracy. It revised legislation, aided by the practice of pre-study. The Trudeau Government was forced to withdraw several bills when amendments proposed by the Senate and its committees proved to be highly contentious.[6] The Senate continued its function as a check on the House of Commons – more accurately on the Cabinet and Prime Minister who dominate and control Commons proceedings – by revising, questioning, holding hearings on, and delaying legislation. Its committees were more useful than ever before and normally conducted higher-quality investigations than committees of the Commons. But the formidable legislative and investigative powers of the Senate were still there, and the institution was thrust back into public consciousness in a series of high-profile, and at times overtly partisan, conflicts following the election of Prime Minister Mulroney's government in 1984.

THE SENATE AS OPPOSITION:
THE MULRONEY YEARS

Nothing from the Diefenbaker period, neither the written record, the analyses of scholars, nor the pontifications of journalists, could have prepared the incoming Progressive Conservative Government of Prime Minister Mulroney for its battles with the Liberal-dominated Senate. By the time of the general election of 4 September 1984, seventy-three senators identified themselves as Liberal, twenty-five as Conservative, and four as independent. But the new House of Commons reflected the public's strong rejection of the previous Liberal Government: Prime Minister Mulroney's Progressive Conservatives held 211 seats, the largest majority a Canadian government has ever enjoyed, while the Liberals were reduced to forty, with the New Democratic Party at thirty, and one identified as "other."

Though the conjunction of a Senate dominated by one party and a Commons dominated by another had occurred several times before in Canadian history, this time there was a crucial difference. John Turner, Leader of the Opposition in the Commons, made Allan MacEachen Opposition Leader in the Senate. MacEachen, who had been a very senior Liberal Cabinet minister with a reputation as a cunning political tactician, lost neither his cunning nor his ardent partisanship upon his elevation to the Senate and to his new role. On the other side of the equation, Mulroney was equally partisan and, backed by his huge majority, was unwilling to view Senate arguments as anything but a politically motivated attempt to obstruct his legislation. This volatile combination generated a series of unusually partisan confrontations between the two Houses the like of which had never been seen before. Mulroney's frequent vitriolic denunciations of the Upper House were taken up by the media, helping to create the perception of the illegitimate Senate.

The Borrowing and Drug Patent Bills

MacEachen dropped the practice of pre-study, giving the Senate both more prominence and stronger tools for resistance to the Commons. In MacEachen's opinion, the Senate was a legislative body, not an advisory one, and should act consecutively with the Commons, not in conjunction with it. To replace pre-study, MacEachen proposed reviving the use of joint conferences between representatives of the two chambers to resolve disputes. The Mulroney Government rejected this proposal, presumably because they did not wish to encourage the exercise of independent Senate power. This set the stage for serious, prolonged, and continuing disputes between the two chambers.

The first skirmish occurred in January 1985, when the Upper Chamber delayed passage of Bill C–11, a $19.3 billion borrowing bill that had been passed under special order by the House of Commons. $12 billion of that sum were for the 1985–86 fiscal year, and Liberal senators objected to this "because the government had failed to tell how the money would be spent. It was like a request for a post-dated blank cheque!"[7] Bill C–11 was passed by the Senate after the tabling of the 1985–86 estimates and was given royal assent on 27 February 1985, but not before the press had strongly criticized the Senate's actions.[8] An argument can be made that the Senate had good reasons for refusing to approve funds for which the government had not presented spending plans[9] but, in a pattern that has consistently repeated itself, the justification for Senate opposition (whether valid or otherwise) was given less weight in the media than the argument that the government's finances were properly the business of the Commons, and the Senate's action was portrayed as mischievous partisan meddling. The real question, however, was why the House of Commons had not raised the "blank cheque" issue itself. Both at this time and later, many Liberal senators were frustrated with what they saw as a lack of critical zeal in the Liberal opposition in the Commons, motivating many of their attacks on government legislation.

Prime Minister Mulroney reacted strongly. On 28 February 1985 he let it be known that the government was shaping legislation intended to curb some of the powers of the Senate. Discussions were already underway with the provinces for a constitutional amendment that would remove the Senate's right to veto money bills. Mulroney said that he had decided to act on Senate reform because a "bunch of Liberal rejects" in the non-elected Senate delayed passage of the borrowing bill for a month after it had been passed by the House of Commons. The government simply dismissed the argument made by the Senate as partisan manoeuvring and claimed that it had cost the taxpayers many additional millions because of its obstruction. The government introduced its constitutional resolution to amend the Senate's powers into the Commons in May. They were debated briefly and then allowed to die. Under this proposal, the Senate would have been able to delay passage of money bills for only thirty days and the passage of other legislation for a maximum of forty-five days. The governments of Manitoba and Quebec refused to support Mulroney's proposal; Manitoba because it wanted the Senate abolished, Quebec because it did not recognize the 1982 Constitution. Senate reform did not die in the minds of the government however and was a recurring theme during the Mulroney years.

In November 1986, Consumer Affairs Minister Harvie Andre introduced legislation in the Commons, Bill C–22, to amend the Drug Patent

Act. The amendments were to give the patent holders of brand-name drugs ten years of freedom from competition for most of the products they brought to market. The Patent Act, a policy of the previous Liberal government, had encouraged competition by producers of generic or no-name drugs, which could make inexpensive copies of brand-name drugs upon payment of nominal fees to the patent holders. Critics argued that, because the prices of patent drugs would rise, the bill would be more damaging to consumers than the government was prepared to admit. The Minister on the other hand argued that benefits would include increased spending on research in Canada by the drug companies. The drug companies lobbied universities, doctors, provincial governments, and, of course, the various actors in the federal government, often in a lavish manner new to Canada.[10]

The Commons debated Bill C–22 for nearly ninety hours, and a Commons committee heard hundreds of witnesses in twenty-two separate sessions. When the bill came before it, the Senate established a committee of five Liberal and three Conservative senators to hold hearings on it. After three months of intensive work, this committee proposed significant amendments to the legislation. In its deliberations, the Senate committee divided along party lines, with Conservative senators defending the government, and Liberals supporting the Senate's proposed amendments.

The government-controlled Commons rejected most of the amendments, and the bill was returned to the Upper Chamber, where Senate Government Leader Lowell Murray declared "the moment of truth has arrived for the Senate. It is up to the Senate now to decide whether to exercise its undoubted constitutional right, which has been exercised rarely, if ever, in modern times, to insist on its amendments, or whether the Senate will bow to the will of the elected House."[11] Conservative senators argued that the Senate had reached the limits of its political legitimacy and that once the Commons had made its voice heard it was time to yield to the will of the Lower House. Liberal senators argued that the reasons given by the Commons for not accepting the Senate's amendments deserved further investigation. They were encouraged by public demonstrations and protests against the bill, by the lobbying efforts of the generic drug industry, and by provincial departments of health.

In the wake of unproductive attempts to seek a compromise with the Hon. Harvie Andre, senators divided along party lines in a series of highly charged debates, and the bill bounced back and forth between the two Houses until 19 November 1987. At this time, Liberal senators followed the advice of John Turner that the will of the Commons must prevail "at the end of the day" and let the Conservative minority pass the bill in the Senate by a vote of twenty-seven to three, with thirty-two Liberals abstaining.[12]

The Drug Patent Bill, though the most important of the Senate's acts of opposition to the decisions of the Lower House, was far from the only one during this period. In 1988, a copyright bill and two controversial immigration bills were disputed on quite reasonable grounds by the Senate, after extensive testimony by witnesses before Senate committees indicated that the copyright bill's provisions for exhibition rights remained problematic and controversial, and many provisions of the immigration bills were deemed to be in violation of both the Charter of Rights and Freedoms and Canada's international commitments to human rights and refugee protection. After a prolonged struggle, the Senate dropped its demands for amendments to the copyright bill, and the immigration bills were passed after the government acceded to the Senate amendments. The Progressive Conservative Government, with its huge majority, could, and did, force legislation through the Commons by using closure and timetabling instruments,[13] but the Liberal-dominated Senate had become a much more difficult and contrary obstacle. Prime Minster Mulroney continued persistent but unsuccessful efforts to reach agreement with the provinces on Senate reform.

The Senate and Free Trade

The Senate achieved its greatest importance in history in 1988, when it refused to pass legislation for a free trade deal with the United States. Here the Senate was replicating its actions in 1913, when it had refused to approve the controversial naval aid bill until the government had won support in a general election.[14] This time Liberal Opposition Leader John Turner reversed the position he had taken on the drug patent bill and asked the Senate to stall the free trade bill until Canadians could vote on the issue. "Call an election and let the people decide,"[15] Turner told the Prime Minister as the Commons passed the legislation under strict closure and timetabling. The government at the time was in the fourth year of its mandate, and an election was drawing near. For his part, Prime Minister Mulroney brushed aside calls for an immediate election and accused the Senate of "hijacking the fundamental rights of the House of Commons"[16] by refusing to pass the legislation. He attacked Turner for abandoning his leadership and handing it over to the unelected Senate. But Turner rejected the suggestion that the Senate and not free trade could become the issue in the next election. "I am the issue," Turner told a press conference "I have asked the Senators to do this and I will take the responsibility."[17]

Not all Liberals approved Turner's position or his use of the Senate to force an election. For example, Liberal Senator Van Roggen broke ranks and resigned his chairmanship of the Senate's Foreign Affairs Committee, saying he supported free trade. Editorial coverage of Turner's move was also mixed. Western newspapers were by and large critical, as exemplified by the *Calgary Herald*'s dismissal of the move as demonstrating "total contempt for the parliamentary tradition of government of the people by the elected representatives of the people."[18] In contrast, eastern newspapers were generally laudatory, as exemplified in the *Toronto Star*'s praise of Turner's "risky but bold move ... [which] has not only shown great personal courage, but also the integrity to insist that this fundamental issue be resolved by Canadians."[19]

It is noteworthy that free trade, and not the action of the Senate in refusing to pass government legislation, was the issue in the 1988 general election, which saw the Mulroney Government returned, though with a much-reduced majority. When Parliament reconvened, the Liberals stood by their commitment to allow the free trade legislation through if the country supported it in a general election, and free trade thus became law on 24 December 1988. Randall White accurately describes the mixed reactions to the Senate's role in the free trade issue:

When Brian Mulroney's new Progressive Conservative government came to office, it complained, with at least some justice, of harassment by the continuing Liberal majority in the Senate ... On the other hand, there are Canadians who still believe that the unreformed Senate, with its unelected Liberal majority, did indeed live up to its highest responsibilities as a body of sober second thought in 1988, when it helped precipitate a federal election over the Canada-U.S. Free Trade Agreement.[20]

The GST Battle and Others

A $33 billion supply bill became the first subject of contention between the two houses in 1989. After the 1988 general election, Parliament did not consider supply during the short period it sat in December. Between then and the beginning of a new session in April, the Mulroney government financed expenditures through Governor General's special warrants without the approval of Parliament, a practice that raised serious questions about parliamentary control of finance. Concerns were expressed in the Commons about both the propriety and legitimacy of the government's use of special warrants in these circumstances, but to no avail. The Senate proposed an amendment to the bill approving these expenditures that implied that the Cabinet had acted improperly in its use of special warrants.

Treasury Board President Robert De Cotret expressed alarm: unless the bill was passed by midnight 15 May 1989, the government would have no cash to pay immediate expenses such as RCMP wages, government suppliers, and veteran's pensions. On 17 May, the Senate backed down and passed the supply bill unamended. It immediately received Royal Assent. In 1997, Parliament enacted a private member's bill sponsored by Peter Milliken, member for Kingston and the Islands, which limited the use of special warrants solely to times when Parliament was dissolved for general elections. This eliminated the possible abuse of special warrants that the Senate had criticized in 1989.

1990 was a more contentious year. The problems began in December 1989, when the still Liberal-dominated Senate established a special committee to consider amendments to the Unemployment Insurance Act, Bill C–21. These amendments were designed to curtail expenditures on unemployment insurance through several contentious provisions affecting the eligibility of seasonal workers, training programmes, and shifting financing of the program towards employers and employees. The government had forced the bill through the Commons. Senator MacEachen, not entirely innocently, alerted his colleagues to the possibility that, if senators were properly to complete their examination of the bill, it would take longer than the government hoped. He said he wanted to avoid a situation of crisis or confrontation that might arise if the Commons suspected that the Senate was using delay as an instrument to block, slow, or frustrate the bill. The Senate committee asked for permission to meet during sittings of the Senate because pressure was coming from government members, and it did not want to be accused of delaying the legislation. Prime Minister Mulroney was having none of these professions of good faith and denounced the Liberal majority in the Senate.[21]

The battle over unemployment insurance took many curious twists, including the passage by the Senate of a bill inspired by MacEachen in which money provisions were "red-lettered," an obscure procedure that involved leaving money clause in red ink, and not as part of the provisions actually passed. The Senate special committee reported that it agreed:

... with the great majority of witnesses before it who condemned the changes to the entrance requirement and benefit structure. The motivation behind these changes appears to be not simply to divert funds to new training programs, but to promote what one witness euphemistically described as, the "adhesion" of workers to their jobs. The government would seem to believe that many of the unemployed are in a position of their own making, and that, with proper "incentives," they would find work or remain in their jobs longer. This, of course, fails to recognize that what is needed is jobs, not incentives to find jobs, or training for jobs that simply do not exist.[22]

Regardless of its other merits, this report was a thinly disguised commentary on Mulroney's earlier election promise of "jobs, jobs, jobs." The committee's recommendations were criticized by Conservative senators for containing money provisions, and the government continued this criticism in the Commons. "We're not going to have this unelected coterie of Trudeauites decide what the policy of Canada is to be in 1990" declared John Crosbie, a senior minister in the Mulroney Government.[23] The

Government House Leader in the Commons, Doug Lewis, accused the Senate of harassment.

Unquestionably, ideological differences between senators appointed by the Trudeau Liberal Government and the Mulroney Conservatives underlay much of this battle over unemployment insurance. At the same time, the Mulroney Government was trying to come to terms with a massive deficit in current spending and the burgeoning public debt. The Chrétien Liberal Government, which succeeded it, had to deal with the same problems and was, if anything, harsher in its reductions to spending on social programmes.

Meanwhile, two other important items of business from the Commons were occupying the Senate. In May 1990, legislation requiring women to obtain the consent of a single doctor for abortion and retaining other abortions as crimes within the criminal code, narrowly passed the Commons in one of its rare "free votes" by 140 to 131. This abortion bill was a compromise. After the Supreme Court had declared the then-existing legislation unconstitutional, the government had proposed five choices to the Commons, ranging from virtually free access to abortion at one end to strict limitation and control at the other. In free votes, the Commons had rejected each of the options. Opinions on abortion were too polarized to allow the compromises and coalitions necessary for a majority to form.[24] Ardent anti-abortionists in the Liberal and Conservative ranks, as well as pro-choicers led by the New Democrats, had campaigned vigorously against the government's bill and hoped to form an alliance to scuttle it. But Cabinet ministers solidly supported the legislation and managed to hold the loyalty of enough Conservative backbenchers to push it through the Commons. As it passed from Commons to Senate, lobby groups on both sides of the issue said they would turn their attention to the Upper Chamber.

Even as the Senate was dealing with unemployment insurance and the contentious abortion bill, a third issue, far more central to the government's economic and fiscal policies, had been the major issue facing the Commons. This was the Goods and Services Tax (GST) – a measure designed to replace outdated taxes on manufacturing with a tax of the sort economists like but taxpayers detest, in effect a general sales tax, or tax on consumption. On 10 April 1990, the Conservative Government, after nine months of rancorous debate and committee hearings, forced the GST bill through the Commons. When it went to the Senate, Liberal Senator Sidney Buckwold, chairman of the Senate Banking Committee, said they would probably hold cross-country hearings on it. On 27 June, Parliament adjourned for the summer. Three major bills – the GST, abortion, and unemployment insurance – were left in the Senate with no hope of becoming law before the fall. When Parliament reconvened, the battles recommenced. On 25 September, the Senate Banking Committee recommended that the GST be scrapped, and, despite a

Conservative filibuster, the committee's report was tabled the following day.

Prime Minister Mulroney took drastic and unprecedented action. On 27 September, unfazed by rising public furor against the new tax, he enlarged the Senate by eight members, claiming that the Liberal senators were undermining the principle of responsible government by blocking the GST and other bills. The move raised the total number of senators to 112 and gave the Conservatives a majority that would eventually get the stalled GST and other bills moving.

In stacking the Senate, Mulroney took advantage of a never before used article in the *Constitution Act, 1867*, section 26:

If at any time on the Recommendation of the Governor General the Queen thinks fit to direct that Four or Eight Members be added to the Senate, the Governor General may by Summons to Four or Eight qualified Persons (as the Case may be), representing equally the Four Divisions of Canada, add to the Senate accordingly.

Only once before, in 1873, had a Canadian government attempted to use this provision, and then the British Colonial Secretary, observing that the Senate had not yet defeated Commons business, refused to advise Queen Victoria to approve the additional appointments. This time, Queen Elizabeth granted approval.

Mulroney's decision to "swamp" the Senate drew angry responses from opposition leaders and most of the provinces. British Columbia and Alberta challenged it in the courts. But "it seems clear that the original intent of section 26 was to provide a "deadlock" mechanism in the event of an irreconcilable clash of wills between the two Chambers," a study by the Library of Parliament had observed the previous month, and "the fact that no such clash occurred in the first 120 years after Confederation invalidates neither the purpose nor the use of section 26 in the appropriate circumstances."[25] This time, there was a serious deadlock between the two Houses, and the Mulroney Government's claim that these were "appropriate circumstances" was upheld by the courts. The Conservatives now, for the first time since they had come into power, enjoyed the support of a majority in the Senate.

The battle over the GST had not reached its conclusion, however. Liberal senators, taking advantage of procedural rules much less stringent than those in the Commons, began a filibuster. At times during the ensuing days, their efforts at delay degenerated into chaos and worse, including shouted obscenities, the ringing of cowbells, the blowing of kazoos, and bitter personal confrontations, with a Liberal senator calling the Speaker a Nazi (the Speaker actually had a distinguished record in the Second World War, unlike the name-calling senator).[26] Liberal senators were indulging in obstruction pure and simple, and it was not obstruction over matters of legislative drafting but over the fundamental principles of legislation that had been passed by the House of Commons. Neither side came out well from this battle. The so-called chamber of sober second thought did not display dignity, did not appear sober, and was not given to much thought of any kind, first or second. On the other hand, the Mulroney Government had proved itself inept at handling Parliament and unable to mobilize the consent of the electorate.

There were renewed calls for Senate reform in the press. An angry Prime Minister Mulroney accused the Liberal senators of "legislative terrorism."[27] By 24 October, the Liberal Party had sunk below the New Democrats, the perennial third party, in the polls, and Liberal Leader Jean Chrétien admitted that the hijinks by Liberal senators in fighting the GST may have contributed to the Party's drop in support.

On 25 October, the GST cleared a major hurdle when the Conservatives, aided by three independents, defeated the Senate Committee report calling for the bill to be killed. The Senate finally passed the bill on 13 December, and it was given Royal Assent the following Monday, the Liberals having succeeded in one last delay by adjourning for the weekend before assent could be given the Friday before. The Senate sat over the Christmas break to catch up on the backlog of work that had accumulated during the prolonged battle over the GST, including the unemployment insurance bill that was then passed as desired by the government.

In June 1991, the Conservative majority in the Senate ensured passage of a package of new rules that gave the government more control over the Senate agenda and reduced the opportunities for filibustering and other delaying tactics.[28] The Liberal senators had boycotted the committee that drafted the rules. This was only the third substantial change to Senate procedure since Confederation, the other two having occurred in 1906 and 1968. Until the post-1984 confrontations, the Senate had traditionally operated on a "gentlemanly" basis; its procedural rules had not been "adhered to with any degree of rigidity and a considerable portion of the Senate's business [was] in fact conducted under suspended rules."[29]

But this was not the end of the Conservative Government's difficulties with the Upper Chamber. On 31 January 1991, the controversial abortion bill came to a vote. The result was an unusual tie, forty-three to forty-three. Cheers went up on both sides of the Chamber when the acting speaker explained that the tie meant defeat of the bill. It had been a free vote, but most Conservatives had voted for it, most Liberals against. Key to the government's defeat was the defection of Senator Pat Carney, a former Conservative Cabinet minister who had been expected to support the government.

Defections from the government side caused the defeat of another item of Conservative legislation in 1993, an act to implement provisions of the budget reducing the number of government agencies by eliminating some and amalgamating others. Contention focused on the proposal to amalgamate the Canada Council, which nurtures cultural and artistic activities, with the Social Sciences and Humanities Research Council (SSHRC), a grant-giving agency that administers funds for research and scholarship and also administers the international programmes of the Department of External Affairs. Both the arts groups and the academic community objected to the amalgamation. The two granting agencies had been separated in 1978 because of their different concerns and needs. Discussion in the Senate was acrimonious, as often happened after the trauma of the GST battle, and a compromise proposal by Senator Frith to divide the bill into two, so that the non-contentious issues could be passed while the Canada Council-SSHRC merger was examined more closely, was defeated by the Conservative majority.

The chairman of the Senate Committee on National Finance, Liberal Senator H.A. Olson, reported on 27 May 1993 that his committee had heard from more than thirty groups of witnesses, many of whom had been refused appearance before the Commons committee. Most testimony was critical of the merger, with witnesses arguing that the distinct voices of the arts and social sciences and humanities research communities would be lost. Conservative Senator Finlay MacDonald agreed with these concerns and offered a spirited defence of the Senate's traditional role:

If ever there was an opportunity, a duty, or a responsibility for the Senate of Canada to make a small contribution to political stability by acting as a counterweight to the House of Commons, today is one day we should reflect upon the reason for our existence...We would be of no value at all, if we were a mere chamber for registering the decrees of the lower house.[30]

The government refused to accept Senator MacDonald's amendment to remove the merger from the bill. But to its surprise, the vote in the Senate on 10 June was a tie, resulting in defeat of the entire bill. While Senator MacDonald had worked quietly to gain the support of four other Tory Senators in voting against it, and others in abstaining, the government whip had not done his homework and had underestimated the strength of the revolt; as a result the entire omnibus bill was lost.

This important event showed once again that senators are less vulnerable to pressure from party whips than are members of the House of Commons and have correspondingly greater freedom to dissent from party positions. Several senators on the government side asserted their independence and, because the sanctions the government can impose on them are much weaker than those members of the House of Commons are liable to, could act on the basis of their studies and beliefs and defeat their own government's legislation.

The period of Conservative rule was drawing towards its close. Prime Minister Mulroney resigned to be replaced by Kim Campbell, who called a national election for 25 October 1993 and went on to receive the most resounding defeat of any government in Canadian history. The massive public rejection of the Progressive Conservative Government proves that they must have done a lot of things wrong, and without doubt the Senate's debates, public hearings, airing of differing viewpoints, and constant questioning of government policies contributed to the swing in public opinion. But how much, it is impossible to say. The Senate, far from being "so sluggish and inert that it seemed capable of performing only the most nominal functions" as Dawson had once described it, was lively and influential during the Mulroney years. The Senate had used its powerful veto more than once and Senate obstruction had led Prime Minister Mulroney to repeatedly demand that the institution be reformed. But Senate reform got lost in his broader and unsuccessful efforts at constitutional amendment.

For much of this period, the Senate was the more interesting house, though the lack of media coverage obscured this from the general public. Parliamentary government, particularly when the party lines and discipline over the private member are as rigid as they are in Canada, requires checks on the government through a vigorous opposition. Government control of proceedings in the House of Commons had by then become so strong that the capacity of the opposition to delay, to examine, to expose faults, and to instigate public discussion was drastically curtailed. The Mulroney Government shortened the time spent on debate of each item of legislation in the chamber,[31] and committee investigation, if anything, became more virulent, partisan, and superficial than before.[32] These problems of weak opposition and government domination still bedevil the House of Commons.

In this 1984–93 period the Senate was often the real focus of opposition to the government. On many crucial issues, both debate and committee investigation in the Upper Chamber were freer, more extensive, and more interesting than in the Lower House. The Senate fulfilled its role as a chamber of sober second thought. On the other hand, in certain instances (though certainly not all) the motivation for its scrutiny of government proposals came from partisan considerations, most visibly during the GST debate. No matter what the motivation, however, nearly all Senate proposals were viewed by the Mulroney Government as partisan meddling and the media's acceptance of this argument contributed to the growth of the public perception of the Senate being illegitimate. Irrespective of the circumstances, the Senate typically found itself in the position of receiving more criticism for being partisan and appointed than praise for its thorough investigations and often principled arguments.

THE SENATE UNDER
PRIME MINISTER CHRÉTIEN

Like Brian Mulroney before him, Prime Minister Jean Chrétien initially faced a Senate whose majority was from the opposition, though this time the Senate majority party was backed by only two members in the Commons. But there was an important difference between 1993 and 1984. The MacEachen Liberal senators had been part of the expansion of government, especially of social programmes, during the 1960s and 70s. They had been on the opposite side of the ideological fence from the Mulroney Conservative Government, and their battles with the Commons had always mixed in with partisanship a measure of fundamental disagreement over the role of government and the vision of the good society. The new Chrétien Liberal Government, on the other hand, placed a much higher emphasis than even the Mulroney Conservatives on reducing government expenditures.

Senator John Lynch-Staunton, the Conservatives' new Senate Leader, at first proposed a much less ambitious role for the Senate than the MacEachen Liberals, saying that the Conservative senators would not use the Upper Chamber as a government-in-exile to defeat legislation, but would do what they could to change bills they felt to be flawed. Jean Charest, the interim Tory Leader, agreed that there were limits to how far the party could push its agenda in the Upper House: "The bottom line is that the House of Commons makes decisions." Nevertheless, some Conservative senators, observing the weakness of the opposition in the Commons, concluded they had to become the real opposition.

Their willingness to act on the basis of this conclusion was shortly to be seen in the process of redistribution of seats in the Commons following the 1991 national census, which was well under way by 1994. Commissions in each province, established by the Mulroney Government, were managing the process. Partly under pressure from the substantial number of Liberal members who were apprehensive over the possible outcomes, the Liberal Government introduced a bill to suspend and amend the process. This delay would have meant that redistribution, enabling electoral boundaries to reflect demographic changes recorded in the 1991 census, would likely have been delayed until after the next election, due in 1997 or 1998. In April 1994, the Conservative Senate majority said they would challenge the Liberal Government's bill. After a long and vigorous fight in the Senate, the objections of senators forced the government to abandon its legislation, and redistribution proceeded under the old act with modifications being made to some boundaries as proposed by the various provincial commissions. The unelected Senate in this instance found itself in the position of opposing both the Government and the House of Commons in defending the principle of the political equality of citizens.

Receiving more notoriety was the issue of privatization of Toronto's Pearson International Airport, the largest and busiest airport in Canada. The Conservative Government had approved a contract to privatize Terminals 1 and 2 at Pearson Airport just before the 1993 election. By this time, the Mulroney Government had become so tainted with allegations of patronage that, regardless of whether this contract made good business sense and had been awarded in a fair manner, suspicions of patronage were strong. The airport deal had become a symbol of the partisanship and influence of lobbyists that voters connected with the Mulroney regime, and Jean Chrétien had made an election promise to scrap it. On 7 July 1994 Conservative senators started a showdown with the new Liberal Government by blocking a bill passed by the Commons that would have killed the privatization deal. Tory senators argued that the bill violated the corporation's constitutional rights, while the Liberals claimed that the Tories were trying to protect their friends who had signed the contract.

After initially holding firm in its determination not to accept significant changes to the bill, in December the Liberal Government accepted some of the changes proposed by the Senate and increased the compensation they were willing to pay to the developers. Conservative senators were not satisfied, however, and in May 1995 the government reluctantly agreed to allow the Senate to hold an inquiry into the Pearson Airport deal. When the session prorogued in February 1996, the Senate and Commons remained deadlocked over the bill.

Early in the new session the Liberal Government introduced a bill identical to the one that had died at prorogation. But on 19 June the Senate defeated this bill. By then the Liberals held one more Senate seat than the Conservatives, but illness, absence, and the key defection of Liberal Senator Herbert Sparrow to the Tory side created a tie vote, forty-eight to forty-eight, the Senate's third tie on important legislation in five years, and caused the defeat. Transport Minister David Anderson said that he was determined to protect taxpayers and would not rule out any options, including stacking the Senate with more government supporters, as Mulroney had to get the GST passed. Within a few weeks, however, the government and the Pearson Development Corporation settled on compensation far lower than the many hundreds of millions that had been rumoured, though allegations persisted of other, hidden benefits to the corporation.

This Pearson Airport bill was unusual, not only in that it was introduced by the government to honour an election commitment but also in that it was highly controversial and based on dubious legal and commercial principles. In particular, many senators opposed the provisions that would have denied the company the right to sue for lost profits as being an abuse of governmental legislative power. In the end it was defeated by the defection of senators from the government's own side.

The Senate delayed other bills as well during this period. A major revamping of unemployment insurance and a new transportation act died in the Senate at the 1996 prorogation, and the Senate also was accused of dragging its feet on a constitutional amendment on secularizing schools in Newfoundland, on amendments to the *Copyright Act*, on a child support bill, and on a sales tax law designed to replace the GST in three Maritime provinces. Many of the Senate's concerns over these bills were reasonable and deserved consideration on their own merits. The debate over Newfoundland schools, for example, involved fundamental questions about the removal of constitutionally protected minority rights, while the debate over child support led to further examination of shared custody. These merits were, however, drowned in the flood of criticism of an unelected Senate thwarting the will of the elected House of Commons. In April 1997, Prime Minister Chrétien appointed two women to the Senate, both strong Liberal supporters, giving the government a clear majority in the Upper Chamber. However, Senate opposition persisted as Liberal senators have, on certain occasions, chosen to challenge the government.

The most recent confrontation between senators and the government occurred in early 2000 on the so-called "Clarity Bill," which established a role for the House of Commons in defining whether the question in a referendum on provincial secession was clear and how large a majority vote in favour of such a referendum question was sufficient to lead to secession negotiations. Several senators on the Liberal side objected to the bill. Particularly contentious to these senators was the clause giving the House of Commons, but not the Senate, a role in settling these problematic questions. Prime Minister Chrétien appointed four new Liberal senators before the Clarity Bill came to a vote, sufficient for one amendment to be barely defeated and the bill itself to pass unscathed. In this instance the Prime Minister's powers of appointment were used to overrule members of his own party in the Senate.

The Senate has continued to play an active role during the tenure of Prime Minister Chrétien, during periods of Conservative and Liberal majority. The Upper House has contributed to parliamentary debate and, at times, has been successful in defeating or amending government legislation. Its efforts to improve legislation have, however, continued to be hampered by the growing perception of illegitimacy.

THE LEGISLATIVE AND INVESTIGATIVE ROLES OF THE SENATE

The tendency of the media and critics of the Senate to concentrate their attention almost exclusively on its rare confrontations with the government and on allegations of partisanship has overshadowed the day-to-day work that senators perform with regards to legislation and special investigations. This is unfortunate as the calibre of both is very high.

The Senate's Legislative Role

No examination of the Senate's role in the legislative process is possible without looking at the broader context of this process as a whole, and no examination as a whole can be done without examining the legislative role of the House of Commons. The primary function of the elected House of Commons, unlike that of the American Congress, does not lie in its legislative role, nor does the Commons perform this function well.[33] The key functions of the Commons lie in the making and unmaking of governments, that is, in supporting a government that retains its confidence, and in providing an opportunity for an institutionally entrenched opposition to criticize the government and propose itself to the electorate as a viable alternative, with the hope that it will defeat and replace the government in the next general election. The notion of "confidence" (which has no counterpart in the American system of separation of powers) is the key to Westminster style parliamentary democracy, and in its ramifications lie many of the complexities and strengths of the parliamentary-Cabinet system of government. In particular, the "fusion" of legislative and executive power in the Cabinet that Bagehot described in 1867 (drawing on an understanding of this aspect of British parliamentary government that had been part of British political thought since at least the late eighteenth century), makes the House of Commons the centre of the ongoing battle between political parties.

Yet in this essential core feature of responsible parliamentary democracy lie also the sources of many of the problems faced by Parliament, as the House of Commons has other functions besides making and unmaking governments. As one of the three parts of Parliament (the others being the Crown and the Senate), the Commons also forms an essential component of the legislative process and has much of the responsibility for holding the government accountable. Moreover, as the centre of national political life, the House of Commons should educate the public through its debates and investigations, should be a training ground for future holders of high political office, should inform the government of the mood and concerns of the public, and should mobilize consent for government programmes through its investigation, review, and ultimate approval of legislation.

Adversarial politics form the lifeblood of the House of Commons. The opposition is as keenly interested in finding fault with the government and claiming that it can do a better job as the government is in demanding recognition for its achievements. The official recognition of "Her Majesty's Loyal Opposition" institutionalizes the constant battle between the parties in the House of Commons as a fundamental aspect of parliamentary democracy. But in Parliament as elsewhere there can be too much of a good thing. The vigour of adversarial partisanship (and its appeal to the media) all too often leads to a situation where the House risks letting the partisan struggles dominate its other functions to the point where they become neglected and badly performed. To prevent this, the Commons as a whole, the political parties, and the individual members should recognize and accept that the Commons has a shared responsibility for functions that extend beyond partisanship, and that to perform these functions well, members and committees must often be bipartisan (or even nonpartisan) when collectively considering issues of legislation and governance that extend beyond party lines. Such recognition of the importance of nonpartisan functions has been hard to find in recent years.

Many of the criticisms of the House of Commons derive from the all too frequent failure of parties and members to accept that some of their tasks involve getting beyond partisanship. The House fails to examine estimates for expenditure in any but a cursory way. Even legitimate criticisms of administration and behaviour by the opposition are vehemently contested and denied by the government. Committees of the House of Commons often become so partisan that they cannot make an effective inquiry into matters of policy and administration. The House degenerates into a battleground of simplistic warfare between the parties; it fails to examine and review legislation and policy issues, and it fails to hold the government to account in any effective way. The media have become more than willing accomplices in this process, encouraging the concentration on scandal-hunting and the superficial rather than on the serious questions facing the country. To paraphrase Shakespeare: the good done by the Commons gets interred and forgotten; the trivial gets reported. Members of the opposition in Parliament, and their parties and leaders, naturally overemphasize the trivial and scandalous while they neglect the serious, important, and nonsensational. The media's obsession with blood on the floor, partisan battles and insistence that any deviation from party lines or dissent by backbenchers is a sign of weakness contribute to the already overwhelming forces making party discipline all-powerful and partisanship virtually the sole determinant of how members of the Commons behave on the floor of the House and its committees alike.

Another criticism enters into a broad overview of the role of the House in the legislative process: much of the membership of the House of Commons is inexperienced and amateur to the point that members cannot perform their functions well.[34] Amateurism in this sense means a lack of political experience before entering the House of Commons, a brief stay in the House itself, and a lack of other qualifications such as higher education, professional qualifications, and work experience indicative of high ability. Particularly on the scores of previous political experience and length of tenure, the Canadian House of Commons is one of the most amateur assemblies among the advanced Western nations. The average member of the Canadian House of Commons serves in the House a little more than four years, compared with more than eight years in Britain, and much longer for members of the American House of Representatives. Short tenure in the House means that many members are still finding their way and are not able to have much influence over parliamentary business before they are defeated or choose to leave.

Normally between forty and sixty percent of members are new to the House following a general election in Canada. The last decade saw both the highest turnover in Canadian history, the election of 1993, when nearly seventy percent of the members elected to the House were new, and the election of 2000, when only thirteen percent of the members returned were serving their first term. Nevertheless, the conclusion that the membership of the Commons by and large is inexperienced and amateur still holds true.

Exacerbating this and the other problems of the Commons is the imbalance in political experience and time in power between the Liberal Party, the perpetual government party, and the fractured and chronic opposition parties. Most of the truly professional politicians are to be found on the government side in the Liberal Party and in particular in the Cabinet. The opposition, especially since the overwhelming defeat of the Conservative government in 1993, has been remarkably inexperienced both in politics generally and in Parliament.

Furthermore, the legislative process is so dominated by the executive, and in particular the central agencies of government, that the government denies the House of Commons the opportunity to perform its legitimate role. Party lines are rigid in the House of Commons. No government has been defeated there by the defection of its own members, on government legislation or any other matter, since the early post-confederation years. The government dominates proceedings in the Commons, including rigidly limiting the time spent debating legislation and studying it in committee. Governments accept few amendments and can and do force legislation through the Commons, even when many of their own members harbour grave doubts about it. Parliament has become so unimportant in the normal processes of governance, including the legislative process, that Savoie's excellent recent study of the concentration of power in Canadian politics makes no mention of it except to describe its weaknesses.[35]

Defenders of the Senate point out that it usefully compensates for several of the major deficiencies in the House of Commons. Its membership is generally far more experienced in both politics and in other professions, and its relative stability of membership gives it a strong advantage in parliamentary experience. It is normally less partisan than the Commons for, as was observed earlier in this paper, government members sometimes vote against their party's position even on government legislation. Amendments are made to bills in the Senate that the government resisted in the Commons. Lower levels of partisanship and party discipline contribute to (with a few notable exceptions, as this paper has shown) a less adversarial style of debate and an approach to investigative work within committees that focuses more steadily, and productively, on substantive issues. All of these claims hold true and have been substantiated in many studies. However these same studies

have come to differing conclusions about the importance of the Senate's role in the legislative process. Reviewing the impact of the Senate
up to 1960, Mackay found that the frequency of Senate amendments to
legislation had diminished during the postwar period, but nevertheless
concluded that the Senate remained virtually indispensable as a revising
chamber. Kunz arrived at a similar conclusion on the basis of a review of
the period 1925–63, noting that voting across party lines had occurred
in a high proportion of votes in the Senate and that the Senate's central
contribution was in the area of technical amendments (corrections of
faulty drafting), which had comprised about seventy percent of its
amendments during the period. Campbell, in contrast, was far more
critical of the Senate, concluding that it had come to function as a
"lobby within," systematically reviewing legislation "from the standpoint
of the interests of big business." Campbell's conclusions, like those of
Kunz and Mackay, suffer from the absence of a detailed analysis of the
total impact of the Senate on legislation that is needed to prove them
convincingly. The examination in this paper of the Senate's activities
from 1984 to 2001 does not support Campbell's contentions and suggests that the focus of Mackay and Kunz on technical revisions only
partially captures the impact of the Senate.

The question that remains is how useful to the legislative process the Senate actually is. No close study has been made of the legislative process as a
whole in Canada to identify the roles played by, and actual impact of, either
the House of Commons or the Senate. Impressionistic evidence suggests
that the House of Commons now amends many fewer bills than in the past
and that the government, perhaps because it has greatly strengthened its
own resources for drafting legislation and consultation with interest groups
on legislation before it is introduced into Parliament, is much more reluc-
tant than in the past to accept amendments proposed by either House. It
also appears that the percentage of Government bills amended by the Senate is small. Heard found that even in the contentious 1984–88 period of
the Mulroney Government the Senate had amended only eighteen out of
248 bills coming to it from the Commons, or 7.3 percent, not far out of line
with the Senate's historic average. The amendments to twelve of these eighteen bills were accepted by the Commons; and the Senate insisted on
amendments to only two out of the remaining six bills for which amendments were not concurred in by the Commons. The Senate passed without
amendment 251 bills out of a total of 269 considered between 1984 and
1990.[36] In other words, only 6.7 percent were amended by the Senate.

The Senate, in dealing with a bill coming to it from the Commons, can
either pass it without amendments, amend it, defeat it, or choose not
proceed with it so that it dies on the order paper without ever being actually defeated. As the examples in the next section show, the Senate can
sometimes decide not to proceed with a bill rather than to vote against

it; the end result is the same, but what the intent of the Senate was can only be discerned from a close look at the actual records of proceedings. The figures given by various authors on the bills rejected by the Senate vary and are not consistent with one another. One of the main reasons for this is how bills that die on the Order Paper are treated, whether they are considered to be bills rejected by the Senate or are simply left out of the total.

Most experienced observers have concluded that Senate committees do a better job than those of the Commons in examining legislation and proposing amendments. The following section will present some examples of legislation that the Senate has introduced or amended in recent years. My intention in presenting them is not to suggest that these examples adequately reflect what the Senate has done on legislation during these years. In fact they discuss only a small sample of its legislative interventions. Nor do I claim that they reflect the distribution of regional, property, individual rights, social issues, and other matters addressed by the Senate in its review of legislation. In the absence of a thorough study of the legislative process in Canada, they stand simply as examples showing that the Senate does, indeed, perform a little-known and badly reported (if at all) function in the legislative process. I present them to illustrate the kind of work that the Senate does in reviewing legislation and how it very often deals with contentious issues in a bipartisan, low-key, and highly informed way quite different from that of the Commons.

DETAILED EXAMPLES OF THE SENATE'S LEGISLATIVE ROLE[37]

The "Son of Sam" Bill. In October 1997, Bill C–220, with unanimous consent and without amendment passed second reading, committee, and third reading stages in the House of Commons all in one day and was forwarded to the Senate. The bill, a private members' bill amending the *Criminal Code* and *Copyright Act* to prevent convicted persons from profiting by writing works describing their crimes, was essentially similar to bill that had died on the Order Paper of the previous Parliament. That bill had received Third Reading in the House despite potentially serious concerns expressed by the House committee that had examined it: that it exceeded the criminal law power, that its effect would reach beyond the incarceration period, and that it addressed a problem that was already being resolved intergovernmentally.

At second reading in the Senate several senators expressed concern that the bill, as reintroduced, had received so little attention in the Commons. Its supporters pointed out that the bill's predecessor had been examined by a Commons committee and, despite the expressed concerns, had been passed unanimously. However, the Senate's Standing Committee on Legal and Constitutional Affairs held thirteen meetings on the bill and examined it in considerable detail, hearing from almost thirty witnesses, including among others representatives from the Canadian Bar Association, the Writers' Union of Canada, the Department of Justice, and the Elizabeth Fry Society.

In its report, the Committee stressed that it was acutely sensitive to the concerns of crime victims that the persons convicted might profit from depictions of those crimes, particularly when the crimes were heinous and sensational, and that it sympathized with the intentions of Mr Wappel, the bill's sponsor. The Committee concluded, however, that the Canadian courts were unlikely to hold that the social ill was of such a scope as to justify the sweeping measures contemplated in the bill. Among its many Charter and legal concerns, the Committee noted that it would undermine the fundamental Charter right of freedom of expression and that the bill would not be restricted to persons convicted of atrocious or heinous crimes, but would have also captured the works of persons such as Gandhi, Malcolm X, Martin Luther King Jr., Nehru, Riel, Garcia Lorca, and Governor General Award winner Roger Caron. Reflecting these concerns, the Committee recommended that the bill not proceed, and the full Senate adopted this recommendation without division.

The Senate's decision on this bill was based on a far more intensive investigation than occurred in the Commons, was dispassionate, involved questions of freedom and rights as well as complex legal issues and the Supreme Court's views on social ills, the proper use of criminal law in a free and democratic society, and such other complex issues as Canada's international obligations under the *Berne Convention for the Protection of Literary and Artistic Work*. The Senate, in acting contrary to general public sentiment on a highly emotional topic, proved that it served a useful and quite different legislative function from the House of Commons.[38]

Sexual Orientation Bills. The federal legal provisions regarding discrimination on the basis of sexual orientation only exist because of six years of persistent effort on the part of the Senate. After the Ontario Court of Appeal ruled in *Haig and Birch* that sexual orientation be read into the *Canadian Human Rights Act*, Senator Kinsella, a Conservative who disagreed with his government's views that this sort of legislation was unnecessary, introduced Bill S–15 into the Senate in order to insert sexual orientation as grounds into the Act. He felt that since the ruling was by an Ontario court, technically it could apply only in that province, making legislation necessary in order to prohibit discrimination on the basis of sexual orientation throughout Canada.

Soon after Bill S–15 was introduced in the Senate, the Minister of Justice, Kim Campbell, introduced a similar bill, C–118, into the Commons. This initially convinced the Senate to delay Bill S–15, but it soon became apparent to the senators that the government did not intend to proceed with C–118 and had simply introduced it as a delaying tactic.

Although the Liberal Government elected in 1993 had included in its platform a promise to introduce similar legislation, it had not done so two and a half years later, in 1996. After the Minister of Justice missed his own deadline for this legislation, Senator Kinsella introduced his own bill, S–2, which would have amended the *Canadian Human Rights Act* by adding sexual orientation in three areas: equal opportunity; discrimination; and allowable affirmative action programmes. This bill passed third reading in the Senate in April 1996, but the Commons did not deal with it at all. Instead, on 29 April, five days after the Senate had passed Bill S–2, the Minister of Justice introduced a more limited bill that left out the affirmative action provision. This bill was passed by the House of Commons and the Senate, receiving Royal Assent on 20 June 1996. After the election, however, the subsequent Bill S–5, which modified the *Canadian Human Rights Act* with respect to disabilities, was amended by the Senate to include sexual orientation as a grounds for affirmative action programs. This bill received approval by the Commons, which apparently did not comment on the substantial Senate amendment and is now part of Canadian law.

In 1998, the Senate reviewed Bill C–37, *An Act to amend the Judges Act and to make consequential amendments to other Acts.* The Judges Act has never contained a definition of "spouse," but Bill C–37 would have added a definition of spouse that would have expressly excluded same-sex couples, despite recent court decisions that such a definition violates the Charter. Both sides of the Senate supported removing the offensive clause, and the House of Commons not only accepted the amendment but commended the Senate for its work.

SUMMARY EXAMPLES OF THE SENATE'S LEGISLATIVE ROLE

Prohibited Degrees of Marriage. On 17 December 1990, Royal Assent was given to Bill S–14, a Senate public bill that removed step-relatives (except brothers and sisters by adoption) from the groups subject to legislation prohibiting marriage between related persons. The change relieved people in this group who desire to marry from the need to obtain passage of a private bill authorizing marriage. The amendment concluded more than six years of convoluted history dating back to 1984, involving four separate attempts by the Senate to remove outdated prohibitions and make Canadian legislation internally consistent.

Witness Protection Programme. In 1996, the government introduced Bill C–13, providing for the establishment of a witness protection programme. One provision of this bill allowed the commissioner of the RCMP to terminate the protection of a person if, "in the opinion of the Commissioner," the witness failed to meet his or her obligations under the protection agreement. The Senate's Committee on Legal and Constitutional Affairs unanimously recommended a change in the wording of that phrase to "if the Commissioner has evidence that" the witness failed to meet those obligations. This was intended to reduce the risk of arbitrary decisions by the commissioner and to provide greater protection for witnesses. The amendment was approved by the House of Commons, with some members commending the Senate for its work.

Bankruptcy. Bill C–5, embodying the second phase of an overhaul of Canada's bankruptcy laws, arrived in the Senate from the House of Commons in October 1996. The Senate Committee on Banking, Trade and Commerce unanimously agreed that the bill made substantial progress with respect to bankruptcy law relating to businesses. However, it sought and obtained a government commitment to develop a database to support future policy development on bankruptcy, as well as fifteen amendments to improve the balance between the rights of creditors and debtors. The Senate also delivered a strong affirmation of the need for public consultation and debate, rather than the more limited technical consultations that government had used.

Drug Policy and Hemp. Bill C–8, legislation intended to allow growing and use of hemp for commercial purposes, reached the Senate from the Commons on 16 March 1996. In reviewing this bill senators from both government and opposition worked together, hearing from more than forty witnesses representing all major stakeholder perspectives during ten meetings on this bill. On the basis of its findings, the committee recommended that a joint Commons-Senate committee be struck with a mandate to broadly review the effectiveness and fairness of Canada's drug policy. In addition, the Senate committee proposed fifteen amendments to the bill, most of which were technical, although one important substantive amendment was a clause decriminalizing hemp, and expanding the potential uses of this versatile crop. The Senate amendments were all agreed to by the Commons and embodied in the final legislation.

The Canadian Wheat Board. Bill C–4, making changes to the structure and powers of the Canadian Wheat Board, was considered by Parliament in 1997–98. The legislation had been rapidly pushed through all stages of consideration in the Commons because the government felt that its substance had been adequately considered by a committee examining similar legislation in the previous Parliament. The Senate Committee on Agriculture and Forestry responded to the fact that several aspects of the bill remained hotly contested, however, and held extensive hearings involving one hundred individuals and thirty farm groups. The committee established that a proposal to allow the Wheat Board to add grains to its mandate reflected an orchestrated attempt by its supporters to influence the Commons committee that had investigated the issue in the previous Parliament and recommended its deletion, along with improvements to transparency and government accountability that were ultimately reflected in the legislation.

Conclusion. The examples provided above, and many others that could have been included, stand in contrast to the more highly publicized confrontations of 1984–2001. They show the Senate performing a legislative role complementary to that of the House of Commons, and making a largely nonpartisan and highly constructive contribution to the legislative process. The problem remains, however, that although the Senate's committee work on legislation is often of a very high quality, it is widely ignored by the media except in unusual circumstances, where adversarial drama produces marketable news.

The Senate's Investigative Role

In recent years partisan warfare in the House of Commons has become more virulent and pervasive, and now only rarely does a committee of the Commons display a consistently nonpartisan interest in an investigation. While the Senate has also demonstrated excessive partisanship on occasion, far more often the Senate and its committees are decidedly less partisan than the Commons, and members of both sides work together to unravel knotty policy problems of public concern.

In carrying out investigative work, the Senate has three advantages over the Commons. First, its members have normally served longer in the Chamber than do members in the Lower House. The normal length of service of the average MP in the Canadian House of Commons is slightly more than four years; the normal senator is appointed in their fifties or early sixties and stays until they reach the retirement age of seventy-five. Although Prime Minister Chrétien has shown a proclivity for appointing persons nearing the age of retirement, it remains true that by and large senators stay in the Upper Chamber longer than members stay in the Lower. This allows them to pursue their interests and concerns over a period far longer than the normal four-year time span between elections to the Commons and the policy cycle dictated by this time horizon.

Second, many senators have a distinguished record of public service and interest in important policy issues behind them when they are appointed. The more relaxed working atmosphere of the Senate allows individual senators to take the initiative in pursuing an investigation of issues important to them, and in this way many of the Senate's most outstanding achievements in investigations are associated with the names of individual senators. The very good and influential Senate investigations into science policy and related issues of thirty years ago in this way are linked with the name of Senator Lamontagne, while Senator Croll led important studies into poverty and related issues.

Third, working conditions in the Senate give its members opportunities to operate outside the confines of party lines and party discipline that members of the Commons often envy. The Senate and its committees, most of the time, are less partisan than the Commons. The possibility of members from one side breaking ranks and voting with the other is always there, and the absence of a rigid rotation of questioning among parties contributes to the achievement of coherent and thorough discussion. While the absence of partisan conflict means that Senate committees, even more than those of the Commons, suffer from lack of media attention, this can be a blessing in disguise because it allows committees to work as cohesive and thoughtful investigating bodies. The results are often impressive, and the track record of the Senate in these sorts of investigations into policy issues in the last forty years, despite all efforts at reforming committees of the Lower House, is far better than that of the Commons. Mackay commended the effectiveness of Senate committee investigations in educating senators and the public about long range trends and problems, while Kunz (although less positive) affirmed the usefulness of an expanded committee role in scrutiny and inquiry, and Campbell found that committee investigative work had been highly effective, although tending to be dominated by business interests.

The following pages provide a relatively detailed case study of Senate committee work in the banking and financial services area, which has been an area of consistent interest for senators, and also describe briefly some recent investigations by other Senate committees. Like the examples of legislative activities in the previous section, they are far from exhaustive. They are presented simply to give some indication of the range, scope, and depth of Senate committee investigations and how these have influenced public discourse, government policy-making, and legislation.

DETAILED CASE STUDY: BANKING AND FINANCIAL SERVICES
Banking and financial services issues often come to the Senate embodied in government legislation passed by the House of Commons, but they can also be examined by the Senate on its own initiative. The process of policy development and change is both long and incremental. The basic legislation remains the same from decade to decade, but in each successive review new circumstances require some changes, or reforms that were previously legislated prove in need of further refinement. Each modification only affects part of the legislative framework, but over time the cumulative impact of incremental changes can produce profound reforms. Many other actors and interests besides the government and Senate become involved. The banking and financial industries themselves take an active role. So do consumer associations and other clientele of financial services industries. Some but certainly not all of these groups would fall within Campbell's notion of a business lobby. In its review of legislation, the Sen-

ate, like the government, must be sensitive to and accommodate the needs of hugely differing and often conflicting interests. The *Bank Act* normally comes before Parliament every decade for updating and review; not only does the Senate scrutinize this important legislation with great care, but often also the introduction of the *Bank Act* itself can be preceded by a Senate Committee study.

In this manner, on 4 October 1989 the Senate Standing Committee on Banking, Trade and Commerce was given the mandate "to study the future of Canadian Financial Institutions in a globally competitive and evolving environment and, in particular, the ownership of such institutions." In April 1990 the committee submitted its report, *Canada 1992: Towards a National Market in Financial Services.* The Committee, after reviewing its 1986 report on the financial services industry, noted that because the financial services sector was undergoing rapid changes, both domestically and abroad, a premium should be placed on flexibility and adaptability. Its report praised the current system and recommended that, although reform was overdue, it should build upon the existing system and should encourage innovation.

In 1991, the government introduced amendments embodying major changes to the legislation governing Canada's financial services sector. In many areas the government's proposals were in accordance with the Committee's. Provisions in the acts continued to ensure Canadian ownership of financial institutions, for example, and the Committee's recommendations against self-dealing, that the Canadian financial services sector adopt the Bank of International Settlements capital-adequacy guidelines and that trust and insurance companies be made to follow the "prudent person" approach to lending, were accepted.

One of the most important of the Committee's recommendations was not accepted by the government, however. The main thrust of the Committee's report had been the need to lower the barriers in the domestic financial market and to create one national Canadian market. Then as now most provinces had their own financial regulatory system; not only were these not entirely in harmony with one another but the costs of duplication – to companies wanting to operate across Canada, or to regulators attempting to control and prosecute abusers of the system – were prohibitive both to the industry and to their clientele. The Committee had urged "all interested parties ...to commit themselves publicly to the eminently reasonable and critically important goal of achieving a single national capital market by 1992," noting that Europe was committed to doing this and arguing that there was no reason why Canada could not do likewise. But nothing in the Acts of 1991, and nothing since, has created a single national capital market, and overlap and duplication continue to exist in the federal and provincial regulatory systems.

In December 1998, the Senate Standing Committee on Banking, Trade and Commerce submitted another study of the state of the Canadian financial services system. In large part its report, *A Blueprint for Change,* was a response to the report of the government's MacKay Task Force on the Future of the Canadian Financial Services Sector. The Committee noted that it generally agreed with the principal thrust of the task force, "the promotion of healthy competition across the full range of financial services, but particularly in banking services."[39] The committee articulated five objectives for the financial services industry:

1 to ensure the safety, soundness, and integrity of the Canadian financial system;
2 to provide a framework for healthy competition in the financial services sector;
3 to foster Canadian control of the key institutions in the financial services sector;
4 to enable consumers to make well-informed decisions and to protect them from improper business practices;
5 to fulfil the stewardship responsibilities of the sector, including achieving the widest possible accessibility to financial services across all regions and income groups.

In June 1999, the Minister of Finance released a white paper, *Reforming Canada's Financial Services Sector,* which set out the government's intentions. Thus, there were three reports to be considered when the *Bank Act* was next updated: the Senate Committee's report, the report of the Mackay Task Force, and the government's own white paper. Many of the Senate's particular concerns were about customer and consumer benefits. One area upon which all three agreed was the need for a national credit union as an alternative to the banks. The Senate Committee, like the task force, desired all Canadians to have equal access to basic banking services, especially low-income people who need to get government cheques cashed, assuring that everyone has the option of direct deposit for all government cheques. Both Committee and task force agreed that banks should be required to give notice of branch closures, and the white paper concurred, proposing four months' notice of branch closing in urban areas and six months in rural areas.

The process of review of financial legislation and of Senate influence on it will continue. In a policy area as complex as banking and the financial services industries it cannot be expected that one single institution – be it the Senate, the Department of Finance, the Canadian Bankers Association, or a task force – can be the single voice that determines outcomes. But the Senate has been a steady, influential voice and many of its concerns, both for the needs of Canadians and the concerns of the financial industries, have been expressed and ultimately accommodated.

OTHER EXAMPLES

The Special Senate Committee on Euthanasia and Assisted Suicide. During the late 1980s and early 1990s, several events dealing with end of life decisions received attention in the media and before the courts. At the same time, public opinion polls have indicated growing support for control by individuals of the dying process while leaving doubts about how well the issues are understood.

In February 1994, the Senate, in response to these public concerns, established a special committee to examine and report on the legal, social, and ethical issues relating to euthanasia and assisted suicide. Reflecting testimony heard over a period of fourteen months from more than one hundred witnesses, and hundreds of additional letters and briefs, the report of the committee, *Of Life and Death*, mirrored the uncertainty of Canadians on the questions of euthanasia and assisted suicide. Nevertheless, it has proven to be an immensely valuable resource for parliamentarians and others. Since its tabling in 1995, more than ten thousand copies of the report have been distributed, and it has been used in courses in medical ethics in departments of medicine, as well as universities, hospitals, and health-care centres.

In 1999–2000, a subcommittee review of developments resulted in the June 2000 report, *Quality of End-of-Life Care: The Right of Every Canadian*. It commended progress in some areas, but chided both levels of government for the slowness in the development of the expertise and medical infrastructure required for the care of people facing death and called for a national strategy for end-of-life care.

Veterans Affairs. In February 1999, the Senate Sub-Committee on Veterans Affairs, with Senator Phillips as chair, issued a report *Raising the Bar: Creating a New Standard in Veterans Health Care*. The sixty-eight recommendations in the report included proposals for improving the delivery of health services, several of which led to changes at specific institutions, including Toronto's Sunnybrook hospital, about which concerns had been raised in the media.

The Sub-Committee has also completed (among many others) studies into the CBC documentary *The Valour and the Horror*, the Canadian War Museum, and the 1994 study *Keeping the Faith*, which resulted in amendments to veterans service legislation to eliminate distinctions between uniformed veterans and civilians who serve abroad in close support of the armed forces in theatres of war or on Special Duty Area missions.

As can be seen, the Sub-Committee on Veterans Affairs has kept a continuing watch over the treatment of veterans by both government and other agencies, and its experience shows the importance of the continuity and perseverance that senators, unlike members of the House of

Commons, can devote to an issue and the success that pressure over a period of years can produce.

Fisheries. Until 1986, Senate studies of fisheries were conducted by the
Senate Committee on Agriculture, Fisheries and Forestry; then in May
1986 a Standing Senate Committee on Fisheries was created to deal
exclusively with fisheries matters. Seven major reports have subsequently been submitted by that committee, including reports on the marketing of fish and issues specific to the three regional fisheries (freshwater,
east coast, and west coast) in 1986, 1987, and 1989. The Committee's
main proposal in 1989, that the precautionary principle of erring on
the side of conservation be broadly applied, has become an important
principle for managing severly depleted fish stocks. Also noteworthy are
reports in 1993, 1995, and 1998 that reiterated principles that have
been broadly echoed in subsequent commission and task force reports:
the need for conservation, industry restructuring, the reduction of
capacity, and an increased role for fishers and fishing communities in
fisheries management. Throughout this period, the Senate Committee
has taken the lead in initiating public discussion of many urgent issues,
served as an important forum for fishers and other key interests, and
achieved a public profile that undoubtedly enhanced its influence on
governments.

Foreign Affairs. The Senate Standing Committee on Foreign Affairs has
performed many thorough studies on areas sometimes neglected by the
Commons, and often of looming importance. Between 1975 and 1982,
the Committee extensively studied Canada-US relations, and its recommendation that bilateral free trade between the two countries be seriously
considered anticipated initiatives subsequently taken by the Mulroney
Government. More recently, the committee's April 2000 report, *The New
NATO and the Evolution of Peacekeeping: Implications for Canada,* explored the
consequences of the new importance of peacekeeping and addressed
some of the issues that had been before the public investigation into the
Somalia affair, such as parliamentary oversight and the role of the Canadian military.

THE SENATE'S ROLE
IN CANADA'S PARLIAMENTARY SYSTEM

In this review of the Senate's activities in the recent past we have seen that
the "Actual Senate" is far different from the "Imaginary Senate" so often
depicted by the media. The modern Senate has evolved over the past fifty
years, working to complement the House of Commons and improve the
quality of governance in Canada, perhaps most importantly through the

development of its committee investigations. The work done by the "Actual Senate" is vital to the effective functioning of Parliament.

Unfortunately, the "Imaginary Senate" is the model usually held up by its critics and the media – in MacGregor Dawson's words, a nearly vestigial body that is "so sluggish and inert that it seemed capable of performing only the most nominal functions."[40] The media and the public focus only on the rare clashes between the Senate and the House of Commons. But this general perception of an inert and lazy Senate does not accurately portray the real Senate and its work, as has been seen in the exploration of the largely nonconfrontational investigative and deliberative roles of the Senate in recent years. As I worked on case studies summarized below, I found myself time and again surprised and even taken aback by the thoroughness, level-headedness, insight, and thoughtfulness of the Senate's review of legislation and investigations into a wide range of social, economic, and other issues. Nothing in the literature on the Senate had prepared me for this. The record of the House of Commons on legislation during this period is no better, while its record of committee investigations is not as good.[41]

In addition, the interests and concerns of senators in their legislative and investigative roles are far broader than suggested in much of the literature, especially Campbell's 1978 portrayal of the Senate as an institutionalized business lobby. In some of the case studies reviewed the actions of the Senate did benefit big business. The investigations of the Foreign Affairs Committee into Canada's trade relationships with the United States and its advocacy of free trade certainly put forward a position whose most obvious beneficiary was big business. But in the Senate's review of banking issues and legislation in the 1989–2001 period, its recommendations responded to the interests of customers of the banks and industry clients as often as to those of the industry itself. The extended, thorough, and influential series of investigations into Canada's fisheries and fisheries industries were concerned with the well-being of the fisheries, the fishers, and fishing communities. Not by any stretch of the imagination could they be considered the work of a pro-business lobby from within. Nor can the studies of Euthanasia and Assisted Suicide, Veterans' Affairs, Peacekeeping, the "Son of Sam" bill, or inter alia the bills on marriage and sexual orientation. Big business is only one of the areas with which senators are concerned and has not been the dominant one in the 1984–2001 period.

The discussion above on the examples of legislative amendments by the Senate, including the "Son of Sam" bill, bankruptcy bills, and the Wheat Board bills, proves that flawed legislation – poorly drafted or based on inadequate consultation – can arrive in Parliament and be passed by the Commons. While the Senate's very occasional amendments hostile to the government garner disproportionate media attention, this should not obscure the role more characteristically played by the Senate: preventing the enshrinement of technically incompetent drafting within the laws of Canada. The fact that the frequency of Senate amendments has declined substantially from the levels typical of a century ago does not indicate the erosion of this role, nor a decline in the effectiveness of the Senate in performing it, but rather that great improvements have been made in the quality of legislative drafting during the past fifty years.[42] Even so, numerous errors still occur and the Senate's revision of legislation remains an important safety feature.

It might be argued that the useful work of the Senate in revising legislation and conducting investigations is more of a symptom of the need to improve the House of Commons, and to reform the legislative and policy-making processes as a whole, than actual proof of the value of the Senate itself. But, if anything, the process of considering legislation by the House of Commons has become more cursory, government-controlled, and partisan (not unconnected phenomena) in recent years. Moreover, the members of the Commons remain by and large short term and amateur, and investigations by Commons committees, despite the efforts and hopes of reformers for more than thirty years, are becoming less thorough and ever more dominated by partisanship. Party leaders control private members and have gained more tools to do so over the past thirty years. As long as these features of Commons proceedings remain, and there is no evidence that they will disappear (quite the contrary they grow stronger), the Senate performs a valuable and even necessary role in the Canadian parliamentary system. That this role has been neglected by most observers, notably in the media, tells more about their powers of observation than it does about what the Senate actually does.

This examination of the Upper House demonstrates that the "Actual Senate" much of the time is a chamber of careful reflection and deliberation whose activities (both legislative and investigative) improve the functioning of our system of government. Although the Senate contributes a great deal to Parliament, it could play an even more significant role as much of its work is currently hampered by the widespread negative impression of the institution in the minds of the Canadian public. The thoughtful deliberations and first-rate investigations that the Senate carries out in an efficient, nonpartisan manner – the normal routine of the Upper House – are largely ignored by the media. Canadians only ever hear about the Senate on the rare occasions when there is a high-profile partisan conflict (such as the GST debate) or when there is a whiff of scandal. The one thing that Canadians do know about the Senate is that it is appointed by the government in power and while this has its benefits – notably much better representation of women, aboriginals, and minorities[43] – these are all obscured by the fact that the unfettered prime-ministerial prerogative of senatorial appointment has all too often degenerated into mere political patronage. As a result of these factors, the Senate lacks public credibility and is widely perceived as being illegitimate.

While a full exploration of Senate legitimacy is beyond the scope of this paper, an acknowledgement of the importance of the problem cannot be avoided in any portrait of the Senate in modern times. Doubts about the Senate's legitimacy are raised constantly, and it is perhaps the most significant impediment that limits the Senate in having greater influence and even in performing its roles more decisively. The need for reform – for the "Hypothetical Senates" – is now treated as an axiomatic truth in discussions of the Senate.

The central contribution of this paper to discussions of reform is its demonstration that the problem does not lie in what the Senate actually does. This paper has shown that the Senate is far from ineffectual and that many senators work very hard at their duties. Though its legislative and investigative activities do not receive much public recognition, the Senate performs a valuable and complementary role to that of the House of Commons in Canada's parliamentary system of government. The real Senate is a far better and more effective legislative body than its critics would have Canadians believe, but its functions and their usefulness are invariably left out of discussions of Senate reform. The work the present Senate does is important enough to demand much more serious consideration in the ongoing debate about reform of Canadian parliamentary institutions.

NOTES

I am very grateful to the Social Sciences and Humanities Research Council of Canada for their support of my research into parliamentary government in Canada. Stephanie Robinson performed invaluable service as research assistant for my work on the Canadian Senate. The sections of this paper entitled "The Senate as Opposition: The Mulroney Years" and "The Senate under Prime Minister Chrétien" draw on my chapter "Not Dead Yet, But Should It Be Resurrected? The Canadian Senate," in Samuel C. Patterson and Anthony Mughan, eds, *Senates: Bicameralism in the Contemporary World*.

1 Campbell, *The Canadian Senate: A Lobby from Within*; Zolf, *Survival of the Fattest: An Irreverent View of the Senate*; McMenemy, "The Senate as an Instrument of Business and Party."

2 For example, Burns, Cody, Crommelin, Galligan, Janda, Lusztig, McConnell, McCormick, Stilborn, White.

3 Kunz, *The Modern Senate of Canada, 1925–1963: A Re-appraisal*, 313–15; Mackay, *The Unreformed Senate of Canada*, 108–9; Hoy, *Nice Work: The Continuing Scandal of Canada's Senate*, 86–9.

4 Davey, *The Rainmaker: A Passion for Politics*, 143.

5 Dobell, "The Senate: New Found Levers of Power?"

6 Marsden, "Doing Its Thing," 447.

7 Davey, *The Rainmaker: A Passion for Politics*, 315.

8 Franks, *The Parliament of Canada*, 193.

9 Heard, *Canadian Constitutional Conventions: The Marriage of Law and Politics*, 93.

10 Robinson, *The Senate of Canada during the Mulroney Years: The Red Chamber Playing the Part of the Loyal Opposition.*

11 Canada. Parliament. Senate. *Debates of the Senate.* 33rd Parliament, 2nd session, vol. 2: 1776 (Senator L. Murray).

12 Gessel, "Confronting the Red Chamber," 18–19; Gessel, "Ending a Bitter Stalemate," 19.

13 Sealey, *Mobilizing Legislation: Losing Consent. Treatment of the House of Commons Under the Mulroney Conservatives.*

14 See Mackay, *The Unreformed Senate of Canda*, 99–100.

15 Canadian News Facts, vol. 22, no. 14, 3849.

16 Canadian News Facts, vol. 22, no. 14, 3849.

17 Canadian News Facts, vol. 22, no. 14, 3849.

18 Canadian News Facts, vol. 22, no. 14, 3849.

19 Canadian News Facts, vol. 22, no. 14, 3849.

20 White, *Voice of Region: The Long Journey to Senate Reform in Canada*, 220.

21 Stewart, "PM Slams 'non-elected' Senate for Tardiness on Jobless Bill."

22 Canada. Parliament. Senate. *Debates of the Senate.* 34th Parliament, 2nd session, vol. 2: 1146–7 (Special Committee of the Senate on Bill C–21, *An Act to amend the Unemployment Insurance Act and the Employment and Immigration Department and Commission Act.* Third and Final Report).

23 Delacourt, "Liberal-Led Senate Throws UI Reforms Back in Tories Lap."

24 Flanagan, "The Staying Power of the Status Quo: Collective Choices in Canada's Parliament after Morgentaler."

25 Dunsmuir, *The Senate: Appointments Under Section 26 of the Constitution Act, 1867.*

26 For a detailed account, see Hoy, *Nice Work: The Continuing Scandal of Canada's Senate*, 163–4.

27 Canadian News Facts, vol. 24, no. 18, 4258.

28 Robertson, *The Rules of the Senate: 1991 Amendments.*

28 Kunz, *The Modern Senate of Canada, 1925–1963: A Re-appraisal.*

30 Canada. Parliament. Senate. *Debates of the Senate.* 34th Parliament, 3rd session, vol. 4: 3368 (Senator F. MacDonald).

31 Sealey, *Mobilizing Legislation: Losing Consent. Treatment of the House of Commons Under the Mulroney Conservatives.*

32 Franks, "Constraints on the Operations and Reform of Parliamentary Committees in Canada."

33 This section draws on my *The Parliament of Canada* (1987). See also my

"Constraints on the Operations and Reform of Parliamentary Committees in Canada" (1997), and *Parliament, Intergovernmental Relations, and National Unity* (1998). Many other observers have made similar criticisms.

34 Atkinson and Docherty, "Moving Right Along: The Roots of Amateurism in the Canadian House of Commons"; Docherty, *Mr. Smith Goes to Ottawa: Life in the House of Commons*; Franks, *The Parliament of Canada.*

35 Savoie, *Governing from the Centre: The Concentration of Power in Canadian Politics.*

36 See Rémillard, in this volume.

37 This section draws on two unpublished analyses of the Senate's work: *Analysis of the Work and Reports of committees of the Senate: 1984–1999,* prepared by the office of Senator Serge Joyal, Summer 1999, and *A Review of Senate Committee Studies,* prepared by the Parliamentary Research Branch of the Library of Parliament, December 1999. In addition, the table and committee staff of the Senate has provided much useful information and many valuable insights into the actual accomplishments of the Senate. I acknowledge my debts to this very able group of servants to Parliament.

38 This issue is far from over. In June 2001 Ontario's attorney general introduced a "Son of Sam" bill into the provincial legislature that would allow the government to seize any profits criminals make when they sell their stories for movies, books, or media appearances. Whether the courts would consider this an intrusion into criminal law, a federal responsibility, or how it might affect Charter rights, were left for the future to determine.

39 Standing Senate Committee on Banking, Trade and Commerce, *A Blueprint for Change: Response to the Report of the Task Force on the Future of the Canadian Financial Services Sector,* para. 80.

40 Dawson, *The Government of Canada,* 279.

41 The problems confronting House of Commons committees and the need for improvement have been examined in many studies. See, for example, Dobell, "Reforming Parliamentary Practice: The Views of MPs."

42 The absence of such improvements in British legislative drafting explains why the House of Lords makes a much greater number of amendments. Heard found that the House of Lords amends nearly 60 percent of the legislation coming to it from the Commons, while in comparison the Canadian Senate had amended less than 4 percent of bills coming to it from the Canadian Lower House. The contrast may be explained by the poor processes of consultation that have been alleged concerning the British pre-parliamentary legislative process in recent years, which result in draft legislation that often needs extensive revision by Parliament, along with what Shell has described as a "legislate-as-you-go" mentality, with ministers not thinking their proposed legislation through carefully enough (Shell, "To Revise and Deliberate: The British House of Lords," 213).

43 Despite being criticized for being unrepresentative, in some ways the Senate is more representative of the Canadian population than is the House of

Commons; 34 percent of senators currently are women, compared to only 20 percent of members in the House of Commons. The groundbreaking "Persons Case" dealt with the rights of women to become members of the Senate, not the elected House of Commons. Similarly, over the years many Canadian minorities achieved their first parliamentary representation in the Senate.

CHAPTER SEVEN

Comparing the Lawmaking Roles of the Senate and the House of Commons

Paul G. Thomas

INTRODUCTION

This chapter compares the relative effectiveness and influence of the Senate and the House of Commons within the Canadian legislative process broadly defined. The original role of the Senate was to complement, not to compete with, the House of Commons, which from the outset was seen as the centre of political life in the country. The elected House of Commons is the confidence chamber in which a defeat of the government on a matter of sufficient political significance results in the calling of an election or another party being asked to assume office. The Senate cannot force the removal of governments. As an appointed body, whose members are perceived to be selected by the Prime Minister mainly on the basis of their past or future service to the governing party, the Senate lacks legitimacy in the eyes of many Canadians. Constitutionally, the Senate is nearly equal to the House of Commons in terms of legislative authority. All bills must be approved by the Senate before they become law. Yet in the past, when there has been an impasse between the two Houses, the Senate has usually deferred eventually to the will of the popularly elected House of Commons. At the beginning of the twenty-first century there are bound to be doubts about the democratic credentials of an appointed upper house, but this fact cannot be taken as conclusive evidence that the Senate is a failure and contributes nothing to the national lawmaking process.

At the time of Confederation, the Senate's original functions were to serve as a house of legislative review and to represent regional interests in the national policy process. Based upon its formal constitutional powers and, even more importantly, upon evolving political practice, the Senate has over the years added two other reasonably discrete and identifiable functions. In support of its legislative responsibilities, the Senate has since the 1960s spent considerable time on the investigation of public policy and its administration. As part of this activity, the Senate has served as a check on the exercise of the discretionary powers granted to ministers and public servants under delegated lawmaking authority from Parliament. Finally, the Senate has provided a growing measure of representation and protection for minorities and other special interests within Canadian society.

This chapter examines Senate activities connected to the above four broad functions – legislative review, regional representation, restraining Executive power, and protecting minorities. Four sets of questions are examined. First, does the Senate engage in independent legislative creativity either by initiating or amending bills? Or, is it merely a ratifying body for Government bills pushed through the House of Commons on the basis of party loyalty and party discipline? Second, does the Senate act as a counterbalance to the centralizing and majoritarian pressures of the contemporary model of cabinet-parliamentary government by providing protection for regional interests within Canadian society? Third, does the Senate through the investigative work of its committees provide a forum for the development of policy ideas that eventually are reflected in legislative proposals? Fourth, does the Senate play a particular role of focusing attention on people in society whose rights and interests are often overlooked – such as the poor, aboriginals, the elderly, veterans, etc.?

Drawing definitive conclusions about the extent and the effectiveness of Senate activity under these four headings will not be possible. Partly this is a result of the limits imposed by the time available to document all of the Senate's activities and by the space limits of a single chapter. Equally important, however, is the fact that the legislative process involves a multitude of different factors that shape behaviour and outcomes at the pre-parliamentary, parliamentary, and implementation stages of the policy cycle. Key parts of this process involving Cabinet and ministerial decision-making are shrouded in secrecy. Neatly separating the contribution of the Senate, in a legislative process that is partly closed, complicated, protracted, interdependent, riddled with pressures from various sources, and constantly changing, is obviously difficult.

This chapter makes three main arguments. First, it is argued that the Senate has more legislative influence than is popularly recognized. Second, it is suggested that for a number of reasons the Senate complements the role of the House of Commons by making a distinctive contribution to lawmaking. Third, it is argued that the Senate serves to restrain and to enforce greater accountability on the political Executive represented by the Prime Minister and Cabinet and on the permanent executive represented by the public service.

On the basis of how they are selected and removed, the varied backgrounds they bring to the job, and the way their attitudes and behaviours are shaped by the procedures and culture of the institution itself, senators adopt a somewhat different perspective on the parliamentary process than do members of the House of Commons. In general, the Senate perspective is less partisan, less majoritarian, less calculating in terms of potential electoral consequences and more balanced in terms of weighting past actions with future considerations. The Senate is still primarily a political body, but the "politics" of the Senate are not as dominated by competitive political parties engaged in the permanent election contest that is the essence of most (although not all) activity in the House of Commons. In an era when governments rely mainly on polling and the advice of the public service to shape policy, they look less and less to Parliament as a place to test their legislation and to search for improvements. Instead, the emphasis is on how to get legislation through as fast as possible and on how to dismiss the arguments made by one's political opponents. At times, the Senate resists this confrontational model of the legislative process and creates greater opportunities to test the validity and acceptability of the legislative plans formulated in the relatively closed world of the political Executive-bureaucratic arena. When the Senate serves as a check on Executive power in this way, it is often accused of acting illegitimately because it is not elected. Conversely, when senators acquiesce too readily in government plans, they are described as grateful party hacks. The truth is more often in the middle. From the outset, the Senate was intended to serve as a counterbalance to the House of Commons, and it continues to serve that role. It clearly could do a better job, but there is no denying that it already makes a worthwhile contribution.

Senate reform has been a popular topic almost since the day the institution was created. However, constitutional and political roadblocks have stood in the way of meaningful reform. Fundamental changes to the Senate, such as the election of senators and changes to its powers, would require a strong measure of federal-provincial agreement that has proven to be elusive. There are limits to how far the Senate can reform itself from within, presuming that the majority of its members wanted to do so and that the government would support particular reforms.[1] In summary, the Senate's contribution to the parliamentary process is determined by the constitutional framework, by external forces and the issues before the government, by current political circumstances (especially the attitude of the Prime Minister and Cabinet), and by the motivations and behaviour of the senators themselves.

The next section discusses the difficulty of conceptualizing and measuring the influence of the Senate within the wider policy process. The third section discusses the formal legislative authority of the Senate. While the Senate has the authority to veto Government bills, the actual use of this power is constrained by political convention. The fourth section examines the Senate's activity in reviewing legislation and the qualities of the Senate's legislative process that enable it to play a complementary role to the House of Commons. As part of this discussion, two familiar criticisms of the Senate's legislative role – that it fails to represent regional concerns and that it acts as a lobby on behalf of business interests – are examined. The fifth section examines the role that the Senate plays in identifying and mobilizing support for policy ideas that eventually become the basis for legislation presented by governments. Investigations by Senate committees are the main forums where this process occurs. The concluding section of the chapter provides an overview of the findings and some general thoughts on how the Senate's legislative role might be strengthened without having to attempt constitutional reform.

UNDERSTANDING PARLIAMENTARY INFLUENCE

Lawmaking is often the main function attributed to Parliament in terms of official interpretations and popular perceptions of the institution. However, according to political scientists, all legislatures perform a number of functions within their respective political systems. Table 1 presents one such typology of functions. Simply put, a function represents the contribution to and the effect upon the political system made by the legislature. A list of particular activities conducted by legislatures that contribute to the fulfillment of the various functions is also shown in table 1. Some of the functions are formally recognized, whereas others are implicit or latent in the operations of the legislatures. The importance of such a typology for this discussion is that the Senate must be seen as a multifunctional institution. Functions overlap in practice, particular activities can contribute to more than one function, there is often a need to balance or "trade off" the various functions, and the priority assigned to functions can shift over time. The inclusion of a particular function or activity in the table suggests nothing about how effectively or ineffectively the Senate operates in terms of the various dimension of its performance.

In practice there is a tension among the various functions ascribed to Parliament. On the one hand, Parliament serves to bring governments into existence through elections to the House of Commons and subsequently sustains them in office through votes of confidence in the Commons. Government business is conducted through the legislation and spending approved by the Commons and the Senate, followed by Royal Assent. Supporting strong governments has always been a role performed by Parliament. In the main, this role is performed by members from the governing party in the House of Commons. The Senate and senators have less responsibility for upholding governments. To balance strong governments, there is a recognized need for an institutionalized, effective, and credible opposition. Parliamentary traditions, procedures, and organization support the right of opposition parties to challenge governments, to express public concern, to enforce the principles of ministerial responsibility, to provide scrutiny of government performance, to represent an alternative government in waiting, and to promote ultimate democratic accountability to the electorate. For Parlia-

Table 1   Functions of Legislatures

---

1 Policy-Making Functions
   • lawmaking
   • control over taxing and spending
   • scrutiny of the government and of the bureaucracy

2 Representational Functions
   • recruiting and identifying leaders
   • dealing with the bureaucracy on behalf of constituents
   • an educational function clarifying policy choices for the electorate

3 Systems-Maintenance Functions
   • creating governments
   • making the actions of governments legitimate
   • mobilizing public support for the outcomes of the policy process
   • management of conflict within the political system
   • contributing to integration with the political system

---

ment to be effective in both its supporting and its critical role requires that members of the House of Commons and senators depart at times from party loyalty and act on the basis of independent judgement of the issues before them. This happens more often in the Senate then in the Commons because the Upper House does not control the fate of governments, senators do not face re-election pressures, and partisanship is more subdued than in the Commons.

Numerous factors, both inside and outside of the political system, can potentially affect the effectiveness of Parliament, including the Senate, in performing all of its functions. To avoid an unduly narrow and unfair assessment of the institution it is necessary to recognize the wider context and constraints under which it operates. At the risk of oversimplification, four broad sets of factors potentially affect the strength of Parliament within the Canadian political system:

• the constitutional arrangements, their impact on how power is distributed, the incentives they create for parliamentarians to engage in certain kinds of behaviours, and the opportunities available to change these written and unwritten "rules of the game";
• the social backgrounds, personal qualities and motivations of parliamentarians;
• the types of issues that arise within society and make it on to the institutional agendas of government in any given period and over time;
• the internal organization, procedures and resources of Parliament.

Of these four broad factors, only the last one can be easily changed in a deliberate and planned fashion and the dominance of Parliament by competitive political parties makes organizational and procedural change difficult because most governments do not want to disturb the existing political equilibrium to their own disadvantage.

Any discussion of the Senate as if it were a unified institution capable of formulating goals and adapting easily to changed circumstances is misleading. The Senate is a political body that contains several types of divisions. Even though partisanship in the Senate is muted compared to the House of Commons, competitive and disciplined political parties still provide the basis for membership and behaviour. Two broad patterns of behaviour are exhibited in the Senate: adversarial, partisan competition and consensual, nonpartisan collaboration. More of the behaviour of the Senate is consensual in nature, especially in relation to noncontroversial legislation and committee investigations, than is true of the House of Commons, where more of an "electioneering" atmosphere prevails more of the time. Although the Senate is usually less partisan than the Commons, the Upper House can never be characterized as nonpolitical for its functions are inherently political in nature.

Given the fact that many senators have previously served as elected representatives in other legislative bodies or as party supporters of some kind, it would be unrealistic to expect them to drop completely their partisan habits of a political lifetime. Besides, most of the ideas, energy, and intensity of parliamentary life come from the adversarial process of parties competing for public support. Would-be Senate reformers often fantasize about the possibility of a completely nonpartisan Senate, but realistically the best that could be hoped for is an institution in which strictly negative partisanship is reduced and the remaining, constructive partisanship is enhanced in quality. Of course, what is negative to what is constructive partisanship is very much a subjective judgement.

While the clash between governing and opposition parties represents the main division within Parliament, there are also disagreements within parties on matters of substance and process. Substantive disagreements can be along ideological, policy, regional, and other lines. At times there are disagreements between the parliamentary leadership of each party and its followers. For example, governments have frequently taken the Senate for granted in different ways and there have been protests to the Prime Minister that the institution must be given the time, resources, and freedom to provide an independent judgement on issues. The popular image of senators as completely docile party loyalists who never question the judgement of their leaders is promoted by the fact that most intraparty disagreements take place in the privacy of the weekly party caucuses or on an informal, unpublicized basis.

In summary, notwithstanding constitutional rhetoric to the contrary, the Senate seldom acts on a unified basis; behaviour is structured mainly along party lines. Traditionally, many government senators did not want to see the institution strengthened if this meant a loss of predictability and Cabinet control over the legislative process. As is discussed below, the past two decades have seen the Senate, including government members, demonstrate more assertiveness and independence from government control.

This chapter is concerned with the effectiveness of the Senate as a law-making body. Its main legislative role is to review government-sponsored public bills that have already undergone debate and perhaps amendment in the House of Commons. Senators also play a direct role and an indirect role in identifying ideas for legislation. A great deal of the Senate's time is, in fact, spent talking about legislation, matters that could lead to legislation, or concerns that arise out of experience with past legislation. However, for many years, scholarly commentators have assumed (or regretfully concluded) that most legislation is initiated and formulated by ministers, working in collaboration with senior public service advisors who, in turn, are carefully attuned to the interests and demands of the groups within society that are most directly affected. Allegedly, over the years there has been a decline in the contribution of Parliament to the formulation and refinement of legislation to the point today that its role consists mainly of ratifying and legitimating decisions reached in the political-executive-bureaucratic core of the political system.

Having accepted that Parliament usually plays a marginal role in law-making, political scientists began to explore possible indirect, nondecisional roles of Parliament within the legislative process and the wider policy-making processes of modern government. In this view, Parliament has merely influence, not real power or real control. Executive leadership, direction, and control is the prevailing pattern. However, the Cabinet and the bureaucracy operate in a wider context of societal and institutional discussion and disagreement over what kinds of legislative actions are needed. Adopting this "discussion model" of policy-making and law-making leads to a recognition that different institutions and actors make different contributions to the development of a policy agenda for government. Parliament is an important participant in this wider discussion process within society. As suggested earlier, Parliament exists to support the government, but also to oversee it. It acts as a check on Executive leadership by criticizing and influencing it and by approving, rejecting, or amending specific legislative proposals. Parliamentary influence is difficult to identify and to measure empirically because it takes different forms, often operates in private, has an impact in an indirect, subtle, and long-term way, and operates amidst a variety of forces swirling around legislation. For a number of reasons, direct and obvious "indicators" of the influence of Parliament, such as the number of bills defeated, delayed, amended, or withdrawn as a result of parliamentary pressure, are not a reliable or comprehensive measure of the institution's contribution to the legislative process.

First, such indicators represent "dumb data" in the sense that they do not speak for themselves, but must be interpreted in light of the context in which Parliament deals with legislation. For example, the number of successful amendments to Government bills approved by the Senate or Commons committee that studied them could be a misleading indicator of parliamentary influence if all of the amendments actually originated in the minister's office or the bureaucracy as a result of last-minute consultations with relevant pressure groups or provincial governments. The fact that the Senate handles most bills after they have been dealt with by the Commons represents a basic limit on the creativity of Senate committees and individual senators, since potential amendments may already have been adopted or rejected by the minister. For both Houses of Parliament to contribute directly to the formulation of laws usually requires a fortuitous combination of circumstances, such as pressures from outside organizations to change bills, a willingness by ministers and their public service advisors to consider amendments, cross-party support perhaps along regional lines, and time to mobilize public opinion regarding proposed legislation.

A second difficulty with direct measures of Parliament's contribution to lawmaking is that they miss the process of anticipation that seems to be involved with the development of bills: anticipation both within ministers' offices and, to a lesser extent, among public service advisors. Successful governing involves, in part, the creation of the appearance of acting on the basis of a widespread consensus. It is for this reason that governments usually consult the outside groups most directly affected by bills before they are tabled in Parliament so as to forestall criticism and to gauge the intensity of opposition. In a similar fashion, the potential reactions within Parliament will be anticipated. The main concern of ministers is the reactions of their own members of the House of Commons and of senators; opposition parties will usually be critical, especially if bills involve matters of partisan disagreement. When ministers anticipate reactions of their colleagues in caucus and when they modify bills on the basis of caucus input, there will be greater pressure on government members of the House of Commons and senators to support bills when they are being debated in both chambers and their committees. In this way, the "pre-parliamentary" process contributes to the appearance that government members are nothing more than "trained seals" who follow the party line.

Third, a "scoreboard" approach based upon a count of bills defeated or changed by Parliament ignores the role of the institution as a "billboard" of public concerns and policy ideas that governments can draw upon in terms of inspiration for legislation. As a public forum for the generation and debate of policy ideas, Parliament at times helps to set the agenda of governments. At other times, it helps to set the parameters of what is politically acceptable and feasible in terms of public policy. On an occasional basis, the Senate is involved in the actual initiation legislation. Only a tiny minority of the bills sponsored by individual members of the House of

Commons or senators ever make it through Parliament to become law. However, there is a little-noticed process in which Parliament, particularly through its committees, serves as an "incubator" of policy ideas that are struggling to gain life in the form of legislation. Sometimes governments adopt such ideas as their own after they have been presented to Parliament over several sessions as private members' bills and resolutions. In summary, Parliament serves as one among a number of forums in which public concerns are expressed, amplified, refined, and acted upon in ways that often escape direct measurement.

Any realistic description of the broad Canadian policy process must begin by acknowledging that prime-ministerial, Cabinet, and ministerial leadership and control forms the predominant pattern. Parliament's role is not to govern, but rather to act as a check on Executive power. It exists to provide oversight of the exercise of Executive power as a basis for enforcing democratic accountability. In practice, Parliament acts mainly to support and to legitimize government proposals for legislation, but it is also expected to criticize, influence, and, on some occasions, amend or reject bills presented by ministers.

THE SENATE'S VETO POWERS

The Senate's formal powers and how they have been utilized in practice will be discussed only briefly because they are covered elsewhere in this volume. The Fathers of Confederation saw the Senate as performing more than a technical revising function within the Canadian legislative process. They saw it as a check on democracy and a stabilizing force to resist rash and impetuous actions by the "popular" and "democratic" element within the House of Commons. Canada's first Prime Minister, John A. Macdonald, said that the Senate should provide "sober second thought in legislation" and should not be "a mere chamber for registering the decrees of the Lower House." The founders of Confederation saw the Senate as independent, complementary, and a controlling influence in the legislative process, not as a subordinate body the House of Commons.[2] The founders' fear of excessive democracy is antiquated in the context of a twenty-first-century democracy, but the notion of a check on the House of Commons is still relevant given the concentration of power in the hands of the Prime Minister and his control over Parliament through party discipline. Restraining a Prime Minister and cabinet may be particularly justified during the first term of a new government, if they are taking highly controversial actions for which they did not seek a mandate during the previous election.

In terms of legislative powers, the Senate was granted nearly equal authority to the House of Commons, with the exception that financial legislation must originate in the Commons. The Senate may initiate other bills, and it must review and approve all bills passed by the House of

Commons before they receive Royal Assent and become law. Both Houses use the same five procedural steps to pass legislation, but how they operate in practice is quite different. The number of Government bills that start in the Senate is small, although it has varied over the years. In theory, the Senate has an absolute veto over all bills, with the exception of constitutional amendments involving provincial legislatures, which it can only delay for up to 180 days. Although the Senate made fairly regular use of the veto early in the twentieth century, more than two decades of non-use after 1940 created the impression that the power to block government legislation has been eroded. However, it is important to recognize that use of the veto, or even the threat of its use, cannot be separated in practice from other Senate actions on Government bills, ranging from review, delay, negotiation, amendment, and defeat.[3] It is the requirement for Senate review of all bills and the potential to reject them that provides the foundation for Senate influence.

Based upon infrequent use of the veto during the postwar period, there has emerged the popular notion that in the event of conflict between the two Chambers of Parliament, the Senate should ultimately defer to the clearly expressed will of the House of Commons. It has been suggested that a political convention in favour of a subordinate role for the Senate now exists. Conventions can be described as extra-legal rules that emerge from the political process over time and represent a restraint on the exercise of power. Since they are general, flexible, and evolutionary, conventions are open to varying interpretations and controversy.[4] There is clearly no justification in history or more recent practice for saying that the Senate must acquiesce, automatically and immediately, once the House of Commons has unequivocally expressed its political will on a particular piece of legislation. That would deny the Senate a useful, complementary role. Exactly when it is legitimate for the Senate to use its veto to defeat a bill remains largely undefined, but past practice suggests such action will be rare. The circumstances when the Senate might invoke its veto to force governments to change their mind include:

- highly controversial bills for which the governments lack an electoral mandate;
- dangerous bills that could do unpredictable and irreparable damage to the national interest;
- bills that violate the *Constitution*, including the *Charter of Rights and Freedoms*;
- bills that violate the fundamental rights of linguistic and other minorities.

While the above list might represent general conditions under which the Senate could legitimately use its veto to defeat or to delay bills, each condition is open to interpretation, and there is no definitive statement of the convention respecting the use of the veto power.

After decades of relative Senate docility, Canadian governments tended to take for granted the expeditious passage of their bills unchanged by the Upper House. During earlier decades, there were several reasons why senators tended to go along with the government's legislative program. First, as the twentieth century progressed, the Senate was seen to lack democratic legitimacy and therefore to have no right to frustrate the clearly expressed will of the popularly elected House of Commons. Second, for most of the past century the Liberal Party had a majority in both Houses of Parliament, and therefore there was little inclination on the part of most senators to frustrate government initiatives through public confrontations. Instead, disagreements could be resolved in the privacy of the party caucus or through other informal channels. Third, the main Canadian political parties have for the most part been pragmatic and non-ideological in their appeal to voters. With some notable exceptions, this has meant that the winning party in federal elections did not come into office with a detailed legislative program. As a consequence, nothing equivalent to Salisbury Convention in the United Kingdom emerged. That Convention suggests that the House of Lords should not defeat or alter beyond recognition any bill that featured prominently in the ruling party's previous general election manifesto.[5] Nothing as definitive as this interpretation of the legitimate role of the Upper House has emerged to date in the Canadian context.

The ambiguity of the convention regarding the Senate's subordination to the Commons led to intense controversy after 1984. The Liberal-controlled Upper House blocked or delayed a series of bills sent over by the Progressive Conservative Government led by Brian Mulroney.[6] It is important to emphasize that we are talking here about the Senate seeking to turn back government legislation by opposing bills in principle, not in attempting to revise them in their technical details. In 1991, on a free vote, the Senate used its veto for the first time in three decades to defeat a Government bill on abortion. On this sensitive moral issue, seven of Progressive Conservative senators joined Liberals and Independents in voting against the bill presented by the Mulroney Government. The Mulroney Government did not seek to reverse this setback by offering a second bill, which suggests that it believed there was not a consensus among Canadians on the issue.

Apart from the unique case of the Abortion Bill, there were numerous other bills that became stalled in the Senate, to the point that Prime Minister Mulroney threatened to place a time limit on the delaying powers of the Upper House. Particularly controversial was the Senate's decision to hold up a money bill for several weeks, forcing the government to spend more on interest payments. However, the most significant incidence of obstruction was the campaign by Liberal senators to block the free trade legislation – a campaign that helped to set the date and the agenda for the 1988 federal election.

After gaining re-election with a second majority, the Mulroney Conservatives introduced the Goods and Services Tax, which the Liberal Senate majority, reacting to widespread outside opposition, refused to pass. In September 1990, Prime Minister Mulroney used the so-called "swamping provision" in the *Constitution Act, 1867* as a basis for the appointment of eight additional senators. Intended as a means to break deadlocks between the House of Commons and the Senate, the "swamping provision" had never been used before. Eventually the logjam in the Senate was broken, but not before the government was forced to retreat on several measures and the Liberal senators were harshly criticized both for exceeding their legitimate authority and for some of their extreme parliamentary tactics. Even today there is still residual bitterness over the partisan battles of the Mulroney era, particularly among a small but influential group of Progressive Conservative senators who identify closely with the former Prime Minister and the policies of his government.

The 1984 to 1993 period illustrates how outside circumstances and the types of issues on the parliamentary agenda influence the behaviour of the various parties within the Senate. It also illustrates how the convention of Commons' supremacy is open to changing and conflicting interpretations in the light of new political circumstances.

The Senate's assertiveness during the Mulroney years was caused by a series of factors: public hostility toward parts of the policy agenda of the Mulroney Government, the partisan desire of Liberals to capitalize on this public opposition, ideological and policy disagreements between the two parties, the personalities and tactical approach of the Liberal leadership in the Senate, and the desire by some senators to halt the perceived erosion of the Senate's powers within the legislative process.

Constitutional conventions are not derived from a single episode; rather agreement on their existence emerges among the relevant political actors over time. Therefore, it is not entirely clear whether the Senate's opposition to the Mulroney Government's agenda represented a transformation of the Senate's traditional role. When the Chrétien Liberals took office in 1993, they also faced an opposition-controlled Senate that proceeded to delay a number of bills. In general, however, the assertiveness of the Senate during the 1993–97 period was less ideologically motivated than during the Mulroney years, in part because the new Liberal Government adopted many of the policies of the former Conservative Government. There was also something of a "revenge" factor in the attempts by some Conservative senators to hold up Liberal legislation. After 1993, Senate obstruction of Government bills was less systematic and objections to bills were more often technical than substantive.

Franks suggests that recent history has produced an institutional culture that is more partisan, but also more individualistic and independent.7 This change is reflected in the increased tendency of Liberal senators to speak and act against the wishes of their government. Several explanations are possible for the willingness of Liberal senators to challenge their government more frequently. First, there is a new generation of senators who see the job as full-time and want to play a meaningful role in the legislative process. Second, there is a recognition among senators that power in the policy process is concentrated in the Office of the Prime Minister and, to a lesser extent, the Cabinet, and that the House of Commons is limited to a marginal role. In these circumstances, the Senate is seen as a countervailing force to the normal pattern of Executive dominance. Third, through appointments made since 1993, the Liberals have gained a secure majority, and Prime Minister Chrétien has appointed a number of individuals who have opted to sit as "Independent" senators. All these developments have contributed to independent behaviour and less predictability in the Senate's handling of government business.

THE SENATE AND LEGISLATIVE REVIEW

To this point, the discussion has focused on the debate over whether the Senate is ultimately subordinate to the Commons in the parliamentary process. In contrast, there is far less controversy over the recognized right of the Senate to amend bills that come over from the House of Commons. Earlier studies suggested that the Senate played an important role as a reviewing chamber to catch faultily drafted legislation and to introduce late amendments that reflected outside interventions.[8] In 1980, a Senate committee offered the following, perhaps not entirely objective appraisal of the Senate's legislative review:

Senators ... do an indispensable job in simplifying and clarifying legislation, saving the taxpayer money, saving the citizen from unfair and unworkable provisions, and saving the citizens and the courts from needless and costly litigation."[9]

Many senators also maintain that they could do an even better job of legislative review if there was better management of the timeline for the passage of bills. They are referring to the fact that bills often reach the Senate so late in terms of the government's timetable, including close to Christmas and summer breaks, that it is not possible for the Senate to give bills the detailed study they deserve.

The Deputy Government Leader in the Senate is responsible for managing the legislative process and for this purpose participates in a weekly meeting that also involves the Government Leader in the Senate, the Government House Leader from the Commons, the Chief Party Whip from the Commons, and staff to these individuals. At these Monday afternoon meetings, the Deputy Government Leader in the Senate communicates potential Senate reactions to bills, warns of possible delays in passage, and, when time is tight, asks the Government House Leader to identify which bills are a priority. These meetings provide an opportunity for the Senate to have influence on the contents and the timing of the government's legislative program, but of course such influence goes unnoticed by the media and the public since it occurs in private.

The argument that the Senate contributes to lawmaking through its review of bills is based on the benefits that flow from several features of the Upper House:

Expertise – the extensive legal, governmental, business, and other experience represented by senators;
Time – a less pressured pace in the Senate, the absence of constituency duties, the lack of the requirement to sustain a government majority, and the greater continuity of membership than in the Commons mean that there is more time to devote to the detailed study of legislation and to committee investigations of topics that could be the basis for future legislation;
Independence – because the Senate is not a confidence chamber, because senators cannot be removed from office, because only one or two senators are placed in Cabinet, because many senators have fulfilled their political ambitions earlier in their lives, and because many have stature based on their backgrounds, senators are more immune than members of the House of Commons from pressures by the government, beyond appeals to loyalty to their party;
Subdued Partisanship – the Senate operates on a less adversarial basis than the Commons because the life of the government is not at stake, members do not face re-election pressures and the stature of individual senators leads to a greater atmosphere of respect and civility;
Procedural Freedom – for most of its history the Senate operated with limited rules, relying on good will and compromises to resolve procedural disagreements; after the upheavals of the 1980s, stricter rules were adopted, but the Senate is still less subject to government control through procedural means and individual senators have more opportunity than members of the House of Commons to raise issues of concern.

It is on the basis of these institutional features that its defenders argue the Senate makes a distinctive contribution to lawmaking and could do even more in this regard if governments showed more respect for the Senate's prerogatives within the legislative process.

The above arguments in favour of the Senate as a "house of review" are plausible, but finding unambiguous empirical evidence to support them is difficult. For example, various studies have been conducted on the percentage of Commons' bills that were amended through Senate review, and on the subsequent extent to which the Commons accepted the changes proposed by the Senate. The proportion of bills amended by the Senate was in steady decline during the latter half of the previous century. Before 1943, the Senate modified 17–25 percent of the bills; from 1942 to 1957 the proportion dropped to 13 percent; and from 1957 to 1988 the proportion dropped to just 4 percent.[10] While there is variation from one session to the next, it has been rare in recent years for more than seven percent of Government bills to undergo amendment in the Senate. It should be noted that in most parliamentary sessions there are eight appropriations or spending bills that the Senate does not attempt to amend because, constitutionally, spending must originate with the Crown (i.e., the Cabinet) and successful amendments would be seen as a serious political challenge to the government.

Judging the impact of the Senate simply from the number of amendments is misleading for a number of reasons. First, detailed attention needs to be paid to the types of amendments proposed and their fate, whether accepted or rejected. Second, bills may be drafted in the Executive-bureaucratic arena with the reaction of the Senate in mind, creating less need for amendments. Third, even when amendments are unsuccessful, we should not discount the benefits that flow from having a public discussion of the issues involved. Fourth, many of the bills introduced by governments are "housekeeping" in nature, amendments to existing legislation to take account of charged circumstances, and they will not evoke much response in the Senate. Finally, when broader, more sensitive issues of public policy are involved with bills, like the Free Trade Agreement in 1988 or the Clarity Bill in 2000, the Senate can attempt major amendments that challenge the principles of the bills, but governments feel obliged to resist changes.

A part of the reason for the decline of the Senate's review function is the improved legislative drafting capacity within the Department of Justice that has meant fewer bills resemble (in the words of the colourful, late Senator Eugene Forsey) a "dog's breakfast" when they enter the parliamentary arena. Since the adoption of the *Charter of Rights and Freedoms* in 1982, the Justice Department has emerged as a central clearing house to ensure that the bills from "line departments" are written in "Charter-proof" language, with the hope of keeping the government out of court.

A further explanation of the above statistics is that they do not reflect an aspect of legislative review by the Senate known as "pre-study" or the Hayden Formula, as it is sometimes called in honour of its inventor and most successful practitioner, the late Senator Salter Hayden. As Chairman of the active and influential Senate Standing Committee on Banking, Trade and Commerce, Hayden began in 1971 the informal practice of acquiring from the minister in charge of a bill and from the Government House Leader, permission to pre-study the subject matter of legislation currently before the House of Commons or an issue requiring government legislation in the near future. Based upon pre-study sessions, the Senate would give advice informally to the ministers in charge of bills and changes would be made during passage in the House of Commons. Occasionally, a bill was even withdrawn and a new bill was substituted based upon the recommendations from the Senate. The pre-study mechanism worked best in terms of influencing government thinking when the Senate did not forsake, but held in reserve, its ultimate right to make amendments. The mechanism was used with particular effectiveness in relation to complicated and technical legislation such as the *Income Tax Act*, the *Bankruptcy Act*, the *Corporations Act*, and many others. In those situations where "pre-study" was used, the public record would not show that the Senate had contributed to the amendments accepted by the responsible minister and adopted by the Commons. From the standpoint of the governing party, the advantage of "pre-study" was that it avoided the potential embarrassment of having bills extensively amended by its own supporters in the Senate. It also gave the Senate committees assigned to conduct the pre-studies something to do early in a session before bills were transferred from the Commons.

While there are recognized examples of the Senate improving bills by means of pre-study, there is also the concern that the practice undermined the normal legislative process. This was the position taken by Liberal Senator Allan MacEachen, a shrewd parliamentarian with many years prior experience in the House of Commons. Earlier in his career, when he was Government House Leader in the Commons, pre-study was seen as a useful way to avoid open conflicts with the Senate and to make it more productive. Upon moving to the Senate in 1984, however, MacEachen convinced his Liberal colleagues to drop the procedure. Pre-study, he argued, made Senate approval automatic, it allowed the chairs of Senate committees to lobby ministers privately on behalf perhaps of narrow interests and it left the public impression that the Senate was incapable of legislative creativity since there was no recognition of its preliminary work on bills. During the first Mulroney Government period (1984–88), when pre-study was dropped, the Senate amended 7.3 percent of the bills, compared with just 4 percent on average during the entire period from 1957 to 1988.[11] Only during Diefenbaker's government (1958–62), again when a large Conservative majority in the Commons faced a hostile Liberal majority in the Senate, did the Senate amendment rate go above 7 percent.

This pattern of amendment activity, especially when viewed alongside of the efforts by Liberal senators to stall the initiatives of the first Mulroney Government, strongly suggests that partisanship is the main driving force in the Senate. However, detailed analyses of the Senate's activities during the three decades prior to 1990 caused Andrew Heard to conclude that partisanship was not the single most important factor behind the level of

Senate amendment activity.[12] Instead, Heard's regression analysis of a number of factors pointed to the size of the government's majority in the House of Commons as the best predictor of the amendment attempts by senators. He offers the hypothesis that governments with large majorities are less likely to accept amendments sought by the opposition in the Commons and that the Senate sees its role as counterbalancing the power of governments to push legislation through unchanged based on strict party voting. Heard cites the example of the Trudeau Liberal Government (1968-72), which saw a relatively large portion (6.1 percent) of its legislation amended even though the Liberals controlled the Senate. In summary, Heard is suggesting that senators, regardless of party, see it as their institutional prerogative and duty to attenuate the normal pattern of Executive dominance in the legislative process, especially when governments are acting without a clear mandate in the face of widespread hostility to particular legislative proposals. The instinct within the Senate opposition to insist upon the right to challenge Government bills is probably stronger in parliamentary situations like that which prevailed after 1993 when the main opposition parties in the Commons were both regional in their focus and appeal. The Progressive Conservative senators claimed that as the only other truly national party, they were in the best position to offer a critical assessment of Liberal legislation.

To this point, the paper has examined the factors that encourage the Senate to amend Government bills, but little has been said about how successful senators are in actually gaining government acceptance of their amendments. If we are interested in the Senate's ultimate influence and contribution to lawmaking, we must know how often Senate amendments are accepted by the government and the Commons. Heard has conducted this kind of analysis over all Parliaments from 1957 to 1988.[13] In the 1984–88 Parliament (Mulroney Government), eighteen of the 248 bills passed by the Commons were amended by the Senate, and twelve of these amended bills were accepted by the House of Commons. Heard's table reveals that this success rate for the Senate in gaining acceptance for its amendments is fairly typical. This finding suggests that it is, in fact, possible for the Senate to change bills. However, it is also necessary to recognize that most amendments proposed by the Senate are technical in nature. Typically, it offers more amendments on bills dealing with specialized matters, that are important but not of widespread public interest. Also, in some instances the responsible minister may, in fact, have arranged for amendments to be passed by the Senate. Finally, the Senate's success in gaining adoption of its amendments may depend crucially on pressures from outside groups.

Even when the government and the Commons refuse a Senate amendment, the process of a Senate committee taking expert testimony and recommending changes draws attention to the contentious features of bills. In this way, the amending process can promote closer examination of aspects of bills by the government, the media, and interested members of the public.

The Senate's Role as a Protector of Regional Interests

This brings us to what many think should be the Senate's principal role in the national legislative process, namely the promotion and protection of regional interests. The failure of the Senate to articulate and to mediate regional interests is widely regarded as its greatest failing. While it is structured along regional lines, as an appointed body the Senate is said to lack the political authority to assert regional wishes against the "democratic will" expressed by votes in the House of Commons. The fact that Senate appointments have been used by prime ministers as devices of party patronage has further discredited the Senate as a protector of regional interests. Allegedly, party loyalty has taken precedence over regional representation. Furthermore, without the requirement of re-election there is supposedly little incentive for senators to keep in touch with public opinion in the regions they ostensibly represent. In short, senators are said to lack visibility and credibility as spokespersons for their regions.

A closer examination of this familiar argument that the Senate has failed as a regional body reveals that it is not altogether persuasive. The necessary qualifications can only be made briefly in the space available here. First, it should be noted that the original intention was to have the Senate represent the views of provincial societies on national legislation. This role is not the same as representing the interests and positions of provincial governments and legislatures. In other words, the Canadian Senate was never meant to be the equivalent of the German Bundesrat, in which the constituent units of the federal system are represented in the Upper House. In Canada's federal system, there are many other forums, such as federal-provincial conferences and the courts, where the interests of provincial governments can be defended. This difference between representing regional perspectives in the national legislative process versus the representation of the interests of provincial governments is often obscured in the rhetoric of political debate. At times, senators find that their interpretation of a province's needs and interests will clash with the views of a provincial government. In such situations, given the publicity-generating capacity of provincial governments, the tendency in the media and among the public is to see the Senate as failing to defend regional interests. It is more accurate to say that such disagreements reflect the different representational roles played by the Senate and provincial governments within our political system.

Despite the original intention to have the Senate serve as a regional protector, the *Constitution Act, 1867* did not spell out this role or provide any mechanism for performing it. The regional structure for Senate membership and the nearly equal legislative powers granted to the Senate reflected the belief that it should act as a brake on the House of Commons on behalf of the smaller provinces. For a number of reasons – including the criticisms presented above – the Senate's regional role has, to say the least, remained underdeveloped. In part, this reflects the fact that protection of regional interests has taken place in other locations within the political system, such as:

- in the courts where early rulings on the division of powers extended the jurisdiction of the provincial governments;
- in the numerous federal-provincial conferences and committees dealing with a wide range of policy issues both national and provincial in scope;
- in Cabinet, which was seen from the outset as a more important forum for regional accommodation than the Senate and has developed this function through mechanisms like the appointment of regional ministers;
- in the elaborate system of private meetings of national, regional, and subregional caucuses attended by both members of the House of Commons and senators from the various provinces that developed over time, especially after the 1960s.[14]

A couple of observations must be made about the effectiveness of these institutional mechanisms for the expression of regional concerns in the national policy process. First, while they may have taken some pressure off the Senate to perform as a regional body, this is not an adequate explanation or justification for its failure to develop institutional procedures and forums to enhance its regional role. Second, the other forums for the expression and accommodation of regional concerns operate mainly in private, leaving the public with the impression that regional representation in national policy-making is non-existent and/or ineffective. A Senate that more frequently expressed and accommodated regional differences in an open manner would probably add to the legitimacy of national policies in all parts of the country.

The weakness of the Senate's regional role is often attributed to the partisan basis for appointment. Senators are said to be beholden to the Prime Minister and/or their party and not to the electorate of their province. Again, this is an exaggeration of the extent to which senators remain purely partisan figures. First, as was suggested earlier, statistical analysis reveals that amendment activity within the Senate is not motivated primarily by partisan considerations. Second, earlier studies revealed that cross-party voting, although low in both Houses, was higher in the Senate.[15] This finding has to be interpreted carefully because formal recorded votes are used infrequently in the Senate compared to the House of Commons. Usually recorded votes are demanded by the Senate Opposition when disagreements within the governing party exist and this contributes to the appearance of more Senate dissent.

Probably no statistical analysis can capture the different partisan climate that *normally* prevails in the Senate compared with the Commons. The word "normally" is in italics because, as we saw earlier, there are times when party lines are rigidly drawn. Perhaps a better indicator of the muted partisanship of the Senate is the role of the party whips within the two Chambers. As in the Commons, the party whips keep members informed of Senate business, the schedule in the Chamber and in the committees, and the requirement to ensure quorum. Traditionally, however, the task of pairing members for recorded votes, a significant function of the Commons' whip, was largely unheard of in the Senate. Moreover, among Senate whips there is less emphasis on bringing party pressures to bear upon independent-minded senators. The psychological pressures to side with one's party are still there, of course, but the whips and the Prime Minister have fewer sanctions to wield against maverick senators. In the past at least, most senators were not regular participants in the caucus processes of the governing party, which meant that there was less onus on them to support party positions developed in such meetings. Some senators have made a point of staying away from caucus to emphasize their independence. Of course, such actions detract from the claim that party caucuses represent important forums for regional input.

Finally, it should be noted that senators may not confront the need to reconcile party loyalty with regional representation because partisanship incorporates regional considerations. In other words, successful mainstream political parties have grasped the need to make their electoral appeals as inclusive as possible and this has required them to accommodate a variety of competing perspectives. As the most frequent governing party during the twentieth century, the Liberal Party in particular developed an organizational culture that emphasized the necessity to integrate regional perspectives into their partisanship. In short, regionalism and partisanship co-mingle on many issues, and through years of service senators develop a national outlook on their role and the issues before them.

Differentiating party and regional issues can be difficult, but it is still possible to identify cases where the Senate has acted in defence of regional interests during the handling of Government bills. The following are some brief examples.

- The *Maritime Code Act* of 1977 threatened to abolish all ports of registry, replacing them with the single port of Ottawa. The Senate's amendments saved the Atlantic Provinces, Quebec and British Columbia from the plan.
- An act to repeal the Department of Regional Industrial Expansion introduced in 1989 was reviewed by a Senate committee that heard from

fifteen witnesses. The committee's five recommendations reflected the fear that the Bill would diminish the national government's commitment and capacity to alleviate regional economic disparities.

- Amendments to the *Unemployment Insurance Act* proposed by the Mulroney Government in 1989 were first strenuously opposed by Liberal members of the House of Commons and the majority of witnesses before a Commons committee because the changes would reduce benefits to seasonal workers in places like the Atlantic provinces. The Liberal-controlled Senate that took up the cause insisted on amendments, but was not very successful.
- A 1997 bill to harmonize the Goods and Services Tax and the provincial sales taxes in three of the four Atlantic provinces was the subject of public hearings (more than two hundred witnesses) conducted by a Senate committee in the region. A unanimous report recommended a number of amendments to delay tax-inclusive pricing and to provide an offsetting tax-credit to low-income individuals. After a long debate, the government and the Commons accepted the changes, in part to meet a deadline for implementation of the new tax.
- On a 1998 bill to amend the *Wheat Board Act*, the Senate's Agriculture and Forestry Committee heard from nearly two hundred individuals and organizations from the Prairies. Based on this testimony, the Committee proposed three amendments and the government accepted them with gratitude.

In addition to its handling of bills, the Senate regularly makes a contribution to regional awareness through the work of its investigative committees (a subject that is discussed below).

In conclusion on the Senate's regional role, it must be noted that the institution has failed to develop any separate procedures or forums to support this role. A 1980 report from a committee of senators dealing with internal Senate reform acknowledged as much. It called for the creation of a standing committee on regional affairs that would hold cross-country hearings on regionally-sensitive issues. Another suggestion was regional all-party caucuses to serve as sounding boards for regional needs and concerns. Whatever the practicality of these two suggestions, they were never acted upon and alternative means of bringing regional issues to the forefront have not been tried. In fairness to senators, they have occasionally collaborated across party lines on an informal basis in order to advance regional interests when threats or opportunities presented themselves. Of course, such all-party groupings are not visible to the media and the public. In summary, there is more regional representation occurring within the Senate than is popularly imagined, but most of it goes unnoticed and the extent of its impact is difficult to measure.

The Senate as a Representative of Other Interests

In addition to being unfairly portrayed as party hacks who have forsaken their regional responsibilities, senators have also been criticized as an influential "lobby from within" acting on behalf of the business community. According to this thesis, influential senators on key committees promote bills and amendments that create a favourable business climate. According to an analysis conducted three decades ago, senators with corporate connections were able to alter legislation that sought to regulate business and to redistribute wealth.[16] The epitome of the "business reviewers" back in the 1960s and 1970s was Senator Salter Hayden, Chairman of the Standing Committee on Banking, Trade and Commerce. That Committee was where much of the lobbying on behalf of business took place. The suspicion that the Senate supports a privileged economic elite has not gone away, as revealed by the fact that journalists track the corporate directorships held by senators and there are regular calls for stricter disclosure and conflict-of-interest rules governing their behaviour.[17]

The thesis that the Senate serves as a business lobby is not entirely persuasive. First, there have always been a significant number of senators with extensive business connections. However, a background analysis of individuals appointed to the Senate by Prime Ministers Trudeau, Mulroney, and Chrétien revealed that 32 percent, 39 percent, and 40 percent of the appointments respectively were individuals with backgrounds in business. In other words, most of the recent appointees to the Senate were not recruited directly from the business community; instead the majority came from other social backgrounds. 80 percent of Trudeau's appointments, 72 percent of Mulroney's, and 55 percent of Chrétien's appointments had held elected political offices before joining the Senate.[18] Given the current anti-politics mood of many members of the public, the elevation of former elected politicians to the Senate is seen as an inappropriate reward for past party service. Such criticism ignores the fact that the Senate is pre-eminently a political body. Senators who bring a understanding of public policy issues and competing perspectives on them can more readily identify what actions are politically feasible. Such senators are also often effective in communication with the public to promote understanding and support for those actions. As politicians, senators (including those with business backgrounds) recognize the need in public policy to reconcile competing values and interests, not to give more powerful groups all that they demand.

Second, the evidence presented to support the portrayal of the Senate as a business lobby is selective consisting mainly of references to the activities of a few senators on one or two committees. Even the original study undertaken by Campbell in the 1970s identified a second group of senators identified as "social investigators" who promoted the cause of less powerful groups in society.

Third, the fact that business interests may have disproportionate access to important Senate forums mirrors the pattern found throughout the policy cycle and the reasons for the business advantage over other groups are many. Surveys of business representatives reveal that they rank senior public servants as their preferred targets of lobbying activity, ahead even of Cabinet ministers. Only after business representatives have failed to convince key decision-makers in the Executive-bureaucratic arena, and perhaps after having stated their case before a Commons committee, do they show up before a Senate committee to oppose bills or to seek amendments. In other words, the Senate is used mainly as an appeal mechanism.

Fourth, rarely can the Senate successfully initiate legislation favourable to any interest. It can prompt, it can delay, it can amend (occasionally), and it can veto (very rarely), but real control over the content of legislation rests with ministers and their public service advisors. Finally, some of the amendments seen as favourable to business could equally be interpreted as the Senate protecting the legal rights of corporations and their shareholders.

The popular stereotype of senators as defenders of corporate interests is also contradicted by its efforts on behalf of less powerful groups within Canadian society. Back in the 1960s, it was a Senate committee that investigated serious poverty in the midst of growing affluence, and, in conjunction with other forces, its report led to a series of new social policies. When comprehensive tax reform was undertaken during the early 1970s, the Senate's committee studying amendments to the *Income Tax Act* pushed for a more redistributive taxation system than did its Commons' counterpart. During the 1980s, Senate committees did important work on retirement age policies and on children in conflict with the law. During the first seven years of the 1990s, five bills providing for protection against discrimination based upon sexual orientation were brought before Parliament. Two of these bills were introduced by Conservative Senator Noel Kinsella. A complicated interplay between the government, the Commons, and the Senate led to the eventual passage of a "gay rights" amendment to the *Canadian Human Rights Act*. As a result of a late Senate amendment that slipped through the Commons unnoticed, the version of the Bill adopted in 1997 provided for the extension of affirmative action programs to victims of sexual discrimination, even though this feature had been deliberately omitted from the Government bill.

To this point, the discussion has focused on the response of the Senate to Government bills that have already received passage by the House of Commons. However, Government bills can also be initiated in the Senate, with the exception of money bills that must begin their parliamentary life in the House of Commons. Money bills involve the raising or expenditure of public funds. While the Senate must eventually pass, defeat, or amend money bills, amendments can only be in the direction of decreasing taxes or spending.

Even with non-money bills there are political constraints on the freedom of the government to introduce bills first in the Senate. First, because the government has greater control of the Commons and its committees, ministers (and often their public service advisors) prefer to start bills there. Prior examination of bills by Senate committees might give ammunition to the opposition parties in the House of Commons. The fact that not all opposition parties in the Commons are represented in the Senate leads to the objection that bills do not receive a full representative review when started in the Upper Chamber. This argument is often combined with a defence of the institutional prerogative of the House of Commons, as the more democratic House, to debate legislation first.

The Government Leader in the Senate has to convince his Cabinet colleagues that the benefits of starting bills in the Senate outweigh the potential disadvantages. The Government House Leader in the Commons, who has overall charge of the government's legislative program, can help in this regard. Former House Leader Mitchell Sharpe (1974–76) was often credited with arranging more preliminary legislative work for the Senate. This practice takes pressure off the Commons' timetable. Bills that are complex and technical rather than partisan are the best candidates for initial review by the Senate, and there have been a number of examples over the years in which the Senate has both improved bills through prior review and saved time in the Commons.

THE STANDING JOINT COMMITTEE ON THE SCRUTINY OF REGULATIONS

One of the consequences of the increased scope and complexity of policy-making during the twentieth century was to force Parliament to pass laws in very general terms and authorize the bureaucracy to refine and to carry out the declared statutory purposes. On the basis of such delegated legislative authority, enormous discretion is granted to the Cabinet, individual ministers, departments, commissions, boards, and other administrative agencies to formulate and to apply rules of various kinds. The results of this delegated rule-making power are described as "subordinate legislation," because they are subject to the enabling act. There are good reasons for the transfer of such powers, such as the lack of parliamentary time and knowledge to legislate intelligently in dynamic new fields of public policy and the desire to take the maximum advantage of the expert knowledge and professional objectivity of the public service. Also, in theory, Parliament can retrieve any delegated lawmaking powers if it discovers abuse by ministers or public servants. Nevertheless, the fact remains that, in quantitative terms at least, the "real lawmakers" have become public servants who formulate and apply thousands upon thousands of pages of regulations that touch on the lives of millions of Canadians everyday. The enabling sections of acts need to be drafted carefully so that they do not confer powers that should only be exercised by Parliament or leave the Executive with more discretion than it needs to accomplish the statutory purposes approved by Parliament; but meeting this test is difficult.

The essential dilemma faced by Parliament is how to balance the need for flexibility and expertise provided by the public service in order to support the accomplishment of public policy goals with the necessity to preserve Parliament's ultimate authority, to protect the rights of parties who are subject to the exercise of delegated rule-making, and to ensure that the vast, largely submerged exercise of discretionary power is subject to ultimate democratic accountability. Parliament has a number of potential checks on delegated lawmaking, but the most important is the Standing Joint Committee for the Scrutiny of Regulations. First created in 1972, the Committee consists of fifteen members (five from the Senate and ten from the Commons) and is co-chaired by an opposition member of the House of Commons and a senator. In general, senators are more involved than members of the House of Commons in the technically difficult and largely unrecognized work done by the Committee. Senators have more time to devote to the detailed study of regulations, and, because they do not face re-election, they are less concerned that the Committee generates almost no publicity. There is not the space here to describe the work of the Committee in detail. A valuable account of the struggle by the Committee to gain co-operation from the government and the bureaucracy is provided by the late Senator Eugene Forsey.[19] His account illustrates how the Executive, partly through habit and convenience, can come to insist on the maximum discretionary authority possible without adequate checks on the exercise of such power.

Since 1973, all Orders-in-Council, regulations, and other statutory instruments of federal departments, boards, and commissions have been referred to the Joint Committee. Regulations are reviewed under thirteen criteria, including whether they exceed the authority granted by the parent act, infringe the rule of law or principles of natural justice, impose a charge or payment without authority, are unclear, or violate the *Canadian Charter of Rights and Freedoms*. It is important to note that this scrutiny pertains only to the form or legality of regulations, not to their effectiveness in achieving policy objectives. There are literally thousands of pages of regulations published annually. To cope with this volume, the Joint Committee employs a staff of several lawyers. Staff members try to correct defective regulations through discussions with the relevant authorities before bringing regulations before the Committee. Even with this advance work, the Committee considers more than one thousand regulations annually, which represent about one quarter of all the regulations published.[20] In response to questionable regulations, the Committee usually recommends changes and works out a compromise with the sponsoring authorities. Since the early 1980s, the Committee has possessed the authority to disallow regulations through a resolution of either the Commons or the Senate. It is the act of declaring a regulation dangerous, more than the actual passage of a resolution to disallow, that provides the Committee leverage with officials. The power has been used infrequently, only five times in the last decade and mainly on Charter issues,[21] but its availability can have a salutary influence on the actions of the Executive.

The work of the Regulations Committee is the most prominent example of a role for the Senate that emerged gradually during the postwar era as a result of the efforts of a small group of dedicated senators. In general terms, these senators have sought to preserve the authority of Parliament and to protect the rights of citizens. By refusing to give officials a "blank cheque" transfer of power, by insisting upon the publication and review of the uses of rule-making powers, and by providing procedural safeguards for individuals and corporations in conflict with administrative authorities, the Senate, through the work of a minority of its members, has sought to uphold the rule of law. Simply put, the rule of law refers to the fact that all actions by government must have a legal basis and that no one, no matter how powerful, is above the law. In an era of Charter challenges, the courts play the most prominent role in preserving this important principle, but it needs to be recognized that the Senate contributes as well.

The Senate and the Initiation of Legislation

The phrase "Government proposes and Parliament disposes" has been used to describe the fact that nearly all bills that make their way through Parliament originate with ministers. For constitutional, procedural, and political reasons, there seems to be limited or no opportunity for Parliament on its own to identify ideas for legislation, to formulate bills, and to arrange for their passage through all stages of the parliamentary process. In the case of the Senate, its role seems to be even more reactive since most of the time it is discussing bills after they have already been debated and sometimes amended in the House of Commons. As was discussed above, the Senate's role of legislative review allows it, under favourable circumstance, to exert some influence on the final shape of legislation. The question to be discussed in this section is whether the Senate on its own is capable of identifying possible ideas for public policy and contributing to the formulation of bills to implement those ideas.

Most knowledgeable observers would say that the Senate rarely, if ever, initiates legislation. In a strict, formal sense this is true. However, such a pessimistic conclusion rests, in part, on an unduly limited interpretation of what constitutes initiation in the policy process. In most instances, the initiation of policy, or more likely today the modification of existing policies, is a complex, extended process involving a series of actors and actions, rather than a decision made at one point in time by a single actor. Initiation involves identifying problems or needs, generating and evaluating ideas for political, technical, and administrative feasibility, seeking agreement on the most appropriate response, and then acting to promote and to implement the idea. These activities can take place simultaneously or chronologically over time in a number of locations throughout the political system. Defined thus broadly, policy initiation is potentially shared among a wide range of actors, including, on occasion, the Senate and its committees. This section seeks to identify how senators contribute both directly and indirectly to the initiation of legislation.

When senators see the need for a law, they can respond individually by introducing bills of their own. However, this method of bringing public policy ideas forward is limited by the fact that such bills cannot involve the expenditure of funds. Bills sponsored by individual senators must make it through the five procedural stages in the Senate and the same procedure in the House of Commons before they can receive Royal Assent and become law. As a courtesy to their sponsors, private members' public bills are usually referred to the appropriate standing committee of the Senate, where expert witnesses can be heard. For example, during the 1997–98 session, nine Senate public bills were referred to committees. The bills covered such topics as a national historical park; *Criminal Code* amendments; tobacco regulation, excise taxes; and the *Canadian Human Rights Act* and aboriginal self-government.[22] Most Senate-sponsored bills never make it into law. However, there have been examples of individual senators using the sponsorship process over several sessions to publicize their ideas, to encourage debate, and eventually to prompt the government into action.

Senate Committee Investigations

A second way that the Senate can serve as an "incubator" for policy ideas struggling to gain a place on the agenda of government is through the conduct of investigations by various types of Senate committees. Before describing the investigative process, some brief background on the Senate committee system is required. The committee system of the Senate is less extensive and does not exactly parallel that of the House of Commons. Table 2 lists the Senate's twelve standing committees and their subcommittees as of the second session of the thirty-sixth Parliament. In comparison, the House of Commons operates twenty standing committees covering broad policy sectors, and a number of these committees use subcommittees to deal with more specialized topics. Table 3 lists the Commons' standing committees during the second session of the thirty-sixth Parliament. Superficially impressive on paper, the Commons committee system has declined in activity and influence during recent parliamentary sessions. Tight control over Commons committees by the government has

Table 2   Standing and Joint Committees of the Senate, Thirty-Sixth Parliament, Second Session

---

Aboriginal Peoples
  Subcommittee on Aboriginal Economic Development in relation to
    Northern National Parks
Agriculture and Forestry
  Subcommittee on Forestry
Banking, Trade and Commerce
Energy, the Environment and Natural Resources
Fisheries
Foreign Affairs
Illegal Drugs (Special)
Internal Economy, Budgets and Administration
Legal and Constitutional Affairs
Library of Parliament (Joint)
Privileges, Standing Rules and Orders
Scrutiny of Regulations (Joint)
Selection
Social Affairs, Science and Technology
  Subcommittee to Update "Of Life and Death"
  Subcommittee on Veterans Affairs
Transport and Communications
  Subcommittee on Communications
  Subcommittee on Transportation Safety

Table 3   Standing and Joint Committees of the House of Commons, Thirty-Sixth Parliament, Second Session

---

Aboriginal Affairs and Northern Development
Agriculture and Agri-Food
Canadian Heritage
Citizenship and Immigration
Environment and Sustainable Development
Finance
Fisheries and Oceans
Foreign Affairs and International Trade
Health
Human Resources Development and the Status of Person with Disabilities
Natural Resources and Government Operations
Official Languages (Joint)
Procedure and House Affairs
Public Accounts
Scrutiny of Regulations
Transport
Industry
Justice and Human Rights
Library of Parliament (Joint)
National Defence and Veterans Affairs

---

created frustration for members of the House of Commons from all parties and caused many of them to limit their participation in the committee system. In short, it should not be assumed that Commons committees are more effective than Senate committees in holding governments to account; in fact, in recent years more independent scrutiny of government performance has probably been provided by Senate committees.

Committees are the real working units of the Senate. Whereas the full Senate usually only meets three days per week – or about sixty to eighty days per year – the committees meet more frequently. For example, in 1997–98 (an election year) the Senate met on sixty-two days and committees had meetings on ninety-five days. The main work of committees is the review of bills and the conduct of investigations. In addition to the standing committees, senators participate on joint committees with the Commons, and at most times the Senate will have several special committees conducting inquiries. Standing committees have also made increasing use of subcommittees to conduct studies of more specialized topics.

Table 4 shows the number of Senate committee meetings and hours involved for the year 1995–96. The report from which the table is derived observed back in 1996 that:

Several problems are inherent in the current committee structure... committees have too many members; absenteeism is high; senators sit on multiple existing committees; and there is an imbalance in the workloads among the various committees."[23]

A further report from the Senate's Privileges, Standing Rules and Orders Committee, tabled in March 1999, called for more flexible committee memberships. More active committees would continue to have fourteen members, while other committees could be cut to ten or as few as six members. Fewer members would reduce pressures on the dwindling Progressive Conservative contingent in the Senate. It would also allow the Senate to add new committees, such as the recently established Standing Committee on Human Rights and Standing Committee on Defence and Security.

The variation in the level of activity of Senate committees and in the degree of commitment by senators to them is duplicated in the Commons' committee system; indeed a recent survey revealed that Commons committees were regarded by many members of the House of Commons as an exercise in futility and a waste of time.[24] In the case of Senate committees, the effective work is done by a minority of members. Estimates by knowledgeable observers suggest that between forty to sixty senators do most of the work within the Senate committee system. This is not a bad percentage compared to the House of Commons. When faced with criticism of the limited sittings of the full Chamber, senators are fond of referring to the

Table 4   Senate Standing Committee Activity, April 1991 to February 1999, average per Year

Standing Committee	Number of Meetings	Hours of Meetings	Number of Bills Referred
Aboriginal Peoples	9.7	16.9	2.2
Agriculture and Forestry	19.6	37.7	2.4
Banking, Trade and Commerce	32.7	75.9	10.4
Energy, Environment and Natural Resources	14.0	26.9	2.9
Fisheries	8.8	14.2	0.1
Foreign Affairs	19.8	34.3	2.2
Internal Economy, Budgets and Administration	20.5	35.4	0
Legal and Constitutional Affairs	37.5	74.6	12.2
National Finance	21.2	33.9	4.6
Privileges, Standing Rules and Orders	6.7	11.4	0
Social Affairs, Science and Technology	36.7	70.2	4.8
Transport and Communications	24.3	52.4	4.1

Source: The Hill Times, 8 March 1999: 9.

much-vaunted role of Senate committees in conducting inquiries. While there is clearly room for improvement, especially if more senators played an active role, there are good reasons for the Senate to be proud of its committee studies.

Senators have been able to undertake committee investigations because they spend less time in the full Chamber on general and legislative debates than does the Commons and because such inquiries can be conducted on a more nonpartisan basis. Unlike Commons committees, the Senate committees do not require prior government approval to begin a study, although informal discussions with the relevant minister usually take place. Several studies have been conducted recently in spite of ministerial objections. The absence of media coverage for Senate investigations means that committee members receive little recognition for their efforts, but it also contributes to a more objective search for the truth on a nonpartisan basis. Immunity from the vagaries of the electoral process means that senators can serve on committees for many years and develop a higher level of expertise in particular fields of public policy than is possible for members of the House of Commons, who change committee assignments frequently and experience a high turnover rate at election time.

Continuity is also found in the position of chairperson of Senate committees. Appointment to these positions is reviewed at the beginning of each Parliament by the Government Leader in the Senate, the Deputy Leader, and the Government Whip. Changes are far less frequent than in the House of Commons, where chairs of committees are rotated through the government backbenches in conjunction with changes among parliamentary secretaries, who serve as paid assistants to ministers. It is far more common in the Senate to find an opposition member chairing a committee than in the House of Commons.

The greater continuity among chairs of Senate committees produces a number of benefits; it allows senators to acquire skills in leading committees; it promotes confidence in the chair among members, and it permits chairs to become both procedural and substantive experts in particular fields. For example, Senator Salter Hayden chaired the Senate Banking Committee for more than twenty years and became an acknowledged authority on tax law and other matters. Committee chairs in the Senate can provide more leadership and control than Commons committee chairs and this can produce more coherent and exhaustive explorations of topics because the balancing of partisan interests does not have to be so strict. For example, most Commons committees apply the ten-minute rule, which requires that questions from representatives of each party and responses from expert witnesses occur in ten-minute blocks of time. In Senate committees, these partisan calculations are less prominent and discussions can flow more smoothly under the leadership of chairs in whom senators from all parties have confidence.

The investigative role of Senate committees has increased during the past several decades for several reasons. First, this type of activity represents the best opportunity for the Senate to have some impact on public policy and programs. Of course, there are no guarantees of success, but under favourable circumstances the reports of Senate committees can have an impact on government thinking. The conditions favouring Senate influence through committee reports are discussed below.

Second, the contemporary Senate has contained a core of younger, more active senators, many appointed during the 1970s and 1980s, who wanted to make a more meaningful contribution to national policy-making and were less willing than an earlier generation of senators to be relegated to a secondary, reactive role.

Third, studies by Senate committees can in some situations represent an alternative to time-consuming and expensive inquiries by royal commissions and task forces. It would be wrong to suggest that Senate committees can match the scope and depth of research conducted by major royal commissions. However, Senate committees hold public hearings, they call for papers and documents to be produced, they examine expert witnesses (government officials, think-tank representatives, business organizations, academics, and others), they hire consultants and other researchers, and they travel inside and outside of Canada to gather evidence. Since the senators are already paid to engage in this type of activity, the additional costs involved are not as great as a royal commission inquiry, which must be built from scratch. Once launched, royal commissions may be difficult for governments to control in terms of the time and expense involved, whereas the budgets and schedules of Senate committees are more within government control.

This difference, along with the patronage basis for Senate appointments, leads to the fear that Senate committee reports will always be less critical of past government policies and less bold in their recommendations compared to reports from more independent bodies like royal commissions and task forces. On the other hand, senators are more likely to consider the political feasibility of their recommendations, and this can increase the prospect of adoption. Furthermore, unlike members of royal commissions, senators do not disperse to other careers once their reports are presented; they remain around to lobby for their implementation. Recently, a number of Senate committees have adopted the practice of following up earlier reports to determine what has happened with their recommendations. Usually this involves inviting responsible ministers and their officials to appear. This practice adds greater meaning to committee work by encouraging senators that their reports do not disappear into a kind of political "black hole."

From 1993–94 to 1997–98, Senate committees undertook 128 special studies or a five-year average of approximately twenty studies annually.[25] It is impossible to convey fully in the space available here the diversity and quality of Senate reports. Table 5 presents a partial listing of the Senate reports produced over the years going back to 1970. A glance at the listing reveals that such studies have covered economic, social, environmental, legal, and other topics of considerable importance to Canadians.

In the category of economic studies, important work has been done over the years by the Senate's Banking, Trade and Commerce Committee, its Committee on Foreign Affairs and its Committee on Social Affairs, Science and Technology. Since the 1980s, the Banking Committee has continued to investigate changes taking place in Canada's system of financial institutions as a result of global competition and deregulation. Its reports have focused on competition between the chartered banks and other financial institutions and on consumer protection issues. In 1982, a study by the Foreign Affairs Committee recommended a bilateral trade agreement with the USA, and after the free trade deal was concluded the committee investigated the experiences of Canadian industries and the operation of the dispute settlement mechanism. Reflecting the fact that economic and social issues overlap, the Social Affairs, Science and Technology Committee has recently examined the impacts of intensified, international competition on economic disparities and social cohesion in Canada.

A tradition of examining social policy issues goes back to the work of Senate committees conducted during the 1960s. The landmark 1971 report from a special committee chaired by Senator Croll prompted an important debate over poverty in the midst of apparent affluence and contributed to the emergence of a number of anti-poverty organizations.

Table 5   Titles of Selected Senate Studies since 1970

The Mass Media (three volumes) (1970)
A Science Policy for Canada (five volumes) (1970–1977)
Poverty in Canada (November 1971)
Canada-United States Relations (three volumes) (1976, 1978, 1982)
Retirement Without Tears (November 1979)
Soil at Risk: Canada's Eroding Future (November 1984)
Youth: A Plan of Action (February 1986)
The Marketing of Fish in Canada (three volumes) (1986, 1987, 1989)
Terrorism (two reports: August 1987, June 1989)
Canada's Land Forces (October 1989)
Petro-Canada (June 1990)
Children in Poverty – Toward a Better Future (January 1991)
The Valour and the Horror (January 1993)
Farm Stress: Its Economic Dimension, Its Human Consequences (June 1993)
The Mandate and Funding of Radio Canada International (June 1994)
Canada's Foreign Policy: Principles and Priorities for the Future (November 1994)
The Aboriginal Soldier After the Wars (March 1995)
Of Life and Death (June 1995)
Farm Machinery: Lost Lives, Lost Limbs (June 1995)
Pull Up! Pull Up! An Interim Report On The Safety Implications of Automated Weather
    Observation Systems (AWOS) (July 1995)
Report of the Special Senate Committee on the Pearson Airport Agreements (December
    1995)
The Atlantic Groundfishery: Its Future (December 1995)
Report on the Special Committee of the Senate on the Cape Breton Development Corpora-
    tion (2 volumes) (1996, 1997)
Wired to Win: Canada's International Competitive Position in Communications (April
    1997)
European Integration: The Implications for Canada (July 1996)
Protecting Places and People: Conserving Canada's Natural Heritage (February 1996)
Of Life and Death (1995)
Airline Industry Restructuring (1999)
Europe Revisited: Consequences of Increased European Integration for Canada (1999)
Forging New Relationships: Aboriginal Governance in Canada (2000)

Similar studies of social problems followed: young people at risk (1986), children in poverty (1991), the farm crisis and its human consequences (1993), and the hardships of Canada's aboriginal veterans (1995). In 1994, a special committee on euthanasia and assisted suicide sought to increase public understanding of this sensitive issue by holding hearings and issuing a valuable report. More than ten thousand copies of the report have been distributed, and it is used extensively for physicians and other health professionals.

Led by Senator Sharon Carstairs, another Senate committee has followed up with a recent report (June 2000) on the absence of adequate policies and financial support for palliative care to people in their final days of life. Also, in March 2000, the Senate Committee on Social Affairs, Science and Technology, embarked on an ambitious multiphase study of the issues facing Canada's health-care system, a topic that is considered too dangerous politically for most elected politicians to tackle in a straightforward manner.

Another category of Senate study might be described as a type of "program evaluation" activity. The Senate committee that has led the way in program evaluation is the Standing Committee on National Finance. Beginning in the early 1970s, the Committee selected a number of departments and programs for systematic in-depth examination. Studies were conducted on fiscal policy (1974), Canada Manpower (1975), Public Works (1982), government policy and regional development (1991), and public service reform (1992). Reflecting on its efforts up to 1991, the National Finance Committee stated that, "it would not be feasible for the Senate to assume the responsibility for the evaluation of all government programs."[26] However, through reviews of selected programs, Senate committees could be an alternative source of advice for ministers who would otherwise be forced to rely on potentially self-serving assessments provided by the public servants who managed those programs and the interest groups who benefited from them. Also, Senate evaluations would not shy away from the political value judgements that are inherent in all program evaluations. Finally, the evaluation work done by Senate committees could be useful in the examination of bills and estimates.

During the 1990s, more Senate committees took up the challenge of evaluating past policies and existing programs, in part because this was seen as a way to reduce costs and improve the effectiveness of programs during a time when government deficits were a growing problem. At the time that Senate committees were improving their scrutiny efforts, Commons committees were declining as a source of program reviews because of the perception that committee studies had no impact. Even though performance reports for more than eighty departments and agencies are now made available annually to Parliament, the rate of utilization by Commons committees has been very disappointing. While Senate committee reviews hardly qualify as scientific and comprehensive evaluations, in general they are seen by most knowledgeable observers to produce more substantive reports than their Commons counterparts. For this reason most public servants will tell you that they would rather spend time discussing their programs with a Senate committee than a Commons committee because the former involves a greater focus on the real issues and there is less partisan gamesmanship involved.

In addition to promoting evaluation activity within the Senate, the National Finance Committee has for thirty years assumed responsibility for examining the Main and Supplementary Estimates of spending presented annually by government to Parliament. The Committee is also authorized to receive the Annual Report from the Office of the Auditor General of

Canada, which examines the financial, accounting, and management issues related to the achievement of economy, efficiency, and effectiveness of operations in the public sector. Concentration of responsibility for financial management issues in a single Senate committee has led to the development of greater expertise. In connection with its examination of the Main and Supplementary Estimates for the fiscal years 1998–99 and 1999–2000, the National Finance Committee held a total of forty-four meetings and examined 127 witnesses.[27] Often, time is at a premium when the Estimates are under study and the reports filed by the Committee tend to be brief, consisting usually of two or three pages. Such reports seek to highlight the main features of the government's spending priorities and to record concerns that senators have raised during the Committee meetings. In recent years, for example, the Committee has expressed concerns about the loss of financial accountability to Parliament arising from poor expenditure forecasting, the increased reliance on Supplementary Estimates voted part way through the fiscal year, the growing percentage (70 percent) of spending that is statutory in nature and not easily changed by Parliament, and the adoption of two-year spending authority for the new Canada Customs and Revenue Agency and the Canadian Parks Agency.[28]

Faced with annual expenditures of more than $150 billion, the National Finance Committee cannot come anywhere close to a comprehensive and intensive examination of the financial issues involved with the far-flung operations of government. Its work on the Estimates, however, has led the Committee to undertake the more systematic evaluations of departments and programs described above. Even acknowledging the limits of its scrutiny of the Estimates, public servants from the Treasury Board Secretariat state privately that they prefer to go before the National Finance Committee than any of the standing committees of the House of Commons. This is mainly because the senators pay more attention to the real financial challenges facing government. Review of the Estimates by the House of Commons occurs under a deadline and most of the sets of estimates that are referred to the appropriate standing committees are simply deemed to have been approved by the deadline often with no actual examination having taken place and no substantive report having been filed. Few members of the House of Commons seem to be seriously interested in the difficult job of understanding government finances, especially since there is little or no publicity or influence arising from careful review of the Estimates before Commons committees. The fact that the Commons' process for voting supply is so inadequate means that even the limited review by the Senate's National Finance Committee is an important source for some review.

It is often suggested that Senate studies of various kinds represent "activity for activity's sake," that the reports produced rarely have any impact on government policy and administrative action. As suggested earlier, this is too pessimistic a conclusion to draw. Most senators are realistic enough not to expect a direct and immediate relationship between their committee recommendations and government action. On the other hand, governments cannot ignore committee reports with complete impunity. Reports from Senate committees both reflect and contribute to the environment of ideas within which policy evolves. Hearings and reports also serve to remind those individuals within the political and the permanent Executive that there are interests and opinions in Parliament and outside that may not have been heard and must be taken into account. The Senate committee inquiry process represents an opportunity to influence Executive thinking and plans before they are fully formulated. Equally important, there is a chance to examine and to criticize government performance in a public forum. As a result, ministers and their public service advisors are obliged, to some extent at least, to boast and confess in public about government performance.

Whether a particular report from a Senate committee will have an impact on government thinking and actions seems to depend on a variety of factors, the relative importance of which seems to vary from case to case. In some instances, the government or a particular minister is genuinely looking for advice, perhaps because existing policy approaches are not working satisfactorily. This appeared to be the case with the Joint Senate-House of Commons Committee on Immigration back in 1975. The Committee's recommendations provided much of the basis for changes to Canada's immigration laws. Similarly, the Senate Foreign Affairs Subcommittee report on Canada's Maritime Command (1982) was helpful to the then Minister of National Defence, Hon. G. Lamontagne, in obtaining Cabinet approval for spending on six new frigates. Lamontagne's successor, Hon. J.J. Blais, was less disposed to accept advice from the Subcommittee and, in fact, sought to keep it from meeting – a contrast that revealed how important ministerial attitudes can be to the success of Senate committee efforts.[29]

A number of factors can potentially contribute to the willingness of ministers to follow the advice of Senate committees. Support from outside of Parliament, especially from those interests most directly affected, adds weight to the recommendations from committees. The quality of Senate reports will affect their prospects for adoption. What qualifies as a quality report involves subjective judgement, but if committees expect their reports to be considered seriously by ministers and the bureaucracy, they must be based as much as possible on thorough and sound analysis. Recommendations must not only be well informed, they must also be seen as financially, administratively and politically feasible. Feasibility often is determined by the closeness of the recommendations to current government thinking and the timeliness of the ideas. In other words, more ambitious plans for which there is not immediate political support will probably be adopted, if at all, in stages over several years. The skills and persistence of senators in lobbying for their ideas (especially inside the governing party) will affect their chances of success.

In summary, Senate committees have done valuable investigative work in the past and, when the circumstances are right, their reports have led to significant government action. Development of the Senate's investigative role has allowed the institution to contribute to policy-making in a manner that is less politically threatening to governments because committee studies dealing with past policies and programs do not directly challenge ministerial reputations in the way that the rejection or amendment of bills does. Senate inquiries represent an important adjunct to its more purely legislative role because they provide background knowledge to allow senators to review government-sponsored bills more intelligently, and they create opportunities for the indirect initiation of legislation.

CONCLUSIONS

This chapter has examined the role played by the Senate and its committees in the national legislative process. Comparisons have been made to the role of the House of Commons and its committees within that process. Contrary to popular belief, the Senate was seen to make a limited, but important contribution to lawmaking, broadly defined. For a number of reasons the Senate brings a distinctive, complementary perspective to the review of government-sponsored bills. Through debates, hearings, delays, amendments, and rare defeats of bills, the Senate may force the Prime Minister and Cabinet to rethink their legislative plans. At times they allow organizations and individuals to be heard when the strictly regimented process of legislative approval in the House of Commons does not. Less and less do governments look to debates in the Commons and the examination of bills in Commons committees as an opportunity to test, improve, and validate their legislative ideas. Instead, the overriding goals are the most efficient possible passage of the overall legislative program and the denial of opposition arguments. Because senators are not preoccupied with re-election, the Senate is normally less partisan and majoritarian in its procedures, culture, and operations than the House of Commons, and this allows it occasionally to slow the Executive juggernaut that normally rolls over the House of Commons. With greater co-operation from governments and more independent-minded senators, the Senate could perform even more effectively as a source of "sober second thought," as a technical revising body, especially for more specialized bills, and as a way to relieve some of the pressures on the Commons through more extensive use of the practice of "pre-study."

As part of its legislative duties the Senate has developed to a limited extent the function of protecting regional, linguistic, minority group, and individual rights. While the Senate has played a greater role in defending regional interests than is generally recognized, it has been too slow to develop formal mechanisms to fulfill this important purpose for which it was originally created. Individual senators have taken actions to promote the rights of minorities of various kinds, but this role has remained underdeveloped. The recently created Standing Committee on Human Rights will strengthen the Senate's commitment to this role. Even though the Senate is still popularly portrayed as representing only Canada's economic and political elites, it has done some valuable work in promoting the cause of more marginal groups within society. Through the largely unrecognized work of legislative review and the Joint Committee for the Scrutiny of Regulations, it has sought to place limits on and to provide supervision of the vast range of discretionary lawmaking authority exercised by ministers and public servants.

The growth of the Senate's investigative activity conducted by its committees has probably been its most notable accomplishment during the past three decades. As was suggested earlier and contrary to the conventional wisdom, Senate inquiries are not purely academic exercises without real results. For a number of reasons Senate committees usually do better investigative work than their Commons counterparts. Senate inquiries resemble in some ways royal commissions and task forces, but they take less time, are less expensive and often have more success in gaining adoption of their recommendations. Reports from Senate committees have been the basis for significant government actions during the past three decades. It requires fortuitous circumstances to produce immediate action on Senate committee reports, but the ideas in such reports became part of the discussion agenda within government. In this way, the Senate can contribute subtly and indirectly to the legislative process.

This chapter has presented a more positive portrait of the Senate's contribution to lawmaking than the prevalent, negative stereotype of a largely useless institution whose members are underworked and overpaid and who can be counted on to acquiesce gratefully to the demands of the Prime Minister since he placed them in a kind of patronage heaven. Like all stereotypes, there is some truth in this popular image of the Senate, but mainly it reflects ignorance and gross exaggeration of what actually takes place within the institution. A more balanced assessment suggests that the Canadian Senate plays a useful and complementary role to the House of Commons. Were governments to use the Senate more appropriately, its contribution to policy-making would be enhanced and perhaps its reputation with Canadians would improve. However, as an appointed body, the Senate will always suffer a credibility problem in a more democratic age. Since constitutional and political obstacles are likely to prevent for the foreseeable future the creation of an elected Upper House, Senate reformers would be wise to concentrate on practical ways to improve the Senate from within. Some possibilities are hinted at in the discussion above, but internal reform is a subject for another occasion.[30]

NOTES

1 Internal and other nonconstitutional reforms are discussed in Professor David Smith's chapter in this volume.
2 As Professor Azjenstat makes clear in her chapter in this volume.
3 Audcent, *The Senate Veto: Opinion of the Law Clerk and Parliamentary Counsel.*
4 Heard, *Canadian Constitutional Conventions: The Marriage of Law and Politics.*
5 United Kingdom, Royal Commission on the Reform of the House of Lords, *A House For The Future*, 39, and Riddell, "The Second Chamber: In Search of a Complementary Role," 405.
6 See Franks, "Not Dead Yet, But Should it Be Resurrected? The Canadian Senate," for a more complete discussion of this period.
7 Franks, "Not Dead Yet, But Should it Be Resurrected? The Canadian Senate."
8 McKay, *The Unreformed Senate of Canada*, and Kunz, *The Modern Senate of Canada, 1925–1963: A Re-appraisal.*
9 Canada, *Report on Certain Aspects of the Constitution.*
10 Heard, *Canadian Constitutional Conventions: The Marriage of Law and Politics*, 89.
11 Heard, *Canadian Constitutional Conventions: The Marriage of Law and Politics*, 90.
12 Heard, *Canadian Constitutional Conventions: The Marriage of Law and Politics*, 91.
13 Heard, *Canadian Constitutional Conventions: The Marriage of Law and Politics*, 90.
14 Thomas, "Les partis et leur représentation des régions."
15 Heard, *Canadian Constitutional Conventions: The Marriage of Law and Politics*, 79.
16 Campbell, *The Canadian Senate: A Lobby from Within.*
17 See Lindgren, "Sober Second Thought or Corporate Lobbyist?"
18 See appendix.
19 Forsey, *A Life on the Fringe: The Memoirs of Eugene Forsey*, chapter 9.
20 McInnes, *Taking It to the Hill: The Complete Guide to Appearing before (and Surviving) Parliamentary Committees*, 78–9.
21 McInnes, *Taking It to the Hill: The Complete Guide to Appearing before (and Surviving) Parliamentary Committees*, 79.
22 Canada. Parliament. Senate. *The Role of Senate Committees in Formulating Public Policy*, 5.
23 Sullivan, "Tory Pressures Liberals to Rejig Committees."
24 Dobell, "Reforming Parliamentary Practice: The Views of MPs."
25 Canada. Parliament. Senate. Senate *Committees Activities and Expenditures, Annual Report 1997–1998.*
26 Canada. Parliament. Senate. The Standing Senate Committee on National Finance, *Program Evaluation Systems in the Government of Canada*, Chair: Fernand E. LeBlanc, January 1991.

27 Canada. Parliament. Senate. The Standing Senate Committee on National Finance, *Second Report*, 2 December 1999.

28 Canada. Parliament. Senate. The Standing Senate Committee on National Finance, *Third Report*, 23 March 2000.

29 Pattee and Thomas, "The Senate and Defence Policy: Subcommittee Report on Canada's Maritime Defence."

30 The chapter in this volume by Professor David Smith is a good starting point.

CHAPTER EIGHT

The Improvement of the Senate by Nonconstitutional Means

David E. Smith

The title of this paper has been chosen with care, and should be so read. What follows is an examination of how to make the Senate of Canada a more effective and, in the public mind, a more credible legislative body. The general thrust of the discussion is on making the institution work better and on achieving this goal by means other than the complex amendment provisions entrenched in Part V of the *Constitution Act, 1982* or the requirements of the so-called "Regional Veto" Act. As much as possible, reference to reform and reforms will be shunned. The source of this pedantry is psychological rather than semantic. Few studies of the Senate do not talk about, if they are not devoted to, its reform. Indeed, "Reform of the Senate" must be one of the hoariest topics in Canadian politics.

Familiarity breeds more than contempt; it encourages inattention. As a result, there is a lot of echo and not much contemplation in what is proposed by way of reform of the Upper Chamber. To the problem of repetition one must also add tunnel vision, as proponents of a particular reform, convinced that their proposed scheme will miraculously transform the Senate, do not consider its overall impact. For instance, those who propose an elected Senate (of whatever variety) propose only that, without acknowledging that the introduction of the elective principle will have both predictable and unintended consequences on Canadian political parties (federal and provincial), voting behaviour, constituency representation, the conventional operation of the Senate, and Parliament as a whole.

It is a law of politics, as it is of physics, that change to one element will lead to compensatory change elsewhere. One reason why reformers are forever frustrated is that they fail to see our political system as a *system* that serves not single but multiple interests. To achieve their goal requires the co-operation of others and sometimes, as in the case of an elected Senate, a very substantial level of federal-provincial agreement. Contrary to the criticisms single-issue proponents make, the status quo confers benefits at the same time as it imposes costs. Those in receipt of the first are unlikely to agree to change without compensation, while reformers, who see only costs, are ill disposed to compromise.

Another reason why reformers make so little headway is that they fail to demonstrate how their favoured reform will produce an improved Senate. This is something they are unable to do because they advance no articulated conception of the Senate's role in the political system. Colloquially phrased, the reformers' approach puts the cart before the horse. They are attempting to remodel the institution without studying the original constitutional blueprint, without considering how the existing legal/political architecture will be affected, and even without having a fully formed conception of what the end product of their efforts will be. Such a strategy is most unlikely to improve the working of the Senate and indeed risks worsening the situation.

The last decade has produced two demonstrations of the inadequacy of this approach. Both the Meech Lake and the Charlottetown accords spoke to Senate reform, yet neither initiative succeeded. While it would be untrue to say that the Senate was a major obstacle to agreement, hindsight makes clear that discussion of the subject suffered from what one writer has labelled a "conceptual" problem.[1] In a critical review of these and other recent Senate reform proposals, Jack Stilborn identifies the problem as an inability "to translate a vision of needs that require Senate reform into a more specific set of roles that can provide a basis for the design of the institution."[2]

When the subject of the Senate arises, it is essential for reformers to recognize the complementary relationship that currently (and necessarily) exists between the two chambers. Reform proposals that do not acknowledge this fact and at the same time offer no alternative constitutional justification for what they propose are destined to fail. In any case, institutional redesign of this magnitude will not happen because conflicting interests, lack of coherent purpose, and an absence of commitment to change stand in its way. It is difficult to say which of these three is the greatest impediment to reformers' success, but it needs to be emphasized that without public commitment, specific reforms are unlikely to happen.

This examination of nonconstitutional means of improving the Senate will begin by distinguishing between constitutional and nonconstitutional improvements. It will then outline a core conceptual vision to guide future reformers, discussing the basic principles that form the foundation for successfully improving the Senate. With this foundation in place, several specific nonconstitutional proposals for improving the Upper House will be considered.

Irrespective of the desirability of constitutional reform, practically speaking, only nonconstitutional improvements can be expected at the present time. There is, in short, a practical need to do something in order to enhance the Upper House and thereby make it a constructive element of

Parliament within *current* constitutional arrangements. Until it again becomes possible to amend the Constitution, it is better to pursue a gradual, cautious strategy, informed by an understanding of the institution's role, to make the most of the current Senate, by using nonconstitutional means. If properly implemented, this approach will bring about significant improvements in the workings of the Upper House.

CONSTITUTIONAL VERSUS NONCONSTITUTIONAL IMPROVEMENT

Of all the methods of improving the Senate, the most labyrinthine is the constitutional amendment process.[3] The obstacles to successfully amending the Constitution are numerous. Section 38 of the *Constitution Act, 1982* lists the general procedure:

1 An amendment to the Constitution of Canada may be made by proclamation issued by the Governor General under the Great Seal of Canada where so authorized by
   a resolutions of the Senate and House of Commons; and
   b resolutions of the legislative assemblies of at least two-thirds of the provinces that have, in the aggregate, according to the then latest general census, at least fifty per cent of the population of all the provinces.

Section 42 of the *Constitution Act, 1982* makes it clear that several important aspects of the Senate would be subject to this 7/50% formula:

1 An amendment to the Constitution of Canada in relation to the following matters may be made only in accordance with subsection 38(1):
   a the principle of proportionate representation of the provinces in the House of Commons prescribed by the Constitution of Canada;
   b the powers of the Senate and the method of selecting Senators;
   c the number of members by which a province is entitled to be represented in the Senate and the residence qualifications of Senators;
   d subject to paragraph 41(d), the Supreme Court of Canada;
   e the extension of existing provinces into the territories; and
   f notwithstanding any other law or practice, the establishment of new provinces.

While the 7/50% formula is itself nearly unachievable, the amendment process is rendered more complex by Section 41 of the *Constitution Act, 1982*, which requires the unanimous consent of the provinces for certain amendments:

An amendment to the Constitution of Canada in relation to the following matters may be made by proclamation issued by the Governor General under the Great Seal of Canada only where authorized by resolutions of the Senate and House of Commons and of the legislative assembly of each province:

 a the office of the Queen, the Governor General and the Lieutenant Governor of a province;
 b the right of a province to a number of members in the House of Commons not less than the number of Senators by which the province is entitled to be represented at the time this Part comes into force;
 c subject to section 43, the use of the English or French language;
 d the composition of the Supreme Court of Canada; and
 e an amendment to this Part.

This section would apply to an attempt to abolish the Senate due to section 41(e), as it would require amending Section 41 to remove the requirements for a Senate resolution and the use of senators as a benchmark for representation in the House of Commons. It has also been argued that the removal of the Senate's veto might require unanimity.[4]

In addition, constitutional amendments are now subject to the "regional vetoes" created by Bill C–110 in 1996. Finally, of course, the 1992 precedent (and in some instances provincial statutes) makes it increasingly likely that any future major constitutional amendment will need to be approved by a national referendum. Taken together, these requirements necessitate an agreement between a very precise combination of federal and provincial governments if an amendment is to be adopted. Given that each of these governments have widely differing interests, political philosophies, and agendas to pursue (to say nothing of the possibility of an election bringing in a new government, with different positions, during the extended period of time required for negotiations), it is perhaps not all that surprising that the constitutional amendment process has become the Gordian Knot of Canadian politics. Until an Alexander emerges to cut through the barriers, the improvement of the Senate is best pursued by nonconstitutional means.

The meaning of "nonconstitutional" should be clarified, since, while convenient, it is technically imprecise. Section 44 of the *Constitution Act, 1982* states that

Subject to sections 41 and 42, Parliament may exclusively make laws amending the Constitution of Canada in relation to the executive government of Canada or the Senate and House of Commons.

Thus, some of the improvements discussed in this chapter are constitutional amendments that can be made unilaterally by Parliament. For the sake of convenience, however, this study uses the term "nonconstitutional" to refer to all changes that can be made to the Senate without resorting to the complex amending formulae[5] and the elaborate federal-provincial negotiations they entail. These nonconstitutional methods are:

1 changes to *The Rules of the Senate* – modifications to the written regulations governing the operation of the Upper House; such decisions are exclusively made by the Senate itself;
2 changes to Parliamentary practice and convention – alterations to the frequently unwritten rules that shape the relationship between the Senate, the House of Commons, and the Executive; some of these practices would be internal to the Senate, while others would affect the House of Commons, the Executive, or any combination thereof; such changes would involve co-operation among all the relevant components of Parliament and could be implemented by various means, including simply reaching an agreement and abiding by it, having one or both chambers adopt a resolution, or by having the Prime Minister publicly state in the House of Commons that a particular practice will be followed;
3 an Act of Parliament – the adoption of legislation to bring about a change in the Senate; as with any piece of legislation, it would need to be passed by both the Senate and the House of Commons;
4 a constitutional amendment under Section 44 of the *Constitution Act, 1982* – the implementation of limited changes to the Constitution as it applies to the executive government, the Senate and the House of Commons; such amendments would require the consent of both Houses of Parliament.

All of these methods require only the development of a clear vision among parliamentarians in order to bring about results.

DECLARATION OF PRINCIPLES

An analysis of failed Senate reform proposals reveals that their shared flaw was the absence of a clear conceptual vision to guide them. Numerous suggestions for reform have been brought forward, but the logic behind all of them was vague and underdeveloped. Proponents typically relied on arguments that went little further than a blanket statement that the Senate must be elected or that the provinces need to select their own representatives. Various reasons for undertaking this or that initiative have been offered, but never with a clearly defined, well thought-out blueprint of the underlying rationale, guiding principles, and ultimate objectives of Senate reform. The lack of any serious analysis has resulted in misguided proposals that would have produced results different than their advocates had intended, even if they had managed to be implemented.

The failure to reform Parliament has limited its ability to effectively control the Executive and undermined public confidence in the institution.

Canadian political institutions, including the Senate, must adapt to changing circumstances if the country is to be properly governed. The many far-reaching developments of recent years, ranging from the excessive accumulation of power by the Prime Minister's Office to the emergence of a culture of rights following the adoption of the *Charter of Rights and Freedoms*, only give further impetus to the need for reform.

To better avoid the mistakes of the past, this examination will lay out the principles from which all specific reform proposals will flow. These principles form an organic whole. They are mutually reinforcing and overlap one another to some degree, but when taken together they provide a firm foundation for Senate reform. Using these guidelines, it is possible to identify both the institutional strengths that should be preserved and the weaknesses that need to be corrected.

1 Canada is a democratic country committed to the rule of law and the preservation of individual rights, as embodied in the Constitution and its Charter of Rights and Freedoms. *The objective of all reform proposals must be to improve the quality of governance in Canada. This must be the cardinal principle of Senate reform.*

2 Political power in Canada is dispersed throughout different institutions and levels of government, which serve to check and balance each other. *All reform proposals must consider the Senate within the context of our political system rather than in isolation. They must preserve the balance and/or correct any imbalances in the dispersal of power.*

3 The Upper House has a distinct meaningful contribution to make to the work of Parliament and is not simply a duplicate of the Lower House. The Senate was designed to complement, not to compete with, the House of Commons. *All reform proposals must recognize the role of the House of Commons under the system of responsible government and must strengthen the complementary relationship between the two Houses of Parliament.*

4 The Fathers of Confederation embedded several characteristics of the Senate within the Constitution that remain vital to the effective functioning of the institution. *All reform proposals must respect the fundamental features and essential characteristics of the Senate: independence, continuity, long-term perspective, professional/life experience, and sectional/minority representation.*

5 The modern Senate has developed distinctive roles within Parliament, notably in its scrutiny of legislation and in its examination of public policy issues. *All reform proposals must strengthen the existing roles of the Senate with regards to legislative revision, scrutiny of the Executive, sectional/minority representation, and policy investigations.*

6 The roles performed by the Senate are essential to the proper functioning of Parliament. *All reform proposals must ensure that the Senate has powers sufficient to carry out its functions, to ensure that its views are adequately considered by the House of Commons.*

7 The Senate requires accomplished individuals from diverse backgrounds in order to function as a chamber of sober second thought. *All reform proposals must ensure that the Senate is composed of members capable of carrying out its assigned roles, in accordance with the fundamental features/essential characteristics of the institution.*

8 People must have confidence in their political institutions if they are to be effective. *All reform proposals must help to improve public confidence in, and thereby enhance the effectiveness of, the Senate.*

These principles do not inherently favour one model for a reformed Senate over any other, but instead highlight the concerns that must be addressed irrespective of the model being proposed. They are the most fundamentally basic requirements for a successful Upper Chamber and any proposal that respects them – be it an elected Senate, a House of the Provinces, or anything else – will help to improve the institution. While in the context of this study, these principles will form the basis of the current nonconstitutional approach towards improving the Senate, they would also apply equally to constitutional reform when it again becomes more feasible. Each principle will now be examined in detail.

Principle 1:
The Objective of All Reform Proposals Must Be to Improve the Quality of Governance in Canada. This Must Be the Cardinal Principle of Senate Reform.

This point may seem obvious, but it is clearly the starting point from which any reform proposal must proceed. If a proposal cannot be shown to bring about an improvement in the quality of Canadian governance, then there is no point in discussing it further. This basic idea of improvement needs to be kept in mind at all times.

Even this most simplistic and straightforward of tests casts considerable doubt on the argument for abolishing the Senate. The driving force behind abolition is not really the desire for improvement so much as frustration with the Senate as it currently exists. The Canada West Foundation, the organization that initiated the campaign for a "Triple-e" (equal, elected, and effective) Senate, maintains that "the popularity of abolition has occurred as a result of the total collapse of support for the status quo."[6] Foundation data show a decline in support for the status quo from about 30 percent in the early 1980s to between 5 and 10 percent at the end of the 1990s.

Senate abolitionists simply view the current Upper House as a useless waste, and a case could possibly be made that removing the Senate would improve Parliament by saving some money and permitting legislation to be adopted more rapidly. Such a proposition is very tenuous, however, as the stated benefits would be minimal – the Senate is not particularly expensive and does not unnecessarily delay legislation. Moreover, no matter what compensating characteristics were given to the new unicameral House of Commons, the abolition of the Upper House would have unavoidable consequences. Canada's Parliament is bicameral, an arrangement of power common to all major federations and most major states.7 At its most general, the defence of bicameralism rests in the role assigned to the Upper House as a chamber of sober second thought, a safety feature that helps limit legislative errors by permitting sequential decision-making. More specifically, in a country as diverse – geographically, socially, or economically – as Canada, there is also reason to be concerned about a one-house Parliament based solely on representation of population. Such a chamber would be overwhelmingly dominated by Central Canada, precisely the scenario that led the Fathers of Confederation to create a bicameral Parliament in the first place. As well, there is the additional concern that a single-chamber Parliament will reinforce the concentration of power now in the hands of the Executive.8 Finally, of course, a change as drastic as abolishing the Senate would require a constitutional amendment, with the unanimous consent of the provinces, to enact. Given these factors, abolition is both impractical and undesirable.

Simplistic as it may seem, it is imperative that any effort to improve the Senate begin with this cardinal principle. Better governance is the ultimate aim and reformers must keep their eyes firmly fixed on this objective.

Principle 2:
All Reform Proposals Must Consider the Senate within the Context of Our Political System rather than in Isolation. They Must Preserve the Balance and/or Correct Any Imbalances in the Dispersal of Power.

The Canadian system of government is a complex, multilayered set of institutions. Among other things, it is composed of elected representatives of the people at the municipal, provincial, and federal levels, forming both the government and the opposition, a judicial system, various departments/ agencies, and the entire civil service. All of these disparate elements interact with one another and for the political system to function properly the proper relationship between each and every part must be maintained.

The Senate is a fully integrated component of the Canadian political system and any effort to modify it must begin by recognizing that the proposed change may well affect other segments of the government machinery or even the system in its entirety. Far too many utopian Senate reforms have been proposed in isolation, without any reference to the House of Commons, the provincial and territorial governments, or indeed anything that exists outside of the Upper House.

That is not to say that successful Senate reforms cannot be wide-ranging. Indeed, many would argue that the current distribution of power in the political system is imbalanced and requires major reforms to correct it.[9] While it is clearly impossible to compensate for every problem in Canadian politics by improving the Senate, a reform proposal that remembers that the Upper House is only one part of a larger whole and that seeks to find the proper balance between those parts will most likely have at least some merit.

Principle 3:
All Reform Proposals Must Recognize the Role of the House of Commons under the System of Responsible Government and Must Strengthen the Complementary Relationship between the Two Houses of Parliament.

The primary function of the Senate is to complement the House of Commons. Because the Senate is not a confidence chamber, it does not compete with the House of Commons in its most important "elective" function, that is, to make and unmake governments. The supremacy of the Lower House is the heart of the entire British parliamentary system.

Rather than compete, the Upper House completes the work of the Lower House in several important ways: revising legislation, conducting special studies, representing the regions and minorities, and scrutinizing the Executive.[10] It is from this activity that the "sober second thought" role of the Senate arises. Redundancy is as central an element of bicameralism as it is of federalism, and Canadian senators, who are free from the pressures of constituency and electoral duties, have the time to consider issues in a manner different from that of the House of Commons.[11] It is one of the paradoxes of modern politics in parliamentary systems that the upper houses are in a stronger position today to carry out the deliberative work of Parliament, which Walter Bagehot described as its expressive, teaching, and informing functions, than is the House of Commons to which Bagehot originally assigned the tasks.[12]

While many have argued that a better balance needs to be struck between the Houses of Parliament, few suggest that the position of the House of Commons should be completely redefined. Even if it was an option, so vast a change – effectively a switch from parliamentary to republican government – would require the redesigning of not just Parliament but of the entire Canadian federation. Such a transformation is clearly beyond the nonconstitutional scope of this study and is beyond the scope of even the most ambitious of the previous failed constitutional reforms.

Efforts to improve the Senate must respect its symbiotic relationship with the House of Commons. It is possible to change the precise nature of this relationship or to leave the relationship as is; it is not possible to discount or ignore the relationship.

Principle 4:
All Reform Proposals Must Respect the Fundamental Features and Essential
Characteristics of the Senate: Independence, Continuity, Long-Term Perspective,
Professional/Life Experience, and Sectional/Minority Representation.

The Fathers of Confederation knew that, if the Senate were to serve as an effective complement to the House of Commons, it could not simply be a duplicate of the Lower House. To that end, they created an Upper House distinguished by fundamentally different characteristics.[13]

It is well-known that the Fathers of Confederation spent more time at Quebec City in 1864 discussing the composition of the Senate than any other institution of government. The reason is with Canadians still: the colonies (now provinces) are manifestly unequal in population. One of the attractions of bicameralism in the 1860s, perhaps the main attraction, was that it permitted a balance or counterweight to "rep-by-pop" enthusiasts such as George Brown. Unlike other federations, which also experienced population disparities among their states or provinces but which used the states and provinces as units for equal representation in the upper chamber, Canada opted for senatorial regions of equal representation, initially three, two of which were provinces in their own right. The reasons for this lay partly in the lessons Canadians drew from the causes of the Civil War in the United States and partly in the value they placed on government being responsible to an elected chamber (Confederation came only thirty years after the Rebellions of 1837). Those reasons notwithstanding, the agreement on the Senate illustrates an important feature of British North American political culture – a tolerance of difference or, phrased more bluntly, a recognition that equality would undermine the federation altogether.[14]

Lengthy tenure, free from the pressures of frequent electoral cycles, gives the Senate experienced members with diverse professional backgrounds who can bring some continuity and long-term perspective to the institution. The importance of these traits becomes clear when one examines the Lower House. A recent study of "life in the House of Commons" reveals an atmosphere of frustration and disenchantment on the part of backbenchers. Turnover of membership is high (excluding the elections of 1974 and 1980, which followed minority governments, the average turnover rate at each election between 1968 and 1993 was approximately 45 percent), and "the opportunity structure is extremely unwelcoming."[15] What this last comment means is that there are few opportunities for members of the House of Commons to get ahead. Being a committee chairman or parliamentary secretary is far less coveted than becoming a Cabinet minister or Cabinet critic. Loyalty to the leader, party and caucus is a necessary but not sufficient condition for advancement. Criticism of the leader is more than sufficient to blight a career. Executive dominance of government and the House of Commons is well documented. Less understood, in part because the Prime Minister nominates them, is the degree of independence senators enjoy. That independence is a product not only of subdued partisanship (every commentator on the Senate remarks invidiously upon the adversarial tone of the Commons and its general absence in the Upper House) but also of distinctive procedures. The manipulation of House committee chairmen and members has no equivalent in the Senate. Where volatility characterizes the former, stability and continuity mark the latter.[16]

When discussing sectional/minority representation, it needs to be remembered that treating the provinces "unequally" in 1867 was not a cause for sorrow. For their part, the Fathers of Confederation did not envision the Senate acting as a house of the provinces. Appointed by the Governor-in-Council for life (until 1965, when mandatory retirement at age seventy-five was introduced), Canadian senators were in a position to be independent of provincial governments, of the people of the provinces, and of public opinion in the country.[17] The federal principle in Canada concerned jurisdiction, not representation. Equality of power in the matter of jurisdiction for the provinces, normally unconstrained by the exercise of superordinate federal power in the form of disallowance or declaratory legislation – that was the view of how Canadian federalism should work. Neither equality of representation nor popular representation of provincial electors was possible.

Nor was the Senate's composition a source of grievance with the founding provinces, since the sectional and regional interests the Senate was expected to protect were not viewed as territorially confined to provinces. A more exact description of the intent of the Fathers of Confederation when it came to designing the Senate is set out in the following comment by Senator Michael Pitfield:

As regards regional representation, I take this term to mean more than geographic representation and to include the representation of what John A. Macdonald called sectional interests. They are the concerns that Canadians in the various regions of our country expect our federal system to protect from the simple representation by population rule that is the basis of the House of Commons. Today these fundamental regional interests include: in the Maritimes, regional industrial policy; in Quebec, language and culture; in Ontario, industrial policy; in the West, resource policy. An appropriately designed second chamber is the classic method of recognizing and protecting such fundamental regional interests, especially in a federation.[18]

An important and nonterritorial variation on this theme is the concept of interest-based constituencies.

Individual senators over the years have become advocates for children, the poor, the aged, visible minorities, prisoners, veterans and illiterates. Their ability to knit together national constituencies of people who might otherwise have an inadequate voice in Parliament can be attributed at least in part to not having to run for election in a geographically defined constituency.[19]

That quotation is drawn from a section of Audcent's report that describes the Senate as a "house of equalization." If in its deliberative role the Senate acts as a house of legislative completion (so to speak), then in its representative role it acts as a house of compensation. From its personnel it can replenish the depleted ranks of a government, witness Mr Trudeau's selection of the three western senators as ministers in 1980. Again, it may inject sectional interests into a debate from which they are being excluded. An example of that role occurred in 1996 when the Senate held extensive committee hearings in Ottawa and St John's on a constitutional amendment to remove protection to denominational education rights in Newfoundland. At issue was the extinction of one of the Terms of Union under which the province had entered Confederation in 1949. The provincial government requested the amendment, and the Government of Canada and the House of Commons complied, with the House devoting only ten hours over two days to debate the resolution. It was left to the Standing Senate Committee on Legal and Constitutional Affairs, which held a month of public hearings, including three days in Newfoundland, to see that members of the affected denominations had a forum for voicing their objections.[20]

The Senate complements the House of Commons by incorporating these five fundamental features/essential characteristics into Parliament. This is not to say that the House of Commons is bereft of experienced, independent-minded members capable of addressing issues (including regional and minority concerns) over the course of many years. There are many such individuals and their work is to be commended. Nevertheless, the central feature of the House of Commons – the electoral cycle with a maximum of five years – works against these important attributes and it is therefore necessary that they be present in the Upper House. A successful proposal for improving the Senate must respect these characteristics.

Principle 5:
All Reform Proposals Must Strengthen the Existing Roles of the Senate with Regard to Legislative Revision, Scrutiny of the Executive, Sectional/Minority Representation, and Policy Investigations

The Senate contributes to Parliament by performing several distinctive roles. Some of these roles were assigned to it during Confederation while others have been institutional adaptations made over the years in order to better complement the House of Commons. These roles are integral to the work of Parliament, and efforts to improve the Senate should strengthen the institution's ability to perform them.

Legislative revision has been the primary function of the Senate since Confederation. The Upper House provides an extra layer of scrutiny, a second set of parliamentary eyes to catch drafting errors or overlooked concerns before faulty legislation is adopted. In the study of bills, the Senate has an advantage over the House of Commons because of its small numbers (105 to 301 in 2002) and because senators have more time, freedom and expert knowledge, as well as greater independence. Senators have no constituency duties, on which studies show members of the House of Commons increasingly devote time and energy, while the nature of their appointment – tenure to age seventy-five and made at the end of a distinguished career or to someone without political ambitions – limits the potential for their judgement to be swayed by outside concerns.[21] It is therefore easier for members of the Upper House to concentrate exclusively on pieces of legislation and the issues that they raise.

The Senate's role in policy investigations is something that it has taken on over the years. As government has become more complex and new issues have arisen, there has been a gradually increasing need for Parliament to examine these issues in detail. While both chambers have taken on this role to some degree, the Senate enjoys the same advantages in this arena as it does in legislative revision. Like royal commissions, investigative studies by the Senate can be the source of public policy, although also like royal commissions, their findings and recommendations may languish unattended to by government, which is free to reject them. Even so, Senate investigations are important because of the diminished capacity of the Lower Chamber and of citizens generally to frame public debate. The Senate provides a forum for broadened participation because its structure and procedures are more encouraging of focused debate and are less susceptible to domination. In short, the Senate provides ballast to a system that seems increasingly weightless. This is an opinion widely shared: "The work of Commons' committees in Canada is now almost as irrelevant as debate in Parliament"[22]; "[M]inisters ... say that Cabinet is no longer where important decisions are made ... 'Rather, it is a kind of focus group for the prime minister'"[23]; "Canadians continue to feel that they do not have much say over what government does and that their elected representatives are not in touch with the people."[24]

Both when scrutinizing legislation and conducting investigations, the purpose of the Senate is to deliberate, to build up its legislative case through debate, to take testimony from witnesses, and to collect a broad range of opinion from Canadians in all walks of life and all parts of the country. In the political marketplace, the Senate's capital, so to speak, lies not in its skill at brokering interests (that clearly belongs to the Commons) but in distilling arguments. While the Senate is not an academic body, the influence it exerts is intellectual in content. This is why the senators spend more time in committee than in the full house; this is why even the institution's critics speak favourably of its work.

It is through its legislative revision and policy investigations that the Senate performs its third function, scrutinizing the Executive. If the primary function of the Senate is to complement the House of Commons, then in its deliberative role it helps to complete the legislative process by forcing ministers and bureaucrats to see problems and re-examine assumptions in government business brought before the Senate. While it is the responsibility of the House of Commons to hold the government to account – ultimately through the confidence convention – this is becoming ever more difficult as the Executive increases its dominance of the chamber. The work that the Senate performs in scrutinizing the government is therefore a useful supplement to that of the Lower House.

The Senate's final role, sectional/minority representation, pervades all of its other functions. The membership of the Senate is selected on a regional basis and tends to provide representation for societal groups that are underrepresented in the House of Commons.[25] Senators are therefore especially conscious of the implications that legislation or policy investigations may have for specific regions or societal groups and can identify particular issues that may have been neglected by the government and the House of Commons.

A recent example of the Senate performing these four functions can be found in its handling of the Clarity Bill (C–20), "an Act to give effect to the requirement for clarity as set out in the opinion of the Supreme Court of Canada in the Quebec Secession Reference." The background and details of the Bill are well-known or easily discovered.[26] No bill in the last decade has been more central to a government's sense of purpose than this one; and no government in recent memory has been as committed as the Chrétien Government to seeing its passage through Parliament. This was why debate in the House of Commons lasted less than two weeks, why witnesses who appeared before a special committee of that chamber were restricted to ten minutes to present their views, and why members of the committee had only ten minutes to respond.

The contents of the Bill and their implications for Canadian unity as well as for the integrity of bicameral Parliament (the Bill conferred the determination of clarity in the matter of a provincial referendum upon the House of Commons alone) are immaterial to this discussion. What is relevant is that the Senate fulfilled its responsibilities of providing both legislative revision and policy investigation (a special committee was established solely to study Bill C–20). Unlike the Chrétien Government's drastic limiting of debate in the House of Commons, the Senate debate lasted three months and witnesses before the Senate Special Committee had, on average, an hour and a half to present their views and answer questions. Clearly, the Upper House was able to provide much more extensive and extended scrutiny of the Executive than was the Lower House in this case. Finally, it is worth noting that one reason for Senate concern with the bill was regionally based. Senators recognised that determination of this matter solely by the Lower House meant, in all likelihood, determination by the members of the House of Commons from Ontario and Quebec, who occupy two-thirds of the Commons' seats.

Although at the end of the day the amendments were defeated and the Senate voted to pass the Bill, the conclusion to be drawn from this incident is not the one critics of the Senate usually draw – that because it failed to thwart the government, the Senate was ineffective. On the contrary, as one inveterate Senate critic, the *National Post*, observed in an editorial: "The surprising thing about the Clarity Bill ... is how drastically the public debate about it has changed since the Liberal government introduced it seven months ago ... For this remarkable development, we have the Senate to thank."[27] It is hard to imagine a more telling affirmation of the value of bicameralism – that it moulds opinion by heightening an awareness of issues and by promoting debate. The editorial in the *National Post*, as well as opinion pieces published in the weeks preceding the vote, confirm this assessment. The same can be said about court decisions as they deal with the *Charter of Rights and Freedoms* or First Nations. This is not to be confused with the subject of judicial activism, which may or may not be the case. Rather, court decisions on rights and freedoms and on Aboriginal self-government stimulate public and academic discussion. In so doing, they inform, educate, and help articulate beliefs and attitudes fundamental to the health of a democracy. The same argument can be made for the role and function of a second chamber. But with this proviso: legislative debate has the potential to improve the framing of law before its passage. Clarifying the intent of legislation reduces the potential exercise of discretion by the courts.

The Clarity Bill is but one example of the importance of the Senate's roles. Rather than diminishing, their importance only seems to be increasing with the passage of time. Successfully improving the Senate will necessitate preserving and preferably strengthening the capacity of the Upper House to perform them.

Principle 6:
All Reform Proposals Must Ensure That the Senate Has Powers Sufficient to Carry Out Its Functions, to Ensure That Its Views Are Adequately Considered by the House of Commons.

In order for the Senate to carry out its functions as a parliamentary chamber, it requires certain powers. In his study, *The Legal, Constitutional and Political Imperatives to Senate Reform*, Senator Serge Joyal lists several: the power to send for persons and papers, the power to administer oaths to witnesses, the power to compel a person to testify, the power to punish for contempt, the power to guarantee the freedom of its members to attend, the power to discipline its own membership, and the power to adjudicate questions of vacancy and membership.[28] These abilities are the basic tools that allow the Senate to conduct its activities on a day-to-day basis. Most significant, however, are its legislative powers.

Except for the requirement that money bills be introduced in the House of Commons and that it can only delay the adoption of certain constitutional amendments for 180 days, the formal legislative powers of the Senate are infinite. It can initiate its own legislation and its consent is required for the adoption of any nonconstitutional legislation. This power is what permits the Senate to perform its functions, as the Executive and the House of Commons must give careful consideration to the concerns of the Upper House. While any element of the Canadian political system, ranging from individual members of the electorate to provincial governments, can protest against a Government bill, no one (save the judiciary if the bill is found unconstitutional) can actually prevent its adoption except for the Senate.

The use of the Senate's powers and the extent to which those powers are appropriate to the functions it performs are central issues in a discussion of improving the Senate. There is no question that the ability to reject legislation, rather than simply to delay or amend it, is exceptional among upper chambers. Certainly, there is no other unelected chamber that possesses similar power. It can be argued that an absolute veto is too strong for any kind of second chamber as even elected bodies that possess it, such as the Senate of Australia, are vulnerable to criticism from government and the public when they contemplate exercising it. Parliamentary democracies based on the Westminster model are strongly imbued with the belief that "governments should be allowed to govern." Opposition, whether elected or appointed, is unpopular.[29] Of course, one cannot overlook the fact that the mere possession of a veto by the Senate, even if it is used infrequently, gives the Upper House influence it might not otherwise possess.

In practice, the fact that the Senate possesses an absolute veto has not led the Upper House to deliberately thwart the will of the elected government. In his study of *The Senate Veto*, the Law Clerk and Parliamentary Counsel to the Senate of Canada presents an appendix entitled "Senate Use of the Veto to Defeat Bills." That list shows that the veto was used forty-four times in the twentieth century and only five times since the Second World War. For those critics who oppose the Senate as currently constructed, that figure may appear excessive, but from any other vantage, it indicates voluntary restraint on the part of senators. They realize that the Senate was given a veto as a final safeguard to be used with circumspection and in accordance with the constitutional principles on which the Senate was founded, and not to systematically obstruct the House of Commons. This is fortunate, as obtaining the level of consent needed to remove the veto through a constitutional amendment will be extremely difficult, as Audcent has observed:

Moving on from the innovative argumer.. with respect to fundamental amendments to the Constitution, conventional interpretation requires that any amendment that affects a matter protected by section 41 of the *Constitution Act, 1982* receive unanimous authorization under the terms of the section.

[...]

Would an amendment dispensing with the advice and consent of the Senate to the enactment of federal legislation affect any element of the Constitution protected by section 41? Arguably yes, under two headings. The first argument is that such an amendment would infringe on the offices of the Queen and the Governor General, protected by paragraph 41(1)(a). The second is that it would be an amendment to Part V of the *Constitution Act, 1982* protected by paragraph 41(1)(e), in particular, to section 44, which refers to the Parliament of Canada and so to its composition.[30]

The extent of the powers that the Senate should possess is a subject that arouses a great deal of debate, but the exact nature of its powers is not important when considering the fundamental principles for the improvement of the institution. All that is required is to consider how the scope of the Senate's powers – limited, unchanged, or expanded from what they are currently – will affect its ability to perform its functions and complement the House of Commons.

Principle 7:
All Reform Proposals Must Ensure that the Senate Is Composed of Members Capable of Carrying Out Its Assigned Roles, in Accordance with the Fundamental Features/Essential Characteristics of the Institution.

The composition of the Senate has long been the primary focus of would-be reformers and, although it has been given a disproportionate amount of attention, it is certainly a key element of any attempt to improve the Senate. This paper has argued that the composition of the Senate is a subordinate question whose answer depends in large measure on agreement about the purpose the Senate should fulfill as a second chamber. That purpose is to complement the House of Commons by bringing distinct institutional characteristics to Parliament (independence, continuity, long-term perspective, professional/life experience, and regional/minority representation) and by performing distinct roles (legislative revision, scrutiny of the Executive, sectional/minority representation, and policy investigation). No matter what method is used to select senators, it must generate a membership possessing the Senate's essential characteristics, capable of fulfilling its roles, and therefore able to complement the House of Commons and improve the quality of governance in Canada. Any proposal capable of achieving this objective is worth considering.

Principle 8:
All Reform Proposals Must Help to Improve Public Confidence in,
and Thereby Enhance the Effectiveness of, the Senate.

People must have confidence in their political institutions if they are to be effective. While it is easy to find widespread criticism of virtually every element of the Canadian political system, there can be no doubt that the Senate is the institution most often attacked as being illegitimate in the eyes of the public. In their minds, senators appointed entirely at the discretion of the Prime Minister are nothing more than supporters being rewarded with a well-paid job that requires no real work and who merely rubber stamp the wishes of the government. Furthermore, on the rare occasions when the Senate might actually think about interfering with government legislation, the Prime Minister can easily stack the chamber with a few more supporters, as the Mulroney Government did with the GST and the Chrétien Government did with the Clarity Bill. On top of this, the recent controversies surrounding the nonattendance of individual senators and the fact that rules that existed at the time (although they have since been changed) provided no penalty for the most infrequent attendees further depreciated the Upper House in the eyes of the public. Finally, one must also add public displeasure at the Senate's response to criminal charges brought against its members.

There are different degrees of validity to these various concerns. Too often critics depict the Senate as a private club whose members act without any regard for interests beyond their immediate personal concern. This is an unfair distortion of how the Senate operates. The vast majority of senators perform their duties diligently and make a positive contribution to the work of Parliament. As in any walk of life, there have been criminals in politics, some in the Senate, some in the House of Commons, and some in provincial legislatures, but criminal activity by senators is exceedingly rare.[31] While the Senate is not responsible to the people or to interests outside of Parliament, it is responsible to Parliament itself. If the Senate possesses a veto on the legislative process, so too does the House of Commons. Laws are made when the three parts of Parliament act as one. All legislative bodies are self-governing institutions that police themselves, and occasionally others, in accordance with the independence historically accorded to Parliament.[32] Likewise, some aspects of Senate attendance policies are far stronger than those of the House of Commons. Unlike the Lower House, from Confederation onward the Senate has listed members in attendance in the daily *Journals,* and since 1990 those names along with committee attendance have been available to the public. While no one is suggesting that the institution is currently perfect and does not need to address the public's concerns, these facts are cited to suggest that the problem is more one of perception than actual practice.

Whatever its cause and extent, however, it is clear that there is a problem: a large segment of the public does not have confidence in the Senate. This is a serious concern as accusations of illegitimacy and inefficiency undercut the good work done by the Upper House.[33] It is, therefore, necessary to improve the Senate – either by making changes or simply by better explaining current mechanisms – so that its legitimacy will be increased in the eyes of the population of Canada. No effort to improve the Senate can overlook this issue if it is to be successful.

Overview

This "Declaration of Principles" can be viewed as a kind of litmus test for any proposal to improve the Senate. If a proposal does not violate any of the principles and accomplishes one or more of their stated objectives, then it should be given serious consideration. If a proposal violates any of these principles, for example by weakening the Senate's ability to revise legislation or by further undermining public confidence in the institution, then more work is required. The proposal in question can either be abandoned, although this should only occur if the idea is so fundamentally flawed as to be completely unworkable, or it can be modified so that its flaws are corrected. Some might disagree over the exact concerns and the relative importance of each principle, but overall they provide a reasonable framework for discussion and ensure that at least some basic analysis is conducted. By taking the time to stop and fully conceptualize reform proposals, one can eliminate unworkable ideas, improve flawed ones, and allow future discussions to concentrate fully on the proposals with the most merit. Such a situation is the only one in which actual improvement of the Senate is possible.

As an example, take the oft-proposed measure of electing the Senate. For the moment, the significant obstacles blocking the constitutional amendment needed to implement such a change will be ignored. Let us begin with the most straightforward version of this proposal: electing senators in precisely the same way as members of the House of Commons. This measure would certainly enhance the Senate's legitimacy in the eyes of the public and, by removing the Prime Minister's power to appoint senators, it would also help counteract the excessive accumulation of power by the Executive. Furthermore, the additional legitimacy deriving from election would enable senators to make greater use of their veto power. Thus, principles 2, 6, and 8 would be well served by this proposal.

On the other hand, an elected Senate would immediately challenge the central principle of the Canadian Constitution, which is government's responsibility to the elected representatives of the people in the House of Commons. An elected Upper House would constitute a rival to the Commons' claim to speak for the people – the two chambers would compete with rather than complement each other, violating principle 3. Senate elections would introduce a tension now absent in relations between the two Houses, as each would have justification for claiming that they spoke for the electorate and had the right to hold the government to account. Conflict between the chambers would require a deadlock-breaking device in the form, for instance, of a joint sitting, a national referendum, or a double dissolution. On this subject, the history of the Australian Senate provides a cautionary note. There, as here, the Constitution requires that appropriation measures be introduced only in the Lower House, but the Upper Chamber refuses to admit of any other limitation on its potential action with regard to financial bills. But there, unlike here, the Senate has used its powers to block the passage of budgetary measures proposed by a government that controls the Lower House. The outcome of that impasse in 1975 was the Governor General's dismissal of the government and the summoning of a new first minister from the ranks of the opposition. The details and propriety of these actions are not relevant to this paper. The events are noted only to underline the possible consequences that the introduction of a second elected chamber might have in Canada.

The election of senators would also have adverse consequences for the essential characteristics of the Senate outlined in principle 4. To begin with, there would be greater sustained partisanship in a manner comparable to the Commons, weakening the independence of senators. Of course, there is partisanship now, as critics never tire of pointing out, usually by referring to the period between 1984 and 1993.[34] There is nothing wrong with this and bicameralism would, in fact, be in jeopardy if the government could not look to supporters there to shepherd its bills through that legislative process. (It is one of the new concerns of Senate critics that were a Canadian Alliance Government to be formed there would be almost no Canadian Alliance senators in the Upper House). All that may be admitted, but it is still the case, as every commentator on the operation of the Senate states, that partisanship there is muted and, sometimes, inverted. It is not uncommon to see senators speaking and even voting in opposition to a bill that originated with a government composed of their party.

Elected senators, like elected members of the House of Commons, would have constituents to serve and a voting base to protect and mobilize. Independent members of the House of Commons are very rarely elected in Canada, and the same would be true of independent senators. Party support at the time of nomination and party resources during campaigns would assume an importance now absent in an unelected chamber – senators desperate for support come re-election time are far more susceptible to pressure from the party Whip. Of course, frequent elections greatly limit the possibilities for long-term perspective and continuity, while minority groups and women would face the same obstacles that limit their ability to elect members to the House of Commons. Moreover, regional representation is not necessarily best served by election either, as can be seen from the experience of the Australian Senate. That body has been exceptional among upper houses in parliamentary systems, as it has been elected since its inception. Indeed, three electoral systems have been employed – plurality, preferential, and, since 1949, proportional. Each change was introduced to respond to unexpected problems that arose with the previous method. From the perspective of Canadian reformers committed to an elected upper house of Parliament, the instructive lesson to draw from Australian experience with just such an institution is that it has never acted as a house of the states. Either its activities were dominated by political parties or it provided a forum for minority party representation. There is no question, as one Australian political scientist has said, that "state identity continues to be a force in Australian politics. But it has been joined by cross-cutting sources of sectional and minority identity."[35] Thus, Australian experience serves as a reminder that the interests of states (or provinces) in a federation are less easily transferred to national politics than reformers may suppose.

In addition, significant segments of the membership of the current Senate would not be present in an elected second chamber, depriving Parliament of valuable resources and violating principle 7. While there are senators who have previously held elected office and might therefore be willing to run in senatorial elections, this is a minority.[36] Many of the distinguished professionals (doctors, teachers, social workers, farmers, journalists, etc.) whose contributions to the work of the Senate are among the institutions greatest assets would not choose to run for election. Another key element of the Senate's membership, those groups underrepresented in the House of Commons because of the mechanics of the electoral system, would also disappear from an elected Upper House. Thus, aboriginals, visible minorities, and women would lose a very significant amount of their Parliamentary representation.[37]

The loss of the essential characteristics and of membership would impede the ability of the Senate to perform its functions, thereby violating principle 5. Dealing with constituency concerns and finding ways of raising their public profile (in order to boost their re-election prospects) would sap significant amounts of time away from legislative revision. Likewise, elected senators would be less interested in conducting lengthy policy investigations, especially on issues that are unlikely to attract the attention of the media and the voters (such as soil erosion) or on matters that are controversial (such as euthanasia). What work is done would be much more heavily partisan, as is the case with the House of Commons. Scrutiny of the Executive would also suffer as the government (or more properly the governing political party and its electoral machinery) would have much more control over the elected Upper House. Finally, as has already been mentioned, societal groups that have traditionally been unable to elect a sufficient number of representatives to the House of Commons (aboriginals, women, etc.) would face the same problems with an elected Senate and regional concerns would also likely fall under the sway of party Whips.

To sum up then, a proposal to elect the Senate in precisely the same fashion as the House of Commons would help to achieve the objectives of principles 6 (adequate powers) and 8 (legitimacy), but would violate principles 3 (complementary relationship), 4 (fundamental features), 5 (roles), and 7 (membership). Furthermore, when one examines more closely the argument concerning principle 2 (correcting imbalances in the distribution of power), that the election of senators and the removal of the Prime Minister's power of appointment would weaken the Executive, the supposed benefits quickly become doubtful as party control over elected members is every bit as strong as its control over appointed ones. On balance, it would therefore seem reasonable to conclude that this proposal would create more problems than it would solve and it would not accomplish the cardinal objective of principle 1 – improving the quality of Canadian governance. In fact, even most proponents of an elected Senate would agree with this assessment as almost no one is proposing that the reformed second chamber be an exact duplicate of the House of Commons.

The challenge is to modify the proposal so that it respects principles 2, 3, 4, 5, and 7 without losing the benefits it brings regarding principles 6 and 8. One possible way of doing this is demonstrated by the ongoing reform of the House of Lords, which, despite having to deal with issues that are irrelevant to the Canadian situation (hereditary peerages, law lords, etc.), has been addressing this very same concern: how to provide a second chamber with the legitimacy of election without sacrificing the advantages gained from appointment.

The proposals contained in *The Second Chamber: Continuing the Reform,* issued in February 2002, are the most recent and address concerns raised with both the earlier Royal Commission report and the government's White Paper. All three focused on the core issues that comprise the "Declaration of Principles."[38] The Committee report proposed a mixed chamber with a majority of elected members (60 percent) and a minority of appointed ones (40 percent). No one party would enjoy a majority in the House of Lords, and 20 percent of the members would be independents with no ties to any political party. The elected element would be elected using proportional representation and the elections would be staggered (with either a third or half the members being elected at any one time). Elected members would serve for a term of two Parliaments and would be ineligible to ever run for re-election or to be appointed to the chamber. The appointed members would be selected by an independent appointments commission, established by statute, which would be responsible to Parliament not the Prime Minister. Half of the appointed members would

be independents with no political ties while the other half would be selected from the political parties according to the percentage of the votes each
received in the most recent Lords election. The political parties would submit lists of possible candidates but the appointments commission would
make the actual decisions. Appointed members would serve a term of ten
years and could not be reappointed or stand for election to the Lords.
Also, both appointed and elected members would not be permitted to
stand for election to the House of Commons for ten years after serving in
the Lords.

The modifications proposed by the report, if placed in the Canadian
context, outline one method for ensuring that the basic "Elect the Senate" proposal respects the "Declaration of Principles." Removing the
Prime Minister's power of appointment and preventing any one party
from having a majority in the Senate would help correct the existing
power imbalance between the Executive and Parliament, in accordance
with principle 2. Using a different electoral system and keeping an
appointed element would ensure that the Senate would not challenge the
primacy of the House of Commons, but rather would preserve the complementary relationship of principle 3. Having staggered elections with
lengthy terms without the possibility of re-election, along with the continued presence of appointed members of whom half would be Independents, would preserve the Upper House's independence, continuity, long-
term perspective, professional/life experience, and sectional/minority
representation, in accordance with principle 4. Likewise, since the elected members would not be focused on re-election and the appointed segment would still provide representation for societal groups inadequately
represented in the House of Commons and independent members with
expertise in many fields, the Senate would still fulfill the roles discussed
in principle 5. The British consensus was that a suspensive veto of one
month for money bills and one year for other legislation would fulfill the
requirements of principle 6. The Senate's absolute veto is appropriate for
the purposes of implementing the federal principle in the Parliament of
Canada. Even if the elections failed to return members of sufficiently
broad expertise and diversity, the appointed senators would ensure that
the chamber continue to satisfy principle 7. Finally, a predominantly elected Senate would curtail charges of patronage and increase the chamber's
legitimacy in accordance with principle 8. A proposal along these lines
might satisfy principle 1 and improve governance in Canada. One must
remember, however, that the political institutions of other nations, however attractive, were created to address the dynamics of their respective systems, and not our own.

This British model is not perfect and certainly would not address all the
problems confronting the Senate. For example, because Great Britain is
not a federation, this proposal does not properly consider the implications for the federal principle, which is fundamental to the Canadian

Upper House. In addition, it does not deal with the underrepresentation of Western Canada under the present distribution of seats. Some might wish to modify certain features of the proposal further – say by having an 80 percent elected / 20 percent appointed chamber – while others might prefer to use altogether different solutions. It is certain, however, that by taking the time to analyze the initial proposal/slogan "Elect the Senate" with the aid of a fully developed conceptual framework (the Declaration of Principles), a proposal could be formulated that respects the constitutional features of our system of government.

NONCONSTITUTIONAL PROPOSALS FOR IMPROVING THE SENATE

Whatever the merits of the Elected-Senate-Based-on-Lords-Reform model just discussed, it is unlikely to be fully implemented in the foreseeable future because of the constitutional roadblocks already mentioned – here is one advantage to Britain's unwritten Constitution! That does not mean, however, that the Senate cannot be improved by various nonconstitutional means in a manner that is consistent with the "Declaration of Principles." It would be wrong to conclude that this approach is a new development. Quite the reverse: "Since 1867, the Senate has constantly evolved to meet new needs and challenges. Most important, it has found ways to check the powers of the Cabinet and its Commons majority without challenging or offending today's democratic culture."[39] The nonconstitutional approach can accomplish a vast number of improvements, some minor and some major. These kinds of changes may not be enough to fully satisfy the wishes of Canadians or the requirements of the "Declaration of Principles," but they would be improvements. Until broader reforms can again be contemplated, we must improve the current Senate as much as possible by using initiatives that can be feasibly implemented within the current constitutional parameters.

Roles and Functions

As has been argued throughout this paper, the first step is to determine what roles and functions the Senate is designed to perform before considering its powers and composition. The Senate is designed to complement the House of Commons, to revise legislation, to scrutinize the Executive, to provide a voice for sectional/minority representation, and to conduct policy investigations. There are several nonconstitutional methods of improving the Senate's ability to perform these roles.

1 THE SENATE COULD ESTABLISH A REGIONAL AFFAIRS COMMITTEE
Given the importance of the Senate's regional dimension, it would make sense to strengthen it by establishing a Standing Senate Committee on

Regional Affairs, which could both examine legislation with a strong regional impact and conduct long-term investigations to identify possible solutions for the different challenges facing individual regions. Representing the sectional interest is one of the fundamental roles of the Upper House, and this measure would significantly enhance its ability to do so. This proposal would not violate any tenets of the "Declaration of Principles." In particular, it would advance principles 4 and 5 by voicing regional/sectional interests and might also enhance their legitimacy in line with principle 8. This measure could be implemented by the Senate itself simply by having the Upper House vote to approve the creation of a new committee.

2 SENATE COMMITTEES COULD SPEND MORE TIME TRAVELLING TO ALL REGIONS OF THE COUNTRY

Senate committees already do travel across Canada in certain instances when they wish to collect more first-hand information. Increasing the frequency with which they do this would help them gain a better understanding of the legislation or policy question being studied. Furthermore, the increased interaction with people across the country would also demonstrate the effectiveness and utility of Senate committees by making their work visible to a greater number of Canadians.

Increased visibility is, however, a two-edged sword and excessive committee travel would seem profligate and quickly undermine the Senate's reputation. Therefore, this proposal could only be implemented in moderation if it is to respect principle 8. With that caveat in mind, this would be an effective way of strengthening the Senate's role in voicing regional/sectional interests and policy investigations according to principle 5. Increasing the travel budget of individual committees would need to be approved by the Standing Senate Committee on Internal Economy, Budgets and Administration and ultimately by the Senate itself. Depending on the extent of the financial expenditures, this measure might affect the overall budget of the Senate, which has to be approved by Parliament.

3 THE USE OF POLICY INVESTIGATIONS BY SENATE STANDING AND SPECIAL COMMITTEES COULD BE INCREASED AND AN INCREASED NUMBER OF SENATORS COULD ACTIVELY PARTICIPATE IN THEM

The policy studies of Senate committees are universally regarded as a major institutional strength. With new issues arising, ranging from emerging technologies to the changing global political environment, the opportunities for augmenting the number of studies performed by Senate committees are certainly present. In addition, the active participation of all senators in such investigations could be assured by requiring senators to be member of at least a minimum number of committees (say three or four) and by stiffening the penalties for not attending meetings.

Increasing the Senate's capacity to conduct policy investigations would directly serve principle 5. Moreover, by bringing Parliamentary scrutiny to bear on matters that the House of Commons has been unable to examine due to its other responsibilities, this proposal would strengthen the complementary relationship discussed in principle 3. Provided it was not pursued in a fiscally irresponsible manner, weakening the Upper House's credibility in violation of principle 8, all of the principles would be respected. The decision to conduct more special studies or to establish more special committees is a decision of the Senate itself – although ultimately budget ramifications may need the approval of Parliament. Policies governing committee participation and penalties for nonattendance are entirely within the discretion of the Senate.

4 THE SENATE SHOULD ENHANCE ITS SCRUTINY OF REGULATIONS AND
   DELEGATED LEGISLATION

A large and ever-increasing amount of political authority is being given to ministers and bureaucrats through the use of regulations and delegated legislation. Only a very small percentage of these instruments are subject to detailed examination by the existing Joint Committee of the Senate and House of Commons for the Scrutiny of Regulations, so there is considerable room for further developing this role. The Senate, which has more time to devote to the issue, could establish its own committee and make a much more concerted effort to study a greater amount of delegated legislation and regulations.

This measure would violate no tenet of the "Declaration of Principles," but it would enhance the Senate's capacity to review legislation and scrutinize the Executive, in accordance with principle 5. By filling a parliamentary void not being addressed by the House of Commons, this proposal would also strengthen the complementary relationship of principle 3. Finally, by reinforcing Parliamentary oversight, this measure would serve principle 2 by counteracting the diminution of Parliament's power. The Senate could create such a committee entirely on its own authority, although it would make sense to collaborate with the House of Commons over the fate of the existing joint committee. That committee could be dismantled or the new Senate committee could be considered a subcommittee that would meet regularly while the full joint committee would only meet every now and then to consider the findings of the subcommittee. This could be accomplished by changes to the current practices and rules of both Houses.

5 THE SENATE COULD INVESTIGATE THE EFFECTS OF INTERNATIONAL
   TREATIES PRIOR TO THEIR ADOPTION BY THE GOVERNMENT

Canada is party to a growing number of international treaties and conventions. These agreements now have widespread impacts across many sectors of society, are binding at both the federal and provincial levels, and are often difficult to withdraw from. They have what has been described as a hobbling effect on Parliament's competencies by limiting its legislative capacity. Currently, however, such commitments can be made unilaterally by the Executive, with Parliamentary approval needed only to enact any changes in domestic legislation required by the terms of the agreements. Given the increasing importance of Canada's international obligations, it would be advisable to examine their implications at least prior to their being ratified by the government, if not sooner.

This would be another task for which the Senate is well suited, as it has the time and expertise needed to conduct such studies. A new committee could be established or the mandate of the existing Senate Standing Committee on Foreign Affairs, which already addresses treaties, could be expanded specifically for this purpose. The mandate should include studying the impact of these treaties on Canada and should also allow the committee to continue monitoring their effects after they have been implemented. The conclusions of the Senate could then be given specifically to the government, the relevant opposition critics, and the House of Commons Standing Committee on Foreign Affairs and International Trade, as well as being made generally available. These reports would offer an opportunity for Parliamentary scrutiny of proposed treaties and could identify concerns that should be addressed. They would offer members of both Houses information to consider when the government attempted to implement any legislative changes.

This proposal would not violate any of the eight principles but it would advance the objectives of principles 2 and 5 by giving Parliament a degree of supervision of the exercise of Executive power. Also, by taking on a task not being performed by Parliament and providing the Lower House with additional information, it would help the complementary relationship of principle 3. The Senate's role would be advisory, so this proposal would simply require the co-operation of the Executive. The Senate could create a committee or expand the Foreign Affairs committee's mandate, but the government would need to agree to delay signing or ratifying treaties until they were studied by the Senate. Otherwise, the treaty obligations would be a *fait accompli*, regardless of any problems that the Senate might identify. The government could express its agreement through a public statement of the Prime Minister or Minister of Foreign Affairs, or it could have the House of Commons adopt a resolution to this effect.

6 THE SENATE COULD MODIFY ITS PRACTICES WHEN PROPOSING
AMENDMENTS OR DEFEATING LEGISLATION, SO AS TO BETTER EXPLAIN
THE RATIONALE FOR ITS ACTIONS

When the Senate amends or defeats a bill, a message is sent to the House of Commons to inform them of the Senate's actions. These messages could be expanded to include an explanation of why the Senate has made amendments or felt it necessary to defeat a bill. These explanations could also then be used to outline the Senate's rationale to the media and the public. By providing short summaries of the concerns raised during the Upper House's examination of a bill, these messages would make the reasons for the senators' decisions clear and easily accessible to those who do not follow their daily deliberations.

This proposal would not violate the "Declaration of Principles" as it simply improves the Senate's methods of communicating its decisions to others. This would advance the objectives of principle 3 by making the members of the House of Commons more aware of the nature of the Senate's concerns, principle 6 by improving the method by which the Senate exercises it powers, and principle 8 by making the public more aware of the good work done by the institution. This measure could be adopted by making changes to current Senate practices without any outside collaboration. The House of Commons could refuse to read such messages, but they would still be made available to the media and the public. The key issue would be identifying the most appropriate means of drafting such messages. Possibilities would include having the Speaker or the Committee that studied the bill submit a proposed message to be approved by the Senate as a whole before being dispatched to the House of Commons.

7 THE SENATE SHOULD INCREASE THE NUMBER OF DAYS IT SITS

In part because it has only one third of the membership of the House of Commons and in part because less time is spent attempting to score political points or impress constituents of voting age, the Senate sits less frequently than does the Lower House. This helps to feed the misperception that senators do not really work. The number of sitting days needs to be increased. This additional time could be used to further some of the additional responsibilities suggested by the other nonconstitutional proposals discussed in this paper. If senators are to conduct additional policy investigations, examine more delegated legislation, or review international treaties, they will also need to spend more time considering and debating their findings in the Senate chamber. This extra time could be obtained either by adding an additional sitting day to each week of the Senate's current schedule or by extending the sitting schedule into the winter and summer recesses taken by the House of Commons.

Increasing the number of Senate sittings would be in line with principles 3, 5, and 8 as it would enable the Senate to better perform its roles and complement the House of Commons, thereby enhancing public confidence in the institution. This measure may have some negative effects on principle 7, as people may be less inclined to serve in the Upper House if they will be kept away from their families and careers for greater periods of time. This would be unfortunate, as the presence of members who are active practitioners of their professions brings many benefits to the Upper

House. In this instance, however, the benefits would outweigh the costs, particularly as not all potential senators will be discouraged by an extended sitting schedule. The Senate's sitting schedule is entirely at the discretion of the senators themselves and can be extended as much as they choose.

Powers

As it possesses an absolute veto over everything short of a constitutional amendment, there is clearly no need to increase the powers of the Senate. The historical record also suggests that the Senate has not abused its powers by using them to deliberately thwart the will of the elected government, suggesting that there is not a pressing need to diminish them. Feasible proposals to reduce the Senate's power can, however, be made provided that the Upper House can still perform its functions, in accordance with principle 6. Of course, even if one were to attempt to do so, it would require a constitutional amendment using at least the 7/50% formula to remove the veto. As such, there is little that can be done nonconstitutionally with regard to the powers of the Senate.

Composition

The composition of the Senate is an important facet of the institution. Its members must possess the abilities and bring the institutional characteristics – independence, long-term perspective, continuity, professional/life experience, and sectional/minority representation – that the Upper House needs to perform its functions. The composition of the Senate can be improved using several different nonconstitutional means.

1 ALL ASPECTS OF THE SENATE APPOINTMENT PROCESS SHOULD BE
TRANSPARENT AND OPEN TO THE PUBLIC
Whatever new measures are implemented concerning Senate appointments, or even if things remain unchanged, one way of enhancing public confidence would be to make the process as open and transparent as possible. The general criteria for selecting senators, the specific reasons for the selection of each individual senator, the rationale for not selecting other candidates, any information about the composition, role, and deliberations of an appointments commission (if one is created); indeed, anything at all related to the Senate appointment process should be publicized and made available.

This proposal would not violate the "Declaration of Principles," as it would not change any facet of the appointments process but would simply make more information available. This would help strengthen public confidence in the Senate, in accordance with principle 8. This measure could be implemented simply by having the Prime Minister voluntarily change current practice and make the information available, but transparency could be made a requirement by an act of Parliament.

2 AN INDEPENDENT VETTING COMMISSION, WHOSE MEMBERS ARE
    SELECTED IN A NONPARTISAN FASHION, SHOULD BE ESTABLISHED TO
    OVERSEE THE APPOINTMENT OF SENATORS; THIS COMMISSION SHOULD
    BE RESPONSIBLE TO PARLIAMENT, NOT THE PRIME MINISTER

The most glaring weakness of the Senate appointment process is the fact that it is perceived as an exercise in patronage. Successive prime ministers have been perceived as abusing their powers and making appointment on the basis of partisanship. The British solution to this problem, developed during the current reform of the House of Lords, is to transfer the responsibility for selecting members of the Upper House to an independent appointments commission. This could not easily be done in Canada, since it would require a constitutional amendment under section 38 of the *Constitution Act, 1982* (7/50%) to formally remove the Prime Minister's power of appointment as the method of selecting senators is specifically mentioned in paragraph 42(1)(b). It might, however, be possible to establish an "Appointments Vetting Commission" that would draw up a short list of four or five candidates from which the Prime Minister would choose. A new convention would emerge by which the Prime Minister would only appoint senators recommended by the vetting commission. The commission would need to be created, and its membership selected in a nonpartisan way, perhaps requiring the consent of the leaders of the government and opposition parties. The membership of the commission could certainly include representatives of the political parties, as it would need a very strong understanding of and sensitivity to the workings of Parliament, but no single party should have an overall majority, as the commission would be charged with making appointments that would be in the best interest of the country and the Senate rather than of the government. This option would coincide nicely with the proposal to develop a set of guidelines to govern the appointment process (composition proposal 4), as the independent commission could then select senators in line with those guidelines and could perhaps also propose any modifications to the criteria that might be needed over time. The formal power of appointment would be in the hands of the Prime Minister, as demanded by the Constitution, but it would be framed by the commission. The result would be the vetting of candidates by an independent body according to pre-established and agreed-upon criteria. A similar process has done much to improve the judicial appointment system.

This proposal would lessen the excessive power of the Prime Minister in accordance with principle 2 and would improve public confidence in the Senate, as required by principle 8. Furthermore, it would enhance the independence of the Senate, as discussed in principle 4, which would in turn strengthen all of the other principles. Moreover, none of the principles would be violated, provided that the commission was established properly. A bill creating such a commission could be adopted by Parliament, or be established through a new convention – resulting from a statement by the Prime Minister or a resolution of the House of Commons – committing the Prime Minister to select only senators from the list of individuals compiled by the appointments commission.

3 SENATORS COULD BE APPOINTED FOR A NONRENEWABLE FIXED TERM OF TWELVE YEARS

It is essential that senators have lengthy terms of office in order to perform their functions, but that does not necessarily have to mean that they be appointed until the age of seventy-five. The current system reinforces the perception that the composition of the Senate is too static, as it theoretically allows someone to sit in the chamber for a maximum term of forty-five years (a person could be appointed at the minimum age of thirty and then sit until retirement at seventy-five), which is clearly too long, even for the needs of continuity and long-term perspective. Such excesses could be avoided by appointing senators for a fixed term of twelve years.

In reality, the historic average term of office for senators is only slightly less than twelve years, so this proposal would not be a radical shift from current practice.[40] Removing tenure until the age of seventy-five would facilitate the appointment of younger senators who would not be considered under the present system because of the public perception of the appointment of a thirty-year-old. Under a fixed term appointment, though, there would be no difference between appointing a thirty-year-old and a sixty-year-old. This broadening of the Senate's membership would not simply help to dispel the retirement-home myth, thus advancing public confidence in the chamber in accordance with principle 8, but would advance the objectives of principle 7 by bringing in new members with skills and perspectives not currently possessed by the Senate. Members would still have the secure lengthy terms needed to guarantee the fundamental features of principle 4 – since Confederation, twelve years is approximately the average length of three parliaments and is nearly double the historic average tenure of members of the House of Commons – and could still perform the institutional roles of principle 5, although shortening the tenure any further would put these principles in jeopardy.[41] In addition, the term of appointment would have to be nonrenewable in order to preserve the independence required by principle 4, as senators might otherwise seek to curry the favour of the Prime Minister in order to be reappointed.

This measure would require a constitutional amendment, as section 29 (2) of the *Constitution Act, 1867* states that a senator shall "hold his place in the Senate until he attains the age of seventy-five years." It could be argued, however, that such an amendment could be made unilaterally by the federal Parliament as it would merely translate the reality of an average tenure of twelve years (i.e., three parliaments) into the Constitution without altering or affecting the "fundamental role and essential characteristics" of the Senate. Taking into account the 1965 amendment that brought the retirement age at seventy-five, and the criteria determined by the Supreme Court in 1980 (in the Senate Reference), it is possible that such an amendment could be made by Parliament alone under section 44 of the *Constitution Act, 1982*. The possibility is at least worth further study, as it raises important issues and does have considerable merit.

4 GUIDELINES GOVERNING THE SELECTION OF SENATORS SHOULD BE DEVELOPED AND MADE PUBLIC; THESE GUIDELINES SHOULD INCLUDE A GENERAL STATEMENT OUTLINING THE DESIRED MEMBERSHIP OF THE UPPER HOUSE

One of the most significant objections to the current appointment process is that senators are picked entirely at the whim of the Prime Minister. Section 23 of the *Constitution Act, 1867*, which outlines the qualifications for senators, was originally very stringent (albeit focused almost exclusively on the nineteenth century view that wealth and property were the proper qualifications for being an effective and trustworthy legislator) but is now insufficient, allowing successive prime ministers to sometimes abuse their power of appointment. To correct these problems, a new set of qualification guidelines should be developed and published, so that when future Senate appointments are made, Canadians could compare them against the pre-established criteria. The electorate would be able to judge both the quality of the criteria and the subsequent appointments as part of the government's record. This would limit the potential for abusing the appointment criteria and process, as a consensus would gradually emerge as to what the appropriate qualifications should be. The specific details of the new appointment guidelines are open to debate. They would have to take into account the Canadian values embodied in the *Charter of Rights and Freedoms* and the fundamental constitutional and organizing principles of the Senate. At the same time, residency requirements would have to remain. Not only are they core components of the Senate's regional representation function, but they are specifically listed in paragraph 42(1)(c) of the *Constitution Act, 1982*.

The appointment guidelines for senators should specifically incorporate the concerns of principle 7, namely that the Upper House be composed of members capable of carrying out its assigned roles in accordance with the fundamental principles of the institution. They should also emphasize that the membership of the Senate is to be complementary to that of the House of Commons, is to be drawn from a broad range of occupations, and is to include in particular members of societal groups that are not otherwise well represented in Parliament.

It is important that the appointment guidelines be drafted with the "Declaration of Principles" in mind and that the criteria not violate any of them. This proposal would clearly further the objectives of principles 3 and 7, and through them those of principles 4 and 5 as well. It would also help principle 8, as by replacing prime ministerial whims with a justifiable rationale for Senate appointments it will enhance public confidence in the Upper House. These guidelines could be adopted in several different ways. To begin with, the Prime Minister could publicly outline them and commit to observing them. Alternatively, they could be adopted as a resolution of the House of Commons, or as a bill adopted by the Senate and the House of Commons. In both cases, these guidelines would still have to respect the existing provisions of section 23 of the *Constitution Act, 1867*. It might also be possible for Parliament to replace the provisions of section 23, except 23(5), which requires senators to be residents of the provinces they represent, with the newer qualification guidelines using a constitutional amendment under section 44 of the *Constitution Act, 1982*.

5 THE APPOINTMENT GUIDELINES SHOULD PREVENT THE APPOINTMENT OF
    LARGE NUMBERS OF SENATORS WHO ARE APPROACHING THE MANDATORY
    RETIREMENT AGE OF SEVENTY-FIVE

Prime Minister Chrétien has demonstrated a marked tendency for appointing senators who are already very close to the mandatory retirement age of seventy-five.[42] Taken too far, this practice would undermine the Senate's continuity and long-term perspective, as well as its ability to perform its assigned functions, due to the rapid turnover in membership. The appointments guidelines should limit the practice in some way. One option would be to impose a maximum age for appointment (for example, no one could be appointed over the age of sixty-five, ensuring a minimum tenure of ten years), while another would be to impose a limit on the number of appointees seventy years or older (for example, no more than 10 percent of the nominees in any given year can be over seventy). If appointment until the age of seventy-five is replaced with appointment for a fixed term of twelve years (see composition proposal 3), then one could set the maximum age for appointment at sixty. Another alternative would be to remove the mandatory retirement age altogether as everyone, irrespective of age, would serve for twelve years, but this would need to be done in conjunction with limiting the number of seventy years or older appointees chosen each year. Otherwise, it would simply worsen the perception of the Senate as being a retirement home.

These measures would not violate the "Declaration of Principles" but would help temper the perception of the ancient Senate, thus enhancing public confidence, in line with principle 8. Moreover, it would prevent the possible loss of the continuity and long-term perspective required by principle 4. The proposals to establish a maximum age for appointment or to limit the number of seventy years or older appointees could be adopted by establishing a convention, laid out in a statement by the Prime Minister or a resolution in the House of Commons, or by having Parliament pass a bill to that effect. Any modification of the mandatory retirement age of seventy-five would, however, require a constitutional amendment under section 44 of the *Constitution Act, 1982*.

6 VACANCIES IN THE SENATE SHOULD BE FILLED WITHIN A FIXED AMOUNT OF TIME

Senate appointments are made entirely at the discretion of the Prime Minister and there have been instances when significant numbers of seats have been left vacant for extended periods of time. As the Senate has only 105 members, even three or four vacancies at one time represent a significant loss of personnel. Outside of Ontario and Quebec, even a single vacancy represents a minimum loss of 10 percent of a province's total Senate representation, while the territories, with only one seat each, would be deprived of any representation in the Upper House. Apart from this inequity, the practice of storing up Senate appointments until a close vote on a key bill is expected and then packing the chamber to ensure its passage (as was done with the Clarity Bill) does nothing to improve the public's confidence in Parliament. Requiring vacancies to be filled within a fixed period of time would help diminish both problems. Even factoring in the time needed for careful consideration of possible candidates (especially needed if the proposal of an appointments commission is taken up) the delay should be no longer than three months at the absolute latest, particularly as work could be done before hand to draw up a pre-prepared list of candidates.

This measure would not violate the "Declaration of Principles" and would help enhance public confidence in the Senate in accordance with principle 8. This measure could be adopted simply by having the Prime Minister publicly commit to respecting it, but could also be made legally binding through an act of Parliament or a constitutional amendment under section 44 of the *Constitution Act, 1982*.

7 THE MEMBERSHIP OF THE SENATE SHOULD INCLUDE A "CROSSBENCH"

The House of Lords has a significant number of independent members that are not affiliated with any political party. Collectively, they are referred to as the Crossbench and, according to the current proposals for Lords reform, they will account for 20 percent of the overall membership. While it is not uncommon to find a few independent senators in Canada (currently there are four), there has never been an institutionalized independent element equivalent to the Crossbench. This should be changed and a fixed number of seats (10–20 percent), divided equally between the regions, should be reserved for independent members.

Clearly, the inclusion of a Crossbench would greatly enhance the Senate's independence in accordance with principle 4, which would also help offset the power of the Executive in line with principle 2. In addition, this measure would enhance public confidence in the Senate, as required by principle 8, by having senators who are clearly not expected to adhere to a party line. The "Declaration of Principles" would be in no way violated by this measure. In theory, the creation of a Crossbench would only require a decision by the Prime Minister to name the required number of independent members. Criteria would need to be established, outlining both the number of independents and what exactly would constitute an independent member. These criteria could be incorporated into the appointment guidelines, discussed in composition proposal 4, to be used by the Prime Minister or vetting commission when making their selections. If so, they should be implemented by the same process – either a declaration, an act of Parliament, or a constitutional amendment under section 44 of the *Constitution Act, 1982*. Such a proposal would need to be further refined and its potential impact considered, but it is certainly worth considering for further study.

8 A MINIMUM NUMBER OF OPPOSITION SENATORS COULD BE ESTABLISHED

In order for the Senate to function properly, there must be a reasonable number of opposition members, enough to sit on the various Senate committees and to challenge the government members in the chamber. While the Senate is not as partisan as the House of Commons, it is still a parliamentary chamber whose operations are organized around the adversarial principle of government and opposition. If the opposition does not have sufficient numbers, then the entire operation of the Upper House could disintegrate, leaving little more than a "registry" for government proposals. Therefore, at a minimum, the opposition parties should always have at least one third (about thirty-five) Senate seats.

This measure would violate no aspect of the "Declaration of Principles" and would in fact strengthen all of the principles. In particular, it would help give the Senate the membership needed to carry out its tasks, in accordance with principle 7, and would enhance public confidence, in accordance with principle 8, by having a significant number of senators being chosen from the opposition parties rather than from among the Prime Minister's supporters. This measure could be implemented by a decision of the Prime Minister to appoint the required number of opposition senators. It could also be incorporated into the proposed appointment guidelines to be used by the Prime Minister or a vetting commission when making selections (composition proposal 4). It would be adopted by whatever means was used to adopt the guidelines, as already discussed.

Accountability

One of the public's major concerns with the Senate is its accountability, and it is therefore important to find ways of enhancing public confidence in the institution. While the Senate is not accountable to the electorate in the same way as the House of Commons, it is accountable to Parliament and the country. Nonconstitutional methods offer several avenues for further improvement.

1 THE SENATE COULD ESTABLISH A CODE OF ETHICS, WITH AN ETHICS
  COMMITTEE TO OVERSEE ITS FUNCTIONING

In contemporary society, the public expects a high level of ethical standards and independence from politicians and has called for further policing of parliamentary behaviour due to incidents that have occurred in the recent past. To alleviate these concerns, the Senate should establish an ethics code in order to clearly delineate what standards members of the Upper House are expected to uphold. As a written document is unlikely to be capable of addressing every possible scenario, an ethics committee should be created to advise and adjudicate on possible violations.

A code of conduct would in no way violate the "Declaration of Principles" and would be of great benefit to principle 8 as it would be a very direct way of addressing the public's concerns about the Senate. The Senate could implement an ethics code and ethics committee by making changes to its rules.

2 THE SENATE SHOULD DEVELOP MORE STRINGENT ATTENDANCE POLICIES

Although the Senate does keep daily attendance records, unlike many other legislatures, the previous laxity of the penalties for absenteeism was demonstrated by former Senator Andrew Thompson and brought about immediate changes to attendance policy. While the penalties have since become more severe, even more could be done. To begin with, section 31(1) of the *Constitution Act, 1867*, which states that senators who fail to attend two consecutive sessions of Parliament will lose their seats, has been rendered obsolete by current practices as a single parliamentary session can now last for several years. It needs to be replaced with a more reasonable timeframe. Failure to attend for more than half of the annual sittings should trigger sanctions. The financial penalty of $120 being deducted from the sessional allowance per day for nonattendance, as stated in section 57(1) of the *Parliament of Canada Act*, should be increased so that failure to attend on a regular basis will actually entail more stringent financial penalties for a senator rather than merely reduce the amount of money they make. Furthermore, the provision of section 57(1) granting twenty-one days of unexcused absences should be reduced to ten days, as a few days absence for personal reasons is acceptable, but over four weeks of sittings seems excessive by public standards. Finally, section 57(3)a of the *Parliament of Canada Act* allows absence for reasons of "public or official business" but does not specify what is meant by this. This provision of the Act should be amended and a tighter definition provided.

None of these measures would violate the "Declaration of Principles," but they would advance principle 8's concern with improving public confidence in the Senate. Poor attendance is a major preoccupation of the public and taking steps to address this concern would be of great assistance in improving the institution's credibility. Many of the measures would require changes to *Parliament of Canada Act* and would therefore require legislation to be adopted by the Senate and the House of Commons. Any alterations to section 31(1) of the *Constitution Act, 1867* would require a constitutional amendment under section 44 of the *Constitution Act, 1982*.

3 THE SENATE COULD DEVELOP A MORE ACTIVE AND EFFECTIVE COMMUNICATIONS PROGRAM

Even with its current perceived weaknesses, the Senate is a highly effective legislative chamber. This is not widely known, however, in part because the Senate has done little to publicize its strengths. There are a variety of techniques that the Senate could implement in order to make the public more aware of the good work it does. One method would be to produce an annual performance report, which could also serve as the basis for an annual debate on the Senate in order to constantly find new ways of improving it. Another measure would be to increase the activities of the Senate's Communications directorate so that it can provide more information to the media, members of the House of Commons, members of the public, educators, and academics. The Senate could make greater use of the internet; for example, an increasing number of senators have created their own websites as a means of communicating with the public. Another possibility, would be to increase television coverage of Senate committee proceedings or to introduce coverage of the debates in the Senate chamber itself (of course, there are many who suggest that the introduction of television coverage of the House of Commons has increased the focus on partisan jabs and ten-second sound bytes to the overall detriment of the quality of debate).

These measures would not violate the "Declaration of Principles" – with the possible exception of the introduction of television coverage – and would all help to better inform the public about the Senate and enhance their confidence in it, in accordance with principle 8. These measures could be largely implemented by the Senate itself, although the budgeting and scheduling of additional television coverage would require co-operation with the House of Commons.

CONCLUSION

The Senate is a more substantial and responsible legislative chamber than its critics allow, and it can be further improved by nonconstitutional means. The reform of Parliament is a never-ending search for ways to improve the quality of legislation and governance for the good of the country. Neither the House of Commons nor the Senate are perfect, and efforts to improve them must continue constantly. Although some of the criticisms of the Senate are unfounded or misguided, others are not; and the institution as it exists currently can be further improved without having to undergo formal constitutional reform. A generation of would-be Senate reformers have futilely devoted themselves to that task. Their efforts consistently failed for two reasons. First, they did not take the time to analyze the institution, identify the problems, and develop appropriate solutions. Mostly, they focused on a single point (most often election) in isolation from the rest of the Senate, Parliament, and the Canadian political system. Second, they attempted to implement their underdeveloped ideas by the Sisyphean means of the constitutional amendment process.

Any effort to improve the Senate must start from first principles. One must decide what the Senate is intended to do before deciding how it should do it. One must consider the Upper House within the context of the broader political system and recognize that the current arrangements bring benefits that should be preserved, such as a more independent chamber and better minority representation, in addition to weaknesses that must be corrected. The "Declaration of Principles" outlined in this chapter is at least a reasonable starting point and is certainly a far more thorough analysis than most would-be reformers have yet provided.

So long as the current constitutional deadlock persists, the only viable option is nonconstitutional improvement and, while it does have limits, this approach can be used to implement very significant changes. Indeed, the present Senate would be unrecognizable to the Fathers of Confederation, even though in constitutional terms little has changed, because of the numerous institutional adaptations brought about by nonconstitutional means. A fully conceptualized nonconstitutional proposal to improve the Senate may not solve every problem and may not satisfy every critic, but it offers a viable means for bringing about reform and strengthening the Canadian political system.

NOTES

1 Stilborn, *Comments on Twenty-Four Senate Reform Proposals Provided for Analysis*, 1; Also Stilborn in this volume. For another valuable perspective, see Seidle, "Senate Reform and the Constitutional Agenda: Conundrum or Solution?"

2 Stilborn, *Comments on Twenty-Four Senate Reforms Proposals Provided for Analysis*, 3.

3 For a detailed examination of the challenges of amending the Constitution, see Joyal, *Legal, Constitutional and Political Imperatives to Senate Reform*. Among other things, he points out that there were only thirty-eight successful consti-

tutional amendments between 1867 and 2000, of which only nine were substantial multilateral amendments. See also James Ross Hurley, *Amending Canada's Constitution: History, Process, Problems and Prospects.*

4 Audcent, *The Senate Veto: Opinion of the Law Clerk and Parliamentary Counsel.*

5 *Constitution Act, 1982,* section 38 and section 41.

6 Stilborn, *Senate Reform in Canada – A Discussion Paper,* 6, citing Canada West
   Foundation, *Taking a Look: Public Opinion in Alberta and Canada on Senate
   Reform.*

7 See the chapter of Professor Ronald Watts in this volume for a more detailed
   examination of bicameralism.

8 For a discussion of the theory of bicameralism, see Riker, "The Justification
   of Bicameralism," and Jaconelli, "Majority Rule and Special Majorities." For
   most of their history, Canadians have thought of bicameralism as a mark of
   national status and maturity. In the words of an early constitutional authority, "unicameral bodies fall into three or four main groups: the parliaments
   of the minor states of southeastern Europe, Servia, Bulgaria and Greece;
   the congresses of Central America, Nicaragua excepted, compose another
   group; the landtags of the Austrian crown lands are one-chambered, and
   so are nearly all the diets of the minor German states, excepting those of
   the free cities." (Quoted in Bourinot, "The Canadian Dominion and the
   Proposed Australian Commonwealth: A Study in Comparative Politics,"
   20.)

9 See, for example, Savoie, *Governing from the Centre: The Concentration of Power in
   Canadian Politics.*

10 For a detailed discussion of the ways in which the Senate performs these
   functions, see the chapters of Professor Gil Rémillard and Professor Paul
   Thomas in this volume.

11 For a discussion of the political value of redundancy, see Landau, "Federalism, Redundancy and System Reliability." Landau noted that "infrastructural"
   weakness applies to individuals and societies as much as it does to institutions.
   For instance, he maintained that "poverty is the absence of redundancy – a
   statement better understood if one notes that a 'subsistence' level consists of
   the bare *minimum* necessary for the sustaining of life. Wealth, of course, constitutes a redundancy" (194). Landau's observation on the political consequences of redundancy was not original to him: "Where no counsel is a people fall; but in the multitude of counsellors there is safety" (Proverbs 11:14).
   The proverb is inscribed in the lobby of the bicameral Parliament of the Australian state of Victoria in Melbourne.

   Game theory offers a parallel insight. In his study of Parliament's response
   to the Mulroney Government's second attempt to fill the void created by the
   Supreme Court of Canada in the *Morgentaler* decision, political scientist
   Thomas Flanagan examines the stalemate that resulted in the Senate in 1990.
   Rational choice analysis helps to explain an outcome he describes as the
   "staying power of the status quo." But he also notes that a bicameral legislature is "another defence" of the status quo. "Contemporary rational choice

analysis," he concludes, "is an extension of older insights into the dynamics of parliamentary procedure" (Flanagan, *Game Theory and Canadian Politics,* chapter 8. See, too, Riker, "The Justification of Bicameralism."

12 Marsh, "Opening up the Policy Process," 12.; Bagehot's discussion is in *The English Constitution,* chapter 5.

13 These characteristics are discussed in detail in the chapter by Professor Gil Rémillard.

14 The same tolerance of difference or retreat from equality has been apparent in the composition of the House of Commons. Whatever principle informs its composition, it is not representation by population. Norman Ward has recorded the intricate balancing of fictive and factual populations; see R. MacGregor Dawson, *The Government of Canada, 5th ed.,* rev. by Norman Ward, chapter 16. If the American model of bicameralism, to which critics of the Canadian Senate are so attracted, is to be a guide, then reform of Commons representation should accompany reform of Senate representation. As it is now, the Canadian House of Commons tries, within its own walls, to balance demands of territory and population. The result is to overrepresent the static as opposed to the expanding parts of the country. By comparison, American politicians are ruthless in the matter of representation. The House of Representatives is the same size today as in 1941, except for the entry of Alaska and Hawaii. As a consequence, New York, the state with the largest contingent of Congressmen in 1941, will, following the redistricting that uses 2000 Census data, trail California by twenty-four seats.

15 Docherty, *Mr. Smith Goes to Ottawa: Life in the House of Commons,* 52, 98. Respectively, 30 and 22 percent of the turnover in 1974 and 1980 were due to "retirement" and not "defeat." That is, in a matter of months, persons who had run in one general election decided not to run again.

16 See the chapter by Paul Thomas in this volume, which lists the benefits that accrue from the Senate's tradition that respects and rewards experience.

17 Canadian experience with an elected upper chamber, the Legislative Council of the United Provinces of Upper and Lower Canada, 1854 to 1867, was not such as to recommend continuation of the experiment in the new federation: "A Comparison of the votes polled in general elections and in the elections for councillors indicates that less interest was taken in the contests for council than for the assembly ... [The Council] still occupied a position of definite subordination to the popular assembly" (McArthur, "A Canadian Experiment with an Elective Upper Chamber," 86–7).

18 Canada. Senate (Commons). *Proceedings and Evidence of the Special Joint Committee of the Senate and the House of Commons on Senate Reform.* 18 October 1983, vol. 30: 26. For more on the origins of national bicameralism, see Janet Ajzenstat's chapter in this volume.

19 Audcent, *The Senate Veto,* 10.

20 See Senate of Canada, *Amendment to the Constitution of Canada, Term 17 of the Terms of Union of Newfoundland with Canada* (13th Report). The reform of Newfoundland's church-run school system proved to be complicated: the Senate refused to endorse the Government's first motion; a new provincial government

came to power; a second provincial referendum on the matter followed; and the Government introduced yet another motion. Throughout these events, however, the Senate held fast to its concern that the voice of affected minorities be heard.

21 Membership in the Senate offers few prospects for political advancement. This is very different from the Australian Senate, where there is a very real possibility of senators becoming ministers. In August 2000 the Government in Canberra numbered forty-two members, seventeen from the Cabinet and twenty-five from the Outer Cabinet. Four senators sit in Cabinet and three in the Outer Cabinet, along with ten parliamentary secretaries drawn from the Senate. Aside from the Government Leader in the Senate, it is unusual today for senators to sit in the Cabinet in Ottawa. In modern times, it is usually only when a party is elected without winning seats in a number of provinces that the Prime Minister will appoint more than one senator to Cabinet. The most recent example is Prime Minister Trudeau's appointment of three senators to his Cabinet in 1980, when the Liberal Party won a majority government without electing a single MP west of Winnipeg.

Tenure in both houses – particularly contrasts in tenure – affects the operation of bicameral legislatures. Partly, this is the result of the different attitudes members of upper and lower houses hold of their roles. See Fenno, *The United States Senate: A Bicameral Perspective.*

22 Delacourt, "More Say at Committee Level, Reports Says," A4.

23 Savoie, *Governing from the Centre: The Concentration of Power in Canadian Politics,* 260.

24 Howe and Northrup, "Strengthening Canadian Democracy: The Views of Canadians," 52.

25 See the appendix for statistics.

26 They are discussed in detail in the chapter of Professor C.E.S. Franks for example.

27 White, "Canadian Nationhood," A17.

28 Joyal, *The Legal, Constitutional and Political Imperatives to Senate Reform,* 15.

29 See Evans, "Accountability versus government control: the effect of proportional representation." "Upper houses," says Evans, "have only one hold over governments, their ability to withhold assent from government legislation" (55). In reply, critics of Australia's Senate (in which each state has twelve members elected using proportional representation) say that even then the House of Representatives is the more "democratically legitimate House" because its constituencies are designed to reflect "one vote, one value" (Coonan, "Safeguard or Handbrake on Democracy?").

30 Audcent, *The Senate Veto: Opinion of the Law Clerk and Parliamentary Counsel,* 63.

31 See the chapter by Senator Murray in this volume.

32 For a study of the House of Commons policing itself and others within its precincts, see Ward, "Called to the Bar of the House of Commons"; see also Ward, "The Independence of Parliament," chapter 5.

33 Professor C.E.S. Franks discusses this concern in his chapter.

34 For a description of this period, see Franks, "Not Dead Yet, But Should It Be Resurrected? The Canadian Senate." See also Franks, this volume.

35 Marsh, "Opening up the Policy Process," 11.

36 See the appendix for statistics.

37 See the appendix for statistics.

38 This discussion of the reports is obviously significantly condensed. It is worthwhile to examine the three studies in their entirety. There are several points on which they concur, notably the appropriateness of the Lords' current roles and powers, as well as the importance of independent members. There are also several points of disagreement. The Royal Commission proposed longer terms for members, while the White Paper leaned towards shorter ones. The exact balance between the elected and appointed members differed in each, and the White Paper also proposed leaving appointments in the hands of the political parties.

39 For a more detailed discussion, see the chapter by Senator Lowell Murray in this volume.

40 See the appendix for statistics.

41 See the appendix for statistics.

42 See the appendix for statistics.

Conclusion: The Senate as the Embodiment of the Federal Principle

Senator Serge Joyal

A constitution embodies a philosophy of values and provides for the institutions to serve them. Parliament is about power: it exists for one reason only – to empower the people of Canada, by serving as the political institution that embodies their collective ethos. From its inception, Canada's constitutional polity has been perceived essentially as a jurisdictional framework. This is no surprise, as federal-provincial tensions have dominated the nation's constitutional discourse since the days of Sir John A. Macdonald. The dearth of academic research on the origin, nature, and purpose of our federal Parliament is due in large part to the preoccupation of legal scholars with the jurisdictional aspects of Canadian federalism. Yet Canada's constitutional architecture is built on much more than the technical aspects of the division of power between jurisdictions. It is first and foremost an institutional framework that expresses the sovereignty of Canada. As Pierre Trudeau concluded at the opening of the Bora Laskin Library in Toronto in 1991:

One final point on historical context: despite decades of political tension
and acrimonious debate between the federal government and the provinces,
the few judgments relating to the provinces' objections would be reached in
a complete intellectual void because there was no body of contemporary
doctrine on the basis of Canadian sovereignty or the nature of constituent
authority.[1]

This intellectual void has resulted in widespread misperceptions of the organic relationship between the Senate and the House of Commons, and between the executive and the legislative branches of government, often obscuring the constitutional checks and balances built into our constitutional architecture.

In contrast to the armed struggle for independence that produced the United States Constitution, Canada's supreme law was the product of a peaceful, orderly, and mature process. And yet, our 1982 Constitution, with its expansive *Charter of Rights and Freedoms*, signifies nothing less than a political revolution. A radical change of seismic dimensions did occur in 1982, shifting the centre of gravity of our political system and fundamentally altering the roles of our national institutions, the relationship between them, and the checks and balances they represent in our system of government. *The Charter of Rights and Freedoms* has become the anchor of Canada's Constitution, as the Supreme Court has recognized:

This Court has noted on several occasions that with the adoption of the *Charter*, the Canadian system of government was transformed to a significant extent from a system of Parliamentary supremacy to one of constitutional supremacy.[2]

The Supreme Court's 1998 opinion on Quebec secession helped fill a doctrinal void. Its landmark decision went far beyond the narrow confines of jurisdictional quibbling and quarrelling that have been the hallmark of Canadian constitutional discourse for too long. For the first time, the court clearly enumerated the founding principles of our constitutional architecture:

Such principles and rules emerge from an understanding of the constitutional text itself, the historical context, and previous judicial interpretations of constitutional meaning. In our view, there are four fundamental and organizing principles of the Constitution which are relevant to addressing the question before us (although this enumeration is by no means exhaustive): federalism; democracy, constitutionalism and the rule of law; and respect for minorities.[3]

The foundation and substance of these principles, which again are not exhaustive, reflect the values of our society, help to define the nature of our national institutions (the executive branch of government and the Parliament of Canada), and help to strike the prevailing institutional balance in our political system. The abundant discourse over the past thirty years on Senate reform has never addressed the application of these founding principles to the proposed alternative solutions. On the contrary, Senate reform has always been viewed within its own exclusive framework, a kind of mantra capable of purging the government and Canadian federalism of all their ills. What, then, is the essential effect of these four principles on the definition of the institution that is the Senate?

The Principle of Federalism

Together with the Charter, the principle of federalism is the central theme underlying the framework of our Constitution. It is, in concrete terms, the recognition of the diverse nature of the constituent elements of our federation. The principle of federalism is essentially the recognition of the linguistic, religious, and socioeconomic differences of Canada's regions and provinces. At its inception, the federal system of government in Canada was devised to accommodate the various needs and bolster the respective strengths of the original partners in Confederation: Upper and Lower Canada, Nova Scotia, and New Brunswick.

As the Supreme Court has recognized, one of the key elements of the Confederation compromise was the creation of a Senate with the necessary legislative power to defend sectional interests.[4] During the Confederation debates, Sir John A. Macdonald stressed the importance of checking the legislative power of governments elected largely by the heavily populated areas of the country:

To the Upper House is to be confided the protection of sectional interests; therefore it is that the three great divisions are there equally represented, for the purpose of defending such interests against the combinations of majorities in the Assembly.[5]

The historical record is emphatic: there would have been no agreement on Confederation without the provision for an Upper Chamber possessing genuine powers capable of counterbalancing the political weight of Ontario's burgeoning population. George Brown, Leader of the Reformers (precursor to the Liberal Party) in Upper Canada at the time of Confederation, was quite candid on this point:

But the very essence of our compact is that the union shall be federal and not legislative. Our Lower Canada friends have agreed to give us representation by population in the Lower House, on the express condition that they shall have equality in the Upper House. On no other condition could we have advanced a step ... and it is quite natural that the protection for those interests, by equality in the Upper Chamber, should be demanded by the less numerous provinces.[6]

This country's original purpose was not to weld the provinces into one, nor to eliminate regional differences. On the contrary, as the Supreme Court has recognized, "the principle of federalism facilitates the pursuit of collective goals by cultural and linguistic minorities."[7] Indeed, there is a compelling argument that if Canada is a federation rather than a unitary state, it is precisely because, at the time of Confederation, Lower Canada was overwhelmingly French and Catholic, while the remainder of British North America was solidly Anglo-Protestant:

The social and demographic reality of Quebec explains the existence of the Province of Quebec as a political unit and indeed, was one of the essential reasons for establishing a federal structure for the Canadian union in 1867.[8]

Nowhere was this more evident than in Quebec, where the Anglo-Protestant minority was guaranteed representation in the Parliament through the creation of carefully drawn minority-majority senatorial districts whose boundaries have remained unchanged since 1867. Quebec is, in fact, the only region whose senators represent specific districts prescribed by the Constitution.[9]

The Senate "embodies the federal principle."[10] In effect, the federal principle requires that a bill obtain a "federal majority" before it becomes law. The population-based House of Commons cannot legislate alone; it must work in tandem with the region-based Senate. Without the requirement of this double majority, the Parliament of Canada would be a unicameral legislative body with no institutional safeguards for the less populous, and therefore less powerful, regions of Canada.

The Democratic Principle

As previously mentioned, the 1998 decision of the Supreme Court in the *Reference re Secession of Quebec* recognized that democracy is a "fundamental and organizing principle of the Constitution."[11] Although democracy is commonly understood to be a form of government in which power resides in the will of the majority, the Supreme Court also recognized that one of the inherent values of a mature democracy is the protection of minority rights. Indeed, the legitimacy of our democratic system depends on the recognition of these rights, many of which are now entrenched in the *Charter of Rights and Freedoms*. It would therefore be a serious mistake to assert that our democratic system of government is strictly based on majority rule, without regard to other constitutional principles. Quite the contrary – the representation of minority interests is a *sui generis* characteristic of Canadian democracy.

This need to balance democracy and equality has influenced the definition of what constitutes a majority in our system of government. This explains why the Fathers of Confederation designed a Parliament in which the will of the majority is represented in the elected House of Commons on the basis of representation by population[12] and in the Senate on the basis of equal representation for each region. Sir John A. Macdonald understood that an appointed Upper Chamber based on regional equality was entirely consistent with the principles of democratic and responsible government:

The members of the Upper Chamber would then come from the people, and should any difference ever arise between both branches, [they] could say to the members of the popular branch – "We as much represent the feelings of the people as you do, and even more so; we are not elected from small localities and for a short period; you as a body were elected at a particular time, when the public mind was running in a particular channel ... We have as much right, or a better right, than you to be considered as representing the deliberate will of the people on general questions, and therefore we will not give way."[13]

In our system of government, a "qualified majority" is required to pass legislation through Parliament: a plurality of votes in the elected House, plus a plurality of votes in the federal Chamber, where the combined votes of the different regions are expressed.

Contrary to widely held opinion, however, the system of apportionment in the House of Commons is not based on the principle of equal representation of voters, but rather on the principle of "effective representation."[14] Legal and constitutional limits have been placed on the principle of representation by population. For instance, the Constitution provides that no province shall have a lesser number of seats in the House of Commons than it has in the Senate.[15] This is one reason why the number of seats attributed to each province is not determined on the basis of population alone.[16] This is the core element of what the Constitution calls "proportionate representation."[17]

The system of electing members to the House of Commons amplifies the cleavages in our federation. This is nowhere more evident than in the distortions caused by the first-past-the-post mode of representation in the past three federal elections. Since 1993, the majority of government MPs have come from one province: Ontario.[18] The domination of Parliament by a single region is precisely what the Fathers of Confederation foresaw and attempted to mitigate. To this end, they created an Upper Chamber in which the regional divisions within Canada were given equal weight, to counterbalance the strength of the heavily populated areas in the elected House of Commons. Far from hindering democracy, the Senate plays a vital complementary role in ensuring a more equitable expression of the voices of Canada's less populated regions.

Constitutionalism and the Rule of Law

According to the principle of constitutionalism, governments must abide by and respect the Constitution from which they derive their authority. This fundamental and organizing principle of the Constitution is clearly outlined in the 1998 decision of the Supreme Court in *Reference re Secession of Quebec*:

The Constitution binds all governments, both federal and provincial, including the executive branch. They may not transgress its provisions: indeed, their sole claim to exercise lawful authority rests in the powers allocated to them under the Constitution ...[19]

In addition to establishing a division of powers between the federal and provincial levels of government, our Constitution provides a system of checks and balances between the executive and legislative branches of government. The complementary relationship in the role, functions, powers, and composition of the two chambers is crucial to the success of Parliament in fulfilling its mandate to make laws for the "peace, order and good government of Canada."[20] Within Parliament, the Senate is the chamber through which the principle of constitutionalism is applied to both the protection of sectional interests and the expression of minority and human rights.

With regard to sectional interests, there is persistent ambiguity, indeed confusion, between the constitutional concept of region and the concept of province. The concept of region refers to a geographical area having various identifiable characteristics of a symbolic, historical, cultural and socioeconomic nature. In the context of the Senate, the equal weight afforded to regions is intended to counter the power of the more densely populated areas of the country in the elected House.[21] With the national interest in mind, the Fathers of Confederation devised an institutional framework in which no single region of the country could be allowed to dominate Parliament by sole virtue of its population. While the boundaries of a province and region are at times co-terminus, a province is primarily a jurisdictional unit, whereas a region encompasses a broader symbolic, cultural, linguistic, and socioeconomic identity. To be cohesive and relevant, government policy at the federal level must reflect this regional dynamic. For this reason, the architects of our Constitution chose to construct a Senate whose membership would be based on a regional rather than provincial basis. In so doing, they avoided the identification of national policies with those of a provincial nature and the confusion of federal jurisdiction with that of the provinces. By reserving the appointment of senators to the federal Crown, the Fathers of Confederation balanced regional and minority interests with the need for the independence of both levels of government. The principle of constitutionalism entrenches regional, linguistic, and cultural diversity in the operations of the Senate and the jurisdictional independence of the two levels of government.

The Principle of Respect for Minorities

Respect for minorities is the fourth fundamental constitutional principle outlined by the Supreme Court in the *Reference re Secession of Quebec*. The protection of minority linguistic, religious, and education rights was the basis for the historical compromise that resulted in Confederation. Indeed, minority rights were "an essential consideration in the design of our constitutional structure even at the time of Confederation."[22] The valid fear of assimilation was a decisive factor in the creation of a bicameral

Parliament with an Upper Chamber designed to protect sectional and minority interests:

Inasmuch as the Act embodies a compromise under which the original Provinces agreed to federate, it is important to keep in mind that the preservation of the rights of minorities was a condition on which such minorities entered into the federation, and the foundation upon which the whole structure was subsequently erected.[23]

As the Supreme Court has noted, expanded protection for the rights of minorities was one of the fundamental objectives behind the inclusion of the *Charter of Rights and Freedoms* in the *Constitution Act, 1982*:

Undoubtedly, one of the key considerations motivating the enactment of the Charter, and the process of constitutional judicial review that it entails, is the protection of minorities.[24]

With the advent of the Charter, the scope of the constitutional protection of rights and freedoms has been broadened in an unprecedented way, encompassing: minority language educational rights (section 23), the equality of men and women (section 28), and aboriginal and treaty rights (section 35), to name a few. As these new categories of rights are added to the Constitution, the role of the Senate as the chamber for the expression of minority rights and human rights within Parliament has been confirmed, broadened, and strengthened. Its composition, functions, and role must now be assessed in light of these increased responsibilities. As a result of the *Constitution Act, 1982*, Parliament has a new and complex role in ensuring the consistency of proposed legislation with the rights and values enshrined in the Charter:

Parliament and the courts are situated differently, in relation to Charter conflicts. Their respective judgments will be influenced by these different points of reference, by the distinct institutional characteristics they possess, and by the specific responsibilities that characterize their roles.[25]

Moreover, as the debates at the time of its adoption reveal, the Charter contains a set of evolving rights.[26] In addition to defining these expanding rights and freedoms, Parliament and the courts must weigh these rights in the balance of "such reasonable limits prescribed by law that can be demonstrably justified in a free and democratic society."[27] This has important ramifications for Parliament, which has the complex task of shaping legislation, public policies, and administrative decisions in accordance with evolving constitutional rights and freedoms, while also determining their reasonable limits. The Senate is particularly apt to play a substantial role in these multifarious deliberations. The House of Commons, whose

members are invariably influenced by electoral concerns, are more susceptible to be swayed by the prevailing public opinion. As the federal
chamber whose role is to protect the rights of minorities, the Senate can
provide a unique contribution to ensuring that federal legislation is consistent with the Charter. That is to say, the Upper Chamber can help, as
Ontario Chief Justice McMurtry put it, "to avoid conflict between Parliament and the Constitution."[28]

According to the *Department of Justice Act*, it is the responsibility of the
Minister of Justice in respect of all Government bills "to ascertain whether
any of the provisions thereof are inconsistent with the purposes and provisions of the *Canadian Charter of Rights and Freedoms*."[29] However, depart-
mental advice received by the Minister remains confidential. Clearly, the
responsibility of ensuring that proposed legislation is consistent with the
Charter should not be the exclusive purview of one minister of the Crown.
Surely Parliament, collectively, must satisfy itself that any given bill is consistent with the Charter before it is enacted. Anything less would amount
to an abdication of its legislative role to the courts. Professor Janet Hiebert
of Queen's University reflects on this point in her groundbreaking text,
Charter Conflicts:

I contemplate the Charter's contribution to the polity more in terms of
compelling critical reflection by all institutions of governance – on how the
normative principle should affect their judgment – than in terms of the
judiciary simply correcting the "wrong" decisions of Parliament.[30]

Understanding the four fundamental and organizing principles mentioned above is essential to an appreciation of the role, functions, and
composition of the Senate in the context of the parliamentary reform.
However, as the Supreme Court noted, they are not exhaustive. For
instance, the principle of debate in Parliament is equally essential. In his
oft-repeated opinion of 1938, Mr Justice Duff reflected on this implication
of the preamble to the *Constitution Act, 1867*:

The preamble of the [*British North America Act*], moreover, shows plainly
enough that the Constitution of the Dominion is to be similar in principle to
that of the United Kingdom. The statute contemplates a Parliament working
under the influence of public opinion and public discussion. There can be
no controversy that such institutions derive their efficacy from the free public discussion of affairs, from criticism and answer and counter-criticism,
from attack upon policy and administration and defence and counter-attack;
from the freest and fullest analysis and examination from every point of view
of political proposals.[31]

The Senate is well suited to serve as the forum for the expression of arguments and counter-arguments, attacks and counter-attacks, since the fate

of the government is not tied to the outcome of its deliberations. Attempts to prevent or unduly limit debate in Parliament clearly undermine this constitutional principle.

Having addressed these principles, how could practical improvements in the operation and composition of the Senate make our parliamentary system more effective and better suited to the country's political development? What is the importance of the Senate's veto, and what ominous unintended consequences would its potential demise entail?

THE LEGISLATIVE INDEPENDENCE
OF THE SENATE

Much of the confusion surrounding the purpose of the Senate stems from an ignorance of the independent legislative role intended for the Upper Chamber by the Fathers of Confederation. Sir John A. Macdonald was unambiguous in expounding on this essential feature of the Senate:

There would be no use of an Upper House, if it did not exercise, when it thought proper, the right of opposing or amending or postponing the legislation of the Lower House. It would be of no value whatever were it a mere chamber for registering the decrees of the Lower House. It must be an independent House, having a free action of its own, for it is only valuable as being a regulating body, calmly considering the legislation initiated by the popular branch, and preventing any hasty or ill-considered legislation which may come from that body, but it will never set itself in opposition against the deliberate and understood wishes of the people.[32]

Both the Senate and the House of Commons are autonomous legislative chambers. Together with the Sovereign, they form the Parliament of Canada.[33] The Queen, the Senate, and the House of Commons must each concur with respect to proposed legislation before it is enacted. In other words, the advice and consent of both chambers are required before the Governor General may grant Royal Assent to a bill in the name of Her Majesty the Queen.

The fundamental purpose of the Senate is to serve as an institutional safeguard, providing review and scrutiny of government legislation and activity, always with a view to sectional interests, the interests of minorities, and individual rights and freedoms. In order to perform these essential functions, the Senate must have real independence from the Executive-dominated House of Commons.

The commonly held view is that the government derives its authority and legitimacy from the House of Commons alone, rather than from Parliament as a whole. This argument raises two questions. First, it does not properly recognize the concept of government accountability in the parliamentary context. Second, it has the insidious effect of subverting the Senate's constitutional role of check and balance.

Responsible Government

Unbalanced criticism of the Senate is most often made in the name of responsible government. It is claimed that when the House of Commons expresses confidence in the government by approving its legislation, any opposition from the Senate is inappropriate. Those who make this argument in order to marginalize the Senate misrepresent our system of government. Responsible government, in the federal context, means that the Executive must have the confidence of the elected House in order to survive. This does not mean, however, that the Senate does not have a legitimate role to play in holding the government accountable by actively challenging the Executive, subjecting its policies to detailed examination and carefully scrutinizing its legislation. Such action is by no means inconsistent with the notion of responsible government. Responsible government does not mean that the Senate cannot challenge the government; it means that the Senate cannot bring down the government.

The evolution of the concept of responsible government in our parliamentary institutions has been rather complex.[34] To achieve a broader understanding of the system, one has to look back at the origins of responsible government in the Westminster model. English historians who wrote on the organization of government followed the lessons provided by the ancients (Polybius among others) on how to organize a sound legislative structure. They concluded that there are three simple forms of government: monarchy, in which laws are made by the One; aristocracy, in which they are made by the Few; and democracy, in which they are made by the Many. According to these historians, each of the forms has major flaws – monarchs eventually treat their subjects as slaves, aristocrats ultimately ignore all interests except their own, and democracy leads to mob rule. The synthesis of these models was "mixed government," in which the legislative function was shared by each of the three forms, with each form serving as a check on the others.

Britain's mixed government is the product of necessity. Over the centuries, a succession of political tensions confirmed that to maintain his government, the King needed the support of two groups: the nobility (Lords) to build an army, and the emerging middle class (Commons) to raise revenues. The most contentious aspect of constitutional evolution in the Parliament of the United Kingdom has been the degree of autonomy enjoyed by each of its three constituent parts. For example, the power of the King to stack the House of Lords with peers in order to secure the passage of legislation was highly controversial. The House of Lords was not seen as an obstacle because the King could always create enough new peers to swamp a stubborn Opposition in that House. Many attempts were made to limit this prerogative, but demands for comprehensive reform went unheeded until the twentieth century.

The major conflict over the structure of mixed government, however, concerned the relationship between the Crown and the House of Commons. Demands were made to exclude all "place-holders" (i.e., those who held remunerated positions at the pleasure of the executive government, including Cabinet ministers) from the House of Commons. It was alleged that the presence of such place-holders corrupted mixed government by hindering the independence of the House. This conundrum was resolved by allowing ministers to sit in either house, while removing many other categories of place-holders. This resulting arrangement proved to be the genesis of responsible government: ministers were henceforth present in Parliament to advance the King's legislative priorities, defend his actions as Head of State, and, perhaps most important, to make requests on his behalf for annual supply. The basic assumption of responsible government – as articulated by Walpole[35] and others – was that Parliament must operate on the assumption that the presence of the King's ministers could influence the House of Commons without corrupting the institution.

Likewise, when the Fathers of Confederation sat down to conceive our Parliament, they reflected at length on the necessity that its chambers be independent from the executive government.[36] They chose the Senate to be the independent chamber. Practical experience had taught the Fathers of Confederations that, in the context of a majority government, the Prime Minister and Cabinet must always have the support of the elected chamber, and will therefore always seek to control its members. The new Canadian Senate would be structured to serve as a counterweight to the elected Lower Chamber. Both houses of our Parliament were therefore endowed with powers and privileges identical to those of the British House of Commons at the time of Confederation.[37]

The level of independence enjoyed by the Senate has enabled it to play a role in one of the crucial functions of our system of responsible government: holding the Executive to account in respect of Government Estimates and supply bills. It is a role that the House of Commons, through an accumulation of changes to its rules and practices, has become ill-disposed to perform.[38]

The doctrine of responsible government has two requirements. First of all, ministers cannot remain in office unless they succeed in obtaining the necessary supply for the executive government from the House of Commons. Secondly, the House of Commons must maintain a level of independence sufficient to conduct a thorough examination of the government's initiatives. The underlying assumption of responsible government is that the House of Commons would be sufficiently independent to exercise meaningful control over the executive government. In the Canadian experience, this assumption has proven to be overly optimistic.

Although the decreasing independence of the House of Commons is visible in other aspects of its operations, nowhere are the consequences more grave than in the study of Government Estimates. The study of Estimates is by far the most important way in which members of the House of Commons can review the success of government policy and the performance of its ministers and public servants. Unfortunately, over the last thirty years the role of the Lower House in the study of Estimates has become a merely symbolic exercise, reducing this aspect of responsible government to an empty shell. Former Professor, MP, and Senator John B. Stewart enumerates reasons for its demise in the House of Commons:

Various explanations may be offered. Let me mention a few. First, the rapid turnover of Members means that many Members never achieve more than a limited understanding of policies and programs. Second, detailed work is far too dull and mundane for many ambitious politicians. Third, detailed work on a committee is not news and is not susceptible to bring a lot of votes. Fourth, some Opposition Members really do not want to suggest improvements in programs and policies; the worse a government's programs and policies are, the greater the chance of defeating that government in the next election. Fifth, a House Leader and a Whip who get their Members to support their estimates and get them through quietly are "smiled" upon by their master. [39]

Since 1968, the members of the House of Commons have three months to examine the details of the Government Estimates.[40] Armed with so-called "supply days" distributed throughout the sitting calendar, the role of the opposition in the study of Estimates has shifted from scrutinizing appropriations to sometimes challenging the policies requiring expenditures. As a consequence, MPs have seemingly come to regard their committee work on Estimates as a farce and a bore, viewing it as a rubber-stamping exercise.[41]

While ominous in itself, the declining role of the House of Commons in the scrutiny of Government Estimates is but a symptom of the Lower Chamber's loss of independence vis-à-vis the government. Over the years, the political culture of the House of Commons has placed systemic obstacles to enforcing the principles of responsible government:

In addition, commentators have long pointed out deficiencies in the handling of Estimates by Parliament, and this sentiment is shared by many Members. The Estimates are an important tool in terms of accountability, and the financial control of the House of Commons. Despite numerous procedural changes over the years, we have been unable to discover a workable solution. There are many reasons for the lack of progress in this area, many of which are *attributable to our political culture*.[42]

What explains the emergence of this political culture? The late former Senator and constitutionalist Eugene Forsey offered a diagnosis of its defects:

Party government tends to spurn constitutional limitations and to seek to overcome them. Parties seek to capture all the organs of the state and to make them work to the party purpose or for the benefit of the party Leader, their principal supporters and their friends. An independently minded House of Commons is an obstacle to this outcome, a strong upper House an even greater one.[43]

Irrespective of the party in power, prime ministers over the past thirty years have exercised overwhelming control over the House of Commons.[44] To become Prime Minister, one must first be chosen Leader of a political party. This means being chosen by a very select body: the delegates at a party leadership convention.[45] Once elected, the Leader is independent of that body, at least until after the subsequent election. Nor can the parliamentary party caucus exert much control over its leadership. Few MPs can seriously claim to have been elected on the basis of their own popularity. The truth is that, to a very great extent, members of Parliament are elected as followers of a party Leader. Furthermore, it is the Leader who has the legal authority to sign the nomination papers of all the candidates of his or her party for election to the House of Commons.[46] In addition to determining the membership of parliamentary and party committees, the leaders of the parties having official status in the House of Commons can appoint members of their caucus to a number of salaried positions.[47] Should such opportunities fail to inspire loyalty, the Leader can always expel from caucus those who drift too far from the party line. In other words, the system provides strong incentive for MPs to follow its unwritten rules.

Party Leaders, as well as Party Whips, often maintain that differences of opinion should be expressed and reconciled in caucus behind closed doors. Though firmly embedded in our political culture, this practice is detrimental to our parliamentary institutions, which find their utility in the process that begins with the public exchange of opposing viewpoints and ends with good government.[48] According to those with wide experience and knowledge of its dynamics, caucus is not exactly the ideal place for anyone wishing to cultivate critical analysis or exert independent points of view:

The one rule of caucus progress and preferment for any caucus Member is to never find himself in the way of having to say "no" to the Leader. Criticism carefully couched. Kind criticism perhaps! But wide open, negative, attacks? Never![49]

Those who do dare to offer an alternative perspective find themselves marginalized. Such members could be deprived of any future opportunities to voice positions challenging the official line and may even be removed from their committees. The peer group environment is such that only the most deeply held personal convictions are likely to survive the pressure placed on individual members:

The classic role, defined by J.S. Mill, of the individual liberty of the Members of Parliament as a check on the Executive, in this tightly contained caucus becomes, per force, sharply reined and curtailed.[50]

This systemic pressure requires that members who intend to deviate from the party line on a given bill or policy must initially raise the issue either in caucus or to the Party Whip or House Leader. As the circle tightens, psychological pressure is added: the notions of "family" and "loyalty" are constantly evoked.[51] Government MPs face the added constraint of having to support their party's legislation in order to maintain the confidence of the House. In this context, "disloyalty has become the metaphor to mean loss of power."[52] As Senator Lynch-Staunton has observed, "responsible government is reversed, with those members of the governing party in the House actually responsible to the Executive."[53] In practice, therefore, the House of Commons (in the context of a majority government) plays only a nominal role in enforcing the concept of responsible government.

To coerce members into supporting their legislation, ministers often insist, without any basis in the convention, that any vote on a Government bill in the House of Commons is a test of confidence in the government. Where parliamentary convention had limited such tests to supply votes, "caucus convention" has expanded the need for rigid party solidarity to any and all ordinary proposed government legislation. There is, as Lord Norton observed,

an inherent conflict in that most Members of Parliament are elected to support and sustain a particular government in office and, at the same time, are Members of an institution (the House of Commons) that is expected to subject to critical scrutiny that very same government.[54]

The far-reaching control exerted by the executive government over its MPs has to a great extent impaired the Lower House in its constitutional duty to scrutinize the activities and legislation of the executive branch.[55] The dominant political culture seems to have effectively neutered the House of Commons.[56] Any real reform of the House of Commons must focus primarily on this problem.

The Senate is markedly different from the House of Commons in its structure and practices. Because the government cannot be brought down by the Senate, there is no need for senators to abandon strongly held convictions and yield to their Party Whip. As they do not campaign for office, senators are not captive to their respective parties for promotions and political favours.[57] In light of the qualifications of its members, the Senate is actually better equipped to hold the executive government accountable for its policies and conduct than is the House of Commons:

why should we try to reduce the powers of the Senate so as to bring those powers into conformity with the theory of responsible government when the House of Commons has lost its capacity to hold the Government accountable?[58]

The Senate is a self-regulating body.[59] The wide range of expertise and experience of senators is widely recognized as an invaluable contribution to the calibre of parliamentary study and debate.[60] To protect and enhance the independence of the Upper Chamber and its members, as well as to improve its effectiveness, some amendments could be made to the *Rules of the Senate* and to the *Parliament of Canada Act.* Any initiative aimed at reforming these Rules must take the following realities of the Upper Chamber into account:

- all senators are equal;
- the executive government is minimally present in the Senate;
- initiatives that would align Senate practices to those of the House of Commons could have a pernicious effect on the nature and role of the Senate;
- each House has its own dynamic and institutional characteristics, and these should be reflected in any proposed improvements.

Standing Committees

Committees are an indispensable component of the Upper Chamber's capacity to review legislation, scrutinize government activities, and study policy issues. They are the link between the legislative branch of government and citizens, public interest groups and experts. Senate committees also serve to galvanize public opinion and refine government policy through a process of in-depth study and debate. In short, the committee work of the Senate is perhaps the best measure of the institution's utility. Observers and analysts[61] of parliamentary committees have concluded that the level of insight, objectivity, and rigour of Senate committees often surpasses that of their counterparts in the House of Commons:

In contrast with the House, the Canadian Senate has long recognized the strength that comes from continuity. Former Senator Salter Hayden, for example, chaired the Banking Committee for over twenty years and was recognized as a national authority on tax law. Continuity of the chair and committee membership has contributed to the ability of some Senate committees to prepare influential reports such as the Croll Committee report on poverty and the Van Roggen report on free trade with the United States.[62]

Membership on committees must be based on a set of well-defined and broadly accepted criteria, such as seniority, area of interest, and aptitude, along with regional and gender-balance considerations. The members of the Selection Committee, which is responsible for the nomination of senators to the various committees of the Upper Chamber, should themselves be selected by the whole Senate through a secret ballot.[63] In addition, rule 85 must be amended to end the abhorrent practice of removing a senator from committee without a valid and written explanation. Compliance with the party line should never be a criterion for committee membership. Senate committees can help stem the tide of public cynicism regarding the political process:

Strong experienced independent committees can stop the erosion of public support for Parliament and provide essential oversight of bureaucracy.[64]

In the same vein, standing committee Chairs and Vice-Chairs should be elected by the committee membership, taking into account the criteria mentioned above. More importantly, additional remuneration for committee responsibilities must be terminated.[65] This new and unfortunate practice creates the impression that assignment to these positions is a payback for loyalty, if not servility, to the Government in the Senate. In addition, these salary "top-ups" run contrary to the principle that all senators are equal. Senate committees have worked well for 136 years without the additional salaries for the positions of Chair and Vice-Chair. Creating these new "place-holders" now adds nothing to the work of Senate committees. It does, however, place an additional tool in the hands of a potentially intrusive leadership.

As mentioned previously, the government's requests for supply appear in both chambers in the form of Estimates. In the Senate, these estimates should be automatically sent to their respective standing committees so that senators may examine the merits of the policies underlying past expenditures, the efficiency and probity with which those past expenditures were made, and the merits of the government's proposed future expenditures. Each committee studying Estimates would be required to report its findings to the Senate. The Senate has the independence and the expertise to provide effective scrutiny of the Estimates in a way that the House of Commons does not.

Likewise, the reports of special studies by Senate committees should be debated by Committee of the Whole in the Senate. During these deliberations, the relevant minister should be called to participate. Reports of the myriad government agencies, which are usually tabled and gather dust on shelves, would also be sent to their respective select committee of the Senate. The Senate should also consider referring the petitions of various citizens' groups to the relevant standing committee of the Senate.

Senate standing committees must be given an expanded role to assist the Senate in fulfilling its constitutional role of protecting minority and human rights. The recent creation of a Senate Standing Committee on Official Languages is a welcome development in this regard.[66] Along with the Senate standing committees on Aboriginal Peoples and on Human Rights, this new committee is essential to enable the Senate to speak for those who would otherwise remain unheard in a majoritarian political culture. Likewise, the Senate Standing Committee on Foreign Affairs should have the added responsibility of assessing, on an ongoing basis, the impact of international agreements on the erosion of parliamentary sovereignty. Most importantly, the Senate Standing Committee on Legal and Constitutional Affairs should focus on ensuring that all proposed legislation can withstand judicial review on Charter grounds.[67]

Institutional Loyalty vs Party Loyalty

Ordinarily, the executive government is represented in the Senate by three senators: the Leader of the Government in the Senate, the Deputy Leader, and the Chief Government Whip. The opposition party with the largest number of seats in the Senate is also entitled to three such positions: Opposition Leader, Deputy Leader, and Chief Opposition Whip.[68] The government is not held "responsible" in the Senate in the sense that its fate is not determined by the outcome of any Senate vote. For this reason, partisanship is not a matter of necessity in the Upper Chamber and is generally frowned upon in Senate debates.

The constitutional duties of a senator, as stated in the Commission of Appointment, do not include loyalty to any party. Notwithstanding public perceptions and political expectations, the constitutional obligations of senators supersede whatever partisan allegiance they may have. This is not merely the statement of an ideal; it is rooted in the constitutional mandate of senators. Despite any assumptions to the contrary, the Commission whereby the Queen summons persons to the Senate of Canada and the Oath of Allegiance to Her Majesty, which one must recite before becoming a senator, are not trifling formalities, nor are they vestiges of the pomp of a bygone era. Indeed, the Commission is a constitutional document,[69] and the Oath is part of the written Constitution of this country.[70] For what compelling reason, therefore, should a senator's constitutional duty under the Commission and Oath give way to party loyalty?

This question may appear theoretical, but it has profound legal implications. According to the Command, a senator is under an order of the Queen to: appear at all times, and without fail, when and where Parliament is sitting; give advice and assist in all affairs of state; and represent a specific region (or district in Quebec).

For this reason, senators do not hold their seats by virtue of a partisan electoral mandate, unlike members of the House of Commons. That is to say, the legal basis of Senate membership is the Command of Her Majesty, not party affiliation. A senator may choose to sit as a member of a party caucus, but it is not because of a legal or constitutional commitment to any particular electoral platform or policy agenda.

Parties, of course, do exist in the Upper Chamber. Most senators belong to one of the two major party caucuses. While party allegiance in the Senate is useful in ensuring a mechanism for weighing arguments and counter-arguments, it is quite distinct from the type of partisanship experienced in the House of Commons. In that chamber, governments and "alternative governments" are formed on the basis of party allegiance. In contrast, the party divisions in the Senate operate in the context of debates based on continuity, bringing long-term perspective to the review of legislation emanating from the House of Commons and to the scrutiny of government activities.

Of course, senators are nominated by the Prime Minister of the day, who has an interest in forming a Senate majority of his own party. As a party Leader, the Prime Minister would expect those he or she has nominated to the Senate to support the government's agenda. There is no guarantee of this, however. Once one is appointed to the Upper Chamber, party allegiance should not be superimposed on the constitutional obligations of a senator.

Where does one draw this line? This situation presents a dilemma: senators must weigh the necessity of upholding the institutional principles of the Upper Chamber with the expectations that they will toe the party line. Senator Jerahmiel Grafstein reflected on this point in his poignant tribute to the late Speaker of the Senate, Gildas Molgat:

It is always difficult to separate one's loyalty and allegiance and still maintain the independence, integrity and objectivity required by the duties of that office. Yet, this is precisely what Gil (Molgat) did. Recently, when importuned to vote on a thoroughly contentious matter (Bill C–20), he refused. Principle and integrity overruled the natural pull of loyalty and allegiance. The full story of Gil Molgat as Speaker is yet to be told, but those of us who know only parts of his story will forever admire his invincible integrity.[71]

There is perhaps no better example of institutional loyalty than that of Senator Molgat. His example provides a perfect illustration of the principles one must maintain in serving as a senator and should be referred to in any definition of the standards by which senators should abide.

Party loyalty is fundamental to any adversarial parliamentary system of government. But blind loyalty has no place in a free and democratic society, nor in a mature party. An appeal to partisan allegiance is often the expedient way of avoiding debate on the merits of a given policy. After all, core commitments and values – on such issues as regional grievances, minority rights, and the Constitution – are agents of cohesion that help shape the identity of a political party. The problem is that party loyalty has become party fealty. We now live in a day when the personal convictions and beliefs of parliamentarians are subject to the pressure of Party Whips.[72] There is no valid parallel between the doctrine of party solidarity and the doctrine of cabinet solidarity. The question should be: is the issue consistent with the mandate and the traditional party policies and values? Loyalty cannot be expected or be enforced by a Whip when it would be inconsistent with the long-held policy and values of a party.

Another question that must be addressed is the partisan work of senators. Some senators hold responsibilities within the structure of their respective parties. Their contribution is often unique due to their experience and previous contributions to public life. It goes without saying that political parties are a core component of our democracy, for better or for worse:

Party is critical to political life, and indeed central to the Westminster model of government, but excessive partisanship is detrimental to Parliament, limiting its capacity to call government to account.[73]

As previously mentioned, the limits on the partisan allegiances of senators flow from their Commission and the Oath. The foremost duty of a citizen who accepts to serve in the Senate is to provide advice and consent in the passage of legislation and scrutinize government policies and activities on the basis of their individual judgment. Senators have a specific mandate to speak on behalf of the sectional interests of their respective regions and to promote minority interests and human rights. Putting personal or partisan ambitions ahead of one's constitutional obligations is, in my view, equivalent to a breach of duty.

Accountability

Senators are not directly accountable to a particular electorate or interest group. Nevertheless they are accountable. First of all, they are individually accountable to the Senate as a whole for the decisions they make under their Commission and Oath. Secondly, senators must collectively give an account of the bills, amendments, motions, reports, studies, conclusions, and recommendations they make to the House of Commons, which, as the other chamber of Parliament, must review their legislative activity. Third, senators are accountable to the people of Canada. They live in their respective regions, participating in the life of their community, profession, and milieu and speaking on issues that relate to their experience and interests. Senators are, as Sir John A. Macdonald said, "men (and women) of the people, from the people."[74] They receive representations in written, electronic, and verbal form. They must be attentive to the concerns raised by the hundreds of witnesses who appear before committee hearings.

The most intimidating court of all is the court of public opinion. This is probably the most demanding aspect of the life of parliamentarians – Canadians can be quite unforgiving of the foibles of their public figures. Senators face an uphill battle to establish and maintain public trust. This is why senators must perform their duty with deep commitment, while maintaining objectivity, independence, and passion for the shared values of Canadians. Clear conflict-of-interest guidelines set forth in a Code of Conduct based on the obligations and responsibilities entailed in the Commission and the Oath of senators would protect and enhance the independence of senators and help instil the confidence of Canadians in the Upper Chamber.

Senate rules and procedures should also be structured to favour the institutional and individual independence and objectivity of the Senate and its members. The reputation of the Senate rests on what its members do, and how they do it. Senators must demonstrate that they are motivated by a sense of moral purpose and public service.

The media generally have shown only passing interest in Senate debates or studies, focusing on the government rather than Parliament. Nevertheless, the Senate can reach out directly to Canadians. To make the Upper Chamber more accessible to interaction with Canadians, and to foster greater public awareness of its work and priorities, the Senate should broadcast its debates. Television and internet coverage of the Upper Chamber would improve public access to the institution and perhaps remove some of the longstanding illusions surrounding the Senate. Citizens will only recognize the credibility of the institution to the extent that they can view and listen to the Senate functioning as a productive and independent house of Parliament.

THE SENATE APPOINTMENT PROCESS: REFORM WITHOUT WRANGLING

Criticisms concerning the appointment of senators are almost as old as the Senate itself.[75] In more recent years, however, the denunciations that accompany the announcement of every new appointment have become increasingly strident.

Whatever the merits or qualifications of a new senator, the media and Opposition parties invariably characterize the appointment as another blatant example of patronage. One might appreciate some of the long-standing grievances vis-à-vis the Senate and its members, especially in western Canada. Nevertheless, the well-established pattern of persistent and intemperate hostility toward the Senate as an institution is neither productive nor warranted. The reality is that senators will continue to be appointed for the foreseeable future. More importantly, such harping criticism ignores the potential good that can come from having an appointed Senate and fails to discern the fundamental difference between representation and "representativeness" in our federal bicameral system.[76]

Overwhelmingly, Canadians view the rich linguistic and ethnic diversity of our people as a source of national pride. The image of Canada as a just society, in which equal rights and equal opportunities for individuals from historically disadvantaged groups are both recognized and affirmed, is an image most Canadians strive to project – as much to ourselves as to the rest of the world. While such noble intentions speak to the strength of our national character, we can no longer remain indifferent to the political reality that in our Parliament the elected chamber consistently fails to adequately reflect the diversity of Canadian society:

While democracy and representation are often confused, there is no doubt that they are in fact very different concepts. At the federal level, the Senate provides an appropriate means to offset the lack of balanced representation produced by our single-vote, single-ballot electoral system. In a country as vast and diverse as Canada, this is a very important feature that should be considered more carefully before reproducing the shortcomings of the electoral system in an elected Senate. To do otherwise would only repeat in the Upper Chamber the same results achieved in all elected legislatures in the country, both federal and provincial.[77]

Appointments to the Senate can serve to reduce this deficit in parliamentary representation. The representation of women is a case in point. On 18 October 1929, the Judicial Committee of the Privy Council decided that women were "persons" in the context of section 24 of the *Constitution Act, 1867* and therefore could be appointed to the Senate.[78] In the sixty-five years from the decision in the "Persons Case" to September 1994, a total of thirty-five women were appointed to the Senate of Canada: an average of one woman appointed every 22.3 months. In marked contrast, twenty-eight women became senators in the period from September 1994 to June 2001: one every 2.9 months. This accelerated pace of appointments under Prime Minister Chrétien has allowed the Senate to substantially overtake the House of Commons in representation of women.[79] Notwithstanding such impressive statistics, one must concede that even at the current high watermark of one third of the Upper Chamber's seats, gender parity in the Senate remains to be achieved.

Indeed, over the past decade, appointments to the Senate have also included individuals from various underrepresented groups, including Aboriginal peoples and Canadians of diverse ethnic origins. This development has enriched the composition of the Senate, enabling the Upper Chamber to better fulfill its role as the embodiment of the federal principle and the voice of minority interests.

However, this trend does not stem from the implementation of clear, well-understood criteria. Although many benefits have been achieved by using the appointment process as a means of improving representativeness, such gains are often overshadowed by a persistent unease over the potential for abuse of the Prime Minister's power to nominate senators.[80] This unease is aggravated by the common perception that citizens are incapable of challenging any such abuse because the power of appointment is an executive one, totally unfettered by the constraints of any remedial or corrective action in either the courts or Parliament. Confronted by this potential for abuse, some believe that it would be better to simply abolish the Senate if it cannot be reformed.

Is it that clear, however, that the power to appoint senators is totally unrestricted and cannot be challenged in court? Apart from the "Persons Case" in 1929, there has been no significant challenge to the power of the Prime Minister to recommend appointments to the Senate. Three separate actions were brought before the courts when Prime Minister Mulroney nominated eight additional senators in 1990, using the provisions of section 26 of the *Constitution Act, 1867* to ensure the passage of the *Goods and Services Tax Act*.[81] However, these three cases dealt with the use of section 26 and the role of Her Majesty, rather than the nominating authority of the Prime Minister. There is, therefore, no established case law on the power of the Prime Minister to advise the Governor General in respect of Senate appointments. It is widely assumed that no one could prevent the Prime Minister from recommending appointments. Nor could the Governor General, it is assumed, refuse to accept a Prime Minister's recommendation to the Senate of any Canadian citizen meeting the basic constitutional and statutory requirements with respect to age and residency. Not surprisingly, this perception of unfettered executive power in the hands of the Prime Minister undermines public confidence in the appointment process.

So are we in some kind of constitutional cul-de-sac? Not at all. A labyrinth perhaps, but not a cul-de-sac. Notwithstanding any perception of absolute prime-ministerial power over the appointment process, there are two paths remaining that offer a way out the maze: one avenue, though unprecedented, is through the courts; the other is through Parliament. Both have the potential to harness executive control of the appointment process so as to further the founding principles of the Senate, while also making the Upper Chamber more representative of Canadian society.

Judicial Means

There has never been a court challenge to the appointment of a senator on the grounds that the appointment violated the institutional principles of the Senate and the values embodied in the Charter. Would it be inconsistent with the fundamental and organizing principles of the Constitution, as set out in the decision of the Supreme Court in *Reference re the Secession of Quebec*, to maintain that such an action is justiciable? Any court challenge to the unrestrained power of the Prime Minister over Senate appointments must rest on the constitutional power of the Governor General to summon individuals to the Senate, established by the *Constitution Act, 1867*. Without the power conferred by section 24 of the *Constitution Act, 1867*, the Governor General would be unable to summon anyone to serve in the Senate. Moreover, sections 24 and 32, respectively, provide that the Governor General can only summon "qualified Persons" or a "fit and qualified Person," that is, individuals who meet the qualifications that are specified in section 23.

This constitutional authority is substantially different from the power vested in the Governor General to make appointments to the Legislative Council following the *Union Act, 1840*.[82] Under the terms of that Act, the Governor General could appoint any person of his choice to the Legislative Council, provided that person was a male British subject having attained the age of twenty-one years. However, in 1856, this executive power was removed as the selection of Legislative Councillors became subject to popular vote.[83] In 1867, yet another system of appointment was devised, this time to select members for the new Senate of Canada. The agreement reached by the Fathers of Confederation on this issue resulted in an executive power of appointment having three important features:

- the power to appoint senators was constitutionalized; that is to say, it was set out in the text of the *Constitution Act, 1867*; this power, therefore, is entirely derived from an explicit constitutional provision, rather than from the common law[84];
- it is the Governor General who has the constitutional responsibility of summoning individuals to the Senate;
- the power to appoint senators, in excess of the maximum specified at section 21, is reserved to Her Majesty on the recommendation of the Governor General.[85]

The responsibility of the Governor General to summon individuals to the Senate was strictly framed in the new Constitution of 1867 so as to support the role, purpose, and functions that the Senate was designed to serve in the new Parliament. Hence, any appointment that would undermine not only the role and function of the Senate but also the principles of federalism and responsible government,[86] would amount to violation by the executive branch of a fundamental principle of the Constitution.

The Fathers of Confederation chose not to replicate the post–1856 elected Legislative Council. Nevertheless, they refused to give the executive government free rein over the composition of the Upper Chamber, as was the case in 1840, by circumscribing the class of persons eligible to serve as senators. At the same time, the Fathers of Confederation declined to make the new Senate a "provincial" chamber based on the

American model, where senators (prior to 1913) were elected by the legislatures of their respective states. The Canadian Senate would be independent (its deliberations not tied to the survival of the government and its members safe from reprisals by their respective party leaders), have a long-term perspective (appointment for life), carry an element of continuity and stability in considering issues (unlike the House of Commons with its regular membership turnover), provide a mature point of view in debate (by limiting the criteria for membership to those who had attained the age of thirty and owned property), and be able to provide a sectional perspective and influence (by structuring the Senate so as to achieve regional balance).

Such characteristics as independence, long-term perspective, continuity, and stability are essential to the proper functioning of the Senate and can only be sustained by the proper use of the power of appointment, as provided for in the *Constitution Act, 1867*. The importance of using functional criteria for selecting members to the Upper Chamber is not lost on those who share our bicameral English parliamentary system. Indeed, the committee of the British House of Commons mandated to explore options for parliamentary reform has observed as much in its recent report on the appointment of members to the House of Lords:

Composition should be driven by function. The second chamber needs to be composed in such a way that it can most effectively discharge its functions, which are essentially those of scrutiny and revision.[87]

In 1980, the Supreme Court acknowledged the relationship between the qualifications for appointment to the Senate and the independent nature and function of the institution:

In creating the Senate in the manner provided in the Act, it is clear that the intention was to make the Senate a thoroughly independent body which could canvass dispassionately the measures of the House of Commons. This was accomplished by providing for the appointment of members of the Senate with tenure for life.[88]

In other words, the appointment of senators and the conditions attached to their appointments are fundamental to the proper functioning of the chamber.

Is it appropriate, therefore, for a Prime Minister to recommend that the Governor General appoint senators whose selection would have the effect of thwarting the role and function of the Senate, thereby preventing the Senate from bringing balanced and sober second thought to legislation?

At some point, a reduction of the term of office might impair the functioning of the Senate in providing what Sir John A. Macdonald described as "the sober thought in legislation." The imposition of compulsory retirement at age seventy-five did not change the essential character of the Senate.[89]

This warning of the Supreme Court in 1980 raises the question of whether abuse of the appointment process could jeopardize the Senate's ability to fulfill its parliamentary obligations. The court did not consider the possibility of a Prime Minister appointing to the Senate only individuals of an advanced age who would be obliged to retire within a few years, if not a few months. There is little doubt, however, that the widespread appointment of septuagenarians to the Senate could only harm the Upper Chamber's ability to bring continuity, stability, and long-term perspective to the consideration of legislation. Let us be clear: the Fathers of Confederation did not intend for the Senate to be a place of temporary employment. It should be obvious to even the casual observer that the appointment of senators to terms that are shorter than the life of one Parliament essentially prevents the Senate from fulfilling its vital role of bringing long-term perspective to the debate of national issues. Yet, over the past ten years this practice has become all too common.[90]

In 1980, the Supreme Court established the criteria for determining the constitutionality of changes to the Senate appointment process. The court found that any modification of the existing appointment power must not alter "the fundamental character of the Senate."[91] This test should be applied in respect of the appointment of senators over the age of seventy. Extending the argument further, would a Prime Minister be entitled to recommend appointments that would effectively impair the operation of the Senate or, conversely, refrain from exercising his power, thus allowing the Upper Chamber to atrophy through the gradual depletion of its membership? Clearly, no such entitlement exists.

Could a Prime Minister use his conventional power as a shield while undermining the very principles of federalism, responsible government, and the protection of minority rights, all of which are defining principles of the Senate? Not with any political legitimacy. Equally illegitimate would be such practices as filling the Senate with members of the same party[92] or allowing all the seats from one part of the country to remain either vacant[93] or stacked with representatives whose political ilk bares no resemblance to that of the local people. Prime-ministerial decisions of this kind would damage the ability of the Senate to operate properly, either by reducing the likelihood of real debate or by depriving a region of its voice in the Senate. Ultimately, no Prime Minister and no Governor General ought to do indirectly what neither can do directly. That is to say, the executive government has no right to cripple the Senate's ability to perform its constitutionally mandated legislative functions.

These examples reveal a truth that has not been generally acknowledged: the executive government cannot undermine the Senate and the institutional principles rooted in the architecture of the Canadian constitution with impunity. The Constitution has established permanent rules and safeguards to guarantee its implementation. No authority is vested in any of its actors that would allow them to disregard its principles. Indeed, all such actors are bound by the constraints of the very Constitution they must uphold:

The Supreme Court of Canada has consistently held that *powers conferred under the Constitution cannot be used so as to run counter to or destroy foundational constitutional principles* ... the power of a legislature to reconstitute itself cannot be used to remove the principle of responsible government underlying parliamentary institutions ... *Built on certain structuring principles*, the Constitution, including its amending formulae, *must be read consistently with these principles*.[94]

Where does one find the authority to enforce these fundamental principles?

Since the adoption of the *Canadian Charter of Rights and Freedoms* in 1982, the executive branch of government is also bound to respect the principles and values enshrined in the Charter. Hypothetically then, would it be constitutional for a Governor General to comply with a Prime Minister's request to appoint only men to the Senate, in light of sections 15 and 28 of the Charter? Is the Prime Minister not bound to uphold the spirit of the equality provisions of the Charter in exercising constitutional powers? What of the many other segments of society that are chronically underrepresented in Parliament? Is there no constitutional obligation on the Prime Minister to ensure that these Canadians are not overlooked in the appointment process? Surely the Prime Minister must acknowledge, sustain, and implement the intrinsic values of the Charter in the performance of constitutional duties?

It used to be asserted that the exercise of prerogative powers was not subject to judicial review. The assertion is belied by the many cases in which the exercise or purposed exercise of prerogative powers has been reviewed by the courts. The courts will determine whether a prerogative power that is asserted by the Crown does in fact exist, and, if it does exist, what are its limits and whether any restrictions on the power have been complied with. The courts will also determine whether a prerogative power has been displaced by statute. *The courts will also require not only that prerogative powers be exercised in conformity with the Charter of Rights and other constitutional norms, but also that administrative law norms such as the duty of fairness be observed.*[95]

If the exercise of Royal prerogative must conform to the Charter and other constitutional norms, *a fortiori* the exercise of an executive power, clearly defined in the text of the Constitution since 1867, must also meet the same constitutional test.

Safeguards exist to protect the integrity of Constitution when it is abused or disregarded. The power of the Governor General to appoint senators is set out in the text of the Constitution. This power of appointment is a constitutional responsibility that is clearly delimited in the *Constitution Act, 1867* and additionally circumscribed by the Charter in 1982. When a Prime Minister, as provided by constitutional convention, advises the Governor General on appointments to the Senate, he is, in effect, exercising an executive power that is no different from any other constitutional power.[96]

Is there a legal imperative to the effect that executive power should not be equally reviewable by the courts by way of a declaratory judgment, in the event that the power were to be abused?[97] Does this mean we must wait until an aggrieved citizen challenges a Senate appointment in court (e.g., where senators are appointed a few months before the mandatory retirement age) before initiating a reform of the appointment system?

Parliamentary Means

Clearly, it would be preferable to circumscribe the executive power exercised by the Prime Minister in accordance with the constitutional principles on which the Senate was founded. There is, in fact, a more commendable way. This option requires the Prime Minister to limit the use of his conventional power so as to comply with the principles of the Constitution and its Charter. The voluntary submission of the Prime Minister to such limits would go a long way to restoring public confidence in our parliamentary institutions. Let us consider two different routes by which Parliament might address this issue.

THE CONVENTIONAL ROUTE

As illustrated in many charts of the appendix, in practice, the nomination of senators is not based on any set of predetermined criteria (see charts on age, profession, education background, gender, minority groups, aboriginal ancestry, etc.). Each successive Prime Minister set his own criteria for appointing senators. Factors such as gender and age, along with various personal objectives and preferences, have determined the selection of appointees. Invariably, the particular pattern followed by a Prime Minister in making Senate appointments emerges over time. It is generally understood that, in any event, such deliberations of the Prime Minister are outside the domain of parliamentary debate or public discussion.

To address these issues that lie at the heart of public hostility to the Senate, the Prime Minister could make a policy statement or put a motion before both houses of Parliament, which would clearly establish the criteria and process to be followed in making Senate appointments. While such a motion would only bind the Prime Minister for the life of the Parliament in which it was adopted, it would nevertheless establish a new framework that would serve as a precedent for successive prime ministers. This approach has limited merit because of the uncertainty of its adoption by future Parliaments.[98]

THE STATUTORY ROUTE

The most effective way to establish a transparent process for appointing senators would be for Parliament to enact a law that would:

- include a comprehensive set of criteria that would reflect the values of the Charter and the institutional principles of our Constitution;
- set a time limit to fill Senate vacancies, similar to the provisions in respect of vacancies in the House of Commons;
- limit any single party to two thirds of the seats in the Senate;
- establish an independent Board of Review, appointed for the life of each Parliament.[99]

This process would confirm the appropriateness of the lists of candidates submitted by the Prime Minister to the Board, from which the Prime Minister would select names of senators to be appointed by the Governor General. All the above elements could be included in an Act entitled, *The Senate Appointments Act.*

This new procedure for appointing senators would parallel the vetting process[100] established for judicial appointments, which is not set by statute[101] but that successive prime ministers have respected in order to reinforce the credibility of the courts and to insulate themselves from criticism of the exercise of their power of appointment. Such reforms would avoid any lengthy and costly legal proceeding brought by an aggrieved citizen convinced of a blatant abuse of the power of appointment, while also negating the need for a parliamentary motion to censure the Prime Minister that would be embarrassing both for the government and for the individuals involved.

THE LEGISLATIVE VETO: MYTH VS REALITY

The Senate's power to veto federal legislation is central to the debate over the purpose and reform of the institution. Although many have spoken or written on this topic, rarely has the discourse or literature resulted in anything novel or comprehensive.[102] There is little academic research available on the debate over the principles that led the Fathers of Confederation to give the Senate the same powers and privileges that the British House of Commons enjoyed in 1867 and to place the two houses on an equal footing in rendering the advice and consent required for the valid enactment of laws.[103] Nor has there been any significant documentation of the veto's use, its various forms or its defining impact on the Senate as an institution.

What is a veto? According to the standard definition, a veto is one of three things: a constitutional right to reject a legislative measure, the rejection itself, or the prohibition of a proposal.[104] For most observers, including politicians frustrated by a Senate that is unwilling to be subservient, the veto is merely a symbol of the Senate's obstinate refusal to bow to the will of elected politicians. When exercised, the Senate's veto is perceived as an act of insubordination rather than the performance of a constitutional duty. Not surprisingly, prime ministers who have encountered a defiant Senate have been the most likely to promote reforms that would curtail its influence.

On 9 May 1985, John Crosbie, then Minister of Justice in the Mulroney Government, introduced in the House of Commons a resolution to amend section 54 of the *Constitution Act, 1867* so as to replace the Senate's power to veto legislation with a "suspensive veto."[105] Eight premiers expressed their support for the resolution, the holdouts being the premiers of Manitoba and Quebec.[106] A change of government in Ontario, however, resulted in the proposal's hasty demise. On 26 June 1985, the new Premier of Ontario, David Peterson, indicated his lack of interest in the Crosbie initiative. The combined reluctance of the governments of Ontario and Quebec effectively killed the proposal. Debate on the issue ceased in the House of Commons, where the resolution eventually died on the Order Paper.

What is the difference between the veto power currently held by the Senate and the suspensive veto proposed by the Mulroney Government? As described by the federal government in 1985 the suspensive veto is, at best, the capacity to delay the passage of financial legislation for no more than thirty days and ordinary legislation for no more than forty-five days.

"Suspensive veto" in this context is a misnomer. Much like "mock chicken," the suspensive veto has the superficial appearance of the real thing, without containing any of its essence. It is not a veto, since it does not include the capacity to reject or prohibit anything. The so-called suspensive veto would essentially enable the Senate to prolong the passage of legislation by thirty days in the case of appropriation and tax bills, and by forty-five days in the case of all other enactments or motions. In practice, the government would simply factor the Senate's token thirty or forty–five day delay period into its legislative calendar.

It is quite plain that the suspensive veto would have the effect of divesting the Senate of its capacity to effectively hold the executive branch to account. The substitution of this non-veto for the real veto currently held by the Senate would also be the death knell for the system of checks and balances that exists between the two houses of Parliament. Wresting from the Senate its power to veto federal legislation would effectively overturn the constitutional order in which Canada has evolved and prospered over the past 136 years. The Senate's existence would be nominal. In practice, all legislative power would be concentrated in the House of

Commons, accelerating the fusion of the legislative branch with the executive government.[107]

Could Canada's Parliament be essentially transformed into a unicameral body,[108] as was attempted in 1985, by the concurrence of the federal government and just seven provinces representing only 50 percent of the Canadian population?[109] Would it not be such a fundamental and structural, change to our parliamentary system that the agreement of all provinces would be required? It is our contention that it is unconstitutional to remove the veto power of the Senate on the basis of the 7/50% amending formula, as proposed in 1985 by the federal government.[110] Amendments of such magnitude require ratification by the federal Parliament and the legislatures of all ten provinces.[111]

Under section 91 of the *Constitution Act, 1867*, the Queen makes laws "by and with the advice and consent" of both houses of Parliament. That is to say, both the Senate and the House of Commons have the power to veto proposed legislation by withholding their required consent. Sections 18, 91, 94 and paragraph 94(*a*) of the *Constitution Act, 1867* confer on the Senate the same legislative powers as those vested in the House of Commons, with the exception at section 53 that appropriation and tax bills may not originate in the Upper Chamber. Just as the House of Commons may refuse to give its consent to a bill from the Senate, the Senate can do likewise for a bill originating in the House of Commons. Each chamber, therefore, is autonomous, having its own legislative veto.

It was clear to the Fathers of Confederation that the Senate must have all the requisite powers to adopt, amend, delay, or defeat legislation in Parliament. Sir John A. Macdonald saw only one limitation to these powers: they should not be used to frustrate the democratic mandate of the government by blocking the enactment of its campaign commitments. In all other cases, the Senate would have the full capacity to, in the words of our first Prime Minister, "canvass dispassionately" the government's legislation. His vision of a Senate with real power was echoed in March 2000 by the late Mr Justice Willard Estey of the Supreme Court of Canada in his testimony to the Senate:

You have a duty. I thought hard about this before coming here. The Senate
has a senior duty to perform. It has to perfect the process of legislation.
That duty must clearly entail, on occasion, an amendment or a refusal or an
automatic approval. All three are within your power. Not only are they
within your power, they are within your duty. You have to scrutinize this
thing and see what is good and bad and purify it. That is why you are here.
The second House invariably around the world is set up as a brake on the
first level of legislation, but the executive branch tags along all the way up
the ladder.[112]

POWERS OF THE SENATE

The Senate's veto is much more than simply the capacity to reject a Government bill. However newsworthy, it is only one of the five powers flowing from the Senate's legislative veto, and one it uses sparingly indeed.[113] The Senate (like the House of Commons) has five legislative powers, which it can exercise concurrently or in isolation:

The Power to Review

The power to review or study legislation is the power most commonly used by the Senate. It is this power that enables the Senate to decide how a bill will be studied, including the assignment of a committee to report on the bill, the number of witnesses who will appear before the committee, and the location of committee hearings. With this power to review, free of constraint, the Senate can examine the proposed legislation, which is often very complex, by calling on recognized experts and, in particular, by permitting the public to voice its opinions fully and objectively. Professor Thomas's analysis has shown that the Senate uses this power differently than the House of Commons. If the Senate had only a limited amount of time in which to review proposed legislation, the quality of its examination would be adversely affected, senators' expertise would not be fully utilized, and the complex issues that are the bread and butter of today's legislators would receive only cursory or even superficial treatment.[114]

The Power to Delay

The power to delay serves two important functions. First of all, it enables thorough debate to take place, through which the public can be alerted to the ramifications and potential pitfalls of proposed legislation. Less direct than defeating a bill outright, the power to delay is nevertheless an effective way of obliging the government to reconsider proposed legislation[115] or to amend it in accordance with the Senate's recommendations in order to guarantee its adoption.[116]

The Power to Negotiate

The power to negotiate, which is inherent in the exercise of the Senate's legislative power, is exercised in a variety of ways (e.g., to obtain the agreement of the House of Commons on amendments to be made to government legislation, to obtain ministerial commitments on tabling subsequent amendments or implementing reports, to secure the establishment of independent advisory bodies, etc.).[117] In short, the Senate uses its negotiation power, derived from its veto power, to produce results for the various sectional and minority interests it exists to protect. Ministers who hope to secure passage of their legislation in a reasonable timeframe are often prepared to accommodate such Senate requirements.[118] Of course, the Senate's power to negotiate does not exist in a vacuum. Without the powers to delay or defeat legislation, it is toothless.

The Power to Amend

The power to amend bills is the most tangible manifestation of the Senate's legislative power. Through its use, the Senate can make a concrete contribution to improving legislation. Amendments may come from committee testimony, from the Government itself noticing an omission or an error, or from a senator on either side of the chamber arguing a principle or acting as the spokesperson for an interest group. The sources are diverse, but the effect is the same: the amendment must go to the House of Commons for its approval.[119] If the House of Commons returns the bill to the Senate without the amendments, the Senate has the option of standing its ground and sending the bill back until the changes are accepted. This capacity to "negotiate" with the House of Commons is the direct expression of the Senate's autonomous legislative power, without which the House of Commons could freely ignore any amendments proposed by the Senate. It follows, therefore, that absent any real power of veto, the Senate cannot amend federal legislation.

The Power to Reject

The power to reject or defeat a Government bill[120] is the most consequential power arising from the Senate's veto. It is also the most controversial. The democratic sensitivities of Canadians are apt to bristle at the prospect of appointed politicians overruling our elected representatives – one reason why this power has been used sparingly and judiciously over the last hundred years.

Without the power to veto legislation, the Senate would be nothing more than an advisory chamber, and little more than an upscale focus group. Its role would be limited to issuing hastily prepared opinions on legislation passed by the House of Commons. Worse than that, the substantive and balanced study of legislation performed by Senate committees would become an empty charade. The citizens of Canada, who currently have the ability to give their input on legislation through the Senate committee process, would have the choice between the party-line/foregone-conclusion committee hearings of the House or the dressed-up therapy sessions of a Senate *sans* veto.

FOUR EFFECTS

Some well-meaning observers mistakenly assume that stripping the Senate of its veto power would only mean removing its power to block or reject a bill. Not so. Abolishing the Senate's veto would mean removing all five of its powers: the powers to study, delay, negotiate, amend, and refuse. The corollary of this would be, in theory, an all-powerful House of Commons, but, in practice, an omnipotent executive government.

Power comes from having options. If the Senate has power, it is because it has the option to initiate its own legislation and approve, reject, or amend legislation proposed by the government. Yet the Senate was not invested with these powers for its own sake. Rather, it holds them in trust for those who are underrepresented in an otherwise majoritarian political culture. The benefits that accrue to the Canadian people as a result of the Senate's possession and use of legislative veto power have four effects.

The Chilling Effect

The simple fact of the Senate's veto power has a chilling effect on the government as well as on the House of Commons, both of which must always consider the scrutiny their legislation will face in the Upper Chamber. The spectre of delay, amendment, or defeat hangs over every bill sent to the Senate by the House of Commons, giving the government every incentive to "get it right the first time." While this deterrent cannot be quantified, its presence is tangible, especially when the government legislates on controversial issues.[121]

The Accountability Effect

Another advantage of the Senate's veto power is the effect it has on the accountability of the government in the legislative process. The Senate can, and often does, take the time necessary to conduct a thorough review of a bill, hearing from all senators who wish to intervene. A Senate committee can hold as many meetings and hear as many witnesses as it thinks fit. This accountability effect compels the government and the House of Commons to provide a detailed explanation and justification of its legislative program. The most striking recent example was Bill C–40, the *Extradition Act*.[122] The issue of the extradition of persons to countries where they may face the death penalty was never raised during debate on the bill in the House of Commons, notwithstanding the serious constitutional, philosophical, and moral significance of the question for Canadian society. The issue was taken up in the Senate, however, where the bill was studied and debated over six months. Although the majority in the Senate defeated amendments to the bill, objections raised by dissenting senators were validated one year later by a landmark ruling of the Supreme Court on extradition and the death penalty.[123]

The Curative Effect

Senate veto power also has a curative effect on defective legislation. For instance, Bill C–7, the Youth Criminal Justice Bill, did not grant young Aboriginal offenders sentenced as adults the right to the same alternative sentencing mechanisms that the courts had recognized for adult Aboriginal offenders. An amendment initiated in the Senate, and subsequently adopted by the House of Commons, rectified this legislative inconsistency. Bill S–41 is another recent case in point.[124] Introduced by the government in the Senate rather than in the House of Commons, its aim was to re-enact regulations and Orders-in-Council passed and published in only one official language. After hearing fifteen witnesses and debating this Government bill over three months, the Senate passed six major amendments altering the essence of the legislation. The bill was subsequently sent to the House of Commons, where it was passed without amendment in less than fifteen minutes!

The Supervisory Effect

Finally, the Senate's veto has a supervisory effect on the legislative activity of the government.[125] Until recently, the average tenure of a senator has been three Parliaments. Such institutional memory and professional experience have enabled the Senate to bring a high standard of legislative rigour to the study of Government bills, particularly when facing an inexperienced government. Senators are more apt to take a less partisan, longer-term view in assessing legislative priorities than the House of Commons, which is more susceptible to prevailing public opinion.[126]

LEGITIMACY OF THE SENATE

Of course, one cannot discuss the positive effects of the Senate's veto power without confronting the sundry and scathing attacks on its legitimacy. Such criticism often lies dormant when the government has a majority in the Senate. When the governing party is defeated at the polls, especially after a long stay in office, it almost invariably retains a majority in the Senate for at least a few years. In these circumstances, the new government is likely to be impatient with an Upper Chamber that is not deferential, placing the Senate in an unenviable "damned if you do, damned if you don't" situation. If it refuses to bless the new government's legislative package, it will most certainly be accused of obstructionism, contempt for the electorate, and possibly even sour grapes. On the other hand, if the Senate passes the entire package without any reservations, it will fail to fulfill its constitutional role of providing sober reflection and holding the government to account.

Has the Senate ever misused its veto? Has it ever blocked bills repeatedly and prevented the elected government from fulfilling its electoral commitments, flouting the traditional limits and the role assigned to it by the Fathers of Confederation? An analysis of the use of the Senate veto over the past century answers these questions while also setting the parameters of what constitutes "legitimate use" of this legislative power.

Since 1900, the Senate has used its veto power forty-four times to reject legislation passed by the House of Commons.[127] In view of the thousands of bills passed by the Senate over the same period, this represents a rather modest percentage. However, an analysis of the forty-four bills by theme or purpose identified five recurring rationales for their rejection by the Senate. As it happens, these rationales do not include narrow partisanship or wanton procedural wrangling. Rather, the Senate has used its veto power judiciously and infrequently, where proposed legislation:

- was of grave detriment to one or more regions;
- breached constitutionally protected human rights and freedoms;
- compromised collective linguistic or minority rights;
- was of such importance to the future of Canada as to require the government to seek a mandate from the electorate;
- was so repugnant as to constitute a quasi-abuse of the legislative power of Parliament.[128]

Notice that each of the five motives listed above reflects aspects of the federal principle that the Senate was created to embody: the representation of sectional interests, the protection of individual rights, the promotion of minority rights, government accountability, and legislative oversight.[129] Far from thwarting our democratic system of government, the Senate veto has been used to ensure its coherence and legitimacy.

Notwithstanding the marked restraint demonstrated by the Senate in using its veto to refuse a bill, the Constitution provides an extraordinary remedy to a Prime Minister experiencing deadlock in the Senate. Section 26 of the *Constitution Act, 1867* authorizes the Queen on the advice of the Governor General (in practice, the Governor General on the advice of the Prime Minister) to appoint four or eight senators in addition to the full membership of the Senate. The purpose of this "swamping power" is to allow the Prime Minister to break a legislative deadlock by securing a government majority in the Senate for the passage of its bills.[130]

Removing the Senate's veto means removing the Senate's power to ensure the adequate representation and expression of sectional interests, minority and linguistic concerns and the rights and freedoms of individual citizens in the legislative process. To do so would be nothing less than a constitutional *coup d'état*, essentially nullifying the federal principle that is at the heart of the Canadian constitutional polity and is embodied in the Senate.[131] Indeed, as the Supreme Court has found, removing the Senate's veto would supplant Parliament with "a new legislative body."[132] In its place would be "a unicameral system of government but with two chambers of Parliament."[133]

In our opinion, the federal government cannot proceed to effectively dismantle one of the three constituent elements of the Parliament of Canada without the agreement of all provincial legislatures.[134] It would be unconstitutional, not to mention unconscionable, to so drastically alter the Confederation covenant without the agreement of the less populated provinces, whose relative lack of clout was one of the chief reasons for creating the Senate in the first place.

Moreover, the elimination of the Senate's legislative veto would also have an impact on the constitutional powers of the Governor General. Since 1867, the Governor General has had to obtain the consent of *both* houses of Parliament before giving Royal Assent to any bill. Remove the requirement of Senate approval and you remove a significant fetter on the power of the Governor General to grant assent.[135] Under the *Constitution Act, 1982*, any amendment affecting the office of the Governor General must be ratified by Parliament and all provincial legislatures.[136]

Furthermore, the removal of the Senate's veto would alter the operation of the amending formula in the Constitution, which cannot be done without the unanimous approval of the provinces.[137] Given these considerations, any constitutional amendment abolishing the Senate's veto under the 7/50% formula would likely be the subject of a lengthy challenge in court. Our constitutional polity successfully maintains an institutional equilibrium designed to safeguard common Canadian values of equality, diversity and responsibility, as enshrined in the Charter. Removing the Senate's veto would gut an essential institution whose aim is to rebalance the inequalities that are present in our society.

CONCLUSION

When pondering the unintended and unfortunate consequences of impulsive Senate reform, one is reminded of the advice offered by an astute observer of the constitutional evolution of Canada. Michael Pitfield is intimately familiar with the executive branch of government, having served as Clerk of the Privy Council for six years and with the Upper Chamber as senator for the past twenty years:

In constitution-making it is important to bear in mind that the first step in reform is almost never the final step. To the contrary, the first steps sets off a process of evolution usually quite rapid at first and gradually petering out. Focusing merely on the change and not on its consequences as far as the eye can see is to invite mistakes and chaos.[138]

Earnest and well-meaning attempts to reform the Senate are to be commended – but they should not serve as the pretence for weakening the
constitutional protection of sectional interests and of minority and human
rights built into our legislative process. The Fathers of Confederation
designed our system of government to reflect a particular set of values.
This set of values is not a replica of the unbridled libertarianism of our
southern neighbours. Enshrined in our Constitution is the expression of
fundamental humanist principles: the recognition and valorization of the
rights of linguistic and cultural minorities; the affirmation, rather than
assimilation, of regional identities; and, more recently, the paramountcy of
human rights and freedoms over government decisions and legislation.
None of these principles can flourish in a society where the system of government is solely preoccupied with the interests of the majority. This
humanist philosophy is reflected in the role accorded to the Senate by our
Constitution.

Abolishing or diminishing the Upper Chamber would have a profound
and nefarious impact on the equilibrium of our constitutional polity and
the effectiveness of its institutions. It would further destabilize the relationship between the executive and legislative branches of government
by undercutting the carefully crafted system of checks and balances
intended to advance the values of Canadian society. The Senate is perhaps the last remaining obstacle to the total domination of Parliament by
the executive government. Its demise would signal the atrophy of parliamentary federalism in Canada and the birth of a less Canadian system of
government.

NOTES

1 Trudeau, *À Contre courant*, 254.

2 *Reference re Secession of Quebec*, [1998] 2 S.C.R. 217, para. 72.

3 *Ibid.*, para. 32.

4 *Reference re Legislative Authority of Parliament in Relation to the Upper House*,
   [1980] 1 S.C.R. 54: 67.

5 Canada. Legislature. *Parliamentary Debates on the Subject of the Confederation of
   the British North American Provinces, 3rd Session, 8th Provincial Parliament of Canada*, 38.

6 *Ibid.*, 88.

7 *Reference re Secession of Quebec*, para. 59.

8 *Ibid.*

9 *The Constitution Act, 1867*, s. 22.

10 Canada. Parliament. Senate. The Standing Committee on Rules, Procedures
   and the Rights of Parliament, Report of the Committee, Tenth Report, March
   5, 2002. (Brief of Professor David E. Smith of the University of Saskatchewan
   on Bill S–34).

11 *Reference re Secession of Quebec,* para. 32.

12 *The Constitution Act, 1867,* s. 52.

13 Ajzenstat et al., *Canada's Founding Debates,* 82–3.

14 *Reference re Provincial Electoral Boundaries (Saskatchewan)* [1991] 2 S.C.R. 158: 160.

15 *The Constitution Act, 1867,* para. 51(*a*).

16 For example, after the readjustment of electoral boundaries the average number of residents per MP will be 108,548 in British Columbia, versus 33,824 in Prince Edward Island; see Representation Formula published in *Canada Gazette,* Part I, EXTRA, vol. 136, no. 1, 13 March 2002.

17 "Proportion*ate* representation," as described above and prescribed by section 52 of *The Constitution Act, 1867,* should never be confused with "proportion*al* representation," which refers to an electoral system in which a party's share of seats corresponds to its share of the popular vote.

18 Ontario's share of government MPs rose from 55 percent in 1993 to 65 percent in 1997, before dropping to 58 percent in 2000.

19 *Reference re Secession of Quebec,* para 72.

20 *The Constitution Act, 1867,* s. 91.

21 Professor Paul Thomas of the University of Manitoba has defined regionalism as a term that refers to "both the distinctive character of defined geographic areas and to people's perceptions of, and identification with, such places. In other words, there is both a tangible, material aspect to regionalism and a symbolic, psychological aspect." Thomas, "Caucus Representation in Canada: Keynote Address to the Canadian Study of Parliament Group Fall Conference on Party Caucuses: Behind Closed Doors."

22 *Reference re Secession of Quebec,* para. 81.

23 *Reference re Legislative Authority of Parliament in Relation to the Upper House,* 48 (excerpt from Lord Sankey in *Re: The Regulation and Control of Aeronautics in Canada,* 70).

24 *Reference re Secession of Quebec,* para. 81.

25 Hiebert, *Charter Conflicts,* xiii.

26 Canada. Parliament. House of Commons. *Debates of the House of Commons,* 32nd Parliament, 1st Session, vol. 7: 7471–6. Ottawa, 19 February 1981. (S. Joyal, MP, on *Resolution Respecting the Constitution Act, 1981*)

27 *The Constitution Act, 1982,* s. 1.

28 McMurtry, "The Role of the Courts in Turbulent Times," 15.

29 *Department of Justice Act,* R.S.C. 1985, c. J–2, ss. 4.1(1).

30 Hiebert, *Charter Conflicts,* xv.

31 *Reference re Alberta Statutes,* [1938] S.C.R. 100: 133 (per Duff, J.).

32 Canada. Legislature. *Parliamentary Debates on the Subject of the Confederation,* 36.

33 *The Constitution Act, 1867,* s. 17.

34 As one authority noted, "We must not be misled by abstract terms ... there is no cut-and-dried institution called responsible government, identical in all

countries where it exists." (Holroyd, J., quoted in Bailey, *Cambridge History of the British Empire*, 395.)

35 Sir Robert Walpole, first and longest serving Prime Minister (1721–42) of the United Kingdom.

36 For further discussion of this issue, see Ajzenstat, in this volume.

37 This is one reason why it is erroneous to equate the role and powers of the Canadian Senate to those of the House of Lords. See also Vile, *Constitutionalism and the Separation of Powers*, ch. 3.

38 Appropriation and tax bills are unique in their capacity to bring down the government; in exceptional circumstances, the Prime Minister may link the fate of the government to other proposed legislation, by announcing to the House of Commons that the outcome of the vote on a particular bill is a matter of the confidence in the government. For instance, on 28 April 1998 Prime Minister Chrétien announced that the approval by the House of Commons of an opposition motion in favour of compensation for victims of Hepatitis c would constitute a loss of confidence in the government. All government MPs were present and voted against the motion, a number of whom were personally distraught at their own government's position. Commentators decried the pressure placed on government caucus members as an abuse of authority.

39 From the text of a letter from John B. Stewart to Serge Joyal, 30 July 2001. Retired Professor of Political Science John B. Stewart of St. Francis Xavier University, Antigonish, Nova Scotia, served as an MP, 1962–68, and as a senator, 1984–99.

40 Prior to their amendment in 1968, the *Standing Orders of the House of Commons* permitted the study and adoption of Estimates in the Committee of the Whole in the House of Commons. Under a 1968 amendment to the *Standing Orders*, the Estimates are "deemed reported" by the various Standing Committees by 31 May and must be adopted by 23 June.

41 Government MP Tony Valeri observed, "Committees must also have the right to oversee spending. MPs today have virtually no influence over how the Government spends money." (Quoted in Fife, "Martin Vows to 'Empower the MP,'" A1.)

42 Kilger, *Report of the Special Committee on the Modernization and Improvement of the Procedures of the House of Commons*, paras. 33–6.

43 Forsey and Eglinton, *The Question of Confidence in Responsible Government*.

44 Lynch-Staunton, "The Urgent Need for Parliamentary – Not Just Senate – Reform," 1: "This is not a partisan statement, let me assure you, for this unfortunate evolution has been going on for some thirty years without interruption."

45 The first major party leadership convention in Canada was held on 7 August 1919. William Lyon MacKenzie King was elected Leader of the Liberal Party of Canada.

46 *Canada Elections Act*, S.C. 2000 c. 9, para. 67(4)(c).

47 In a parliamentary system in which the number of government MPs rarely surpasses 170, there are more than eighty-seven appointed positions for which embers receive an additional salary: thirty-seven ministers, twenty-seven parliamentary secretaries, Speaker, Deputy Speaker, Whip, Deputy Whip, sixteen Chairs (three are from the opposition) and three Vice-Chairs of committees, for a total of eighty-seven.

48 For further discussion, see Rémillard, in this volume.

49 From the speech of former Senator Allan J. MacEachen on the occasion of his retirement from the Senate.

50 Grafstein, "The Mystery of National Caucus," 17.

51 "'The Liberal party is a family and people who try to tear it apart and split it apart are playing with fire' said Peter Donolo." (Milnes and Torip, "Survey 'Saddens' Chrétien," A1.)

52 Grafstein, "The Mystery of National Caucus," 15.

53 Lynch-Staunton, "The Urgent Need for Parliamentary – Not Just Senate – Reform," 7.

54 Great Britain. *Strengthening Parliament: Report of the Commission to Strengthen Parliament*, 6.

55 Savoie, *Governing from the Centre: The Concentration of Power in Canadian Politics.*

56 On 3 March 2000, the Leader of the Government in the House of Commons gave a Notice of Motion that proposed to limit to one the number of amendments to Government bills a private member could introduce at Third Reading. The motion was withdrawn after strong opposition was voiced on both sides of the House. Had the motion been successful, the executive government would have, for all intents and purposes, assumed the legislative power of the House of Commons at Third Reading.

57 Professor Rémillard's chapter has identified and explained the characteristics of Senate membership that are necessary for the review of government legislation and the scrutiny of Executive spending.

58 Stewart, letter to the author (see note 39).

59 *New Brunswick Broadcasting Co. v. Nova Scotia (Speaker of the House of Assembly)* [1993] 1 S.C.R. 319.

60 Great Britain. *Strengthening Parliament: Report of the Commission to Strengthen Parliament*, 15.

61 See also the chapters by Franks and Thomas in this volume.

62 Dobell, "Reforming Parliamentary Practice: The Views of MPs," 14.

63 Senate of Canada. *Rules of the Senate*, subsection 85(1).

64 Grafstein, "The Mystery of National Caucus," 30.

65 *An Act to amend the Parliament of Canada Act, the Members of Parliament Retiring Allowances Act and the Salaries Act*, S.C. 2001, c. 20.

66 The Senate adopted a motion to this effect on 10 October 2002.

67 James Kelly, Professor of Political Science at Brock University, suggests this proposal in Kelly, "Guarding the Constitution: Parliament and Judicial Roles under the Charter of Rights."

68 These six positions receive an additional salary. They add to the sixteen

Chairs and three Vice-Chairs, Speaker and deputy Speaker, for a total of twenty-four senators of the governing party who are paid more than their colleagues.

69 The author's Commission reads: "KNOW YOU, that as well for the especial trust and confidence We have manifested in you, as for the purpose of obtaining your advice and assistance in all weighty and arduous affairs which may the State and Defence of Canada concern, We have thought fit to summon you to the Senate of Canada and We do appoint you for the Division ("Region of" Kennebec) in Our Province of Quebec. AND WE do command you, that all difficulties and excuses whatsoever laying aside, you be and appear for the purposes aforesaid, in the Senate of Canada at all times whensoever and wheresoever Our Parliament may be in Canada convoked and holden, and this you are in no wise to omit."

70 The *Constitution Act, 1867*, Schedule V: "I *A.B.* do swear, That I will be faithful and bear true Allegiance to Her Majesty [Queen Elizabeth II]."

71 Canada. Parliament. Senate. *Debates of the Senate*, 2001, 204.

72 The debate on Bill C–40 (*An Act respecting extradition, to amend the Canada Evidence Act, the Criminal Code, the Immigration Act and the Mutual Legal Assistance in Criminal Matters Act and to amend and repeal other Acts in consequence*, 36th Parliament, 1st Session; S.C. 1999, c. 18) was particularly regrettable. This legislation contains a provision allowing for the extradition of persons to countries where they charged with capital offences. Votes in either chamber on the issue of capital punishment have traditionally been a matter of conscience, and hence free votes. The refusal by the government leadership to recognize the nature of the issue and to allow a free vote was wrong on moral as well as political grounds.

73 Great Britain. *Strengthening Parliament: Report of the Commission to Strengthen Parliament*, 8.

74 Ajzenstat et al., *Canada's Founding Debates*, 81–2.

75 David Mills, member of the House of Commons (Lib. – Bothwell, ON) in the government of Alexander Mackenzie, introduced the following motion to reform the Senate on 13 April 1874: "That the present mode of constituting the Senate is inconsistent with the Federal principle in our system of government, makes the Senate alike independent of people, and of the Crown, and is in other material respects defective, and our Constitution ought to be so amended as to confer upon each Province the power of selecting its own senators, and of defining the mode of their election," House of Commons, *Journals* 1874, 52. Mr Mills later served as Minister of Justice and Attorney General of Canada in the government of Sir Wilfrid Laurier while a member of the Senate. Alexander Brady, distinguished professor of political economy at the University of Toronto, raised similar concerns over the Senate appointment process in 1958: "[The Senate's] relative lack of popular favour is partly attributable to the fact that its appointments have been frankly drawn into the system of party spoils" (Brady, *Democracy in the Dominions*, 72).

76 Professor David Smith, in his upcoming book on bicameralism in Canada,

discusses at length how the composition of an Upper Chamber serves to compensate for the lack of representation of certain groups in the elected Chamber. As he ably explains, there is a structural function attributed to representation in a bicameral federal system, which he describes as "representational protection" (Smith, *Federalism*).

77 Joyal, "The Senate: The Earth Is Not Flat," 6.

78 *Edwards v. Attorney-General for Canada*, [1930] A.C. 124; The significance of this ruling cannot be overstated; it was the first decision in Canadian case law to recognize that our constitutionally mandated parliamentary institutions must evolve to reflect changes in Canadian society, thereby affirming that the Constitution is a living document, the interpretation of which is not shackled to the sociocultural context of the era in which it was written.

79 Appointments of women to the Senate per Prime Minister, as of 15 December 2002, are as follows: Chrétien, 31; Mulroney, 13; Trudeau, 12; St-Laurent, 4; Diefenbaker, 2; King, Bennett, Pearson, and Clark, 1 each. See appendix 1, chart C2.

80 "The public is no longer prepared to tolerate the cynical abuse of authority," Stevens, "Prime Minister Has Done Terrible Harm to Senate," B3.

81 *Re Appointment of Senators* (1991) 78 D.L.R. (4th) 244 (B.C.C.A.); *Weir v. Canada (Attorney General)* [1991] N.B.R. (2d) 337 (N.B.C.A.); *Singh v. the Queen* [1991] 3 O.R. (3rd) 429 (O.C.A.).

82 *Union Act, 1840*, (UK), 4 Vict., c. 35, s. IV.

83 *An Act to change the Constitution of the Legislative Council by rendering the same Elective*, (1856) 20 Vict., c. 140 (Canada).

84 "Royal prerogative consists of the powers and privileges *accorded by the common law to the Crown.* The prerogative is a branch of the common law, because it is the decisions of the courts which have determined its existence and extent" (Hogg, *Constitutional Law of Canada*, 13). "Royal prerogative is the residue of discretionary or arbitrary authority, which at any given time is left in the hands of the Crown" (Dicey, *Introduction to the Study of the Law of the Constitution*, 424).

85 *The Constitution Act, 1867*, ss. 26–7.

86 The Governor General could refuse to appoint new senators once the House of Commons had been dissolved. As the late author, professor, and Senator Eugene Forsey observed, "there are times when a Governor General would be entitled to reject even a usual Senate appointment, for example, where a government defeated at the polls tried to fill Senate vacancies before the new Government took office," quoted in Dunsmuir, *The Senate: Appointments under section 26 of the Constitution Act, 1867*; see also Forsey, "Appointment of Extra Senators under Section 26 of the *British North America Act*," 159–67.

87 Great Britain. *The Second Chamber: Continuing The Reform : Fifth Report Of Session 2001-2002*, 2.

88 *Reference re Legislative Authority of Parliament in Relation to the Upper House*, 77.

89 *Ibid.*, 76–7.

90 See appendix, chart B–3. Eighteen senators over the age of seventy were

appointed in the eight-year period from 31 August 1994 to 31 August 2002.
28 percent of Prime Minister Chrétien's appointees to the Senate had
attained the age of seventy before the date of their appointment. In contrast,
as of 1 September 2002, the average age at appointment of Prime Minister
Chrétien's nominees to the Supreme Court of Canada is fifty-five years. The
figure rises slightly to 55.3 years for his nominees to the Federal Court of
Appeal.

91 *Reference re Legislative Authority of Parliament in Relation to the Upper House,* 77.

92 In the 135 years following Confederation, Conservative prime ministers have
appointed 311 members of their own party (under its various incarnations:
174 Con, 102 Prog-Con, 29 Lib-Con, three Ind-Con, two Unionist, one Nat-
Con) to the Senate, along with fifteen Liberals (fourteen Lib, one Ind-Lib),
four Independents, and one other (Reform). Liberal prime ministers have
appointed 424 members of their own party (419 Lib, three Ind-Lib, one Lib-
Prog, one Lib-Ref) to the Senate, along with nine Conservatives (eight Prog-
Con, one Unionist), seven Independents, and three others (two Nat, one
Socred). In other words, Conservative prime ministers have given 94 percent
of their Senate appointments to Conservatives, while Liberal prime ministers
have given 96 percent of their Senate appointments to Liberals.

93 In the 1st Session of the 37th Parliament (29 January 2001 to 16 September
2002), there were anywhere from eight to thirteen vacancies (7.6 percent to
12.4 percent) in the Senate at any given time.

94 Howse and Malkin, "Canadians Are a Sovereign People: How the Supreme
Court Should Approach the Reference on Quebec Secession," 193–4.

95 Hogg, *Constitutional Law of Canada,* 15–16.

96 *Re Appointment of Senators,* 245: "Furthermore, s. 26 contains executive powers,
and, as such, should not be interpreted using a doctrine which was developed
to determine when a general power to legislate may be invoked."

97 While "decisions made by the Governor in Council in matters of public convenience and general policy are final and not reviewable in legal proceedings" (Dickson, J., in *Thorne's Hardware Ltd. v. R.* [1983] 1 S.C.R. 106: 111),
"the mere fact that a statutory power is vested in the Governor in Council
does not mean that it is beyond judicial review." (Estey, J., in *Attorney General
of Canada v. Inuit Tapirisat of Canada,* [1980] 2 S.C.R. 735: 748).

98 As the Supreme Court observed in *Re Amendment of the Constitution of Canada,*
"It is because the sanctions of convention rest with institutions of government
other than Courts, such as the Governor General or the Lieutenant Governor, or the houses of Parliament, or with public opinion and ultimately, with
the electorate, that it is generally said that they are political,"882–3.

99 For instance, such a board could be composed of: 1) a retired senator from
each of the two main parties represented in the Senate; 2) a retired member
of Parliament representing the party with the largest number of members in
the House of Commons that is not represented in the Senate; and 3) two
other Canadians of good report, whose achievements have caused them to be
honoured as Companions of the Order of Canada.

100 While federal judicial appointments are made by the Governor General on the advice of the federal cabinet, potential appointees must first be vetted by independent committees drawn from the legal profession and established for their respective jurisdictions. Selection criteria guiding the federal judicial appointment process include merit, maturity, and objectivity. In addition, federal government policy requires that the judicial appointments "represent a broad cross-section of Canadian society. To achieve this, the appointment of women and individuals from cultural and ethnic minorities should be encouraged." (From Department of Justice, Commissioner for Federal Judicial Affairs, "A New Judicial Appointment Process," 5)

101 For instance, former Chief Justice Pierre Michaud of the Québec Court of Appeal has called for changes to the *Judges Act* (R.S.C. 1985, c. J-1) that would establish a consultative committee for evaluating potential appointees to the Supreme Court of Canada, comprised of the Chief Justice of Canada, the President of the Canadian Bar Association, and representatives of the law faculties from the candidate's region (Trudel, "Pierre A. Michaud partage son expérience,"18–19).

102 The following reports devote only a few pages to the subject: Canada. Parliament. Senate. *The Special Joint Committee of the Senate and of the House of Commons on the Constitution of Canada: Final Report* (Molgat-MacGuigan), 1972; Canada. *Report on Certain Aspects of the Canadian Constitution* (Lamontagne), 1980; Canada. Parliament. Senate. *Joint Senate/House Committee Report on Senate Reform.* (Molgat-Cosgrove), 1984; Canada. Parliament. *Renewed Canada: Report/ratio of the Special Joint Committee of the Senate and the House of Commons on the Renewal of Canada* (Beaudoin-Dobie), 1992.

103 With the exceptions at section 53 of the *Constitution Act, 1867* and section 47 of the *Constitution Act, 1982.*

104 Barber, *The Canadian Oxford Dictionary*, 1616.

105 *Journals* of the House of Commons, 1985, 595–7.

106 In a letter dated 9 May 1985, the Lévesque Government in Québec announced that although it agreed with the substance of the resolution, it refused to participate in any ratification process that might be construed as tacit acceptance of the *Constitution Act, 1982.* Manitoba Premier Howard Pawley, a New Democrat, supported the outright abolition of the Senate.

107 What Bagehot calls the 'efficient secret' of the English Constitution, "the close union, the nearly complete fusion, of the executive and legislative powers" (Bagehot, *The English Constitution*, 8).

108 It should be noted that while section 47 of the *Constitution Act, 1982* provides for the amendment of the Constitution without the approval of the Senate, in no case can the House of Commons singlehandedly amend the Constitution of Canada. Depending on the nature of the constitutional amendment, ratification will also be required either by seven provinces representing 50 percent of the population of Canada (sections 38 and 42), by all provinces (section 41), by the particular province(s) concerned by the amendment (section 43), or, where only the federal government is con-

cerned, by the Senate (section 44). In this sense, under the *Constitution Act, 1982*, the provincial legislatures have assumed the Senate's veto power over constitutional amendments in all matters except those of purely federal jurisdiction.

109 That is to say, by the ratification of a constitutional amendment in the House of Commons and in the legislatures of seven provinces representing at least fifty percent of the population of Canada; *Constitution Act, 1982*, s. 38.

110 For further discussion of this issue, see the legal opinion of the Law Clerk and Parliamentary Counsel of the Senate: Audcent, *The Senate Veto*, 63–70.

111 *Constitution Act, 1982*, s. 41.

112 Canada. Parliament. Senate. Standing Committee on Aboriginal Peoples. *Proceedings of the Standing Senate Committee on Aboriginal Peoples*

113 Since 1991, the Senate has defeated four bills emanating from the House of Commons; see appendix.

114 To understand how this power of review is exercised in practice, one need only examine the progress of Bill C–7 (*An Act in respect of criminal justice for young persons and to amend and repeal other Acts*; S.C. 2002, c. 1), which the Senate studied and debated from 5 June to 18 December 2001, hearing sixty-three witnesses in committee.

115 The controversial Bill C–16 (*An Act respecting Canadian citizenship*, 36th Parliament, 2nd Session) was held in the Senate for five months, ultimately dying on the Order Paper at the dissolution of the 36th Parliament. The government did not reintroduce this legislation after its re-election in November 2000.

116 In his chapter, Professor Franks gave a number of examples of debates in which this delaying power was used.

117 Hiebert, *Charter Conflicts*, 133: "The Senate committee agreed to report Bill C–3 without amendments on the basis of an undertaking by the Solicitor General that the Government would introduce legislation to address some of the committee's concerns, particularly in relation to privacy. Also included in this undertaking was the creation of an independent advisory committee with representation from the Office of the Privacy Commissioner to oversee the administration of the DNA data bank, the requirement of an annual report by the Commissioner of the RCMP to the Solicitor General on the operation of the DNA data bank, the promise of legislation to bring within the ambit of the DNA data bank those offenders who are convicted in the military justice system, and a provision for parliamentary review every five years."

118 In accordance with concerns raised in a Senate Private Member's Bill (Bill S–8, *An Act to maintain the principles relating to the role of the Senate as established by the Constitution of Canada*, 37th Parliament, 1st Session), section 18.1 of the *Canada Elections Act* (S.C. 2000, c. 9) was amended by S.C. 2001, c. 21 (*An Act to amend the Canada Elections Act and the Electoral Boundaries Readjustment Act*) [Bill C–9 (37th Parliament, 1st Session) at s. 2].

119 Recent examples of Senate amendments approved by the House of Commons include Bill C–33 (*An Act respecting the water resources of Nunavut and the*

Nunavut Surface Rights Tribunal and to make consequential amendments to other Acts, 37th Parliament, 1st Session; S.C. 2002, c. 10), Bill C–7 (*An Act in respect of criminal justice for young persons and to amend and repeal other Acts*; S.C. 2002, c. 1), and Bill C–24 (*An Act to amend the Criminal Code (organized crime and law enforcement) and to make consequential amendments to other Acts*, 37th Parliament, 1st Session; S.C. 2001, c. 32).

120 Bill C–28 (*An Act respecting certain agreements concerning the redevelopment and operation of Terminals 1 and 2 at Lester B. Pearson International Airport*, 35th Parliament, 2nd Session) was defeated by a vote of 48–48 in the Senate on 19 June 1996. Bill C–43 (*An Act respecting abortion*, 34th Parliament, 2nd Session) was defeated on 31 January 1991 by a vote of 43–43 in the Senate.

121 For further discussion, see the chapters by Franks and Thomas, in this volume.

122 See note 75.

123 *United States v. Burns*, [2001] 1 S.C.R. 283.

124 37th Parliament, 1st Session (*An Act to re-enact legislative instruments enacted in only one official language*, S.C. 2002, c. 20).

125 For further discussion, see Rémillard, in this volume.

126 Audcent, *The Senate Veto*, 24–5.

127 Ibid.

128 From the text of my letter to former Senator Jacques Hébert, 27 August 1998; see also Audcent, *The Senate Veto*, 26.

129 Kunz, *The Modern Senate of Canada, 1925–1963: A Reappraisal*, 336–7.

130 Of course, the government must be within four or eight seats of a Senate majority for this swamping power to be effective. This is because section 28 of the *Constitution Act, 1867* places the final limit on Senate membership at 113, while the current maximum number of senators is 105. This may explain why section 26 has been used only once since Confederation – by Prime Minister Mulroney in 1990 to secure passage of the *Goods and Services Tax Act* (Bill C–62, 34th Parliament, 2nd Session).

131 See Frémont and Boudreault, "Supraconstitutionnalité canadienne et sécession du Québec."

132 *Reference re Legislative Authority of Parliament in Relation to the Upper House*, 72.

133 Bogdanor, *Power to the People: A Guide to Constitutional Reform*, 119.

134 It is no more possible to remove the Senate's veto on the basis of section 38 the *Constitution Act, 1982* than it is to strip the House of Commons of its legislative veto on through the same 7/50% amending formula.

135 Audcent, *The Senate Veto*, 65.

136 *The Constitution Act, 1982*, paragraph 41(1)(*a*).

137 Ibid., paragraph 41(1)(*e*).

138 From the preface by Senator Michael Pitfield, in this volume.

Database and Charts on the Composition of the Senate and the House of Commons

Jonathan Nagle

Intelligent and informed discussion of Senate Reform has long been limited by the absence of hard information about the institution. This lack of data feeds mistaken assumptions, permits half-truth (and outright lies) to go unchecked, and is largely responsible for the confusion that surrounds the issue. What has long been needed are concrete facts upon which to base a comprehensive evaluation of the Senate.

To that end, over the past two years we have undertaken extensive research on the Senate and the House of Commons. A group of nine researchers thoroughly examined material contained in the Library of Parliament, the *Canadian Parliamentary Guide,* the *Canadian Parliamentary Handbook,* and biographical newspaper clippings in order to extract as much information as possible about Canadian parliamentarians. Using this material, we have constructed a comprehensive database containing biographical information on senators and members of the House of Commons, including their political experience, professional background, awards, education, and date of birth. This database contains far more information and can generate far more graphs than can be accommodated in this appendix, which includes only a small sample of the most relevant statistics.

When this project was initially undertaken, no alternate source of information existed. During the research and development phase, however, the Library of Parliament began the creation of its own database, enabling us to collaborate with them, exchanging and verifying data in order to strengthen both systems. The creation of our database required six steps:

1 research
2 data entry
3 creation of queries
4 review of statistical gatherings
5 creation of charts
6 interpretation of charts.

1 RESEARCH

It was decided from the outset that we would limit our focus to the period from 1940 to the present. It was judged that this would give us a solid historical perspective on Parliament, and the necessary research could be conducted within a reasonable amount of time. The researchers gathered as much information as possible on each and every parliamentarian, both senators and members of the House of Commons, using the sources previously mentioned. While these resources provided a wealth of data, it was not always possible to find complete information in all statistical categories. For example, it was not always possible to identify whether parliamentarians had prior political experience or whether they were part of a minority group. Even with these limitations, we were able to accurately complete statistics for a wide range of categories.

Special attention has been given to the period from 1968 to the present and primarily to the Senate appointments of Prime Ministers Trudeau, Mulroney, and Chrétien. The information concerning this period is more abundant, these three prime ministers each made a substantial number of Senate appointments, and the 1965 constitutional amendment replacing tenure for life with tenure until the age of seventy-five was already in place, so all their appointments were on the same footing.

2 DATA ENTRY

The data entry process was done using Microsoft Access. Standardized forms were designed to minimize the risk of human error. For example, a combination of textual description and field restrictions were used to ensure that all dates were entered in *month/day/year* format. Furthermore, the entered data was then reviewed in order to catch any errors.

The data on the Senate is updated with each new appointment to the Upper House (last updated 7 July 2002), while the House of Commons has been updated to include the results of the November 2000 election. The data entry categories are as follows:

1 Parliamentarian:
   A–Name; B–Gender; C–Most Recent Parliamentary Role;
   D–Date of Birth; E–Place of Birth; F–Born in Canada;
   G–Born outside of Canada
2 Education:
   A–Number of Bachelor Degrees; B–Number of Masters Degrees;
   C–Number of PhDs; D–University Name; E–College Name(s) and
   Other(s)
3 Awards Received:
   A–Order of Canada (OC, CM, CC); B–Privy Council Member;
   C–Other

4 Professional Experience:
  A–Profession before Parliament; B–Career after Parliament
5 Political Experience:
  A–Former MP; B–Federal Assistants; C–Federal Organizations and
  Parties; D–Provincial Political Experience; E–Provincial Assistants,
  Advisors and Cabinet Directors; F–Provincial Organizations and
  Parties
6 Municipal Experience:
  A–Mayor or Councilor

3 CREATION OF QUERIES

At this stage of the project, with the data assembled and inputed, we could then begin to use it to answer questions about Parliament. We would begin by deciding what we wanted to know – for example, the average age of Prime Minister Chrétien`s Senate appointments or the average tenure of members of the House of Commons since 1940. We would then use Microsoft Access to generate a query on that question –using it to separate the relevant data from the mass information contained in the database. Nearly any question related to the composition of Parliament (using the data entry categories) can be used to generate a query. We have already created well over 150 queries with only the most relevant to the chapters having been included in this appendix.

4 REVIEW OF DATA

We had experienced professional Information Technology specialists review the structure and layout of our database. They retraced the initial procedures used by our data programmers, reviewing the data and queries, in order to find and correct any errors that had initially slipped through the cracks. Furthermore, we had a thorough review of the initial research conducted in order to assure the quality and accuracy of the information entered into the database. All of these measures helped to ensure that the database was both comprehensive and accurate.

5 CREATION OF CHARTS

With the database compiled and the specific information required isolated by the query, the next step was to present the statistics in a fashion that could be quickly understood. This was done by transferring the results from a query (or series of queries for more complex questions) into Microsoft Power Point, which could display the information in the form of charts of various kinds (pie charts, bar graphs, etc.).

6 INTERPRETATION OF CHARTS

The charts were reviewed by a professor of statistics, as well as by the Library of Parliament, in order to be certain that proper methodology was used and that no errors had crept in. This statistical expertise permitted us to determine which characteristics of Parliament could be accurately represented by charts and which type of chart was best suited for depicting the information.

EXPLANATION OF THE CHARTS

As already stated, the purpose of the database and the charts is to provide a factual basis for discussions about the Senate. The stereotypical view of the Senate – a chamber filled with old white male former politicians who sit there year after year without doing any work – has been repeated so often that it is now simply accepted at face value. When one actually examines the facts of the situation, however, it quickly becomes apparent that this common perception of the Senate is inaccurate.

The attached charts have been grouped together under four headings: Tenure, Age, Societal Diversity, and Professional Experience. The Tenure charts show that, while senators do have a longer average tenure than members of the House of Commons, it does not begin to approach the near-eternity that critics suggest. Moreover, unlike the wide fluctuations that can occur in the membership of the House of Commons, the rate of turnover in the Senate is fairly consistent, bringing some continuity and institutional memory to Parliament.

The Age charts demonstrate that, while, on average, senators are older than members of the House of Commons, the Upper House is not the geriatric ward/retirement home that it is often made out to be. The charts on Societal Diversity reveal that senators are drawn from all segments of society and that several important groups, notably women and aboriginals, are better represented in the Senate than in the House of Commons.

Finally, the charts on Professional Experience indicate that while there are indeed many senators who sat in provincial houses of assembly or the House of Commons prior to their appointment to the Senate, there is also a significant number who have never been elected to public office. Rather than being comprised entirely of professional politicians, the membership of the Senate is comprised of people with a wide variety of professional experiences.

SECTION A — TENURE

Chart A–1: Number of Years per Parliament

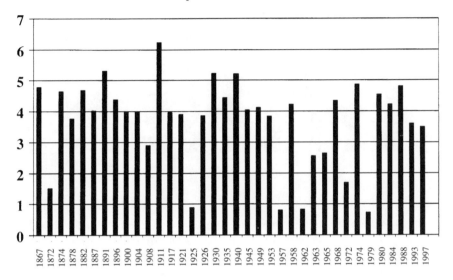

Chart A–2: Average Number of Years per Three Parliaments

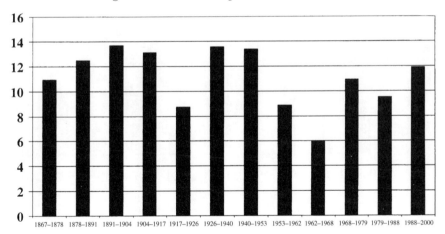

Chart A–3: Number of Senate Appointments by Prime Minister

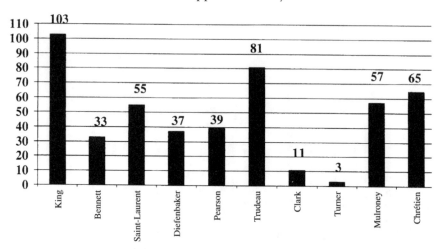

Note: Kim Campbell did not appoint any senators and is therefore not included

Chart A–4: Turnover Rate in the House of Commons and the Senate on
            Election Dates since 1968 (percentages)

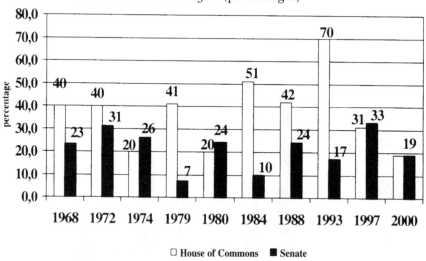

Percentage of members who left the chamber between one election and the next
(e.g.: 23% of Senators left between 1968 and 1972)

Chart A–5: Average Length of Tenure for Members of the Senate and the House of Commons on Election Dates

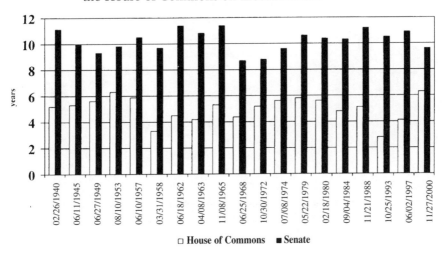

SECTION B — AGE

Chart B–1: Average Age of Senators upon Appointment by Prime Minister

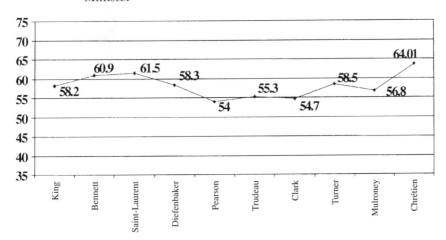

Note: Prime Ministers are listed in order of when they were *first* elected

Kim Campbell did not appoint any senators and therefore is not included

Chart B–2: Average Age of Senators at the Beginning of Each Year

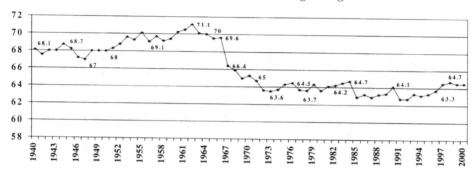

Chart B–3: Age of Senators upon Appointment by PM Trudeau,
            PM Mulroney, and PM Chrétien

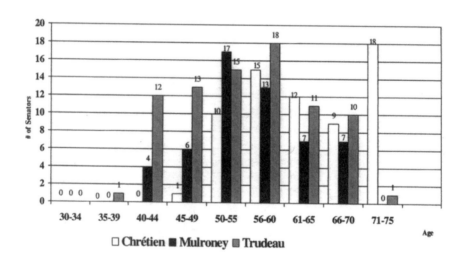

Chart B–4: Breakdown of Prime Minister Chrétien's Sixty-Five
Appointments by Age

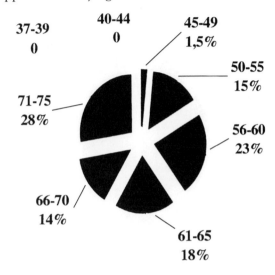

37-39
0

40-44
0

45-49
1,5%

50-55
15%

71-75
28%

56-60
23%

66-70
14%

61-65
18%

Chart B–5: Breakdown of Prime Minister Mulroney's Fifty-Seven
Appointments by Age

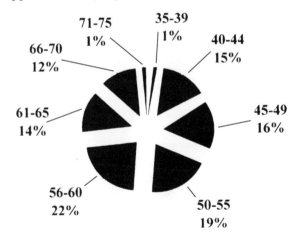

71-75
1%

35-39
1%

66-70
12%

40-44
15%

61-65
14%

45-49
16%

56-60
22%

50-55
19%

Chart B–6: Breakdown of Prime Minister Trudeau's Eighty-One Appointments by Age

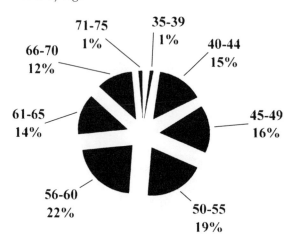

SECTION C − SOCIETAL DIVERSITY

Chart C–1: Visible Minorities in the House of Commons and the Senate at the 27 November 2000 Election

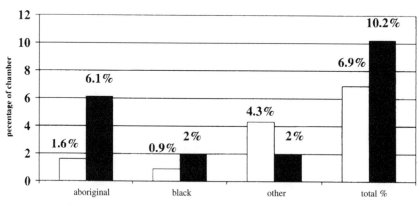

327

Chart C–2: Women in Canadian Parliament (percentage)

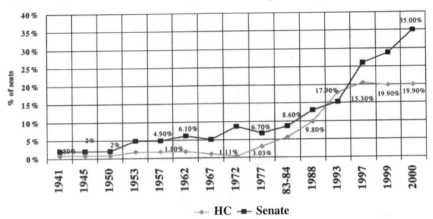

— HC — Senate

Note: Currently 35% of the Senate (out of 97 total members) are women and 19% of the House (out of 301 total members) are women as of 22 October 2000

SECTION D — PUBLIC OFFICE

Chart D–1: Senators Who Had Been Elected to Public Office Prior to Appointment to the Senate, 1970

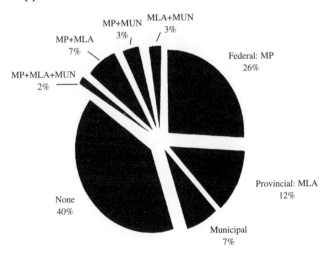

Note: Elected to city council, to a provincial legislature, to the House of Commons, or to multiple offices

Chart D–2: Senators Who Had Been Elected to Public Office Prior to Being Appointed to the Senate, 1980

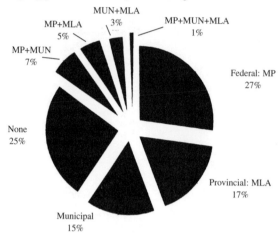

Note: Elected to city council, to a provincial legislature, to the House of Commons, or to multiple offices

Chart D–3: Senators Who Had Been Elected to Public Office Prior to Being Appointed to the Senate, 1990

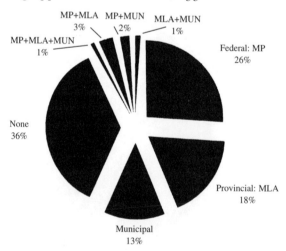

Note: Elected to city council, to a provincial legislature, to the House of Commons, or to multiple offices

Chart D–4: Senators Who Had Been Elected to Public Office Prior to
          Being Appointed to the Senate, 2000

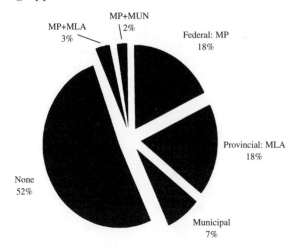

MP+MUN
2%

MP+MLA
3%

Federal: MP
18%

Provincial: MLA
18%

None
52%

Municipal
7%

Note: Elected to city council, to a provincial legislature, to the House of Commons,
or to multiple offices

Bibliography

ARTICLES AND MONOGRAPHS

Ajzenstat, Janet. *The Political Thought of Lord Durham.* Kingston and Montreal: McGill-Queen's University Press, 1988.

Ajzenstat, Janet, Paul Romney, Ian Gentles, and William D. Gairdner, eds. *Canada's Founding Debates.* Toronto: Stoddart, 1999.

Alberta. Legislative Assembly. Select Special Committee on Senate Reform. *Report of the Alberta Select Special Committee on Senate Reform.* Chairman, Dennis Anderson, S.l.: s.n.; Edmonton, AB: Clerk's Office [distributor], 1985.

Alen, A. and R. Ergec. *La Belgique fédérale après la quatrième réforme de l'État de 1993.* 2e éd. Brusells: Ministère des Affaires étrangères, du Commerce extérieur et de la coopération au développement, 1998.

Archer, Jeffrey and Graham Maddox. "The 1975 Constitutional Crisis in Australia," in *Government, Politics and Power in Australia: An Introductory Reader, 3rd Ed.* Dennis Woodward, Andrew Parkin, and John Summers, eds. Melbourne, Australia: Longman Cheshire, 1985.

Archer, Keith et al., eds. *Parameters of Power, Canada's Political Institutions.* Toronto: Nelson, 1995.

Atkinson, Michael M. and David C. Docherty. "Moving Right Along: The Roots of Amateurism in the Canadian House of Commons," in *Canadian Journal of Political Science*, vol. 25, no.2, June 1992: 459–80.

Aubry, Jack. "Trio in Cabinet Quietly Hope to Scrap Senate," in *The Montreal Gazette*, 31 May 1999: A9.

Aucoin, Peter. "Accountability: The Key to Restoring Public Confidence in Government," in *Timlin Conference*, Saskatoon, University of Saskatchewan, 6 November 1997.

Audcent, Mark. *The Senate Veto: Opinion of the Law Clerk and Parliamentary Counsel.* Ottawa: Senate of Canada, 1999.

Bagehot, Sir Walter. *The English Constitution.* Paul Smith, ed. Cambridge: Cambridge University Press, 2001.

Bailey, Sir Kenneth. *Cambridge History of the British Empire*, vol. 7. Cambridge University Press, 1933.

Bakvis, Herman and William M. Chandler, eds. *Federalism and the Role of the State*, Toronto: University of Toronto Press, 1987.

Barber, Katherine. *The Canadian Oxford Dictionary*, suppl. Toronto: Oxford University Press, 2001.

Barnhart, Gordon. *Administrative Relationship of the Clerk of the Senate to the Committee on Internal Economy, Budgets, and Administration*. February 1990. (Unpublished.)

Basta, L. *Federalism and Multiethnic States: The Case of Switzerland*. Fribourg, Switzerland: Institut du Fédéralisme Suisse, 1996.

Beaudoin, Gérald, *Le Fédéralisme au Canada*. Wilson & Lafleur, 2000.

Bellavance, Joël-Denis. "Senator Files Defamation Suit against Bloc MP," in *National Post*, 12 May 1999: A8.

Bédard, Pierre. *Le Canadien*, Novembre 1806.

Blache Pierre. "Droit de vote, représentation, démocratie, égalité et citoyenneté," in *Le Devoir*, 13 December 2001: A7.

Bogdanor, Vernon. *Power to the People: A Guide to Constitutional Reform*. London: Victor Gollancz, 1997.

Bogdanor, Vernon. *Devolution in the United Kingdom*. Oxford and New York: Oxford University Press, 1999.

Bonenfant, Jean-Charles, *La Vocation manquée du Sénat canadien*. Les Cahiers des Dix, vol. 37. Québec City: Éditions Laliberté, 1972.

Bourinot, John G. *Federal Government in Canada*. Baltimore: Johns Hopkins University Press, 1889.

Bourinot, John G. "The Canadian Dominion and the Proposed Australian Commonwealth: A Study in Comparative Politics," in *Transactions of the Royal Society of Canada*, section 2,1895.

Brady, Alexander. *Democracy in the Dominions: A Comparative Study in Institutions*. Toronto: University of Toronto Press, 1958.

British Columbia. *Reform of the Canadian Senate*, British Columbia's constitutional proposals: papers, no. 3. Victoria, BC: Queen's Printer, 1978.

Brown, Jim. "MPs Plan Demonstration against the Senate on June 8," in *The Montreal Gazette*, 28 May 1999: A10.

Browne, G.P. *Documents on the Confederation of British North America: A Compilation, Based on Sir Joseph Pope's Confederation Documents, Supplemented by Other Official Material*. Carleton Library Series, Toronto: McClelland et Stewart, 1969.

Burke, Edmund. "Speech to the Electors of Bristol" (3 November 1774), in *The Works of the Right Honourable Edmund Burke*. 6 vols. London: Henry G. Bohn, 1854–56.

Burns, R.M. "Second Chambers: German Experience and Canadian Needs," in *Canadian Federalism: Myth or Reality?* J. Peter Meekison, ed. Toronto: Methuen, 1977, 188–215.

Campbell, Colin. *The Canadian Senate: A Lobby from Within*. Toronto: Macmillan, 1978.

Canada. *La Chambre de la fédération*. Cabinet du ministre d'État chargé des relations fédérales-provinciales. Ottawa: Queen's Printer, 1978.

Canada. *Constitutional Reform: House of the Federation*. Ottawa: Government of Canada, 1978. (Minister responsible was the Hon. Marc Lalonde, Minister of State for Federal-Provincial Relations.)

Canada. *Parliamentary Debates on the Subject of the Confederation of the British North American Provinces*. 3rd Session, 8th Provincial Parliament of Canada, Hunter, Rose & Co. Parliament Printers, Quebec, 1865 (photographic reproduction of the original, Ottawa, 1951).

Canada. *Royal Commission on the Economic Union and Development Prospects for Canada*, Report. Ottawa: Queen's Printer, 1985. (Macdonald Commission Report.)

Canada. *Shaping Canada's Future Together: Proposals*. Ottawa: Government of Canada, Privy Council Office, Minister Responsible for Constitutional Affairs, 1991. (Minister was the Hon. Joe Clark.)

Canada. *To Build the Future of Canada Together: Proposals*. Ottawa: Minister for the Provisioning and Canada Services, 1991.

Canada. *Consensus Report on the Constitution: Charlottetown*. Queen's Printer, 28 August 1992.

Canada. *Draft Legal Text* [of the Consensus Report on the Constitution]. Ottawa: Government of Canada, 1992.

Canada. "Responsive Institutions – Fact Sheet," in *Our Future Together: Notre avenir ensemble*. Ottawa: Government of Canada, 1992.

Canada. Constitutional Conference (1968). *The Constitution and the People of Canada: An Approach to the Objective of Confederation, the Rights of People and the Institutions of Government*, Ottawa: Queen's Printer, 1969.

Canada. Department of Finance. *Reforming Canada's Financial Services Sector: A Framework for the Future*. Ottawa: Department of Finance, 1999.

Canada. Department of Justice. *Reform of the Senate: A Discussion Paper*. Presented to the Special Joint Committee of the Senate and House of Commons on Senate Reform by the Hon. Mark MacGuigan, Minister of Justice. Ottawa: Government of Canada, 1983.

Canada. Legal and Constitutional Affairs Committee. *Report on Certain Aspects of the Canadian Constitution*. Ottawa: Queen's Printer, 1980. (Lamontagne Report.)

Canada. Legislature. *Parliamentary Debates on the Subject of Confederation of the British North American provinces, 3rd session, 8th provincial Parliament of Canada*. Québec: Hunter, Rose & Co., 1865.

Canada. Library of Parliament. *A Review of Senate Committee Studies*. Ottawa: Parliamentary Research Branch of the Library of Parliament, December 1999.

Canada. Parliament. *Report of the Special Joint Committee of the Senate and of the House of Commons on a Renewed Canada*. Ottawa: Queen's Printer, 28 February 1992. (Beaudoin-Dobbie Report.)

Canada. Parliament. House of Commons. *Debates of the House of Commons*, 32nd Parliament, 1st Session, vol. 7: 7471–6. Ottawa, 19 February 1981.

Canada. Parliament. Senate. *Debates of the Senate*. 33rd Parliament, 2nd session, vol. 2: 1776. Ottawa, 2 September 1987. (Senator L. Murray.)

Canada. Parliament. Senate. *Debates of the Senate.* 34th Parliament, 2nd session, vol. 2, 1146–7. Ottawa, 14 February 1990. (Special Committee of the Senate on Bill C–21, *An Act to amend the Unemployment Insurance Act and the Employment and Immigration Department and Commission Act.* Third and Final Report.)

Canada. Parliament. Senate. *Debates of the Senate.* 34th Parliament, 3rd session, vol. 4: 3368. Ottawa, September 3 June 1993. (Senator F. MacDonald.)

Canada. Parliament. Senate. *Debates of the Senate.* 36th Parliament, 2nd session, vol. 138, no. 38, Ottawa, 23 March 2000. (Senator J.B. Boudreau.)

Canada. Parliament. Senate. *Debates of the Senate.* 37th Parliament, 1st session, vol. 139, no. 12, Ottawa, 1 March 2001. (Senator J. Grafstein.)

Canada. Parliament. Senate. *Debates of the Senate.* 37th Parliament, 1st session, vol. 139, no. 15, Ottawa, 17 April 2002. (Senator S. Joyal.)

Canada. Parliament. Senate. *Debates of the Senate.* 37th parliament, 1st session, vol. 139, no. 32, Ottawa, 3 May 2001. (Senator S. Carstairs.)

Canada. Parliament. Senate. *The Special Joint Committee of the Senate and of the House of Commons on the Constitution of Canada final report,* Ottawa: Queen's Printer, 1972. (Molgat-MacGuigan report.)

Canada. Parliament. Senate. *Joint Senate/House Committee Report On Senate Reform.* Ottawa: Queen's Printer, January 1984. (Molgat-Cosgrove Report.)

Canada. Parliament. Senate. *Senate Committees Activities and Expenditures, Annual Report 1997–1998.* (Prepared by the Committees and Private Legislation Directorate.) Ottawa, 1998. www.parl.gc.ca/36/1/parlbus/commbus/senate/com-f/annual-f/repannual98-f.htm [10 September 2002].

Canada. Parliament. Senate. *Senate Committees Activities and Expenditures, Annual Report 1999–2000.* (Prepared by the Committees and Private Legislation Directorate.) www.parl.gc.ca/36/2/parlbus/commbus/senate/com-F/annu2000-f/annualoopart1-f.htm#FINANCES_NATIONALES [10 September 2002].

Canada. Parliament. Senate. *Senate Report,* vol. 1, no 1. Ottawa: January 2001.

Canada. Parliament. Senate. *The Role of Senate Committees in Formulating Public Policy.* November 1999. www.parl.gc.ca/36/2/parlbus/commbus/senate/com-F/pub-F/public-f.htm [10 September 2002].

Canada. Parliament. Senate. Committees and Private Legislative Directorate. *A Legislative and Historical Overview of the Senate of Canada,* revised, 1989. Third and Final report of the Special Committee of the Senate on Bill C–21. Ottawa: Queens Printer, 31 March 1993.

Canada, Parliament. Senate. Standing Committe on Aboriginal Peoples. *Proceedings of the Standing Senate Committee on Aboriginal Peoples,* 2nd session, 36th Parliament, no. 7, 23 March 2000. [Ottawa: The Committee, 1997.]

Canada. Parliament. Senate. The Standing Committee on Rules, Procedures and the Rights of Parliament, Report of the Committee. *Tenth Report.* 5 March 2002. (Brief of Prof. Smith on Bill S–34.)

Canada. Parliament. Senate. The Standing Senate Committee on National Finance. *Program Evaluation Systems in the Government of Canada,* Chair: Fernand E. LeBlanc, January 1991.

Canada. Parliament. Senate. The Standing Senate Committee on National Finance. *Second Report.* 2 December 1999.

Canada. Parliament. Senate. The Standing Senate Committee on National Finance. *Third Report.* 23 March 2000.

Canada. Parliament. Senate. The Standing Senate Committee on National Finance. *Third Report.* 22 March 2001. www.parl.gc.ca/37/1/parlbus/ commbus/senate/com-f/fina-f/rep-f/rep03mar01-f.htm [10 September 2002].

Canada. Parliament. Senate. The Standing Senate Committee on Social Affairs, Science and Technology. *Study on the State of the Health Care System in Canada. Work Plan. (August 2001).* www.parl.gc.ca/37/1/parlbus/commbus/senate/Com-e/SOCI-E/press-e/work_plan-e.ht m [10 September 2002].

Canada. Senate (Commons). *Proceedings and Evidence of the Special Joint Committee of the Senate and the House of Commons on Senate Reform.* 18 October 1983, vol. 30.

Canada. The Task Force on National Unity. *A Future Together: Observations and Recommendations.* January 1979 (co-president, Jean-Luc Pepin; co-president, John P. Robarts).

Canada Gazette, part 1, EXTRA, vol. 136, no. 1, 13 March 2002.

Canada West Foundation. *Taking a Look: Public Opinion in Alberta and Canada on Senate Reform,* September 1998. www.cwf.ca/abcalcwf/doc.nsf/publications

Canadian News Facts, vol. 22, no. 14, 4 August 1988.

Canadian News Facts, vol. 24, no. 18, 21 October 1990.

Caro, Robert A. *Master of the Senate: The Years of Lyndon Johnson,* New York: Alfred A. Knopf, 1982.

Central Intelligence Agency, *The World Factbook 2002.* Washington, DC. www.cia.gov/cia/publications/factbook

Charbonneau, Guy. "A Second Chamber; Not a Secondary One," in *Canadian Parliamentary Review,* no. 8, 1985–86: 16–18.

Cloutier, Edmond, ed. *Dominion Provincial and Interprovincial Conferences from 1887 to 1926,* Ottawa: Imprimeur du Roi, 1951.

Cobb, Chris. "MostWant to Vote on Judges: 'There needs to be some review', Argues Alliance Critic," in *National Post:* A1. (Environics poll released 4 February 2002.)

Cobbett, William, ed. *The Parliamentary History of England, 1066–1803,* 36 vols., London: T.C. Hansard, 1806–1820.

Codding, G.A. *The Federal Government of Switzerland.* Boston: Houghton Mifflin, 1961.

Cody, Howard "Lessons from Australia in Canadian Senate Reform," in *Canadian Parliamentary Review,* vol. 18, no.2, 1995: 19–25.

Cohen, Andrew. "Renegade Senators Deserve Accolades." *Financial Post,* June 18, 1993.

Constitution Unit. *Checks and Balances in Single Chamber Parliaments: A Comparative Study.* London: Constitution Unit, School of Public Policy, 1998.

Constitution Unit. "Lords Reform Stage Two: Wakeham or What?" in *Monitor: The Constitution Unit Bulletin*, no. 17, December 2001: 1–2.

Coonan, Helen. "Safeguard or Handbrake on Democracy?" in *Deadlock or Democracy?* Brian Costar, ed. Sydney: University of New South Wales Press, 2000, 12–28.

Coyne Andrew. "The Second Charter of Rights," in *National Post*, 8 February 2002: A15.

Coyne, Andrew. "House of Commons – Rest In Peace," in *National Post*, 1 December 2001.

Craig, Gerald, ed. *Lord Durham's Report: An Abridgement*. Toronto: McClelland and Stewart, The Carleton Library, 1968.

Craven, G. "The States – Decline, Fall or What?" in *Australian Federation: Towards the Second Century*. G. Craven, ed. Melbourne. Australia: Melbourne University Press, 1992.

Crommelin, Michael. "Senate Reform: Is the Game Worth the Candle?" in *UBC Law Review*, vol. 23, no. 2, 1989: 197–213.

Davey, Keith. *The Rainmaker: A Passion for Politics*. Toronto: Stoddard, 1986.

Dawson, R. MacGregor. *The Government of Canada*. 5th Ed. Norman Ward, ed. Toronto: University of Toronto Press, 1979.

Delacourt, Susan. "Liberal-Led Senate Throws UI Reforms Back in Tories Lap," in *Globe and Mail*, 15 February 1990: A1.

Delacourt, Susan. "More Say at Committee Level, Reports Says," in *Ottawa Citizen*, 1 May 2000: A4.

Department of Justice. Commissioner for Federal Judicial Affairs. *A New Judicial Appointment Process*. Ottawa: 1988.

Descoteaux, Bernard. "Un Nécessaire contrepoid," in *Le Devoir*, 1 November 1999: A8.

Dicey, Albert Venn. *Introduction to the Study of the Law of the Constitution, 10th Ed.* London: Macmillam, 1959.

Dobell, Peter C. "The Senate: New Found Levers of Power?" in *Parliamentary Government*, vol. 8, no. 2, 1988): 14–17.

Dobell, Peter C. "The New Senate," in *Policy Options*, vol. 10, no. 3, April 1989: 29.

Dobell, Peter C. "Reforming Parliamentary Practice: The Views of MPs," in *Policy Matters*, vol. 1, no. 9, 2000: 154.

Dobell, Peter C. "An Elected Senate: Relations with the House of Commons," in *Parliamentary Government*, no. 41, June 1992: 18–21.

Docherty, David C. *Mr. Smith Goes to Ottawa: Life in the House of Commons*. Vancouver: University of British Columbia Press, 1997.

Le Droit, "Dion dit non au Sénat élu," 6 July 1998.

Duchacek, I. *Comparative Federalism: The Territorial Dimension of Politics. Revised Edition*. Lanham: University Press of America, Center for the Study of Federation, 1987.

Dunsmuir, Mollie. *The Senate: Appointments Under Section 26 of the Constitution Act, 1867*. Ottawa: Research Branch, Library of Parliament, August 1990.

Elkins, D. *Beyond Sovereignty: Territorial and Political Economy in the Twenty-First Century*. Toronto: University of Toronto Press, 1995.

Elton, David. "The Charlottetown Accord Senate: Effective or Emasculated?" in *The Charlottetown Accord, the Referendum, and the Future of Canada.* Kenneth McRoberts and Patrick J. Monahan, eds. Toronto: University of Toronto Press, 1993.

Harry Evans, Clerk of the Senate. "Accountability versus Government Control: The Effect of Proportional Representation," in *Deadlock or Democracy?* Brian Costar, ed. Sydney: University of New South Wales Press, 2000, 48–57.

Richard F. Fenno, Jr., *The United States Senate: A Bicameral Perspective.* Washington: American Enterprise Institute for Public Policy Research, 1982.

Fife, Robert. "Martin Vows to 'empower the MP': Free Votes, More Money: Plan Seen as Rebuke to Concentration of Power by Chretien," in *National Post*, 26 July 2002, A1.

Fink, Zera. *The Classical Republicans: An Essay in the Recovery of a Pattern of Thought in Seventeenth-Century England, 2nd Ed.* Evanston, IL: Northwestern University Press, 1962.

Flanagan, Thomas. "The Staying Power of the Status Quo: Collective Choices in Canada's Parliament after Morgentaler," in *Canadian Journal of Political Science*, vol. 30, no. 1, March 1997: 31–53.

Flanagan, Thomas. *Game Theory and Canadian Politics.* Toronto: University of Toronto Press, 1998.

Fleiner, T. and N. Schmitt, eds. *Vers une Constitution européenne: L'Europe et les expériences fédérales.* Fribourg: Institut du Fédéralisme Fribourg Suisse, 1996.

Fondation Bertelsmann. "Disentanglement 2005. Ten Reform Proposals for Better Governance in the German Federal System," in Bertelsmann Comission, *Governance & Constitutional Policy.* Gütersloh: Bertelsmann Stiftung Publications, 2000. www.bertelsmann-stiftung.de/publisher.cfm?lan=EN&nId=60 [8 August 2002].

Forsey, Eugene. "Appointment of Extra Senators under Section 26 of the British North America Act," *Canadian Journal of Economics and Political Science*, no. 12, 1946: 159–67.

Forsey, Eugene. "The Canadian Senate," in *The Parliamentarian*, vol. 63, no 4, October 1982: 276.

Forsey, Eugene. *Speech to the Canadian Bar Association*, Halifax, 19 August 1985. (Unpublished.)

Forsey, Eugene. *A Life on the Fringe: The Memoirs of Eugene Forsey.* Toronto: Oxford University Press,1990.

Forsey, Eugene. "No-More than a Triple E Senate is Needed," in *Politics: Canada.* *7th Ed.* Paul Fox and Graham White, eds. Toronto: McGraw-Hill Ryerson, 1991.

Forsey, Eugene and G.C. Eglinton. *The Question of Confidence in Responsible Government,* 1985. (Unpublished.)

Forum des Sénats du Monde. *Le Bicamérisme dans le monde: situation et perspectives.* Paris: Service des relations internationales du Sénat, 2000.

Franks, C.E.S. *The Parliament of Canada.* Toronto: University of Toronto Press, 1987.

Franks, C.E.S. "Representation and Policy-Making in Canada," in *Canada's Centu-ry: Governance in a Maturing Society: Essays in the Honour of John Meisel.* C.E.S. Franks, J.E. Hodgetts, O.P. Dwivedi, Doug Williams, and V. Seymour Wilson, eds. Montreal: McGill-Queen's University Press, 1995.

Franks, C.E.S. "Constraints on the Operations and Reform of Parliamentary Com-mittees in Canada," in *The Changing Roles of Parliamentary Committees: Working Papers on Comparative Legislative Studies.* Lawrence D. Longley and Attila Agh, eds. Appleton Wisconsin: Research Committee of Legislative Specialists, Inter-national Political Science Association, 1997, 199–207.

Franks, C.E.S. *Parliament, Intergovernmental Relations and National Unity.* Kingston, Ontario: Institute of Intergovernmental Relations, Queen's University, 1997. (A study originally prepared for the Privy Council Office, 1997.)

Franks, C.E.S. "Not Dead Yet, But Should it Be Resurrected? The Canadian Sen-ate," in *Senates: Bicameralism in the Contemporary World.* Samuel C. Patterson and Anthony Mughan, eds. Columbus, Ohio: Ohio State University Press, 1998, 120–61.

Frémont, Jacques and François Boudreault. "Supraconstitutionnalité canadienne et sécession du Québec," in *N.J.C.L.*, no. 8, 1997: 163. http://canada.justice.gc.ca/fr/ps/const/replyqa5.html [30 September 2002].

Frith, Royce. Letter to the Editor of the *Globe and Mail,* 14 May 1990.

Frith, Royce. *Hoods on the Hill: How Mulroney and His Gang Rammed the GST through Parliament and Down Our Throats.* Toronto: Coach House Press,1991.

Gagnon Lysiane. "Le Syndrome Dutoit-Boilard," in *La Presse,* 25 July 2002: A13.

Galligan, B. "An Elected Senate for Canada? The Australian Model," in *Journal of Canadian Studies,* vol. 20, no. 4, Winter 1985–86: 77–98.

Garner, J. *The Franchise and Politics in British North America, 1755–1867.* Toronto: University of Toronto Press, 1969.

Garran, Sir Robert. *The Cambridge History of the British Empire, Vol. 7, Part 1.* Cam-bridge University Press, 1933.

Gessel, Paul. "Confronting the Red Chamber," in *Maclean's,* vol. 100, 24 August 1987: 18–19.

Gessel, Paul. "Ending a Bitter Stalemate," in *Maclean's,* vol. 100, 30 November 1987: 19.

Gibbins, Roger. *Regionalism: Territorial Politics in Canada and the United States.* Toronto: Butterworths and Co., 1982.

Gibbins, Roger. *Conflict & Unity – An Introduction to Canadian Political Life. 3rd Ed.* Scarborough, ON: Nelson Canada, 1994.

Gigantès, Philippe D. and Susan Erlington. *The Thin Book Reforming the Senate.* Ottawa: Gigantès, 1998.

Gillmor Don and Pierre Turgeon. *Le Canada: une histoire populaire.* Montreal: Éditions Fides, 2000.

Gosford, Lord. "Report of 1837 on British North America," in *British Sessional Papers*, House of Commons, vol. 24.

Goudappel, F.J. *Powers and Control Mechanisms in European Federal Systems: A Comparative Approach to the Form of Government of the European Community.* Rotterdam: Sanders Instituut, 1997.

Grafstein, Jerahmiel. "The Mystery of National Caucus," *Allan J. MacEachen Conference 2001,* St. Francis Xavier University, 2001. (Unpublished.)

Great Britain. *Press Reaction on the Report of the Royal Commission on the Reform of the House of Lords, A House for the Future,* London, Central Office of Information, 2000.

Great Britain. *Strengthening Parliament: The Report of the Commission to Strengthen Parliament.* London, Conservative Party, 2000.

Great Britain. *The House of Lords: Completing the Reform.* A Government White Paper. 7 Novembre 2001.

Great Britain. *The Second Chamber: Continuing The Reform: Fifth Report Of Session 2001-2002.* Report and Proceedings of the Committee / House of Commons. UK: Public Administration Select Committee, 2002.

Great Britain. Parliament. House of Commons. British Sessional Papers. *Report of the Commissioners Appointed to Inquire into the Grievances Complained of in Lower Canada: Presented to Parliament by His Majesty's Command,* vol. 24: 6 [London: anon., 1837].

Greene, Richard. "The Information Explosion and the Senate," in *Canadian Parliamentary Review,* vol. 9, no. 4, Winter 1986–87: 19–21.

Hamilton, Alexander, James Madison, and John Jay. *The Federalist.* Cambridge: Harvard University Press, 1961.

Heard, Andrew. *Canadian Constitutional Conventions: The Marriage of Law and Politics.* Toronto: Oxford University Press Canada, 1991.

Hiebert, Janet L. *Charter Conflicts,* Montreal: McGill-Queen's University Press, 2002.

Hogg Peter. *Constitutional Law of Canada, 3rd Ed.* Toronto: Carswell, 1992.

Holmes, J. et C. Sharman. *The Australian Federal System.* Sydney and Boston: George Allen and Unwin, 1977.

House of Lords. House of Lords Appointment Commission. *Annex A: Criteria Guiding the Assessment of Nominations For Non-Party Political Members Of The House Of Lords.* www.houseoflordsappointmentscommission.gov.uk/criteria.htm [14 August 2002].

Howe, Paul and David Northrup, "Strengthening Canadian Democracy: The Views of Canadians," in *Policy Matters* (Institute for Research on Public Policy), vol. 1, no. 5, July 2000: 52.

Howse, Robert and Alissa Malkin. "Canadians Are a Sovereign People: How the Supreme Court Should Approach the Reference on Quebec Secession," in *Canadian Bar Review,* vol. 76, 1997.

Hoy, Claire. *Nice Work: The Continuing Scandal of Canada's Senate.* Toronto: McClelland and Stewart, 1999.

Hurley, James Ross. *Amending Canada's Constitution: History, Process, Problems and Prospects.* Ottawa: Canada Communications Group Publishing, 1996.

Jackson, Robert J. "Remarks to the Special Joint Committee of the Senate and

House of Commons on Senate Reform," in *Contemporary Canadian Politics: Readings and Notes*. Robert J. Jackson, Doreen Jackson, and Nicholas Baxter-Moore, eds. Scarborough: Prentice-Hall Canada, 1987, 178–82.

Jackson, Robert J. et al. "The Senate,"in *Politics in Canada: Culture, Institutions, Behaviour, and Public Policy*. Robert J. Jackson, Doreen Jackson, and Nicholas Baxter-Moore, eds. Toronto: Prentice-Hall, 1986, 340–51.

Jaconelli, Joseph, "Majority Rule and Special Majorities," in *Public Law*, 1989: 587–616.

Janda, Richard. *Re-Balancing the Federation Through Senate Reform: Another Look at the Bundesrat*. Background studies of the York University constitutional reform project, no. 11. Toronto: York University Centre for Public Law and Public Policy, 1992.

Jeffery, C., ed. *Recasting German Federalism: the legacies of unification*. London; New York: Pinter, 1999.

Johnson, Brian D. "Lessons of the Red Chamber: inside the Senate," in *Equinox*, no. 16, July/August 1984: 26–47.

Joyal, Serge. "The Senate: The Earth Is Not Flat," in *Cité Libre*, February 1999.

Joyal, Serge. *Analysis of the Work and Reports of committees of the Senate: 1984–1999*. Prepared by the Research Group of Senator Serge Joyal. Ottawa: Parliament of Canada, Summer 1999.

Joyal Serge. *Legal, Constitutional and Political Imperatives to Senate Reform*. Ottawa: The Senate of Canada, February 2000.

Joyal, Serge. "The Senate You Thought You Knew," speech by Serge Joyal to a meeting of the *Canadian Political Science Association*, 29 July 2000.

Juberias, C.F. "A House in Search of a Role: The Senado of Spain," in *Senates: Bicameralism in the Contemporary World*. S.C. Patterson and A. Mughan, eds. Columbus, Ohio: Ohio State University Press, 1999, 260–300.

Kelly, James. "Guarding the Constitution: Parliament and Judicial Roles under the Charter of Rights," in *Canada: The State of the Federation, 2002*, Harvey Lazar, Peter Meekison, and Hamish Telford, eds. Montreal: McGill-Queen's University Press, 2002.

Kent, Tom. *A Public Purpose: An Experience of Liberal Opposition and Canadian Government*. Kingston: McGill-Queen's University Press, 1988.

Kilger, B., ed. *Report of the Special Committee on the Modernization and Improvement of the Procedures of the House of Commons*. June 2001.

Knowles, Valerie. *First Person: A Biography of Cairine Wilson, Canada's First Woman Senator*. Toronto: Dundurn Press, 1988.

Kriesi, H. *Le Système politique suisse, 2e éd*. Paris: Economica, 1998.

Kunz, F. *The Modern Senate of Canada, 1925–1963: A Re-appraisal*. Toronto: University of Toronto Press, 1965.

Lamey, Andy. "The Charter Rescues Equality from the Mob," in *National Post*, 16 July 2002: A18.

Landau, Martin. "Federalism, Redundancy and System Reliability," in *Publius*, vol. 3, no. 2, Fall 1973: 173–96.

Landes, Ronald G. "The Legislative Branch of Government: Representation and

Legitimation," in *The Canadian Polity: A Comparative Introduction.* Scarborough: Prentice-Hall, 1983, 150–95.

Lapointe, Renaude. "The Role of the Canadian Senate," in *Journal of Parliamentary Information,* vol. 21, no. 4, October-December 1975: 596–606.

Lazar, Harvey, Peter Meekison, and Hamish Telford, eds. *Canada: The State of Federation, 2002,* Montreal: McGill-Queen's University Press, 2002.

Leclerc, Wilbrod. "A 'Useless' Senate Rebuffs Transport in Examination of the Maritime Code Act," in *Optimum,* no. 9, Summer 1978: 46–50.

Lee, Frances E. and B.I. Openheimer. *Sizing Up the Senate: The Unequal Consequences of Equal Representation.* Chicago, IL: University of Chicago Press, 1999.

Lemco, Jonathan and Peter Regenstrief. "Let the Senate Be: There Is Not Enough Support for the Effort or Cost of Reforming or Abolishing the Senate, which Gives Some Useful Public Service and Usually Knows Its Place," in *Contemporary Canadian Politics: Readings and Notes.* Robert J. Jackson et al., eds. Scarborough: Prentice-Hall, 1987, 183–7.

Leonardy, U. "The Institutional Structures of German Federalism," in *Recasting German Federalism: The Legacies of Unification.* C. Jeffery, ed. New York: Pinter, 1992, 3–22.

Lijphart, Arend. *Democracies: Patterns of Majoritarian and Consensus Government in Twenty-One Countries.* New Haven: Yale University Press, 1984.

Lijphart, Arend. "Bicameralism: Canadian Senate Reform in Comparative Perspective," in *Federalism and the Role of the State.* H. Bakvis and W.M. Chandler, ed. Toronto: University of Toronto Press, 1987.

Lijphart, Arend. "Foreword: 'Cameral Change' and Institutional Conservatism," in *Two Into One: The Politics of National Legislative Cameral Change.* Lawrence D. Longley and David M. Olsen, eds. Boulder: Westview Press, 1991, XI.

Linder, W. *Swiss Democracy: Possible Solutions to Conflict in Multicultural Societies,* New York: St Martin's Press, 1998.

Lindgren, April. "Ethics and the Senate: Sober Second Thoughts on Conflict," in *Ottawa Citizen,* 14 January 1995: B3.

Longley, Lawrence D. and David M. Olsen, eds. *Two Into One: The Politics and Processes of National Legislative Cameral Change.* Boulder: Westview Press, 1991.

Lusztig, Michael. "Federalism and Institutional Design: The Perils and Politics of a Triple-E Senate in Canada," in *Publius,* no. 25, Winter 1995: 35–50.

Lynch-Staunton, John. "The Urgent Need for Parliamentary – Not Just Senate – Reform," in *Canadian Club,* 28 March 2000.

Lynch-Staunton, John. "The Role of the Senate in the Legislative Process," in *Canadian Parliamentary Review,* vol. 23, no. 2, Summer 2000: 10–12.

Mackay, Robert A. *The Unreformed Senate of Canada.* London: Oxford University Press, H. Milford, 1926. (Reprinted Toronto: McClelland and Stewart, 1963.)

Macdonald, John A. Canadian Legislative Assembly, 6 February 1865, in *Canada's Founding Debates.* Janet Ajzenstat et al., eds., 80.

Macdonald, John A. *Parliamentary Debates on the Subject of the Confederation of the British North American Provinces,* 3rd session, 8th Provincial Parliament of Canada, Québec: Hunter, Rose & Co., Parliamentary Printers, 1865, 88.

Macdonald, John A. *House of Commons Debates*, vol. 3, 4th Session: 926 (1 June 1872).

MacGregor, Ian. *A History of Senate Reform in Canada, 1867–1957*. Kingston: Queen's University, 1957. (Unpublished Master's thesis.)

Macpherson, C.B. *The Real World of Democracy*. Ottawa: Canadian Broadcasting Corporation, 1965.

Madison, J., A. Hamilton A. and J. Jay. *The Federalist Papers* [1788]. I. Kramnick, ed. New York: Penguin Books, 1987.

Manfredi, Christopher P. "La Charte et le caractère distinct du Québec." in *Cité Libre*, vol. 38, no. 4, Autumn 2000.

March, Roman R. *The Myth of Parliament*. Scarborough: Prentice-Hall of Canada, 1974.

Marissal, Vincent. "Le Sénat a trop de pouvoirs, soutient l'ex-sénateur Hébert," in *La Presse*, 13 August 1998: B1.

Marleau, Robert and Camille Montpetit. *House of Commons Procedure and Practice*. Ottawa: House of Commons; Montreal: Cheneliere/Mcgraw-Hill, 2000.

Marsden, Lorna R. "Doing Its Thing – Providing 'Sober Second Thought': The Canadian Senate, 1984–1990," in *Politics: Canada. 7th Ed.* Paul Fox and Graham White, eds. Toronto: McGraw-Hill Ryerson, 1991, 446–54.

Marsh, Ian. "Opening up the Policy Process," in *Representation and Institutional Change: 50 years of Proportional Representation* (Papers of Parliament, no. 34). Marian Sawer and Sarah Miskin, eds. Canberra: Department of the Senate, 1999, 187–97.

Marshall, Geoffrey, ed. *Ministerial Responsibility*. Oxford, UK: Oxford University Press, 1989.

Massicotte, Louis, and Françoise Coulombe. *Senate Reform*. Ottawa: Research Branch, Library of Parliament, April 1988.

Mastias J. and J. Grangé. *Les secondes chambres du parlement en Europe occidentale*. Paris: Economica, 1987.

McArthur, Duncan. "A Canadian Experiment with an Elective Upper Chamber," in *Transactions of the Royal Society of Canada*, vol. 24, 1930, section 2, 86–7.

McCauley, Janet Marie. *The Senate of Canada: Maintenance of a Second Chamber through Functional Adaptability*. Ann Arbor, Michigan, University Microfilms International: 1983. (Thesis (PhD) Pennsylvania State University, 1983.)

McConnell, H. "The Case for a 'Triple E' Senate," in *Queen's Quarterly*, no. 95, Autumn 1988: 683–97.

McCormick, Peter. "Canada Needs a Triple E Senate," in *Politics: Canada. 7th Ed.* Paul Fox and Graham White, eds. Toronto: McGraw-Hill Ryerson, 1991, 435–9.

McCormick, P., E.C. Manning, and G. Gibson. *Regional Representation: The Canadian Partnership: A Task Force Report*. Calgary: Canada West Foundation, 1981.

McGee, Thomas d'Arcy. *Notes sur les gouvernements fédéraux passés et présents*. Saint-Hyacinthe: des Presses à Pouvoir du "Courrier de Saint-Hyacinthe," 1865.

McInnes, David. *Taking It to the Hill: The Complete Guide to Appearing before (and Surviving) Parliamentary Committees*. Ottawa: University of Ottawa Press, 1999.

McMenemy, John. "The Senate as an Instrument of Business and Party," in

Politics: Canada. 7th Ed. Paul Fox and Graham White, eds. Toronto: McGraw-Hill Ryerson, 1991, 454–63.

McMurtry, Roy. "The Role of the Courts in Turbulent Times," in *Canadian Club*, 3December 2001.

McNairn, Jeffrey L. *The Capacity to Judge, Public Opinion and Deliberative Democracy in Upper Canada, 1791–1854.* Toronto: University of Toronto Press, 2000.

McRae, K.D. *Conflict and Compromise in Multilingual Societies.* Waterloo, ON: Wilfrid Laurier University Press, 1983.

McRoberts, Kenneth and Patrick J. Monahan, eds. *The Charlottetown Accord, the Referendum, and the Future of Canada,* Toronto: University of Toronto Press, 1993.

Mill, John Stuart. *"Considerations on Representative Government"* (1861), in *Essays on Politics and Society by John Stuart Mill.* J.M. Robson, ed. Toronto: University of Toronto Press, 1977.

Mill, John Stuart. *On Liberty: Representative Government, The Sujection of Women: Three Essays.* London: Oxford University Press, 1960.

Milnes, Arthur and Rob Torip. "Survey 'sadden' Chretien camp," in *The Kingston Whig-Standard,* 30 July 2002.

Montgomery, Charlotte. "No Action Yet on Liberal « Rejects » Tory Plan to Reform Senate Languish," in *The Globe and Mail,* 12 December 1985: A3.

Moore, Christopher. *1867: How the Fathers Made a Deal.* Toronto: McClelland et Stewart, 1997.

Morgan, Edmund S. *Inventing the People: The Rise of Popular Sovereignty in England and America.* New York: Norton, 1988.

Morin, Jacques-Yvan and José Woerling. *Les Constitutions du Canada et du Québec, tome premier, 2e édition.* Éditions Thémis, Montreal, 1994.

O'Brien, Gary. "Legislative Influence of Parliamentary Committees: The Case of the Senate of Canada, 1984–1991," A paper presented to the Annual Meeting of the Canadian Political Science Association, Montreal Quebec, June 1995.

Olson, David, and C.E.S. Franks, eds. *Representation and Policy Formation in Federal Systems.* Berkeley: Institute of Governmental Studies Press, University of California, 1993.

O'Neal, Brian. *Senate Committees: Role and Effectiveness.* Ottawa: Research Branch, Library of Parliament, June 1994.

Ontario. Advisory Committee on Confederation. *Report of the Advisory Committee on Confederation.* Toronto: Advisory Committee on Confederation, 1978–79.

Pattee R.P. and Paul G. Thomas. "The Senate and Defence Policy: Subcommittee Report on Canada's Maritime Defence," in *Parliament and Canadian Foreign Policy.* David Taras, ed. Toronto: Canadian Institute of International Affairs, 1985, 101–20.

Patterson, S.C. and A. Mughan, eds. *Senates: Bicameralism in the Contemporary World.* Columbus, Ohio: Ohio State University Press, 1999.

Patzelt, W.J. "The Very Federal House: The German Bundesrat," in *Senates: Bicameralism in the Contemporary World.* S.C. Patterson and A. Mughan, eds. Columbus, Ohio: Ohio State University Press, 1999.

Pawelek, Nancy. "The Conscience of Parliament: The Second Chamber Contemplates Its Future," in *Parliamentary Government*, no. 5, 1984: 8–10.

Pearlstein Steven. "O Canada! A National Swan Song? U.S. Economic, Cultural Weight Threaten Nation's Identity," in *Washington Post*, 5 September 2000: A1.

Pelletier, R. " Federalism and Upper Houses: Searching for a Solution," in *Centralizing and Decentralizing Trends in Federal States*. C. Lloyd Brown-John, ed. Lanham: University Press of America, 1988.

Pelletier, Réjean. "La Réforme du Sénat canadien à la lumière d'expériences étrangères," in *Les Cahiers de Droit*, vol. 25, no. 1, March 1984: 9–13.

Quebec Liberal Party, Constitutional Committee. *A New Canadian Federation*. The Liberal Party of Quebec, Montreal, 1980.

Rémillard, Gil. *Le Fédéralisme canadien*. Montreal: Québec/Amérique, 1983.

Riddell, Peter. "The Second Chamber: In Search of a Complementary Role," in *The Political Quarterly*, no. 40, October-December 1999: 404–10.

Ridges, Edward Wavell. *Constitutional Law of England*. London: Stevens, 1937.

Riker, William H. "The Justification of Bicameralism," in *International Political Science Review*, vol. 13, 1992: 101–16.

Robertson, G. *An Elected Senate: Our Best Hope for Real Reform*. Paper presented to a Colloquium on Constitutional Law 1982: A Year After, Québec, 26 March 1983.

Robertson, G. *A House Divided: Meech Lake, Senate Reform and the Canadian Union*. Ottawa: The Institute for Research on Public Policy, 1989.

Robertson, Gordon. *The Missing Balance in Canadian Federation in Federalism for the Future*. Wilson & Lafleur, 1998.

Robertson, James R. *The Rules of the Senate: 1991 Amendments*. Ottawa: Library of Parliament, Research Branch, June 1991.

Robinson, Stephanie. *The Senate of Canada during the Mulroney Years: The Red Chamber Playing the Part of the Loyal Opposition*. Kingston: Queen's University, Department of Political Studies, 1996. BA thesis, 1996.

Roblin, Duff. *Speaking for Myself, Politics and Other Pursuits*. Winnipeg: Great Plains Publications, 1999.

Roebuck, John Arthur. *Colonies of England, A Plan for the Government of Some Portion of Our Colonial Possessions*. London: John W. Parker, 1849.

Romney, Paul. *Getting It Wrong: How Canadians Forgot Their Past and Imperilled Confederation*. Toronto: University of Toronto Press, 1999.

Rose, Michael. "Reluctance in the Red Chamber," in *Maclean's*, vol. 98, 4 March 1985: 34.

Ross, Sir George. *The Senate of Canada: Its Constitution, Powers and Duties Historically Considered*. Toronto: Copp Clark, 1914.

Russell, M. *Reforming the House of Lords: Lessons from Overseas*. Oxford: Oxford University Press, 2000.

Russell, M. and R. Hazell. *Commentary on the Wakeham Report on Reform of the House of Lords*. London: The Constitution Unit, University College London, 2000.

Russell, Peter. *Constitutional Odyssey: Can Canadians Become a Sovereign People?*, 2nd Ed. Toronto: University of Toronto Press, 1993.

Sabetti, Filippo and Harold M. Waller. "Introduction: Crisis and Continuity in Canadian Federalism," in *Publius*, vol. 14, no. 1, Winter 1984: 1–8.

Saunders, Cheryl. *The Constitutional Framework: Hybrid, Derivative but Australian.* Papers on Federalism No. 13. Melbourne: Centre for Comparative Constitutional Studies, University of Melbourne, 1989.

Savoie, Donald. *Governing from the Centre: The Concentration of Power in Canadian Politics.* Toronto: University of Toronto Press, 1999.

Scharpf, Fritz W. 1988. "The Joint Decision Trap: Lessons from German Federalism and European Integration," in *Public Adminstration*, no. 66: 239–78.

Scheiber, H.N., ed. *Perspectives on Federalism: Paper from the First Berkeley Seminar on Federalism.* Berkeley: Institute of Governmental Studies, University of California, 1987.

Schmitt, N. *Federalism: The Swiss Experience. Federalism: Theory and Application Vol. 2.* HSRC Publishers: Pretoria, 1996.

Sealey, Ellen. *Mobilizing Legislation: Losing Consent. Treatment of the House of Commons Under the Mulroney Conservatives.* Kingston: Queen's University, Department of Political Studies, 1995. BA thesis, 1995.

Seidle, F. Leslie. "Senate Reform and the Constitutional Agenda: Conundrum or Solution?" in *Canadian Constitutionalism, 1791–1991.* Janet Ajzenstat, ed. Ottawa: Canadian Study Parliament Group, 1992, 91–122.

Senate of Canada, *Amendment to the Constitution of Canada, Term 17 of the Terms of Union of Newfoundland with Canada* (13th Report). Standing Senate Committee on Legal and Constitutional Affairs, 7 July 1996.

Senate of Canada. *Rules of the Senate.* Ottawa: Senate of Canada, 2002

Senate Standing Committee on Banking, Trade and Commerce. *A Blueprint for Change: Response to the Report of the Task Force on the Future of the Canadian Financial Services Sector.* Chairman: Michael Kirby, December 1998.

Sharman, Campbell. "Second Chambers," in *Federalism and the Role of the State.* Herman Bakvis and William M. Chandler, eds. Toronto: University of Toronto Press, 1987, 82–100.

Sharman, Campbell. "The Senate and Good Government," in *The Senate and Good Government and Other Lectures in the Australian Senate Occasional Lecture Series, 1998*, no. 33. Canberra: Dept. of the Senate, Parliament House, 1999, 153–70.

Shell, Donald. "To Revise and Deliberate: The British House of Lords," in *Senates: Bicameralism in the Contemporary World.* Samuel C. Patterson and Anthony Mughan, eds. Columbus: Ohio State University Press, 1999, 199–224.

Sifton, C. "The Foundation of the New Era," in *New Era in Canada: Essays Dealing with the Upbuilding of the Canadian Commonwealth.* John Ormsby Miller, ed. London: Dent, 1917.

Simpson, Jeffrey. *Spoils of Power: The Politics of Patronage.* Toronto: Harper & Collins, 1988.

Simpson, Jeffrey. *The Friendly Dictatorship.* Toronto: McClelland & Stewart Ltd., 2001.

Sinclair, B. "Coequal Partner: The U.S. Senate," in *Senates: Bicameralism in the*

Contemporary World. Samuel C. Patterson and Anthony Mughan, eds. Columbus: Ohio State University Press, 1999, 32–58.

Smiley, D.V. "Federalism and the Legislative Process in Canada," in *The Legislative Process in Canada: The Need for Reform*. William A. W. Neilson and James.C. MacPherson, eds. Toronto: Butterworth,1978.

Smiley, D.V. *An Elected Senate for Canada? Clues from the Australian Experience*. Discussion Document no. 21. Kingston: Institute of Intergovernmental Relations, Queen's University, 1985.

Smiley, D.V. *The Federal Condition in Canada*. Toronto: McGraw-Hill Ryerson, 1987.

Smiley, D.V. and R.L. Watts. *Le Fédéralisme intra-étatique au Canada*. Ottawa: commission royale sur l'union économique et les perspectives de développement du Canada, vol. 39, 1986

Smith, David. "The Canadian Senate in Bicameral Perspective," chapter 5 in *Federalism*. (Forthcoming.)

Smith, Jennifer. "Canadian Confederation and the Influence of American Federalism," in *Canadian Journal of Political Science*, no. 21, September 1988: 443–63.

Sokolsky, Joel. "Overload and Marginality: Parliament and Defence Policy in the 1980s." A paper presented to the Biennial Meeting of the Association of Canadian Studies in the United States, San Francisco. 17–20 November 1989. (Unpublished.)

Sproule-Jones, Mark. *Governments at Work: Canadian Parliamentary Federalism and its Public Policy Effects*. Toronto: University of Toronto Press, 1993.

Statistics Canada, *Health Statistics at a Glance*. Ottawa: Statistics Canada, 1999.

Statistics Canada. *Outline of the Statistics on Health*. Ottawa: Statistics Canada, 1999.

Stevens, Geoffrey. "Prime Minister Has Done Terrible Harm to Senate," in *Toronto Star*, 18 September 1990: B3.

Stewart, Edison. "PM Slams 'non-elected' Senate for Tardiness on Jobless Bill," in *Toronto Star*, 14 December 1989.

Stewart Patterson, D. "Senate Showdown on Drug Patent Bill is Delayed," in *Globe and Mail*, 3 September 1987: A4.

Stilborn, Jack. *Comments on Twenty-Four Recent Senate Reform Proposals Provided for Analysis*. Ottawa: Parliamentary Research Branch, Library of Parliament, 5 July 1995.

Stilborn, Jack. *Senate Reform in Canada – A Discussion Paper*. Ottawa; Parliamentary Research Branch, Library of Parliament, 28 July 1999.

Stilborn, Jack. *The Legal Constitutional and Political Imperatives to Satisfy for Reform of the Senate of Canada and a Dismissal of the Abolition Proposal*. Draft. Ottawa: Research Branch, Library of Parliament, 2000.

Stilborn, Jack. *Senate Reform Proposals in Comparative Perspective*. Ottawa: Research Branch, Library of Parliament, November 1992.

Strauss, Leo. *What is Political Philosophy? and Other Studies*. Glencoe, IL: Free Press, 1959.

Sullivan, Ann. "Tory Senator Pressures Liberals to Rejig Committees," in *The Hill Times*, 28 October 1996.

Taras, David, ed. *Parliament and Canadian Foreign Policy*, Toronto: Canadian Institute of International Affairs, 1985.

Thomas, Paul G. "Les Partis et leur représentation des régions," in *Les Partis politiques au Canada: représentativité et intégration.* Herman Bakvis, ed. Toronto: Dundurn Press, 1991.

Thomas, Paul G. "Caucus on Representation in Canada: Keynote Address to the Canadian Study of Parliament Group Fall Conference on Party Caucuses: Behind Closed Doors." Ottawa, 21 November 1997.

Toulin, Alan. "Quit Stalling on UI, Mulroney Tells Senate," in *Financial Post*, 15 December 1989: B2.

Tremblay, Manon and Caroline Andrew, eds. *Femmes et représentation politique au Québec et au Canada.* Montreal: Éditions du remue-ménage, 1997.

Trickey, Mike. "Jewish Congress Argues against Sunset Clause for Anti-Terrorist Bill," in *The Ottawa Citizen*, 6 November 2001: A4.

Trudeau, Pierre-Elliott. *À Contre-courant: textes choisis, 1939–1996.* Montreal: Éditions Stanké, 1996.

Trudel, Clément. "Pierre A. Michaud partage son expérience," in *Journal du Barreau*, vol. 34, no. 14: 18–19.

Tsebelis, G. and J. Money. *Bicameralism.* Political Economy of Institutions and Decisions Series. Cambridge: Cambridge University Press, 1997.

Uhr, J. "Generating Divided Government: The Australian Senate," in *Senates: Bicameralism in the Contemporary World.* S.C. Patterson and A. Mughan, eds. Columbus, Ohio: Ohio State University Press, 1999, 93–119.

United Kingdom. *Report of the Royal Commission on the Reform of the House of Lords.* London: The Stationery Office, 2000.

United Kingdom. Royal Commission on the Reform of the House of Lords. *A House For The Future*, January, 2000. (Chairman: Rt. Hon. Lord Wakeham.)

Van Loon, Richard S. and Michael Whittington. *The Canadian Political System: Environment, Structure and Process, 3rd Ed.* (rev.). Toronto: McGraw-Hill Ryerson Ltd., 1981.

Vile, M.J.C. *Constitutionalism and the Separation of Powers, 2nd Edition.* Liberty Fund, Incorporated, 1998.

Vipond, Robert C. *Liberty and Community, Canadian Federalism and the Failure of the Constitution.* Albany, NY: State University of New York Press, 1991.

Waite, P.B. *The Confederation Debates in the Province of Canada, 1865.* Toronto: McClelland and Stewart, 1963.

Ward, Norman. *The Canadian House of Commons: Representation.* Toronto: University of Toronto Press, 1950.

Ward, Norman. "The Independence of Parliament," in *The Canadian House of Commons: Representation.* Toronto: University of Toronto Press, 1950.

Ward, Norman. "Called to the Bar of the House of Commons," in *Canadian Bar Review*, May 1957: 529–46.

Ward, Norman. *The Public Purse, A Study in Canadian Democracy.* Toronto: University of Toronto Press, 1964.

Watts, R.L. *New Federations: Experiments in the Commonwealth.* Oxford: Clarendon Press, 1966.

Watts, R.L. "Second Chambers in Federal Political Systems," in *Ontario Advisory*

Committee on Confederation, Background Papers and Reports, Vol. II. Toronto: Queen's Printer, 1970, 315–55.

Watts, R.L. "Divergence and Convergence: Canadian and US Federalism," in *Perspectives on Federalism: Paper from the First Berkeley Seminar on Federalism.* H.N. Scheiber, ed. Berkeley: Institute of Governmental Studies, 1987, 179–213.

Watts, R.L. *Executive Federalism: A Comparative Analysis.* Research Paper 26. Kingston: Institute of Intergovernmental Relations, Queen's University, 1989.

Watts, R.L. "The Federative Superstructure," in *Options for a New Canada.* R.L. Watts et D.M. Brown, eds. Toronto: University of Toronto Press, 1991, 309–36.

Watts R.L. "Regional Representation in National Institutions," in *Regionalism: Problems and Prospects.* E. Villers et J. Sindane, eds. Pretoria, South Africa: Human Sciences Council, 1993, 155–70, 192–8.

Watts, R.L. "The Reform of Federal Institutions," in *The Charlottetown Accord, the Referendum, and the Future of Canada.* Kenneth McRoberts and Patrick J. Monahan, eds. Toronto: University of Toronto Press, 1993, 17–36.

Watts, R.L. "Representation in North American Federations: A Comparative Perspective," in *Representation and Policy Formation in Federal Systems.* D.M. Olson and C.E.S. Franks, eds. Berkeley, Californie: Institute of Governmental Studies Press, 1993, 291–321.

Watts, R.L. "The Organization of Legislative and Executive Institutions: The Comparative Relevance for Europe of Canadian Experience," in *Vers une Constitution européenne. L'Europe et les expériences fédérales.* T. Fleiner and N. Schmitt, eds. Fribourg: Institut du Fédéralisme, 1996, 155–84.

Watts, R.L. *Comparing Federal Systems, 2nd Ed.* Kingston: Institute of Intergovernmental Relations, 1999.

Wheare, K.C. *Federal Government, 4th Ed.* London: Oxford University Press, 1963.

Wheare, K.C. *Legislatures.* London: Oxford University Press, 1968.

White, Randall. *Voice of Region: The Long Journey to Senate Reform in Canada.* Toronto: Dundurn Press, 1990.

Whyte, Kenneth. "Canadian Nationhood," in *National Post,* 1 July 2000: A17.

Wirick, Gregory. "Of Warhorses, Pastures, and Power: An Interview with Allan J. MacEachen," in *Parliamentary Government,* no. 7, 1988: 11–13.

Wudel, D. "A Job Description for Senators," in *Policy Options,* no. 7, April 1986: 22–3.

Yaffe Barbara, "The Trough-Meister Pulls Out a Plum," in *Vancouver Sun,* 15 June 2001: A14.

Zolf, Larry. *Survival of the Fattest: An Irreverent View of the Senate.* Toronto: Key Porter Books, 1984.

LEGISLATION

Statutes:

An Act to amend the Bankruptcy and Insolvency Act, the Companies' Creditors Arrangement Act and the Income Tax Act, S.C. 1997, c. 12 (Bill C-5)

An Act to amend the Canada Elections Act and the Electoral Boundaries Readjustment Act, S.C. 2001, c. 21 (Bill C-9)

An Act to amend the Canadian Wheat Board Act, S.C. 1998, c. 17 (Bill C-4)

An Act to amend the Criminal Code (organized crime and law enforcement), S.C. 2001, c. 32 (Bill C-24)

An Act to amend the Judges Act and to make consequential amendments to other Acts, S.C. 1998, c. 30 (Bill C-37)

An Act to amend the National Defence Act and to make consequential amendments to other Acts, S.C. 1998, c. 35 (Bill C-25)

An Act to amend the Parliament of Canada Act, the Members of Parliament Retiring Allowances Act and the Salaries Act, S.C. 2000, c. 20 (Bill C-28)

An Act to amend the Patent Act and to provide for certain matters in relation thereto, S.C. 1987, c. 41 (Bill C-22)

An Act to amend the Unemployment Insurance Act and the Employment and Immigration Department and Commission Act, S.C. 1990, c. 40 (Bill C-21)

An Act to change the constitution of the Legislative Council by rendering the same elective (1856) 20 Vict., c. 140 (Canada)

Anti-terrorism Act, S.C. 2001, c. 41 (Bill C-36)

Bank Act, S.C. 1991, c. 46

British North America Act, 1867 (UK) 30-31 Vict., c. 3, [R.S.C. 1985, App. II, No. 5]; also cited as the *Constitution Act, 1867*

Canada Customs and Revenue Agency Act, S.C. 1999, c. 17 (Bill C-43)

Canada Elections Act, S.C. 2000, c. 9 (Bill C-2)

Canada Evidence Act, R.S.C. 1985, c. C-5

Canadian Charter of Rights and Freedoms, Part I of the *Constitution Act, 1982*

Canadian Environmental Protection Act, 1999, S.C. 1999, c. 33 (Bill C-32)

Canadian Human Rights Act, R.S.C. 1985, c. H-6

Clarity Act, S.C. 2000, c. 26 (Bill C-20)

Comprehensive Nuclear Test-Ban Treaty Implementation Act, S.C. 1998, c. 32 (Bill C-52)

Constitution Act, 1982, being Schedule B to the *Canada Act 1982* (UK), 1982, c. 11 [R.S.C., 1985, App. II, No. 44]

Constitutional Amendments Act, S.C. 1996, c. 1 (Bill C-110)

Controlled Drugs and Substances Act, S.C. 1996, c. 19 (Bill C-8)

Department of Justice Act, R.S.C. 1985, c. J-2

DNA Identification Act, S.C. 1998, c. 37 (Bill C-3)

Extradition Act, S.C. 1999, c. 18 (Bill C-40)

Judges Act, R.S.C. 1985, c. J-1

Legislative Instruments Re-enactment Act, S.C. 2002, c. 20 (Bill S-41)

Maritime Code Act, S.C. 1977-78, c. 41

Marriage (Prohibited Degrees) Act, S.C. 1990, c. 46 (Bill S-14)

Nunavut Waters and Nunavut Surface Rights Tribunal Act, S.C. 2002, c. 10 (Bill C-33)

Parliament of Canada Act, R.S.C. 1985, c. P-1

Quebec Act, 1774 (UK), 14 Geo., III, c. 83 [R.S.C. 1985, App. II, No. 2]

Union Act, 1840 (UK), 3-4 Vict., c. 35 [R.S.C., 1985, App. II, No. 4]

Witness Protection Program Act, S.C. 1996, c. 15 (Bill C-13)

Youth Criminal Justice Act, S.C. 2002, c. 1 (Bill C-7)

Unenacted Bills:

Bill S-2, *An Act to amend the Canadian Human Rights Act (sexual orientation)* (35th Parliament, 2nd Session)

Bill S-8, *An Act to maintain the principles relating to the role of the Senate as established by the Constitution of Canada* (37th Parliament, 1st Session)

Bill S-15, *An Act to amend the Canadian Human Rights Act (sexual orientation)* (34th Parliament, 3rd Session)

Bill S-31, *An Act to better assist the Senate to serve Canadians by restoring its rights, opportunities and functions* (36th Parliament, 2nd Session)

Bill C-16, *Citizenship of Canada Act* (36th Parliament, 2nd Session)

Bill C-28, *Pearson International Airport Agreements Act* (35th Parliament 2nd Session)

Bill C-60, *Constitutional Amendment Act* (30th Parliament, 3rd Session)

Bill C-108, *An Act to amend the Canadian Human Rights Act* (34th Parliament, 3rd Session)

Bill C-220, *An Act to amend the Criminal Code and the Copyright Act (profit from authorship respecting a crime)* (36th Parliament, 1st Session)

CASE LAW

114957 Canada Ltée (Spraytech, Société d'arrosage) v. Hudson (Town), [2001] 2 S.C.R. 241

Attorney General of Canada v. Inuit Tapirisat of Canada, [1980] 2 S.C.R. 735

Dixon v. British Columbia (Attorney General), (1989) 59 D.L.R. (4th) 247, (1989) 4 W.W.R. 393, 35 B.C.L.R. (2d) 273, 15 A.C.W.S. (3d) 121 (B.C.S.C.)

Edwards v. Attorney-General for Canada [The Person's Case], [1930] A.C. 124

New Brunswick Broadcasting Co. v. Nova Scotia (Speaker of the House of Assembly) [Donahoe], [1993] 1 S.C.R. 319

Re the Regulation and Control of Aeronautics in Canada, [1932] A.C. 54

Reference re Alberta Statutes, [1938] S.C.R. 100

Reference re Appointment of Senators Pursuant to the Constitution Act, 1867, (1991) 78 D.L.R. (4th) 245 (B.C.C.A.)

Reference re Authority of Parliament in Relation to the Upper House [The Senate Reference], [1980] 1 S.C.R. 54

Reference re Provincial Electoral Boundaries (Sask.), [1991] 2 S.C.R. 158

Reference re Resolution to Amend the Constitution, [1981] 1 S.C.R. 753

Reference re Secession of Quebec, [1998] 2 S.C.R. 217

Singh v. Canada, [1991] 3 O.R. (3rd) 429 (O.C.A.)

Thorne's Hardware Ltd. v. The Queen, [1983] 1 S.C.R. 106

United States v. Burns, [2001] 1 S.C.R. 283

Weir v. Canada (Attorney General), [1991] N.B.R. (2d) 337 (N.B.C.A.)

Contributors

PROFESSOR JANET AJZENSTAT publishes in the field of public law and Canadian political history. Her works include *Canada's Founding Debates*, edited with William D. Gairdner, Ian Gentles, and Paul Romney (Stoddart, 1999); *Canada's Origins: Liberal, Tory, or Republican?*, edited with Peter J. Smith (Carleton University Press, 1985); and *Canadian Constitutionalism, 1791–1991* (Canadian Study of Parliament Group, 1992). She has held research grants from the Social Sciences and Humanities Research Council of Canada and the Donner Canadian Foundation. In 1985, she was awarded the Jules et Gabrielle Léger Prize for the study of the monarchy and Canadian parliamentary institutions. She taught public law and political philosophy in the Department of Political Science at McMaster University for eight years. In 2000, she retired as a full professor.

PROFESSOR C.E.S. FRANKS's works include explorations into public administration, government accountability, aboriginal self-government, relations between governments and aboriginal peoples, the public service, Canada's north, issues affecting nuclear energy, and politics in India. He has written or edited thirteen books, including *The Parliament of Canada, The Canoe and White Water*, and *Dissent and the State*, and has conducted many studies for royal commissions, for Parliament, and for government agencies. Among his academic honours, Professor Franks has been elected a fellow of the Royal Canadian Geographical Society and the Royal Society of Canada. He has taught at Queen's University for more than thirty-five years in the Department of Political Studies and was cross-appointed as a professor to the School of Physical and Health Education. He is currently an emeritus professor of both departments.

THE HON. SERGE JOYAL, PC, has worked extensively on Canadian political and constitutional issues. He was a Member of the House of Commons from 1974 to 1984. During that time he served as vice-chair of the Public Accounts Committee and as Parliamentary Secretary to the President of

Treasury Board. He was the co-chair of the Joint Committee of the Senate and the House of Commons on the patriation of the Canadian Constitution (1980–81) before becoming Minister of State (1981) and Secretary of State of Canada (1982–84). To mark the patriation of the BNA Act, he published "Constitution 1982." Senator Joyal holds an Honourary Doctor of Laws Degree from Moncton University (1984) and was named a Chevalier of the French Légion d'Honneur in 1995 and an officer of the Order of Canada in 1996. He was summoned to the Senate in 1997.

THE HON. LOWELL MURRAY, PC, has considerable experience in Canadian politics and constitutional deliberations. Among other things, he has served as chair of the Standing Senate Committee on National Finance, the Standing Senate Committee on Social Affairs, Science and Technology, and the Standing Senate Committee on Banking, Trade and Commerce, as well as co-chair of the Joint Committee of the Senate and House of Commons on Official Languages. Senator Murray also served as the Leader of the Government in the Senate (1986–93), Minister of State for Federal-Provincial Relations (1986–91), and Minister responsible for the Atlantic Canada Opportunities Agency (1987–88). He was summoned to the Senate in 1979.

PROFESSOR GIL RÉMILLARD is the author of many works on the subject of Constitution, including *Le Fédéralisme canadien: éléments constitutionels de formation et d'évolution* (1980). He was Professor of Law, Laval University (1972–85). Professor Rémillard has been involved with Provincial politics and constitutional negotiations for many years. He held many offices during his political career, including the responsibilities of Quebec's Minister of International Relations (1985–88), Minister responsible for Canadian Intergovernmental Affairs (1985–93), and Minister of Justice, in charge of the Reform of the Quebec Civil Code (1992). He was awarded the Médaille du Barreau du Quebec in 1994. Since 1994, Professor Rémillard has been teaching at the Quebec National School of Public Administration and Counsel at Fraser Milner Casgrain LLP.

PROFESSOR DAVID E. SMITH has worked extensively on the subject of Canadian politics, having written numerous works on the topic, including *The Invisible Crown: The First Principle of Canadian Government* (1995) and *The Republican Option in Canada: Past and Present* (1999). He was Visiting Professor of Canadian Studies in Japan (1981–82). He served as Chairman of the Aid to Scholarly Publications Programme, Social Sciences Federation of Canada (1993–94) and President of the Canadian Political Science Association (1994–95). He was a recipient of a Jules et Gabrielle Léger Fellowship in 1992 and of a Killam Research Fellowship in 1995–97. Professor Smith is currently a professor in the Department of Political Studies at the University of Saskatchewan.

DR JACK STILBORN currently combines consulting work as a policy researcher on intergovernmental issues with work as an Analyst in the Research Branch of the Library of Parliament, where he has been a specialist in Canadian political institutions and intergovernmental relations since 1985. During this period, he has provided research and analysis to a range of parliamentary committees, including the constitutional committees of the early 1990s, and authored parliamentary research publications on Senate reform, Parliament, intergovernmental relations, and public service reform. Dr Stillborn also worked for an interval as advisor with the Ontario Ministry of Intergovernmental Affairs.

PROFESSOR PAUL G. THOMAS's works have focused on public administration, parliamentary reform, and federal-provincial relations. He co-authored *Canadian Public Administration: Some Problematic Perspectives* (1982; 2nd ed. 1987) and is associate editor of Canadian Public Administration, having served as editor from 1993 to 1996. Professor Thomas's academic honours include the 1983 University of Manitoba Excellence in Graduate Teaching Award and the 1994 Lt Governor's Medal for Public Administration in Manitoba. He is currently a professor in the Department of Political Studies at the University of Manitoba.

PROFESSOR RONALD L. WATTS has worked for more than forty years on the comparative study of federal systems and on Canadian federalism. He has written or edited more than twenty books, monographs, and reports and more than sixty articles and chapters in collaborative collections. His most recent book is *Comparing Federal Systems* (2nd ed. 1999; French edition 2002). On several occasions he has been a consultant to the Government of Canada during constitutional deliberations, most notably 1980–81 and 1991–92, and has been an advisor to governments in several other countries. He is currently principal emeritus and professor emeritus of Political Studies at Queen's University, where he has been a member of the academic staff since 1955 and was principal and vice-chancellor 1974–84. He has received five honourary degrees and was promoted to Companion of the Order of Canada in 2000. He is a fellow and a former director of the Institute of Intergovernmental Relations at Queen's University.

Index

abolition of the Senate: arguments for and against, xxii, xxviiin11, 87, 107, 111, 140, 235–6, 292; effect of on parliamentary workings, 140, 235–6, 245, 307. *See also* reform

Aboriginal: land claims and self-government, xxi, 139–40, 149, 215, 243; offenders, 304; rights in the *Constitution Act, 1982,* xviii; senators, 80, 121, 139, 147, 151, 291, 320; veterans, 221. *See also* minority representation

Aboriginal Peoples, Standing Committee on, 287

abortion, 161, 163, 199

absence. *See* attendance

academic literature on the Senate, xviii-xix

accountability: of each level of government, 94, 136; methods of increasing, 264–6; of non-elected authorities, 134; in origin of the Senate, 3; quest for resulting in concentration of power in the Cabinet, 24; of senators, 33, 99, 289–90; through decentralization, 105; through parliamentary parties, 145–6; through veto, 303–4

An Act to amend the Bankruptcy and Insolvency Act, the Companies' Creditors Arrangement Act and the Income Tax Act (Bill C-5), 176

An Act to amend the Canadian Human Rights Act (sexual orientation) (Bill S-2 and Bill S-15), 174–5

An Act to amend the Canadian Wheat Board Act (Bill C-4), 176–7, 183, 209

An Act to amend the Criminal Code and the Copyright Act (profit from authorship respecting a crime) (Bill C-220), 167, 173–4, 183, 187n38

An Act to amend the Criminal Code (organized crime and law enforcement) (Bill C-24), 316n119

An Act to amend the Judges Act and to make consequential amendments to other Acts (Bill C-37), 175

An Act to amend the Patent Act (Bill C-22), 156–8

An Act to amend the Unemployment Insurance Act and the Employment and Immigration Department and Commission Act (Bill C-21), 160

An Act to better assist the Senate to serve Canadians by restoring its rights, opportunities and functions (Bill S-31), xxviiin19

An Act to maintain the principles relating to the role of the Senate as established by the Constitution of Canada (Bill S-8), xxviiin19

activity reports of the Senate's work, 123

administration of the Senate, 134, 148, 163, 253

age of appointment, 259, 261, 295, 312–13n90, 323–6. *See also* retirement

agencies, government, 163–4